BEGONIAS

BEGONIAS

Cultivation, Identification, and Natural History

MARK C. TEBBITT

Published in association with
Brooklyn Botanic Garden

TIMBER PRESS

Mention of trademark, proprietary product, or vendor does not constitute a guarantee or warranty of the product by the publisher or author and does not imply its approval to the exclusion of other products or vendors.

All photographs by the author unless otherwise stated.
Line drawings by Paul Harwood unless otherwise indicated.

Published in 2005 by
Timber Press, Inc.
The Haseltine Building
133 S.W. Second Avenue, Suite 450
Portland, Oregon 97204-3527, U.S.A.
www.timberpress.com

Printed through Colorcraft Ltd., Hong Kong

Library of Congress Cataloging-in-Publication Data

Tebbitt, Mark C.
Begonias : cultivation, identification, and natural history / Mark C.Tebbitt.
p. cm.
"Published in association with Brooklyn Botanic Garden."
Includes bibliographical references and index.
ISBN 0-88192-733-3 (hardback)
1. Begonias. I. Title.
SB413.B4T43 2005
635.9'3627—dc22

2005001411

A catalog record for this book is also available from the British Library.

To my mother and father

Contents

Preface

Like many gardeners, my first experience of *Begonia* involved one of the ubiquitous hybrid cultivars. As a young child I remember planting tuberous begonias in my parents' garden and then watching them for days afterward as their pom-pom-like flowers came into bloom. Later, after Venus's flytraps and bromeliads had stimulated my interest in exotic houseplants, I grew hybrid rex and cane begonias on my bedroom windowsill. All helped to fire the imagination of a budding botanist, and as often happens, led to a wider interest in the genus. Years later when I had the opportunity to study *Begonia* for my doctoral thesis, I jumped at the chance to learn more. At that time I was lucky to work closely with the staff and plants of the Glasgow Botanic Garden in Scotland. This beautiful city garden has one of the world's largest collections of *Begonia* species and cultivars, and working with the collection heightened my appreciation for the genus's enormous diversity. Three years of constantly studying these plants did little to dampen my interest in *Begonia*, and ultimately led to a staff position at Brooklyn Botanic Garden, where happily I have been able to continue my taxonomic research on the genus and its closest relatives.

During the course of my career I have spent a great deal of my time identifying begonias and have often found my attempts frustrated by the general lack of published, detailed species descriptions. Rather than easing the problems of identification, books about *Begonia*, written for a popular audience, have tended to focus almost exclusively on their cultivation, with different begonias being emphasized in different parts of the world. American books typically discuss how to cultivate a wide range of species and hybrids. Paramount among these works is Mildred and Edward Thompson's *Begonias: The Complete Reference Guide*, which for many of us has become a standard reference. On the other hand, most European, Australian, and New Zealand works focus on the cultivation of the tuberous hybrids, since these plants have gained an almost cult-like following in those parts of the world. This dichotomy appears to have arisen in part because introducing species from Mexico and Central America into the United States and Canada has been relatively easy, but it is also due to climatic factors, as much of the United States has proved too warm for the successful cultivation of most tuberous hybrids. Given the large size and enormous horticultural appeal of the genus, surprisingly few books about begonias provide a means to accurately identify even the most commonly cultivated *Begonia* species. Even more surprising is the fact that the last monograph of *Begonia*, Alphonse de Candolle's account of the Begoniaceae in volume 15 of the *Prodromus Systematis Naturalis Regni Vegetabilis*, was published as long ago as 1864; therefore, modern-day botanists, like gardeners, lack a convenient means of identifying the species.

Given this sizable gap in the literature, my primary goal in writing this book was to provide detailed yet accessible information that will allow a variety of readers to identify, and hence learn more, about the cultivated *Begonia* species. I hope that this book will also provide enthusiasts with interesting and practical background information on many other aspects of the cultivated begonias, including their natural history, a subject which likewise has received little previous attention.

The descriptions that appear in this book were made using a combination of cultivated living plants and dried herbarium material. While writing the species accounts I discovered that a few of the cultivated species were misnamed, unidentified, or, in a couple of cases, new to science. I hope the resulting revisions facilitate the accurate naming of these begonias and stimulate further research on this large and taxonomically poorly studied genus.

Acknowledgments

This book has greatly benefited from the guidance and knowledge of many people. From Brooklyn Botanic Garden (BBG) I would particularly like to thank Adrian Bennett, who assisted me in the production of the book and whose editorial and linguistic skills and scholarly attention to detail are greatly appreciated, and Paul Harwood, who provided most of the beautifully drawn artwork, as well as a good sense of humor. I am also grateful to Britta Husack and Kathy Crosby for translation of German texts, Jinshuang Ma for translation of Chinese texts, and Alessandro Chiari for maintaining my research collection of begonias. I would also like to thank BBG President Judy Zuk and Vice President for Science Steve Clemants for supporting this project. The Stanley Smith Horticultural Trust, USA, is also gratefully acknowledged for its financial support.

Several people helped improve one or more of the chapters. For this I wish to acknowledge my wife Laura Steger Tebbitt, as well as Kathy Crosby, Niall Dunn, Patricia Jonas and Janet Marinelli of BBG, and the following members of the American Begonia Society (ABS): Howard and Barbara Berg, Mike Flaherty (Gazebo Plants and Flowers), Jack Golding, Mike Kartuz (Kartuz Greenhouses), Richard and Wanda Macnair, Don Miller, Morris Mueller, Thelma O'Reilly, and Johanna Zinn. I am also grateful for the information and plant material supplied by Trefflé Courchesne, Édith Morin, and Janique Perreault (Montreal Botanical Garden); Euan Donaldson, David Menzies, and John Stevenson (Glasgow Botanic Garden); Beth Castellon, Dina Gallick, and Darrin Duling (New York Botanical Garden); Bill Claybaugh (ABS), Ron Determann (Atlanta Botanical Garden), Eric Hammond (Heronswood Nursery), Dave Horak (BBG), and W. Scott Hoover (ABS/New England Tropical Conservatory); and Carrie Karegeannes, Toby Lothman, and Gene and Ann Salisbury (ABS). I also wish to thank Piers Trehane for advice on cultivated plant nomenclature and Liz Steger-Hartzman (Liz Steger Photography) for advice on photographic issues.

The following botanists kindly provided their assistance and in some cases graciously allowed me to consult their unpublished research: Kerry Barringer and

Gerry Moore (BBG), Luc Brouillet (Montreal Botanical Garden), Laura Forrest (Southern Illinois University, Carbondale), Will Goodall-Copestake, Pete and Michelle Hollingsworth, Mark Hughes and Vanessa Plana (Royal Botanic Garden Edinburgh), Ruth Kiew (Singapore Botanic Gardens), Tracy MacLellan (University of the Witwatersrand, Johannesburg), F. MacRoni (Concord Village, Brooklyn, New York), Ching-I Peng (National Museum of Natural Sciences, Taiwan), Martin Sands (Royal Botanic Gardens Kew), Stephen Smith (United States National Herbarium), Marc Sosef, Hans de Wilde, and the late Jan Doorenbos (National Herbarium Nederland, Wageningen University branch), Susan Swensen (Ithaca College, New York), and Keith Watson (Kelvindale Museum, Glasgow).

A number of photographs and line drawings appear with the generous permission of the photographers and artists, who are individually and gratefully acknowledged in the text.

I also wish to acknowledge the following institutions for the use of their resources: New York Botanical Garden; Brooklyn Museum of Art; United States National Herbarium; Harvard University Herbarium; Montreal Botanical Garden; Glasgow Botanic Garden; Royal Botanic Garden Edinburgh; Royal Botanic Gardens Kew; Natural History Museum, London; National Museum of Natural History, Paris; Botanical Museum, Berlin-Dahlem; and the Wageningen and Leiden University branches of the National Herbarium Nederland.

I hope that I have not omitted anyone who has contributed to this book, and apologize if I have.

1

Introduction

How *Begonia* got its name

Despite *Begonia*'s current horticultural popularity, the discovery of the first members of this genus was hardly accompanied by great fanfare. As the seventeenth century drew to a close, few people probably even noticed when French botanist Charles Plumier named and illustrated six new plant species and in 1700 published them in a friend's book as the genus *Begonia*. Plumier chose the name to honor Michel Begon, who had served as governor of the French Antilles from 1682 to 1685. He was no doubt motivated to do so by the fact that Begon had recommended him to King Louis XIV of France for the position of plant collector in the French Caribbean.

The Caribbean proved rich pickings for Plumier. Not only did he discover begonias there but also *Fuchsia* and frangipani, the latter of which Carl Linnaeus named in his honor as the genus *Plumeria*. Plumier's name *Begonia* was not without rival, however, as three other names had earlier been published for species now recognized as members of this genus: *Totoncaxoxo coyollin* (*Begonia gracilis*) from Mexico, *Tsjeria-narinampuli* (*B. malabarica*) from India, and *Aceris fructu herba anomala, flore tertrapetalo albo* for a Caribbean species now called *B. acutifolia*. Despite the prior existence of these names, and the later publication of a few additional ones, the name *Begonia* was adopted by Linnaeus in his *Species Plantarum* of 1753, and this work is used by modern-day botanists as a starting point for accepted botanical names.

Since the discovery of the first begonias, numerous plant hunters have continued to collect specimens of new and interesting species, and the genus is now known to occur in almost every region of the earth with a tropical or subtropical climate. The one notable exception is the lush rain forests of northern Australia. Presently around 1500 wild species of *Begonia* are recognized, making this genus one of the largest among the flowering plants. Six others probably contain more species—*Astragalus* (milk-vetches), *Euphorbia* (spurges), *Senecio* (groundsels and ragworts), *Solanum* (potatoes), *Piper* (peppers), and *Carex* (sedges)—but in my clearly biased opinion, these lack the horticultural versatility and charm of the begonias.

Begonias in cultivation

Early introductions: Asia and Europe

Begonia has a long and distinguished history in cultivation, which began at least as long ago as 1400 with the cultivation of *Begonia grandis* in its Chinese homeland. This frost-hardy species is currently a popular ornamental plant throughout the world, but it, like many other early garden plants, may originally have gained recognition for its medicinal rather than its aesthetic properties. Even today, *B. grandis* and several other begonias are employed as medicines in their native lands where their astringent properties are utilized to clean wounds, reduce swelling, and treat a variety of diseases. Many other begonias are locally eaten as vegetable greens or drunk as herbal teas. The rather bitter tasting, purple tea made from the locally famous *B. fimbristipula* of southern China can even, on occasion, be purchased in Asian markets in the United States.

Although the hardy begonia had long been grown in China and was introduced into Japanese gardens in 1641, other members of the genus were not widely cultivated until European plant collectors began introducing them into their patrons' stove houses during the eighteenth century. The first living begonia to reach European shores was a Jamaican species, *Begonia minor*, which William Brown sent to Kew Gardens in 1777. In the years immediately following Brown's introduction, others began to trickle into cultivation. In those days the introduction of tropical plants was fraught with difficulties. Seed was largely considered an unreliable means of introducing these exotic plants since little or nothing was known about the conditions necessary for germination. Instead, whole plants were usually dug

Begonia tea made from the Chinese *B. fimbristipula*. Photo by Liz Steger Photography

up from the wild and transported via sailing ship to Europe. Not surprisingly, few of these survived the long and difficult ocean voyages and those that did were highly valued.

This haphazard means of transporting plants was revolutionized in 1835 when English inventor Nathaniel Ward demonstrated that portable glass houses could provide plants with a constant moist atmosphere, even temperature, and protection from salt spray during shipping. These Wardian cases greatly improved a plant's chances of survival and revolutionized the plant collecting business. Once they became widely used the number of successful plant introductions increased drastically, and by 1847 somewhere between 70 and 80 *Begonia* species were being cultivated within Europe.

Remarkably, many of these early introductions have remained popular in cultivation into the twenty-first century. Some of these particularly significant nineteenth-century introductions that have played an extensive role in the production of the most popular hybrid cultivars include: *Begonia veitchii* (1867), *B. schmidtiana* (1878), and *B. socotrana* (1880). Inevitably, during this golden age of plant introduction, which was being financed by Europe's industrial revolution, a few species entered cultivation as unsuspected but, as it turned out, welcome stowaways among other plants. Notable examples include: *B. cucullata* (1821), *B. rex* (1856), and the exquisitely scented *B. lubbersii* (1880).

Though the problems associated with transporting plants had largely been solved by the introduction of Wardian cases, plant collecting in the 1800s was still a difficult and often dangerous occupation. Many of those responsible for discovering and introducing the first begonias to Europe led lives as colorful as the exotic species they collected. At that time, like now, most collectors were employed either by the large botanic gardens or the leading nursery firms. Richard Pearce, who collected for both Veitch and Sons and William Bull Nurseries, deserves particular mention. During his distinguished and adventurous career he introduced three South American begonias of particular horticultural merit. Records of his travels are scarce, but we do know that like many other plant collectors his life was cut short after catching a tropical fever. He left us, however, with a variety of good garden plants, including three begonias that were subsequently hybridized to produce the *Begonia* ×*tuberhybrida* cultivar group: *B. boliviensis*, *B. pearcei*, and *B. veitchii*.

Of all the perils to be faced while searching for tropical plants, catching a tropical fever was for many nineteenth-century collectors the greatest fear, since at that time few effective treatments were known. Gustav Mann, for instance, one of Kew's many gardener–plant collectors, wrote of this fear in a letter to the garden's director, William Hooker. At that time Mann was on a collecting trip to Clarence Peak on the West African island of São Tomé:

> The trees were much overgrown by Orchids, Ferns and Begonias, while moss hung a foot in length from the branches . . . I regret very much that I could not stop some days longer, but I ran the risk of making myself a cripple for life . . . To stop there in the wet season is quite impossible, and would be certain death.

Mann was certainly prudent to worry. After descending from the mountain he developed a fever from which he was lucky to recover a few days later. We gardeners must thank him for risking his life. During his trip up the mountain he collected two of the finest African begonias now in cultivation: *Begonia prismatocarpa* and *B. mannii*.

Since Mann's trip up Clarence Peak, new generations of collectors have continued to search the world's tropical regions for begonias. More recent introductions of note include: *Begonia bowerae* (the eyelash begonia, 1948), *B. masoniana* (the iron-cross begonia, 1952), and *B. soli-mutata* (the instant suntan begonia, 1974).

Early introductions to North America

Though we have detailed knowledge about the introduction of begonias to Europe, we know little about their first appearance in North America; however, after 1850 many begonias seem to have arrived soon after being introduced in Europe. American interest in the genus increased so dramatically during the nineteenth and twentieth centuries that by the 1920s, when Europe was recovering from the ravages of World War I, most new introductions began to enter cultivation in the United States and from there were introduced to Europe. This trend continues to this day. With the founding of the American Begonia Society in 1932, *Begonia* popularity soared, and an even greater range of new species was introduced into cultivation, particularly from the relatively accessible regions of Mexico, the West Indies, and Brazil. Now at the start of the twenty-first century, a significant proportion of the new introductions to both North America and Europe are facilitated by the American Begonia Society's seed exchange, the practice of introducing new plants via seed having largely replaced the older method of transporting plants used during the early 1900s.

Methods of cultivation: a short history

Generations of gardeners have witnessed enormous changes in the methods used to cultivate begonias. At the turn of the eighteenth century, when the first begonias were being introduced into Europe's gardens, they were grown exclusively in the stove houses of Europe's largest and wealthiest botanic gardens. The precursors of our modern-day glasshouses, stove houses were coal heated and typically constructed of stone and timber with a few panes of glass arranged along one side. Toward the end of the eighteenth century an increasing percentage of their surface area was comprised of glass. In time, the stone walls were replaced by cast and then wrought iron, allowing an even greater use of glass. Despite the fact that such building materials became increasingly common with industrialization, not until the early 1900s did glasshouses become widely affordable, making the hobby of cultivating begonias and other tropical plants possible for the average person.

As glasshouses became less expensive, so too did the tropical plants being cultivated in them. By the late 1840s these exotics became plentiful and cheap enough that they could be grown widely outdoors in temperate areas as summer bedding. Begonias were a relatively late addition to the list of plants, but some of the hybrid begonias have found a place among the most popular of all summer bedding plants. Particularly popular are the hybrid Semperflorens begonias that resulted from crossing *Begonia cucullata* with *B. schmidtiana* and the *B.* ×*tuberhybrida* cultivars that resulted from crossing several tuberous species. Indeed these plants are so widely grown, some outdoor gardeners apparently think they are all the genus has to offer and as a result exhibit the symptoms of overexposure in their general negativity toward all things begonia. Nevertheless the group's reputation as an outdoor garden plant is being saved, as an ever increasing number of new *Begonia* species are currently gaining favor as either tender or marginally hardy garden plants.

Around the same time that begonias were first used as summer bedding they were also beginning to be grown as houseplants. Following the introduction of household central heating in the mid nineteenth century, begonias were increasingly grown indoors. Plants with dramatic leaves were particularly favored and members of the *Begonia* Rex-cultorum group, which have some of the most colorful leaves of all houseplants, were particularly popular in Victorian homes. Flowering houseplants were less common. They had earlier been deemed too difficult to grow indoors after repeated failed attempts to get roses and other cool-climate natives to flower. As frustrated homeowners turned to foliage plants, nurserymen promoted the idea that it was more sophisticated to grow "non-flowering" foliage plants and that flowers were frivolous. Furthermore, since flowers and sex are intricately related, the introduction of foliage plants made it safe for young Victorian ladies with lots of spare time to pursue botanical interests in their parlors, without fear of conversations becoming too risqué.

By the end of the nineteenth century, times had changed and tropical plants with attractive flowers had become popular indoor subjects. Paramount among such begonias were the *Begonia socotrana* hybrids, of which the Reiger hybrid group is currently the most popular. In fact, their compact habit and large showy flowers make them among the most commercially important of all winter-flowering houseplants today. They are, nevertheless, rather difficult to grow year-round in the home and are usually treated as temporary houseplants and discarded once they have finished flowering. More accommodating in the usually dry interiors of our homes are those begonias like *B. venosa* and *B.* 'Erythrophylla', which have thick, fleshy vegetative parts. Of course these plants do not produce the intense floral displays of the *B. socotrana* hybrids.

A late nineteenth-century development that allowed an even greater number of showy-flowered begonias to be permanently cultivated in the home was the terrarium. Enclosed terrariums could be used to grow humidity-loving plants such as the gorgeous yellow-flowered *Begonia prismatocarpa*. After years of disfavor, glass containers have come back into vogue; and nowadays, with the use of artificial lighting specifically designed to promote plant growth, these mini gardens can be situated almost anywhere in the home. This return to indoor, contained-atmosphere gardening is probably a result of the increasing urbanization of the world, which is leaving many gardeners with no access to a conventional glasshouse, a trend likely to continue for the foreseeable future.

Future possibilities

Pitcher plants, nasturtiums, and other tropical plants once loved by the Victorians have now dropped out of fashion, but gardeners continue to grow begonias generation after generation. Why should this be so? For one thing, begonias are generally easy to grow, and a small but carefully selected collection can produce flowers throughout the year. Another factor is their versatility as both foliage and flowering plants. But above all, many of the species have proven easy to hybridize, resulting in an endless supply of new cultivars.

Since the late eighteenth century more than 400 of the 1500 natural species have been introduced into cultivation, and from these, thousands of hybrid cultivars have been developed. Hybridization of begonias began in the early 1800s, soon after the first species arrived in Europe, and has continued ever since. Some early hybrid cultivars such as 'Ricinifolia', 'Erythrophylla', and 'Phyllomaniaca' are, amazingly, still widely cultivated today. Though many begonia hybrids have enormous commercial value (sales of Semperflorens begonia hybrids in the United States during 2003, for example, amounted to well over $60 million), many others do not, but instead are popular plants that have been passed along from one gardener to another, remaining in cultivation simply through the generosity of generations of enthusiasts. Interestingly, these pass-along plants are those that have endured in cultivation the longest, while the commercial hybrids have tended to succumb to the whims of gardening fashion relatively soon after their introduction.

A trend taking shape now at the start of the twenty-first century that is likely to further increase the popularity of begonias as garden plants is the introduction of new cold-tolerant species collected from relatively high altitudes, particularly in China. Although few of these are likely to approach the cold hardiness of *Begonia grandis*, which easily survives temperature plunges to 14°F (–10°C), some, like *B. formosana*, *B. pedatifida*, and *B. emeiensis*, have proved to be winter-hardy in the Pacific Northwest and the Carolinas and are likely to do well in other regions with similar mild climates.

As a vast array of promising wild species remain to be introduced into cultivation, the horticultural future of the genus looks extremely bright. Imagine, if you will, the horticultural potential of one yet-to-be-introduced species, *Begonia balansana* (Plate 1). In its native habitat, this compact rhizomatous species produces an almost continuous display of showy pink, or in a few cases white, flowers, curious crown-shaped fruit, and beautiful net-veined leaves. Recent molecular research indicates that this species is closely related to *B. rex*, suggesting that it may be possible to hybridize *B. balansana* with members of the Rex-cultorum group and thereby introduce striking new characteristics into this commercially important group of hybrids. *Begonia balansana*, unfortunately, also serves to illustrate the importance of conservation, because like several other members of the genus, this Vietnamese species exists in just one tiny patch of forest, situated in an advancing sea of tropical agriculture (Plate 2). With the destruction of the world's forests increasing at an alarming rate, we gardeners must help conserve those cultivated begonias with small wild distributions by carefully maintaining and propagating them in cultivation. Similarly, collecting seeds and never whole plants from the wild is essential when introducing additional species into cultivation. Otherwise these vulnerable species may be lost forever.

2

General cultivation techniques

In nature, begonias are found throughout much of the tropics and subtropics at a range of altitudes and in a variety of habitats. Not surprisingly then, different species often prefer markedly different conditions in cultivation. A plant that naturally grows perched upon the trunks of trees in the humid, high elevation rain forests of western Africa would not be expected to thrive under the same growing regime as, say, one from a semi-arid hillside in northern Mexico. Consequently, it is important to choose those species that are suited to your available growing conditions, or alternatively to modify the growing conditions to suit the kinds of plants you wish to grow. One secret of successfully growing begonias is to recognize what type of conditions a particular plant is likely to need. Clues can be inferred from a plant's appearance, as well as knowledge of its natural habitat. For example, begonias with naturally pale or particularly thin or pustulose leaf surfaces are adapted to higher humidity and relatively low light levels. A dense covering of reddish hairs on the leaves also signifies a similar preference for these conditions. Conversely, a plant with thick leaves, or leaves that are either hairless or covered with silvery white hairs will prefer less humid, brighter conditions. Each of these features performs a particular physiological function adapting the plant to its environment. Pustulose leaf surfaces, for example, are an adaptation to low light conditions, because the cone-shaped pustules help capture scattered light, allowing more of it to be retained and used in photosynthesis. Conversely a covering of silvery white hairs reflects light away from the leaf so that less reaches the inside, an advantage for plants in bright sunlight, since excess sunlight can damage the leaf. Also we can predict that a species growing naturally at high altitudes will prefer a cooler temperature compared to one from lower altitudes. For this reason, I have presented habitat information along with each species description in chapter five.

In a book written for a broad spectrum of growers, as this one is, being specific about cultivation techniques is impossible The most appropriate way to grow begonias depends to a large extent upon the precise conditions a grower is able to provide, and this will often be dictated, at least to some extent, by local climate. For information on how to grow begonias in a variety of climates the *Begonian*, a bimonthly publication of the American Begonia Society, is unrivalled. It regularly includes practical tips from growers living in a wide variety of geographical areas. It also offers information on growing begonias under specialized conditions, such as in a terrarium or greenhouse, under florescent lights, or outdoors in a garden. A great deal of cultural information specific to begonias is also available in the numerous specialized books on this subject, many of which are listed in the bibliography at the back of this book.

Regardless of where, or how, you grow begonias it is of paramount importance to pay close attention to your plants and to know how a healthy individual of a particular species should look throughout the year. You must not only be able to identify the plants you are growing but also recognize a plant that is growing poorly from one that is in its natural semi-dormant or dormant winter phase. If you think a plant is ailing, look at it closely and determine why. Only after its symptoms have been diagnosed should treatment commence. This chapter and the cultural information that follows each species' description in chapter five will provide some of the basic information necessary to grow a range of begonias. There is, however, no substitute for experience; talk to other growers, read about the species you are growing, and above all, expect to lose a few plants every once in a while and learn from your mistakes.

Temperature, light, and humidity

The three variables of temperature, light, and humidity are interrelated and must be supplied in the correct balance for healthy plant growth. Most begonias, however, can adapt to a wide range of growing conditions, allowing several species to grow together in the same area. This chapter discusses the optimum conditions for the majority of begonias. Chapter five mentions when optimum conditions for a particular species differ from the norm.

Optimum temperatures for most begonias are in the range of 55 to 85°F (13–29°C), with nighttime temperatures, which are more critical, lower than the daytime temperatures. As a rule, those species from higher elevations or subtropical locations generally require temperatures at the lower end of the range even during the day, and those from lower elevations or tropical locations require temperatures at the mid to higher end of the range. Greenhouse growers may install wet pads and fans to decrease temperatures, or they can, less expensively, douse the greenhouse floor with ice-cold water in the morning whenever a hot day is expected.

Even though many begonias naturally grow on the forest floor, in cultivation they require well-lit conditions. Much, however, depends upon the climate in which the begonias are being cultivated. In warm sunny areas, as a general rule, begonias should not receive bright direct sunlight and light should either be indirect (scattered off surrounding objects) or filtered (for example, by netting or trees). In northern regions this shading is often necessary during the spring and summer but in the fall and winter most begonias will need far less or even no shading. To find out the best way of growing begonias in your area talk to other local growers or join a regional begonia group. In the home, plants grown under natural sunlight on a windowsill will often perform best when provided with a south-facing position in the winter and an east-facing one in the summer.

As different *Begonia* species require different amounts of light for optimum growth, learning to recognize when a plant is being grown under the wrong light levels is important. Determining if a plant is growing poorly as a result of too much or too little light can sometimes be a little tricky because both extremes can result in unnaturally pale foliage, poor growth, and a lack of flowers. As a general rule, plants grown in too dark a location will have unnaturally pale foliage that is stretched toward the brightest light source. However, plants receiving too much light will often have pale, bleached leaves with dry, brown margins. Overly bright conditions will cause a few species, rather than becoming bleached, to develop unsightly amounts of red or purple pigment in their stems and leaves. Once you have made a diagnosis and moved a plant to an area with more favorable light it should soon recover and put on new growth.

The vast majority of begonias require a relative humidity between 40 and 60 percent. Relative humidity is a measure of the amount of moisture in the air compared with the maximum amount that the air could contain at that temperature. In general, warmer air has the potential to hold more moisture than colder air does. Symptoms of a plant grown in an environment lacking sufficient humidity are crispy, brown leaf margins (Plate 3b), and in extreme cases leaf and flower bud drop. Splashing water on the floors each morning is a useful way to increase the humidity levels in a greenhouse; and, if the water is cold it will also help reduce atmospheric temperatures. In the home, where you cannot water the floor, group plants close together or grow them on humidifying trays. These trays contain a layer of pebbles to which you periodically add water to a level slightly below the top of the pebbles. The potted plant sits on top of the pebble layer so that it is not in direct contact with the water but benefits from the rising water vapor. Begonias requiring particularly humid conditions are often grown in contained atmospheres, sometimes even within a greenhouse setting. Many of these species are listed in appendix C. Symptoms of plants grown under conditions that are too humid are increased susceptibility to fungal and bacterial diseases, including leaf rot. Install fans in the home or greenhouse and open greenhouse ventilation to reduce humidity.

Choice of container and growing medium

Many begonias are relatively shallow rooted and require only shallow pots. However, taller-growing, cane-like, and shrub-like species have a tendency to become top heavy and for that reason often need deeper pots, sometimes with rocks added for ballast. Some growers with greenhouses in relatively cool northern areas tend to prefer porous clay pots to plastic or glazed pots, because they allow excess water to evaporate from the growing medium. Warm-climate growers tend to prefer plastic pots, because they hold moisture in the growing medium and need less frequent watering. Furthermore, clay pots are heavier to lift and more difficult to keep clean. Consider the costs and benefits of each type of container before choosing one over the other.

As a rule most begonias will need repotting only once their roots have filled the container they are growing in. When repotting begonias, and most other tropical plants, move them into a container that is only slightly larger than the existing one, otherwise excessive moisture may accumulate in the medium and cause the roots to rot. If a larger pot is not available or desired shave off the roots and soil on the sides and bottom of the root ball and put it in the same size pot with some fresh growing medium around the edges. The growing media for most pot- or container-grown begonias should be slightly acidic (pH 5.8–6.8), light, well aerated, and free draining. A number of appropriate soil-less mixes are available in nurseries and garden centers, but some growers prefer to make their own mix, some favoring loam- (good-quality topsoil) based, or peat-based mixes. Others prefer a mix containing these two components or more. Sphagnum peat is particularly useful in mixes since it creates acidic conditions. The addition of sand, grit, bark, or perlite will promote good drainage and increase air circulation around the roots. For plants grown in greenhouses in plastic pots I recommend a potting mix used by the staff of the United Kingdom's National Begonia Collection at Glasgow Botanic Garden:

7 parts sphagnum peat
2 part grit (small, sharp stones)
1 part bark
a little slow-release fertilizer
a little ground limestone

Plants grown in terrariums, however, require a very different mix, which I discuss under "Contained atmospheres and artificial lights" later in this chapter.

Water and fertilizer

The amount of water to give the plants will vary depending on your specific growing conditions. Numerous factors, including the climate, growing medium, and type of container, will all influence how much water a plant needs at a particular time. As a general rule, most begonias grown in pots should be watered as soon as the top half-inch of their growing medium becomes dry to the touch, but not before. Over watering and lack of adequate atmospheric humidity are probably the two most common reasons that begonias and other tropical plants are lost. When plants need watering the growing medium should be watered sufficiently to allow excess water to drain from the bottom of the pot, since deep watering like this will promote a healthy, well-developed root system. The water should be just warm to the touch. Very cold or hot water can send a plant into a state of shock. Special care should be taken not to over water rhizomatous, rex, or tuberous begonias, particularly when they are in a state of dormancy or slowed growth. The most common symptoms of over watering among all begonias are leaf drop, root rot, and wilted stems. Somewhat confusingly, wilting is also a symptom of under watering, as are yellowing leaves and flower buds that fall before they open. If in doubt, knock a plant out of its pot and check to see if the potting medium is either overly wet or dry.

While plants are actively growing they will benefit from the regular application of a water-soluble fertilizer containing a 20-10-20 mix of the three major plant macronutrients: nitrogen (N), phosphorus (P), and potassium (K). Always read the instructions that come with the fertilizer, as over application of fertilizer can damage roots. Do not apply fertilizer to newly repotted plants for about one month or to sick or dormant plants, because they are particularly susceptible to root damage. Also remember that a soil-less potting mix will need more frequent fertilizer application than will most soil-based mixes. Some growers prefer to add time-release fertilizer pellets to the growing medium instead of, or in some cases combined with, liquid fertilizer. Experiment to find which method best suits your situation.

Pinching, pruning, staking, and labeling

Pinching, or removal of stem tips, promotes side branching and will result in a bushier plant. Regular pinching, starting when a plant is young, is important if mature plants are to be compact and attractively shaped. It is particularly useful for the cane-like begonias because it will promote branching toward the base of their stems. Pruning, or the removal of whole stems or large parts of stems, is generally needed less frequently and is normally only carried out when an old stem upsets the balance of a plant or when a plant has become too large for its growing area. Some growers in warmer climates recommend severely pruning older cane-like begonias in late winter or early spring to produce bushier plants. Occasionally, inner stems may also be removed to promote air circulation within a plant and thereby prevent diseases associated with excessive humidity.

Staking is often necessary for taller begonias and those with naturally floppy stems. It should be carried out early in the life of a plant long before it becomes a necessity, so that the mature plant will have a more natural appearance and the stakes and ties will be as unobtrusive as possible. In order to obtain a graceful shape, each of the plant's main stems should have its own stake and each stake should be positioned as close to its stem as possible, preferably on the side facing away from the viewer. Green bamboo stakes and clear plastic ribbon ties are often used for staking, as these materials blend relatively unobtrusively into the foliage.

Every plant in a collection should have a label with its name and any other information you deem useful, such as its source and date of acquisition. Many growers use plastic labels and write on them with pencil. Permanent ink is often a less-than-permanent solution and I do not recommend it. Small, inexpensive devices designed to punch plant names into strips of durable, sticky-backed tape that are then fixed onto plastic labels also work well and are widely available.

Contained atmospheres and artificial lights

Perhaps the easiest way to grow a wide range of begonias is in a greenhouse or, in warm climates, in a shade, or lath, house. However, for those growers with no access to a greenhouse or shade house, contained-atmosphere and artificial-light gardening provide means of cultivating humidity-loving species in the home. In my home and office, I grow begonias in a wide variety of glass and clear plastic containers, including converted fish tanks, goldfish bowls, and large glass cookie jars. The top of each container is sealed with either plastic wrap or a pane of glass so that humidity can build up inside. The containers are then positioned under horticultural fluorescent lights. Such containers can alternatively be placed near a window, but careful positioning is essential since direct sunlight can stew plants, quickly turning them into something resembling cooked spinach. Under artificial strip lights situate plants requiring particularly bright light closest to the center of the light where light levels are most intense. Timers may be used to provide 14–16 hours of light per 24 hours. This can be reduced temporarily to 12 hours a day for two months in early winter to encourage flower production in winter and early spring bloomers.

The general care of plants in contained atmosphere gardening is slightly different from that involved with other methods. In particular, many growers use an especially porous growing medium composed of chopped, long-fiber sphagnum moss and a small amount of perlite. Prepare the sphagnum for the mix by immersing it in boiling water to sterilize it, letting it cool, then cutting it with scissors into roughly 2.5-cm-long pieces. Then blot the wet sphagnum with newspapers or paper towels to remove any excess water before mixing it with the perlite. Before adding the growing mix to the container, line the base with a 6-mm layer of small charcoal pieces. The charcoal is said to absorb soluble salts and other impurities before they have a chance to build up and damage young roots. On top of the charcoal layer add 2.5–7.5 cm of the chopped sphagnum-perlite mix. Because this growing medium is still moist at this point it usually does not need any additional water after planting. Even when established, plants in contained atmospheres will need less frequent watering than those in other situations. With these enclosed containers, the only way to determine when to water is to touch the surface of the growing material to see how moist it is. Add water only when it becomes dry. Some growers recommend using distilled water or rainwater when watering contained atmospheres. Sealed containers will need watering only a few times a year, a great asset for someone who travels a great deal. If a particularly dense build-up of condensation occurs on the inside of the container soon after watering, too much water has been added. A turkey baster or paper towels may be used to remove the excess water. Afterward, leave the lid off for a few hours to rectify the problem. Aside from occasional watering, the care of enclosed containers is minimal. If plants are left for a year or longer without changing the growing medium, check to see that the pH level has not dropped too low. If the pH has fallen below 5.8, ground limestone may be gradually worked into the growing medium until the pH is raised to the correct level. Fertilizing begonias grown in terrariums is rarely necessary, but some growers find that the addition of fertilizer will produce more active growth and larger plants. Sometimes after fertilizer has been applied mold will grow on the surface of the growing medium. This, however, typically does no harm to the plants and can be removed easily. The periodic removal of fallen blooms or any leaves that touch the sides of the container is also necessary before they start to decay.

A few *Begonia* species have gained the reputation of being difficult to grow because they require high humidity coupled with relatively low temperatures in the range of 62 to 65°F (16–18°C). I am told that these plants perform well when grown in contained atmospheres placed under lights in the basement of a house, where it is often slightly cooler. Examples include *Begonia acaulis, B. variabilis,* and *B. versicolor.* Another useful trick for reducing the temperature inside a terrarium is to set the lights to come on only at night when conditions are usually cooler. That way the extra heat produced by the lights will not push the air temperature above damaging limits. A fan can also remove any excess heat produced by the lights.

For many growers light stands provide a space-saving means of cultivating a wide variety of begonias indoors. Plants are usually positioned close together on trays with artificial lights suspended above them. A sheet of plastic draped around the light stand, while looking unattractive, will help to increase humidity levels and allow a greater range of species to grow. Much has been written on the subject of gardening under artificial lights and a few of the more helpful books are listed in the bibliography.

Propagation

Propagation is among the most rewarding aspects of growing plants. Not only is it an inexpensive and convenient means of introducing new plants into your collection but it is also gratifying to witness a tiny seed or cutting become a mature plant covered with flowers. Propagation is also a good way to safeguard rare or particularly valued plants. Keeping backup plants reduces the risk that you will lose all stock of a particular species or hybrid as a result of an unforeseen mishap. In addition, it allows you to swap spare plants with friends, who will usually be more than happy to give cuttings back to you if your plant dies.

Propagation methods range from the simple, such as dividing a large plant into two or more smaller ones, to the more complex, including such techniques as seed or tissue culture. The method most commonly used for begonias is stem cuttings. To prepare a stem cutting, use a sharp, sterile knife to remove from the tip of a healthy, actively growing stem or branch 5–15 cm of non-flowering stem with roughly two to five nodes. Trim off the lower leaves, then place the cut end, which should be just below a node, in the rooting mix. Before doing this, be sure that the basal node has a dormant growth bud, not a scar left from an inflorescence, which will be reluctant to produce roots. Roots should form at the cut end after a few weeks. Leaf cuttings are another means of propagation that works well for those begonias with a rhizome, but it is not suitable for many of the cane-like and shrub-like begonias. For leaf cuttings, remove a young healthy leaf with about 2.5–5.1 cm of its petiole, or leaf stalk, still attached and place it in rooting medium so that the petiole is below ground but the leaf blade is not covered. With large leaves it is often necessary first to trim the leaf blade to a smaller size to prevent the cutting from losing excess moisture through having an overly large surface area. After a few weeks, a new plantlet will form at the cut end of the petiole and can then be potted up and grown to maturity. Cuttings of all kinds are usually rooted in a highly friable, soil-less mix that is kept slightly moist. Mixes made from equal parts peat and sharp, salt-free, sand or equal parts perlite and vermiculite both work well. Some growers also add chopped sphagnum moss to their mix when propagating the more difficult species. Rooting in water is even possible for some cane-like and shrub-like begonias. Regardless of the rooting medium used, most begonia cuttings need ample atmospheric humidity and often benefit from being grown in an enclosed, transparent container or under a mist unit. An enclosed container should be placed in a well-lit area away from direct sunlight. Artificial lights are commonly used for propagating begonias in the home. Adding rooting hormone to the cut ends is rarely necessary, but the fungicide present in most rooting hormone can be beneficial. Some growers alternatively soak all their begonia cuttings in a 5 percent bleach solution for 5–10 minutes to help prevent rot.

Seed propagation is also a valuable technique because many begonias are conveniently obtained only via seed. The American Begonia Society's seed fund is a particularly good source of rare or hard-to-find species. *Begonia* seeds are small and should be sown in a draft-free place since they have the tendency to blow away—most are adapted for wind dispersal. To sow begonia seeds, first prepare a seed tray or pot with a suitable sterile seed mix such as one comprised of equal parts sand and peat. To sterilize the seed mix place it in an oven at 60–70°F (16–21°C) in a shallow baking pan covered with aluminum foil for about an hour. Level and gently firm the surface of the seed mix and use warm water to thoroughly wet it. You can either use a watering can or soak the pot in a tray of water.

After the pot has drained thoroughly, sow the seeds by sprinkling them evenly across the surface of the moist medium. This can be done by putting a small amount of seed on a small sheet of paper folded lengthwise and gently tapping the paper as the seeds roll off onto the medium. *Begonia* seeds need light to germinate, so they should not be covered with the medium. Place the container with the seeds in a humid, well-lit environment. A pane of glass or plastic film placed on top of the container will help increase humidity. The seeds of many *Begonia* species will start to germinate within two to three weeks, but some take up to a year. Seedlings are best transplanted once they have developed their first or second true leaf. At that time, they should be carefully transplanted into new trays or pots so that they are about 1.3 cm apart. I use a slender, pointed piece of bamboo cane to transplant the seedlings without damaging them. With this tool I gently lift the seedlings out of the original seed mix and position them in a small, ready-made hole in the new medium. Similar utensils such as a narrow, sharpened plant label will work equally well. After the seedlings have been transplanted, the humidity should be gradually decreased to approximate that which the adult plant will receive. Once the seedlings have reached about 3.8 cm in height they should be transplanted a second time, so that each plant occupies its own 8-cm pot. Repotting is repeated each time the young plant reaches the limits of its new pot. With most *Begonia* species, plants will reach flowering size in as little as six months to a year. With all forms of propagation, always remember to add labels to trays and pots to provide a record of what is being propagated and a means of learning from each experience. Recording on the label the date the seed was sown is especially beneficial.

Pests and diseases

Fortunately, most pests and diseases of begonias are generally problematic only in large greenhouse collections, and even then problems can usually be prevented by purchasing healthy, pest- and disease-free material and maintaining suitable, hygienic conditions for cultivation. Additional practices that will greatly reduce pest and disease outbreaks include avoiding overhead watering, which can spread certain pests and diseases, using sterilized potting soils, and regularly removing dead and dying leaves and flowers from plants and benches. Growers who maintain frequent monitoring should encounter few pests or diseases and will be able to easily control any that do arise before they become a serious problem. Following is a list of the most serious pests and diseases of begonias, some of which are illustrated in Plates 3, 4, and 5.

Pests

Mealy bugs. This common pest is covered with a distinctive crumbly, soft, white wax and secretes a characteristic cottony or wooly substance over its egg clusters. If infestations are localized, remove adults and young by wiping affected areas with a cotton swab dipped in rubbing alcohol or by dipping the plant in a solution of soapy water and alcohol. Continue treatment as long as necessary. Biological control, horticultural oils, and insecticidal sprays are also available and can be used to treat large infestations that sometimes occur in greenhouses.

Mites. A number of tiny mite species can be problematic. Two of the worst offenders are the broad mite and the cyclamen or begonia mite. Usually, the first sign of their presence is damaged young leaves that are tightly rolled inward at their margins and otherwise brittle, discolored, and crinkled (Plate 4). Remove and destroy any infected plant parts and then spray with an acaricide specifically recommended for the control of the problem mite. General insecticides rarely prove effective at controlling mites. In greenhouse conditions, where these pests are most problematic, quarantine new plants to prevent infestations.

Broad mite.

Red spider, or two-spotted, mites can also attack begonias. Infested leaves are yellow speckled and, if the infestation is severe, may be covered with a wool-like substance on their undersurfaces. Control these mites with the beneficial predatory mite *Phytoseiulus persimilis* or an acaricide.

Nematodes. Two kinds of these microscopic, worm-like creatures parasitize begonias: leaf nematodes and root nematodes. Leaf nematodes are more of a problem in glasshouse culture because they require moist, humid conditions to move from plant to plant. Major symptoms of this pest include the presence of reddish brown, dead lesions on the leaves, stunted growth, and the overproduction of red or purple leaf pigments. Infestations can be prevented by good hygiene. Most importantly, avoid introducing infected plants to your collection. Remove dead and dying material from plants and benches as this can harbor leaf nematodes, and avoid overhead watering as the splashing water can transport nematodes between plants.

Various species of soil-borne nematodes attack the roots of begonias causing them to develop swollen galls or become gnarled and distorted. The foliage of affected plants appears discolored, lacks vigor, and wilts under stress. Such plants are also susceptible to secondary attack by pathogenic fungi and bacteria. The best form of control is to destroy affected plants. In the open garden avoid

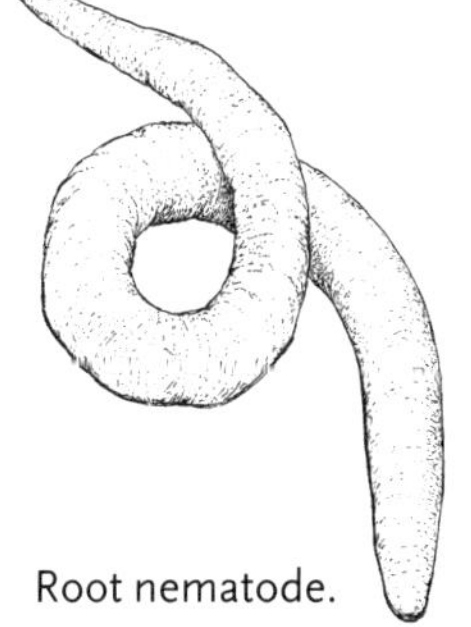

Root nematode.

replanting begonias in contaminated soil. In the case of pot grown plants, infestations may be prevented and controlled by routinely sterilizing potting soils and washing plant pots.

Scale Insects. Scale insects are small oval insects that are easy to identify by the armor-like covering of wax and old cast-off skins that protect the adults and eggs. Two unrelated kinds feed on begonias: soft scale which characteristically produce honeydew, and hard scale which are usually more heavily armored and do not produce honeydew. Treat infestations in the same way as described for mealy bugs. If you do use chemical sprays, bear in mind that they are most effective at killing the juvenile "crawler" stage of the life cycle, so time applications accordingly.

Slugs and snails. Often the first sign of slugs or snails is a glistening, silver trail of mucus and rounded holes in the leaves of a prized plant. Slugs and snails are usually only a problem in the open garden, where they can be controlled by a variety of methods. For example, a sprinkling of soot or diatomaceous earth around the base of the susceptible plants will deter these pests. For a more permanent solution, set beer traps or routinely walk around the garden with a flashlight on a damp night, when these pests are active, and remove them. Removing dead and dying plant material and other debris from the garden will also make it a less hospitable place for slugs and snails. I do not recommend most slug pellets because they can be harmful to pets and wild birds.

Weevils. The adults and larvae of both the vine weevil and the lesser strawberry weevil feed on begonias but in most areas the former species is the worse offender. Adults of both species measure up to 1.3 cm in length and have a darkly colored, swollen abdomen and an elongated head with two jointed antennae. They feed at night producing a characteristic notched pattern on the edges of leaves. During the day they hide in crevices and in mulch. As with slugs and snails, one method of controlling these pests is to routinely walk around the garden or greenhouse at night and remove them by hand. The weevil grubs resemble fat, white housefly maggots and cause more damage to plants than do the adults. They feed on roots and tubers, causing plants to suddenly wilt or collapse. Most chemical treatments focus on the larvae, as chemical control of the adult weevils is difficult. When infestation is widespread, some authorities recommended working insecticides into the potting medium whenever plants are repotted. In less severe cases, appropriate liquid insecticides may be watered into the potting mix. As a preventive measure, this is usually done periodically from late July to October when weevil

Adult and larval vine weevil.

larvae are most abundant. In a contained greenhouse situation biological control of the larvae with beneficial parasitic nematodes is also effective. To prevent unexpected infestations, always examine the roots of severely wilted plants for larvae and routinely tidy the greenhouse to reduce the number of potential hiding places for the adults.

Whiteflies. These small, powdery white, moth-like insects infest the undersurfaces of the uppermost leaves and if disturbed fly rapidly around the top of the host plants. Affected leaves are often yellow spotted and covered with sticky honeydew. In cases of severe infestation, leaf drop may occur. Adult whiteflies are attracted to a specific shade of yellow and can be trapped on commercially available sticky boards of that color. The tiny predatory-parasitic wasp *Encarsia formosa* can also be used to control the larval stage in greenhouses. Treatment with suitable insecticides is possible but may be problematic because several strains of whitefly have evolved resistance to commonly used brands.

Diseases

Bacterial leaf spot. This disease produces water-soaked areas on the leaves that are surrounded by yellow rings. The spots turn brown and then black and eventually cause leaf drop. In some cases associated stem rot also occurs. Bacterial leaf spot is most often seen during the summer months when temperature, humidity, and rainfall levels are high. The best management is to avoid introducing infected plants to your collection. Once the disease is present, remove and destroy any affected leaves or stems and in extreme cases spray plants with a bacterial leaf spot treatment. Avoid splashing water on the leaves when watering because this will benefit the bacteria. Since the disease quickly spreads through wounded Rieger hybrids, do not remove affected leaves from these cultivars. Instead, spray the whole plant with a bacterial leaf spot treatment.

***Botrytis* blight.** This fungal disease produces gray moldy patches on leaves, stems, and buds. *Botrytis* thrives under cool, wet, humid weather, especially in the presence of dead, damaged, or dying plant tissues. It can be managed by spacing plants to facilitate good air circulation, by providing good ventilation of greenhouses, and by continually removing and destroying dead and dying leaves and flowers. Fungicide sprays are also available.

Powdery mildews. These minute fungi produce unsightly white powdery patches on leaves, stems, and buds (Plate 3d). Like *Botrytis*, powdery mildews prefer cool temperatures, high humidity and wet leaves, but unlike that disease, they favor healthy plants. However, they may be problematic when plants are stressed due to under watering. In a greenhouse, good air circulation and ventilation are effective preventive measures, as is avoidance of overhead watering. Restricting watering to the morning so that water unwillingly splashed on leaves will quickly evaporate also helps. Severe cases may be treated with a fungicide.

***Pythium* root rot.** This fungal disease attacks the roots and stem bases of adult plants and cuttings. Affected plants at first have a slightly wilted appearance, followed by yellowing of their lower leaves. As the disease progresses, roots and stems turn black and mushy, leading to the death of the plant. The use of sterilized potting soil and appropriate fungicides will control this disease. Giving cuttings less water and providing plants with good drainage are effective preventive measures.

***Rhizoctonia* crown rot.** A sign of this fungal disease is the presence of brownish mold spreading from the soil to the infected stem base, a condition that will eventually lead to the collapse and death of the stem. *Rhizoctonia* is usually found only on plants that have been damaged or are stressed by high temperatures or poor growing conditions. Maintenance of hygienic conditions and good cultural practice should prevent fungal growth. Fungicide sprays are also available.

Viral diseases. A variety of viruses can attack begonias, causing among other symptoms, yellow mottling of the leaves (Plate 3a), pale yellow rings or spots, leaf malformation, and stunted growth. If you suspect the cause is a virus, destroy all affected plants. Always use sterilized soil and maintain good aphid control to reduce the spread of viruses. Aphids are not usually a serious pest of begonias, but controlling them with soapy water or suitable insecticides is important because they can transfer viral diseases via their syringe-like mouth parts.

3

The genus *Begonia* and its relatives

Begonias in the wild

Throughout most of the world's tropical and subtropical regions, begonias grow in a wide variety of ecological niches, ranging from the mist-splashed sides of waterfalls to the moss-covered branches of trees. Wherever a suitable location is found, a different *Begonia* species seems to have evolved to occupy the space. With just more than 1500 species comprising the genus, individual species are, not surprisingly, usually restricted to very small geographical areas. *Begonia malachosticta*, which is grown for its polka-dotted leaves, illustrates the small distribution and high degree of ecological specialization typical of many wild begonias. It makes its home on a single hill on the island of Borneo, and there only in limestone crevices between altitudes of 75 to 150 m. This is precisely where the tree canopy lets in just the right amount of light.

Currently so little is known about how new species of *Begonia* evolve that we can only speculate as to why so many occupy such small areas. One possibility that looks increasingly likely is that most *Begonia* species have a very poor ability to disperse their seeds, and as a result different populations isolated by even small distances can evolve into new species as a result of random genetic changes. Most begonias employ wind and water runoff to disperse their seeds, both of which are relatively inefficient means of dispersal. A small number, however, have evolved animal-dispersed fruits and have much larger distributions. Animals, such as birds and bats, enable larger numbers of seeds to be routinely carried much longer distances than most begonias' individual seeds could be transported by either rainwash or the faint breezes that typically penetrate the understory of the rain forest. In fact, the record for the largest natural distribution of any begonia is held by *B. longifolia*, an animal-dispersed species that is found from eastern China westward to the Himalayas and southward to Indonesia, a distance of several thousand miles. Widely distributed species, like this, often vary in minor vegetative and floral features from one part of their range to another, and for this reason are often subdivided into either subspecies or varieties. Subspecies are distinguished by a greater number of features and a higher level of geographic separation between their different populations than varieties are.

Though many *Begonia* species are ecological specialists, restricted to undisturbed tropical forest, some are able to inhabit disturbed areas, such as road cuts and secondary growth forest, and are thriving in these times of large scale destruction of the tropical forests. Two such species, *B. nelumbifolia* and *B. heracleifolia*, are commonly found today throughout tropical Mexico and Central America wherever forests have been dissected by roads. Before the roads arrived they were probably restricted to open areas by rivers or small forest glades created by localized storm damage. *Begonia hirtella* and *B. ulmifolia* are particularly notable colonists. Such is their love of disturbed habitats, they have repeatedly escaped from cultivation and become weeds far outside their natural ranges. Indeed, *B. hirtella* has naturalized almost throughout the tropics and is just as likely to become a greenhouse weed, if given the chance.

Though begonias are found naturally throughout much of tropical and subtropical Africa, Asia, and the Americas, the greatest number of species occur in the humid montane forests of South America and mainland Asia. Just one tropical region of any size lacks begonias—Australia. Possibly one day someone will dis-

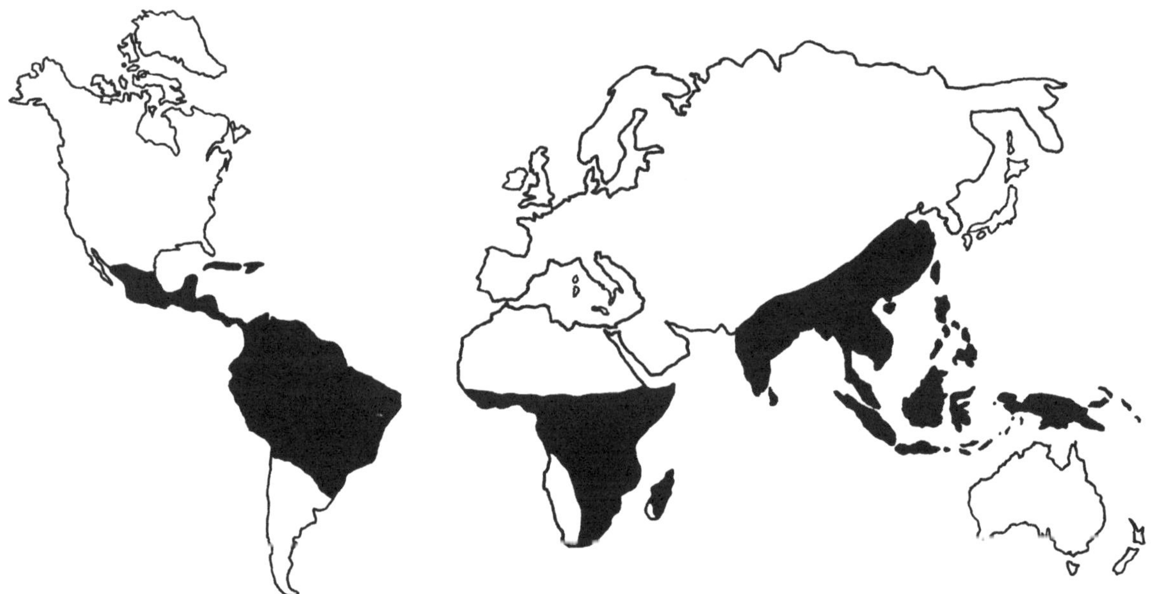

Natural worldwide distribution of the genus *Begonia*.

cover a few begonias in the rain forests of remote northeast Queensland, but chances are the genus has just not had enough time since it first evolved in Africa to colonize this distant continent. Indeed, if you follow the migration route that *Begonia* probably took from Africa into mainland Asia, and from there southward through Malaysia and Indonesia to Papua New Guinea and the Solomon Islands immediately to the north of Australia, you will find a marked decrease in taxonomic diversity as you approach Australia.

Though no begonias are recorded from Australia, those keen to see begonias in the wild will be pleased to know that elsewhere the genus is easy to locate wherever tropical forests are left standing. Those searching for wild begonias in such areas should simply travel to the nearest waterfall marked on their map, because there, with a little luck, wild begonias will very likely be found (Plate 6).

Begonia's defining characteristics

The distinctive asymmetric leaves, fleshy jointed stems, and showy flowers of most cultivated begonias make them among the easiest of all ornamental plant genera to recognize. Nevertheless, some species do not exhibit any of these features and can only be identified as begonias by a combination of subtle botanical characteristics. One such plant is *Begonia bogneri*, a curious Madagascan species with short, thin stems, grass-like leaves, and diminutive flowers. However, even this species is easily recognized as a *Begonia* because it possesses a combination

Leaf of *B. scharffii* and *B. bogneri* plant.

of less conspicuous morphological and cellular features that are characteristic of all begonias and provide the botanical basis for recognizing the genus. These include alternate stipulate leaves, separate male and female flowers, petal-like sepals, centripetal stamen development, inferior ovaries, cellular calcium oxalate crystals, and seeds with a seed lid and collar cells and very little endosperm.

Structural variation among begonias

Since *Begonia* contains hundreds of species with a wide range of environmental preferences, accurately identifying individuals in cultivation is important if you wish to discover more about their particular horticultural requirements. Though recognizing a plant as belonging to the genus *Begonia* is easy (see "*Begonia*'s defining characteristics"), the identification of the species, and particularly the cultivars, is often much more time consuming. This chapter provides a useful resource for identifying cultivated begonias.

Because the range of form and structure found within *Begonia* can be daunting, I have described the most important taxonomic features here to help navigate the descriptions in chapter five. Most of these are easily observed with the naked eye, but some of the floral characters require the use of a good-quality hand lens, and a few of the features associated with the ovary require that this organ be transversely sectioned. Even so, all these anatomical characters can be easily distinguished with a little practice. An illustrated glossary of technical terms is provided at the back of the book.

Habit

In those species with above-ground stems, the growth habit may be prostrate, upright, scrambling or climbing. Several of the larger, shrubby begonias have woody stem bases and can reach a height, or spread, of up to 3.5 m, but even so, true trees are not found in the genus. At the other extreme are those species that lack aerial stems and have leaves that arise directly from an underground tuber or rhizome, or from an extremely short, ground-level stem. Species with aerial stems are usually evergreen, but some tuberous begonias have a dormant period during which the aerial growth dies back. *Begonia crassicaulis* and its relatives are particularly interesting since they have deciduous leaves that are produced each year, on

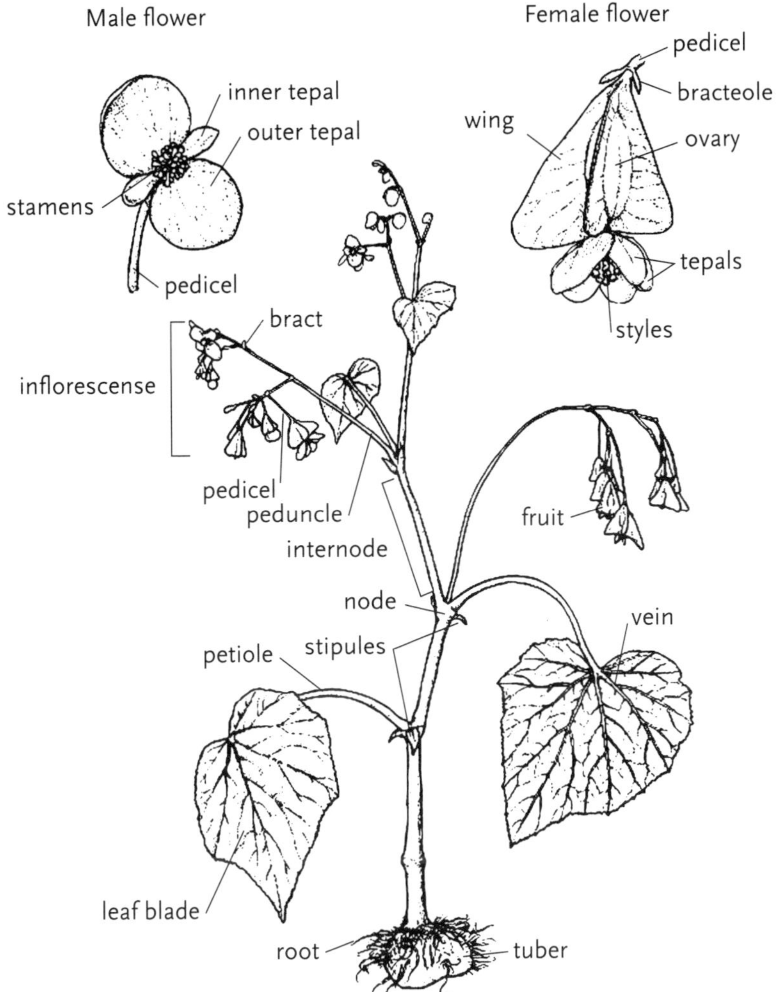

Parts of a *Begonia* plant, using the example of *B. grandis*.

persistent thickened stems, after the plant has flowered. Most begonias are perennial but a few, such as *B. hirtella*, are annual and must be propagated annually from seed. Nevertheless, this latter species seldom requires our assistance since it grows prolifically from seed and can become a greenhouse weed.

The general habit of a plant often provides a useful means of narrowing down a species' identity to a handful of possibilities. Characteristics of the leaves, flowers, and fruits may then be used to determine the exact species.

Leaves

The popular image of a begonia leaf as oblique, asymmetric, and ear-like in shape is somewhat misleading, as symmetric leaves are found in several species, including *Begonia herbacea*, and peltate leaves are also characteristic of some begonias, like *B. lubbersii*. Others, such as *B. bipinnatifida*, have deeply dissected fern-like leaves or, as in the case of *B. luxurians*, palmately compound leaves. The arrangement of veins in the leaf also varies and may be palmate (for example, in *B. oxyloba*), palmate-pinnate (*B. maculata*), or pinnate (*B. parilis*), depending upon

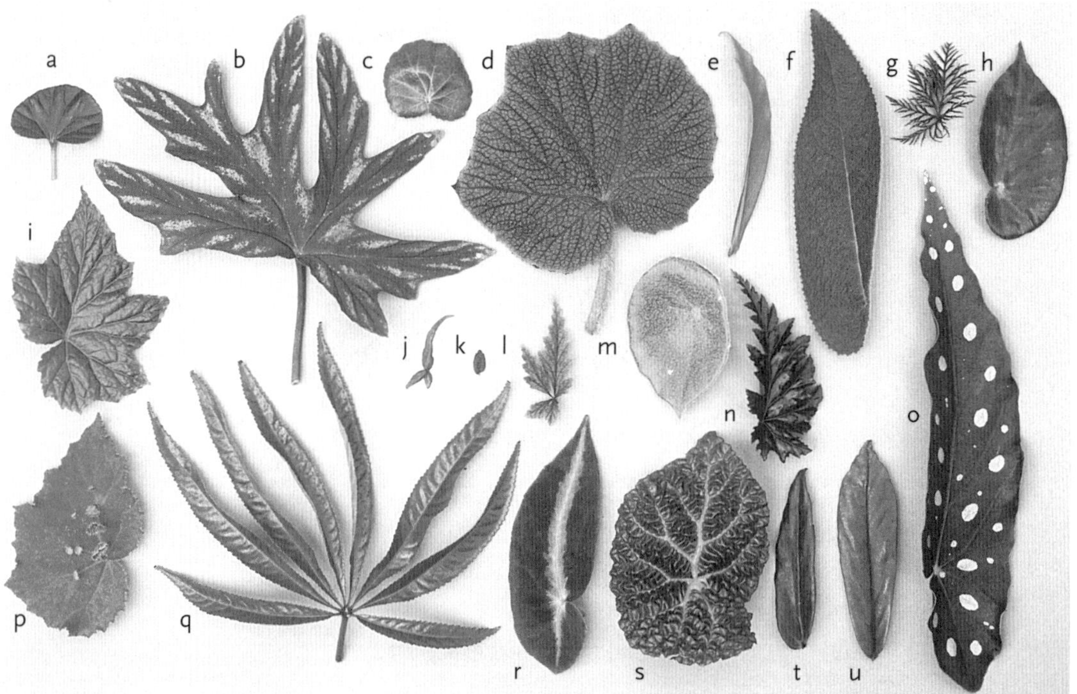

A diverse selection of *Begonia* leaves: **a**) *B. fischeri* var. *malvacea*, **b**) *B. aconitifolia*, **c**) *B. rotundifolia*, **d**) *B. acida*, **e**) *B. herbacea*, **f**) *B. egregia*, **g**) *B. bipinnatifida*, **h**) *B. sanguinea*, **i**) *B. oxyloba*, **j**) *B. dregei*, **k**), *B. foliosa*, **l**) *B. polilloensis*, **m**) *B. peltata* var. *peltata*, **n**) *B. serratipetala*, **o**) *B. maculata*, **p**) *B. hispida* var. *cucullifera*, **q**) *B. luxurians*, **r**) *B. listada*, **s**) *B. gehrtii*, **t**) *B. komoensis*, **u**) *B. parilis*, illustrating much of the diversity of begonia leaf outlines. Leaf outlines may, for example, be ovate in *B. gehrtii* and *B. hispida* var. *cucullifera*, angular-ovate in *B. maculata*, ovate (in outline) with palmately compound bipinnatifid lobes in *B. polilloensis*, circular in *B. rotundifolia*, circular (in outline) with palmate lobes in *B. aconitifolia*, circular (in outline) with palmately compound lobes in *B. luxurians*, oblong-lanceolate in *B. egregia*, and angular-obovate in *B. parilis*. Likewise, leaf bases may vary from truncate in *B. fischeri* var. *malvacea* to cordate in *B. acida* (and several of the other species) and wedge-shaped in *B. parilis*.

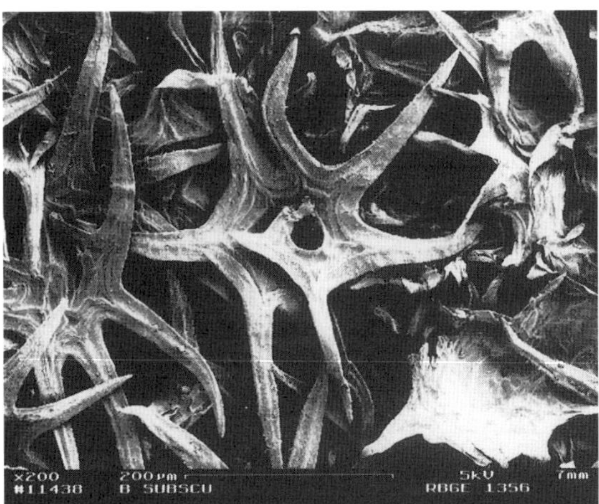

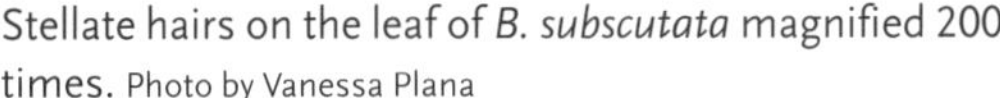

Stellate hairs on the leaf of *B. subscutata* magnified 200 times. Photo by Vanessa Plana

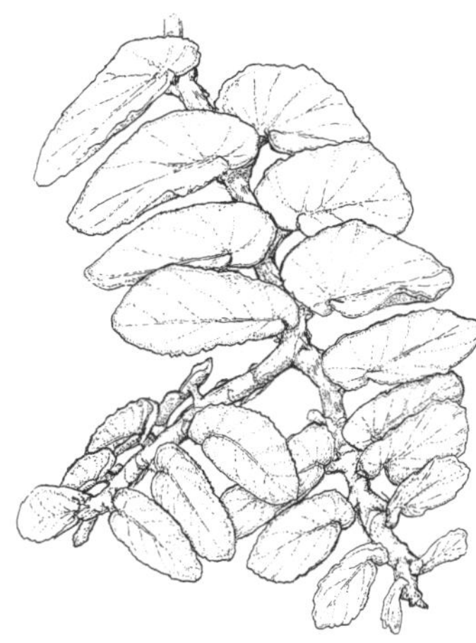

Begonia thelmae with a distichous leaf arrangement.

the species. Leaf surfaces, and other plant parts, are often covered with a variety of hairs, which in some African species often take the form of beautiful, microscopic, star-shaped or circular scale-like structures.

The arrangement of leaves in the majority of species is alternate, but in a few Asian species yet to be introduced into cultivation, the upper leaves are opposite. In two diminutive Burmese species, *Begonia adenopoda* and *B. burmensis*, which have sadly been lost from cultivation, some of the leaves are arranged alternately along a short stem, while the rest form a whorl atop the stem. Whorled leaves are also found in those species that lack stems. *Begonia thelmae* and several of the cane-like species have leaves arranged in two staggered rows along each side of the stem, a state known as distichous. Most species have several leaves, but a few, such as *B. dioica*, have only one or two.

Inflorescence

An enormous variety of flower arrangements occur in *Begonia*. In some species, inflorescences develop at the ends of branches and are called terminal inflorescences, and in others they develop in the leaf axils along the length of each branch and are called axillary inflorescences. In some species both arrangements are found on the same plant. Because the structures of the inflorescences themselves are so varied, botanists working on *Begonia* sometimes use a simplified classifica-

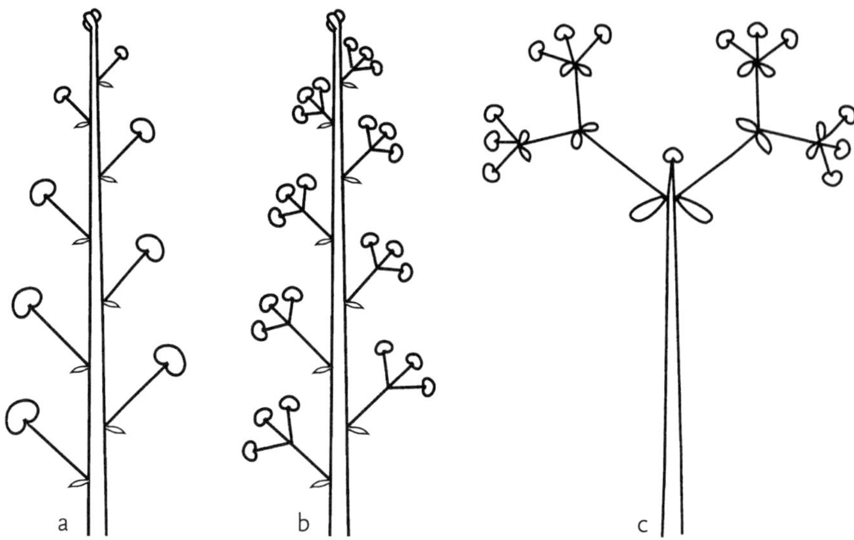

Basic inflorescence types: **a**) and **b**) racemose, **c**) cymose.

tion that recognizes two basic inflorescence types: racemose and cymose. A racemose inflorescence is characterized by a continuously growing, dominant central axis. A cymose inflorescence, on the other hand, lacks a central axis that dominates the lateral branches. Most species of *Begonia* have cymose inflorescences but a few, including *B. grandis, B. gracilis,* and *B. modestiflora,* have racemose inflorescences. In *B. chlorosticta* and related species the male inflorescence is often racemose, but the female flowers are paired or solitary. The individual flowers of *Begonia* are always unisexual, and the position of the male flowers in relation to the female flowers is variable among species. An inflorescence may possess flowers of both sexes; or the two sexes may be on separate inflorescences; or in the case of *B. roxburghii* and a handful of other species, they are consistently on separate plants. As the male and female flowers of a particular plant frequently mature at different times, observing a plant over a period of time is often necessary in order to determine the true structure of its inflorescence.

Petals and sepals

The majority of flowering plants have flowers with easily identified whorls of green sepals and brightly colored petals, but in *Begonia* the sepals and petals are both brightly colored and, therefore, often difficult to distinguish. Anatomical research has shown that both sepals and petals are present in some begonias, but since they are often difficult to tell apart they are widely referred to collectively as tepals.

The number of tepals in a flower varies considerably among species, and even within a plant of a particular species this number usually differs between the male and female flowers. Flowers typically have two, three, four, or five tepals, but some of the tuberous South American species have up to eleven. Tepals are usually free but in a few species they are basally joined in the male, the female, or both flowers. *Begonia ampla* is an example.

Flower color

Most *Begonia* species have white or pink tepals but in some species they are yellow, orange, or red. These yellow-, orange-, and red-flowered species have been important in the development of many modern-day cultivars. Yellow flowers are common in Africa, occurring in approximately 30 percent of the species from that continent. The only yellow-flowered begonias outside Africa are the South American *B. pearcei* and *B. lutea* and the Asiatic *B. xanthina* and *B. flaviflora*. Cultivated orange-flowered species include the South American *B. dichroa*, the Asian *B. cathayana*, and the African *B. sutherlandii*. Cultivated red-flowered species include the South American *B. boliviensis*, *B. corallina*, *B. maculata*, and *B. coccinea* and the Asian *B. chitoensis*. Some red-flowered South American species, including *B. boliviensis* (Plate 34) and *B. fuchsiaflora* (Plate 7), are hummingbird pollinated and have characteristic tubular flowers. However, unlike typical hummingbird-pollinated plants these begonia flowers do not produce nectar and must rely on deception rather than reward to attract hummingbirds. The bee-pollinated flowers typical of most other begonias similarly trick pollinators into visiting their pollen-less female flowers. In this case the female flowers mimic the male flowers, which do offer their visitors pollen rewards.

Scent

Several begonias have pleasantly scented flowers that help attract insect pollinators. Fragrance in begonias is usually most noticeable on sunny days during the early morning and is often strongest in the female flowers. Among the most powerfully scented species is the Brazilian *Begonia integerrima*, which like most other fragrant begonias has a sweet, spicy smell. Other pleasant smelling, cultivated species from the western hemisphere include *B. egregia*, *B. hydrocotylifolia*, *B. lubbersii*, *B. minor*, and *B. venosa*. Scented Asian species include *B. deliciosa*, *B. dipetala*, *B. masoniana*, and the particularly fragrant *B. roxburghii*. The African species *B. dregei* and *B. meyeri-johannis* also have pleasantly scented flowers. Some fragrant species have been used in developing the many scented hybrid cultivars, including *B.* 'Martha Floro', whose scent comes from *B. lubbersii*; *B.* 'Sweet Dreams', from *B. integerrima*; and *B.* 'Honeysuckle', from *B. dichroa*. As fragrance varies from plant to plant, it is not considered a helpful character for identifying begonias.

Stamens

The male reproductive organs of *Begonia* are highly variable and exhibit several characters that can help with identification. Because of the small size of *Begonia* stamens most of these characters can be seen only with a hand lens or dissecting microscope. One characteristic that is more readily observed is the shape of the stamen cluster, which can range from a symmetric, or actinomorphic, sphere or cone to an asymmetric, or zygomorphic, mass that resembles a bunch of bananas. Also easily observed and equally important is whether or not the connective tissue

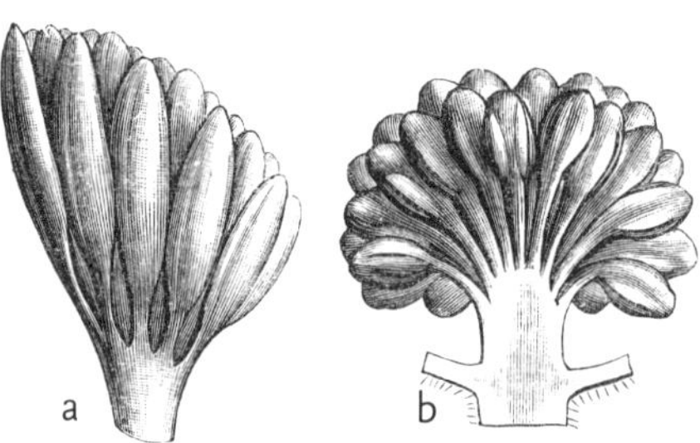

Stamen arrangements: **a**) clustered like a bunch of bananas, **b**) in a symmetric mass. Reproduced from Warburg, O. (1894) Begoniaceae. In: A. Engler and K. Prantl (Eds.) *Die Natürlichen Pflanzenfamilien*, ed. 1, 3, 6a: p. 128, Wilhelm Engelmann, Leipzig

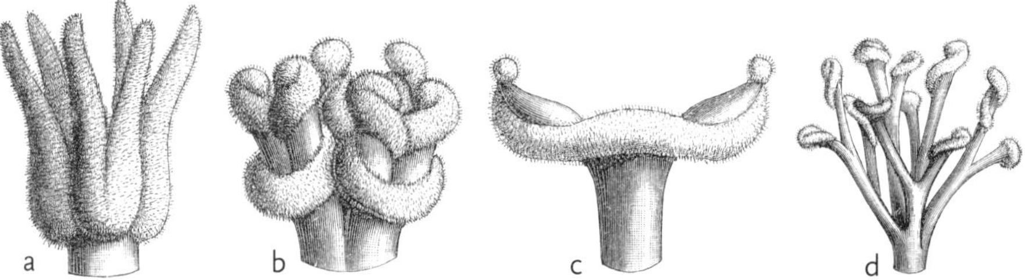

A selection of the diversity found in the styles and stigmas of *Begonia*: **a**) *B. foliosa* var. *miniata*, **b**) *B. dregei*, **c**) *B. fusca*, **d**) *B. thomeana*. Reproduced from: Warburg, O. (1894) Begoniaceae. In: A. Engler and K. Prantl (Eds.) *Die Natürlichen Pflanzenfamilien*, ed. 1, 3, 6a: p. 129, Wilhelm Engelmann, Leipzig

that binds the two pollen sacs together projects beyond the pollen sacs. Other useful taxonomic characteristics relate to the anther's method of dehiscence, the stamen-to-filament length ratio and whether or not the filaments are fused together.

Styles and stigmas

The female reproductive organs (styles, stigmas, and ovaries) show a great deal of variation and provide botanists with many important taxonomic features. Most *Begonia* species have three styles, but some have two or four, or in rare instances up to seven. They may be simple, once-branched (examples a, b, and c), or multi-branched (example d). The stigmatic tissue can be crescent-shaped or contracted near the style apex, but in most species it is arranged in a straight or spiral band (examples b, c, and d). In a few begonias, including the commonly cultivated *B. foliosa* var. *miniata* (example a), the stigmatic tissue covers the entire surface of the style.

Ovaries

Many features of the ovaries are important in the classification and identification of *Begonia* species. Taxonomists put particular emphasis on the different types of placentation, the arrangement or configuration of the ovule-bearing placentae. The genus exhibits both axillary and parietal placentation patterns, which are usually readily distinguished. A few, predominantly African, species, however, have parietal placentation that superficially appears axile. Fortunately, these species are otherwise distinct so their identification is rarely made problematic by this cryptic arrangement. With practice, you can distinguish all placentation types in a mature ovary by transversely

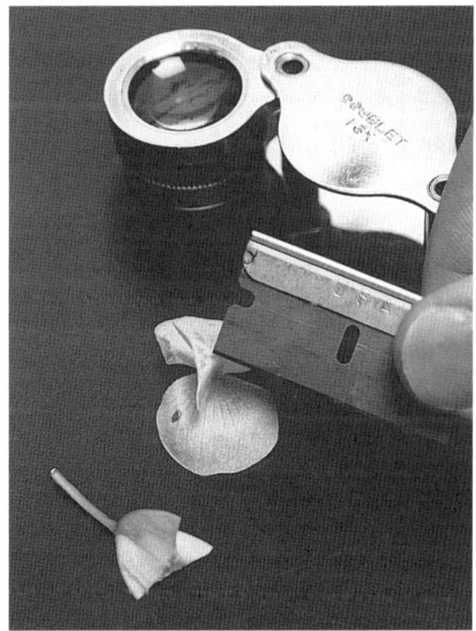

Sectioning a begonia ovary to determine its type of placentation and number of placental branches. Photo by Liz Steger Photography

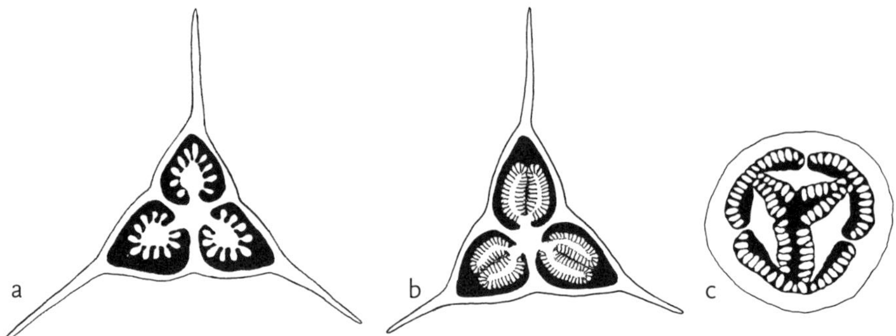

Ovary placentation types: **a**) axile placentation, with entire placentae; **b**) axile placentation, with bifid placentae; **c**) parietal placentation, with branched placentae.

sectioning it midway along its length with a sharp knife or razor blade. Transverse sectioning of the ovary is also necessary to distinguish the number of locules, or compartments, in the ovary and determine the number of placental branches found in each. Within *Begonia,* the number of ovary locules varies from one to six, with two or three being most common. Often the number of locules corresponds to the number of styles, but this is not always the case. For instance, *B. imperialis* and its closest relatives usually have three styles but only two ovary locules. In ovaries exhibiting axillary placentation the form of the placental branches varies from fused, a state known as entire, to two or more branched. In a few species the placental branches appear to be entire because their inner surfaces are pressed together and not covered with ovules. This is relatively rare, however, and among the species presently cultivated is found only in *B. albo-picta, B. ampla, B. corallina, B. integerrima, B. lubbersii, B. maculata, B. pseudolubbersii, B. radicans, B. salicifolia, B. solananthera,* and *B. undulata.* The relative size and shape of the ovary wings, when present, are also taxonomically important and readily observed.

Fruit

Taxonomists consider the fruit to be among the most important organs for the identification of *Begonia* species. The type of fruit, method by which the seeds are released, and orientation of the fruit stalk, whether it is upright, nodding, or pendulous, are all important taxonomic features. The fruit of most begonias is a dry, winged capsule, but a few species have burr-like, horned fruits (Plates 8 and 9) or fleshy, berry-like fruits (Plate 165). Most species with dry, winged capsules have wind-dispersed seed, but some species from Asia, like *B. rex* and *B. hatacoa*, have evolved to disperse their seed in a more ingenious manner. In these species, two small wings on the back of the inverted capsule trap falling raindrops; when enough water has accumulated it causes the capsule to nod up and down thereby shaking out the seeds. Horns and fleshy fruit coatings are both adaptations to animal dispersal: horns catch in the fur of passing animals which shake the seeds out through special holes in the capsules, and fruits with fleshy coatings are attractive to birds and mammals, which eat them whole and later disperse the seeds unharmed in their droppings. Many of the fleshy fruits have attractively colored surfaces that signal to their animal dispersers they are ripe and good to eat. In some epiphytic African species, such as *B. loranthoides* (Plate 143) and *B. cavallyensis* (Plate 144), the fleshy fruits split open when they are ripe, and the internal placentae, rather than the fruit walls, are attractively colored. In these animal-dispersed species, fruit colors may be white, pink, yellow, orange, or red. *Begonia* species with berry-like fruits are largely restricted to Africa and include *B. ampla*, *B. mannii*, and *B. salaziensis*. A few Asian and Central American species also have berry-like fruit and are also occasionally cultivated; these include *B. roxburghii*, *B. longifolia*, and *B. leprosa* from Asia, and *B. oaxacana* from the Americas.

Seed

The seeds of *Begonia* and its closest relative, *Hillebrandia*, are unique in the plant kingdom, since they possess a ring of collar cells between a seed lid and the remainder of the testa cells. As the seed germinates, the developing root system pushes open the seed lid and causes the collar cells to split apart, providing a gap through which the seedling emerges.

Despite their consistency in structure, *Begonia* seeds show a great diversity in size, shape, and surface texture. Compared to other plants, begonias have very small seeds, with the mean seed length ranging from 0.2 mm in *B. iucunda* to 2.3 mm in *B. ebolowensis*. In fact, they are so small that observation of many of their taxonomically important features is possible only with a scanning electron microscope.

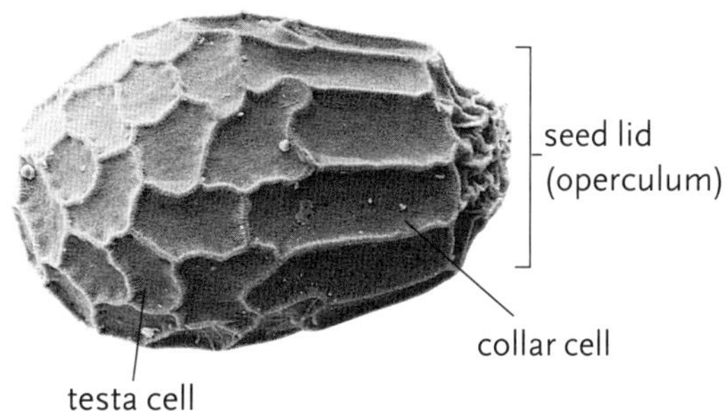

Scanning electron micrograph of a typical wind-dispersed *Begonia* seed magnified 100 times.

As with the fruit, *Begonia* seeds are themselves variously adapted to wind, water, or animal dispersal. Wind-dispersed seeds are usually small and either have buoyant air-filled cells or pronounced surface ornamentation that helps catch air currents. The latter feature is also found in some water-dispersed seeds. In contrast, most animal-dispersed begonias tend to have relatively large seeds that lack surface ornamentation. In these species the whole fruits rather than the individual seeds are dispersed and therefore seed size and ornamentation are not as constrained by evolutionary pressures. Some epiphytic African begonias, like *B. mannii*, have seeds with a fleshy aril-like structure that is thought to be attractive to animal dispensers.

Chromosome number

Chromosome numbers are notoriously difficult to count in *Begonia* since the chromosomes are very small and often accompanied by fragments that are easily mistaken for true chromosomes. Unfortunately, these difficulties have led to the publication of many erroneous counts. Nevertheless, if this data is used cautiously, knowledge of chromosome numbers is of value to both the begonia breeder and botanist.

Many botanical subgroups recognized within *Begonia* appear to be characterized by particular chromosome numbers. This feature is often indicative of a close evolutionary relationship among such species, and also a good indicator that they can be successfully hybridized in cultivation. In the wild, changes in chromosome number are probably important means by which new *Begonia* species evolve, but unfortunately, few studies have looked at the role of chromosomes in *Begonia* evolution. Those chromosome counts deemed reliable are included in this book at the end of each species description.

Classification

Botanical classification

Since *Begonia* is such a large genus, its species have traditionally been classified into smaller, more manageable groups or "sections." The current classification by Jan Doorenbos and colleagues, published in 1998, recognizes 1403 species of *Begonia* subdivided into 63 sections. This treatment bases its findings largely on the earlier classifications of Alphonse de Candolle (1864), Otto Warburg (1894), and Edgar Irmscher (1925), but its ancestry can be traced as far back as Johann Friedrich Klotzsch's study of 1855. Though the modern classification is an improvement on these earlier works, it is unlikely to be the last word in *Begonia* taxonomy, as at least 19 species still have not been assigned to a section (for example, see *B. boisiana* and *B. thelmae*) and many more species have only recently been published, or await publication. Indeed three new sections have been added since its publication. Nevertheless, future classifications will probably resemble the present system quite closely since several of the sections and almost all the species are well defined.

Of the 66 sections of *Begonia* currently recognized, each is restricted to a single continent. The majority contain between one and 30 species, although the largest, section *Petermannia*, contains just more than 200. In modern taxonomic treatments, each section is ideally composed of a distinct evolutionary lineage and contains species that share a number of unique characteristics.

In the early days of classification, the characters that were considered important in delimiting *Begonia* sections were found mostly in the flowers and included features of the styles, stigmas, ovaries, and fruit. Botanists also emphasized the number of tepals in the male and female flowers. In modern taxonomic studies of *Begonia*, additional characters such as seed and pollen micro-morphology, chromosome number, and DNA sequence data are increasingly being used alongside the traditional characters.

One reason taxonomists have subdivided the genus into sections is that these smaller groups speed and simplify the identification process. Rather than blindly matching up an unknown plant with each of the more than 1500 species in the genus, you can more simply first determine the section of an unknown plant and then work through this much smaller group to determine which species it is. The division of the genus into sections also gives users the ability to predict characteristics of unfamiliar species, such as the cultural requirements of a newly introduced species or whether two species are likely to produce hybrid offspring. This ability is possible because the species within a section share numerous features, having inherited them from their common ancestor. The descriptions in chapter five of this book list the botanical section assigned to a species directly after its name.

Horticultural classification

Understandably, most gardeners and horticulturists have shied away from the sectional classification of *Begonia* because the botanical terminology necessary to identify species to a section can be daunting. In 1903, Adolphe Van Den Heede devised a separate horticultural classification with four easily recognized groups: tuberous, herbaceous, shrub, and stemless or rhizomatous. These groups have proved useful pigeonholes because their defining characters can be easily observed, and the species within each usually have similar cultural requirements. Heede's simple classification has been modified several times since its conception, and today, a century later, the horticultural classification includes additional groups based on parentage and growth habit. The American Begonia Society currently recognizes eight groups: cane, shrub, rhizomatous, Semperflorens-cultorum, tuberous, Rex-cultorum, trailing or scandent, and thick stemmed. In contrast, growers in Europe recognize five different groups: Elatior, Lorraine, Semperflorens-cultorum, tuberous, and foliage. The differences in the two systems reflect the fact that Europeans predominantly grow certain hybrid cultivar groups, while North Americans tend to grow a wider range of species and hybrids. For the purpose of this book I have adopted the horticultural classification system recognized in the United States since this system is more applicable to the plants treated here. In chapter five, the horticultural group that each species has been assigned to is listed next to its botanical section. In a few cases, when a particular species had either not been assigned a horticultural class or had obviously been placed in the wrong class, I have assigned the species to a new horticultural group.

Hillebrandia sandwicensis (Begoniaceae).

Related plants

The begonia family

Begonia belongs to the family Begoniaceae, which also contains one other genus, *Hillebrandia* (Plate 10). That genus is represented by a single, rarely cultivated species, *H. sandwicensis*, unique to the Hawaiian islands of Kauai, Mauai, and Molokai. The species grows in wet seepage areas and by streams in tropical rain forest (Plates 11 and 12) but sadly is declining because its fleshy rhizomes are a favored food of feral pigs. In appearance, *Hillebrandia* closely resembles *Begonia*, but it differs in its more numerous and more readily distinguished sepals and petals, its semi-inferior ovary, fruits that open between the styles, and microscopic characteristics of its pollen and seed. These features, along with evidence from DNA sequence studies, suggest that *Hillebrandia* is a relatively old genus that was derived from the same ancestral stock as *Begonia*. People seldom cultivate *H. sandwicensis*, but it is not difficult to grow as long as it has a cool, moist position in semi-shade and its tuberous rhizomes can dry out slightly during the summer and autumn months when they become dormant.

Until 2003 the begonia family contained a third genus, *Symbegonia*, but the approximately 12 species included in that genus are now considered to belong to the genus *Begonia*. At least three of these species are found in cultivation and are discussed under *B. symsanguinea*.

Related families

Since the 1990s, DNA-based studies have led to some unexpected discoveries concerning the wider evolutionary relationships of the begonia family. Botanists had traditionally found the family difficult to classify within larger taxonomic schemes; its species share obvious features only with the cucumber (Cucurbitaceae), datisca (Datiscaceae), and tetrameles (Tetramelaceae) families. These three families, like the Begoniaceae, are morphologically isolated from the rest of the plant kingdom. We now know, based on DNA sequence evidence, that the Begoniaceae is related to a diverse group of plant families, collectively known as the order Cucurbitales. The Cucurbitales include the cucumber, datisca, and tetrameles families as well as three other families that were not traditionally linked with the begonias:

Datisca cannibina (Datiscaceae): **a**) habit, **b**) flowering branch, **c**) male flower, **d**) female flower.

the Anisophylleaceae, Coriaceae, and Corynocarpaceae. These seven families that make up the Cucurbitales are remarkably different in appearance.

Datiscaceae (datisca family). The family Datiscaceae contains a single genus, *Datisca*, with two herbaceous species, *D. cannibina* (Plates 13 and 14) from mainland Asia and *D. glomerata* from western North America. *Datisca cannibina* is occasionally offered for sale in the United States as a "hardy begonia" and looks superficially like cannabis (*Cannabis sativa*).

The members of the Datiscaceae are the closest living relatives of the Begoniaceae, yet despite their close relationship, these families are morphologically very different. This suggests that they parted from their common ancestor many millions of years ago. If any intermediate species once existed, they, like the immediate common ancestor, have long since become extinct. No fossilized remains of the Begoniaceae or Datiscaceae have ever been found, which is unfortunate since these could be used to directly date the origin of the families. Instead, we must content ourselves with a rough estimate of their age, which can be determined by comparing levels of DNA sequence change present in these and other closely related families, such as Tetramelaceae and Coriaceae, for which radio carbon dateable fossils are available. Results of this method estimate that *Begonia* evolved roughly 26–42 million years ago, a time when many modern-day groups of mammals were first beginning to inhabit North America, and when herds of the now extinct, rhinoceros-like brontothere dominated the Great Plains.

Tetramelaceae (tetrameles family). The Tetramelaceae contains two genera, each with a single species: *Tetrameles nudiflora* and *Octomeles sumatrana*. Both these species are massive trees that grow wild throughout much of tropical Asia and, in the case of *T. nudiflora*, northeastern Australia. Once included within the Datiscaceae, these species have only relatively recently been recognized as a separate family, a change based on new evidence from DNA sequence data. The members of both Tetramelaceae and Datiscaceae share a number of unusual microscopic features with the begonias, including the presence of a distinct seed lid, which is pushed open as the seed germinates. In fact, it was such shared features that

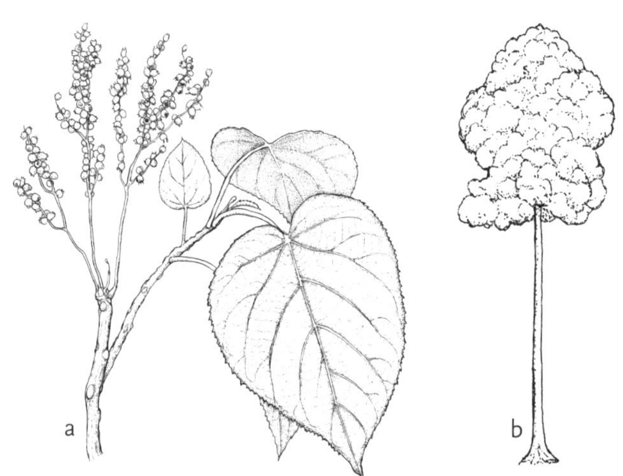

Tetrameles nudiflora (Tetramelaceae): **a**) flowering branch, **b**) habit.

originally led botanists to group these three families in traditional flowering-plant classifications.

Cucurbitaceae (cucumber family). The cucumber family shares several characteristics with the begonia family, including unisexual flowers, inferior or semi-inferior ovaries, and twisted stigmas. A number of unique features, however, distinguish the members of the cucumber family, particularly their characteristic stamens and vascular systems. The family contains about 90 genera and 700 species and includes many economically important species, such as cucumber, pumpkin, squash, and watermelon. Most species are herbaceous perennials that climb by means of tendrils. Their aerial parts are damaged by frost, and the relatively few species encountered outside the tropics have either an annual life cycle or winter storage tubers.

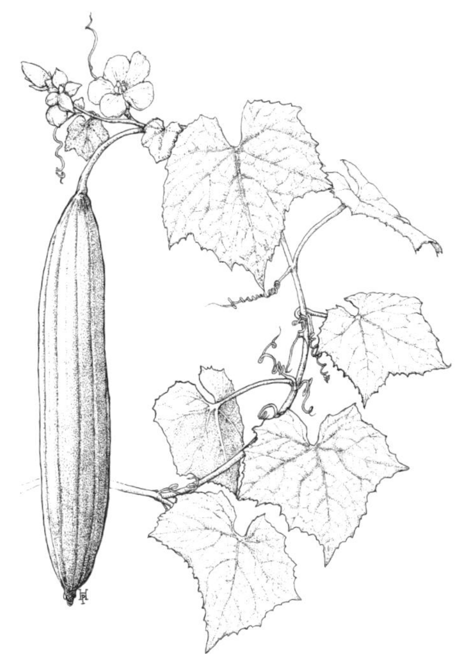

Luffa acutangula (Cucurbitaceae).

Anisophylleaceae (anisophyllea family). This family contains four genera of tropical trees and shrubs from wet lowland primary forest: *Anisophyllea*, with 30 widespread species; *Combretocarpus*, with one Malaysian species; *Poga*, with one West African species; and *Polygonanthus*, with two Amazonian species. None of them are widely cultivated and the family, as a whole, is poorly understood taxonomically. Some botanists even doubt if *Polygonanthus* belongs in the family. The name *Anisophylleaceae* is derived from *aniso*, meaning "unequal," and *phylla*, meaning "leaves," and refers to the asymmetric leaves found in some species of the family.

Corynocarpaceae (karaka family). The single genus of the family, *Corynocarpus*, contains five species of evergreen trees from tropical and warm temperate regions of the southwest Pacific, including Australia and New Zealand. None are widely cultivated. *Corynocarpus* was allied with at least 13 different families prior to its classification near the Begoniaceae. Despite sharing no obvious morphological characters with the Begoniaceae, it is clearly related to the families in the order Cucurbitales on the basis of numerous shared DNA sequence characters.

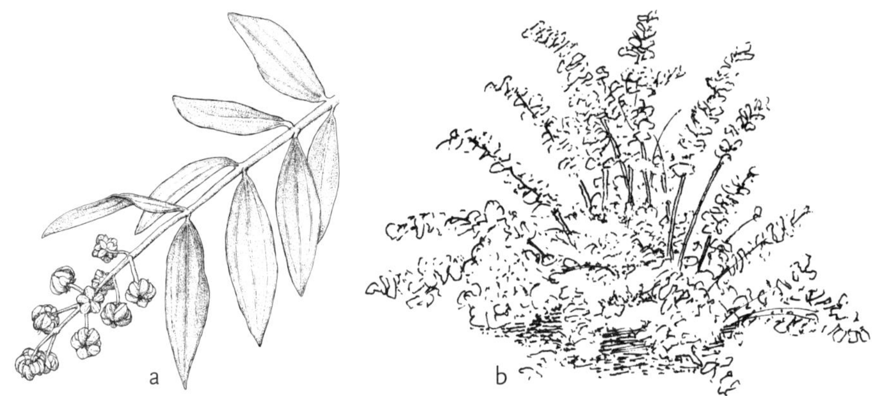

Coriaria myrtifolia (Coriariaceae): **a**) fruiting branch, **b**) habit.

Coriaceae (coriaria family). This family contains a single genus, *Coriaria*, with five species of attractive deciduous or evergreen shrubs that are occasionally cultivated in areas with mild winters. *Coriaria* has an interesting wild distribution that represents one of the most unusual patterns among the flowering plants. It is dotted across Central America, western South America, the Mediterranean, New Guinea, and New Zealand, and from the Himalayas eastward to southern Japan. Despite this wide distribution it is notably absent from Australia and most of Africa. Certain coriarias are reported to be hallucinogenic, and the leaves of *C. myrtifolia*, when crushed in water, have been used as a fly poison. The name *Coriaria* means "leather" and relates to the fact that some species were used in tanning leather. The members of Coriaceae show little resemblance to the begonias; however, *Coriaria* and *Datisca* share a common feature as both have symbiotic relationships with nitrogen-fixing bacteria that live in specialized root nodules.

4

Identification

This book presents a variety of ways to identify *Begonia* species in cultivation. Perhaps the easiest method is to look through the color photographs to make a visual match with your plant. Afterward, double check the name you have arrived at by comparing your plant with the relevant description in chapter five. This approach usually works well, however, only for species with particularly distinct features; the majority of begonias need a more precise method. For this reason, this chapter provides a sectional key and short descriptions of the cultivated botanical sections, the latter of which are referenced to the species-level keys and descriptions in chapter five.

Using the multi-access key

I decided not to present a dichotomous key to all the cultivated begonias for two reasons. Firstly, the list of cultivated species is forever changing, and secondly, if I had restricted such a key to just those species currently in cultivation during this snapshot in time it would be very long and unwieldy. Instead, I decided to write an easy-to-use multi-access key to the sections and then provide several shorter, more technical, dichotomous species keys along with the species descriptions.

To use the multi-access key, construct an initial shortlist of sections on a piece of paper by choosing from the key a particularly distinct characteristic of your plant and noting which sections have that feature. Next eliminate sections from this shortlist by looking at additional characteristics of the unknown plant and crossing out the sections not listed for these characteristics. You may observe the characteristics in any order and combination, and you may compare as many or as few characters as you wish. If a particularly large section contains a particular character trait that belongs to only a single cultivated species, then that species is listed in parentheses along with its section. Three species included in the key, *Begonia boisiana*, *B. malabarica*, and *B. thelmae*, have not yet been classified within a section so are treated individually. One other, *B. taiwaniana*, is likewise problematic to place in the existing classification and is also treated individually.

Once you have used the key to identify the section of the unknown plant, or you have narrowed the choice down to a handful of potential sections, look at the relevant short sectional descriptions that follow the key. These descriptions will confirm that you have reached the correct section or will further narrow down the search. After each of the sectional descriptions is a list of the included species known to be in cultivation, and in many cases, a point of reference to a species-level key in chapter five. Use the keys in chapter five to arrive at a final identification of your species and then, whenever possible, check that the plant matches the relevant description and photograph(s).

Key to the sections of Begonia represented in cultivation

(See chapter three and the illustrated glossary for explanations of botanical terms.)

Plant climbing or trailing: *Baryandra, Gireoudia* (*B. mazae* and *B. purpusii*), *Solananthera, Tetraphila, Wageneria*; not yet classified *B. thelmae*

Plant rhizomatous: *Baryandra, Begonia, Chasmophila* (rhizome subterranean), *Coelocentrum, Diploclinium, Gireoudia, Leprosae, Loasibegonia, Monopteron, Parvibegonia* (*B. crenata*), *Platycentrum, Pritzelia, Quadrilobaria, Reichenheimia, Ridleyella, Scutobegonia, Sphenanthera, Tetraphila, Trachelocarpus, Weilbachia*

Plant tuberous: *Augustia, Barya, Chasmophila, Diploclinium, Erminea, Eupetalum, Knesebeckia, Parvibegonia, Peltaugustia* (not tuberous but has small bulb-like structures at base of stem), *Quadrilobaria, Quadriperigonia, Rostrobegonia*

Plant lacking a rhizome or underground tuber: *Augustia* (*B. dregei* has a swollen caudex), *Begonia, Cyathocnemis, Diploclinium, Donaldia, Doratometra, Filicibegonia, Gaerdtia, Gireoudia, Haagea, Hydristyles, Knesebeckia, Lepsia, Mezierea, Parietoplacentalia, Peltaugustia, Petermannia, Pilderia, Platycentrum, Pritzelia, Quadriperigonia, Rossmannia, Rostrobegonia, Ruizopavonia, Scheidweileria, Solananthera, Sphenanthera, Squamibegonia, Tetrachia, Tetraphila, Trendelenburgia, Wageneria, Weilbachia*; not yet classified *B. boisiana, B. malabarica*, and *B. thelmae*; section uncertain *B. halconensis* and *B. taiwaniana*

Petiole with a ring of hairs where it joins blade: *Augustia, Baryandra* (sometimes inconspicuous), *Gireoudia, Knesebeckia, Rostrobegonia* (sometimes inconspicuous), *Scheidweileria, Pritzelia* (*B. caraguatatubensis*), *Platycentrum* (*B. circumlobata*)

Leaves peltate: *Diploclinium, Gaerdtia* (*B. lubbersii*), *Gireoudia, Leprosae* (*B. leprosa*, rarely peltate), *Loasibegonia, Peltaugustia, Petermannia* (*B. amphioxus*), *Pritzelia* (*B. paulensis*), *Reichenheimia, Ridleyella, Scutobegonia, Tetrachia, Tetraphila*

Leaves palmately compound: *Gireoudia, Petermannia, Platycentrum, Scheidweileria*

Flowers yellow, orange or red: *Augustia* (*B. sutherlandii*), *Barya* (*B. boliviensis*), *Baryandra, Chasmophila, Eupetalum, Gaerdtia, Lepsia* (*B. foliosa* var. *miniata*), *Loasibegonia, Petermannia, Platycentrum, Pritzelia* (*B. coccinea*), *Reichenheimia* (*B. coriacea*), *Ruizopavonia, Scutobegonia, Solananthera* (*B. radicans*), *Tetraphila*

Inflorescence racemose: *Diploclinium, Parvibegonia, Petermannia, Pilderia, Quadriperigonia*

Male flowers with two tepals: *Augustia, Chasmophila, Cyathocnemis, Diploclinium, Donaldia, Doratometra, Filicibegonia, Gireoudia, Haagea, Hydristyles, Knesebeckia* (*B. aconitifolia*), *Loasibegonia, Mezierea, Monopteron, Petermannia, Pilderia, Quadrilobaria, Reichenheimia, Rossmannia, Rostrobegonia, Ruizopavonia, Scutobegonia, Squamibegonia, Tetrachia, Trachelocarpus, Weilbachia*

Stamen mass asymmetric and often resembling a bunch of bananas: *Chasmophila, Erminea, Filicibegonia, Gireoudia, Haagea, Loasibegonia, Mezierea, Petermannia, Ridleyella, Scutobegonia, Squamibegonia, Tetrachia, Tetraphila, Weilbachia*; not yet classified *B. boisiana* and *B. malabarica*

Stamen mass symmetric: *Augustia, Barya, Baryandra, Begonia, Coelocentrum, Cyathocnemis, Diploclinium, Donaldia, Doratometra, Eupetalum, Filicibegonia, Gaerdtia, Hydristyles, Knesebeckia, Leprosae, Lepsia, Mezierea, Monopteron, Parietoplacentalia, Parvibegonia, Peltaugustia, Petermannia, Pilderia, Platycentrum, Pritzelia, Quadrilobaria, Quadriperigonia, Reichenheimia, Rostrobegonia, Ruizopavonia, Scheidweileria, Solananthera, Sphenanthera, Tetraphila, Trachelocarpus, Trendelenburgia, Wageneria*; not yet classified *B. thelmae*; section uncertain *B. halconensis* and *B. taiwaniana*

Anther connectives projecting: *Augustia, Begonia, Cyathocnemis, Donaldia, Doratometra, Erminea, Gireoudia, Hydristyles, Knesebeckia, Lepsia, Mezierea, Pilderia, Platycentrum, Pritzelia, Rostrobegonia, Ruizopavonia, Scheidweileria, Solananthera, Sphenanthera, Tetrachia, Tetraphila, Trachelocarpus, Trendelenburgia, Weilbachia*; not yet classified *B. boisiana* and *B. thelmae*; section uncertain *B. halconensis* and *B. taiwaniana*

Anther connectives not projecting: *Barya, Baryandra, Chasmophila, Coelocentrum, Diploclinium, Doratometra, Eupetalum, Gaerdtia, Gireoudia, Haagea, Knesebeckia, Leprosae, Loasibegonia, Mezierea, Monopteron, Parietoplacentalia, Parvibegonia, Peltaugustia, Petermannia, Quadrilobaria, Quadriperigonia, Reichenheimia, Ridleyella, Ruizopavonia* (*B. holtonis*), *Scutobegonia, Squamibegonia, Tetrachia, Tetraphila, Wageneria*; not yet classified *B. malabarica*

Female flowers with two tepals: *Chasmophila, Cyathocnemis, Filicibegonia, Gireoudia, Haagea, Loasibegonia, Mezierea, Quadrilobaria, Rossmannia, Ruizopavonia, Scutobegonia, Squamibegonia, Weilbachia*

Female tepals fused at base: *Petermannia* (occasionally), *Squamibegonia, Symbegonia*

Bracteoles present: *Begonia, Cyathocnemis, Diploclinium, Donaldia, Doratometra, Eupetalum, Gaerdtia, Gireoudia, Hydristyles, Knesebeckia, Lepsia, Peltaugustia, Pilderia, Pritzelia, Quadriperigonia, Reichenheimia* (*B. coriacea*), *Rossmannia, Rostrobegonia, Ruizopavonia, Scheidweileria, Solananthera, Tetrachia, Trendelenburgia, Wageneria*; not yet classified *B. thelmae*; section uncertain *B. taiwaniana*

Ovary locules two: *Monopteron, Parvibegonia, Petermannia* (*B. amphioxus* occasionally), *Platycentrum, Ridleyella, Weilbachia*

Ovary locules four or five: *Loasibegonia, Mezierea, Scutobegonia, Sphenanthera, Squamibegonia, Tetrachia*

Placentae parietal or pseudo-axile, at least in central part of ovary: *Coelocentrum, Mezierea, Parietoplacentalia, Tetraphila*

Placentae entire: *Augustia, Chasmophila, Doratometra, Erminea, Filicibegonia, Gaerdtia* (*B. edmundoi*), *Haagea, Leprosae, Lepsia* (*B. foliosa* var. *miniata*), *Loasibegonia, Peltaugustia, Pilderia, Platycentrum* (occasionally in *B. pavonina*), *Pritzelia, Reichenheimia, Ridleyella, Rostrobegonia, Ruizopavonia* (*B. holtonis*), *Scheidweileria, Scutobegonia, Trachelocarpus, Trendelenburgia, Wageneria*; not yet classified *B. boisiana, B. malabarica*, and *B. thelmae*

Placentae bifid, ovules present between branches: *Augustia* (*B. dregei* var. *princae*), *Barya*, *Baryandra*, *Begonia*, *Coelocentrum*, *Cyathocnemis*, *Diploclinium*, *Donaldia*, *Doratometra*, *Eupetalum*, *Gaerdtia* (*B. dichroa*), *Gireoudia*, *Hydristyles*, *Knesebeckia*, *Leprosae*, *Lepsia* (*B. foliosa* var. *miniata*), *Mezierea*, *Monopteron*, *Parietoplacentalia*, *Parvibegonia*, *Petermannia*, *Platycentrum*, *Pritzelia* (*B. paulensis*), *Quadrilobaria*, *Quadriperigonia*, *Rossmannia*, *Rostrobegonia*, *Ruizopavonia*, *Sphenanthera*, *Tetrachia*, *Tetraphila*, *Weilbachia*; section uncertain *B. halconensis* and *B. taiwaniana*

Placentae bifid, ovules absent between branches: *Gaerdtia*, *Squamibegonia*, *Solananthera*

Fruit fleshy and lacking well-developed wings when mature: *Leprosae*, *Mezierea*, *Parietoplacentalia*, *Sphenanthera*, *Squamibegonia*, *Tetraphila*

Sectional classification of the cultivated species

Classification follows Doorenbos et al. (1998), with minor modifications. The asterisk (*) signifies that a detailed description of the species appears in chapter five.

section *Augustia*

A section of 12 species from tropical East Africa, closely related to section *Rostrobegonia*. It is identified by its combination of being tuberous (or having a swollen stem base in the case of *B. dregei*), having anthers with projecting connectives, having usually entire placentae (bifid in *B. dregei* var. *princae*), and by the lack of a tuft of hairs at the junction of the petiole and blade (occasionally present in *B. dregei* and *B. sutherlandii*). *Begonia dregei* and *B. sutherlandii* are commonly cultivated members.

Cultivated species: *B. brevibracteata*, *B. dregei**, *B. geranioides*, *B. sutherlandii**

section *Barya*

A section of three Andean species, one of which is commonly cultivated and readily identified by its pendent, scarlet flowers with lanceolate to lanceolate-ovate tepals that project forward.

Cultivated species: *B. boliviensis**

section *Baryandra*

A section containing a single epiphytic, rhizomatous species from the Philippines.

It is easily identified by its glossy green leaves; orange flowers; and large, red, flattened hairs on its stems, petioles, and inflorescence stalk.

Cultivated species: *B. oxysperma**

section *Begonia*

A section of about 65 species predominantly distributed in the West Indies and Brazil. Section *Begonia* is difficult to distinguish from a number of other New World sections, particularly *Doratometra* and *Knesebeckia*. However, section *Begonia*, as represented in cultivation, can be identified by the following, admittedly long, combination of characters: plants perennial, lacking tubers, petiole joining leaf blade at an angle and lacking a ring of hairs below point of attachment with blade, leaf venation palmate or palmate-pinnate (never pinnate), male flowers with four tepals, anthers oblong, longer than the filaments, connectives projecting, bracteoles two to three, female flowers with five tepals, placentae bifid. Apart from certain members of this section, only some species of section *Cyathocnemis* also have three bracteoles, making the identification of those species of section *Begonia* with this characteristic somewhat easier. Several of the species in this section are common in cultivation.

Cultivated species: *B. acutifolia, B. admirabilis, B. banaoensis, B. bissei, B. cubensis**, *B. cucullata**, *B. descoleana, B. fischeri, B. glandulifera, B. lomensis, B. minor, B. mollicaulis**, *B. obliqua**, *B. plumieri, B. rotundifolia**, *B. schmidtiana**, *B. schulziana, B. subvillosa, B. venosa**

section *Chasmophila*

a section containing a single tropical West African species that is rarely cultivated and easily recognized by its yellow flowers, non-peltate leaves, and sausage-shaped underground tubers.

Cultivated species: *B. iucunda*

section *Coelocentrum*

A section of 12 rhizomatous species from southwestern China and northern Vietnam that is distinguished by a combination of female flowers with three or four tepals and winged ovaries with parietal placentation. A single species is commonly cultivated.

Cultivated species: *B. masoniana**

section *Cyathocnemis*

A section of about 20 Andean species that is recognized by having two tepals in both the male and female flowers and the basal-most bracts fused into a cup-shaped structure that surrounds the first branching point of the inflorescence. Three of the species are infrequently cultivated.

Cultivated species: *B. bracteosa, B. cryptocarpa, B. cyathophora**

section *Diploclinium*

A widespread Asian section containing about 140 species. As currently recognized the section is very difficult to delimit as it lacks any unique defining features. Most species have three-locular ovaries and bifid placentae and are either rhizomatous or tuberous, but these characteristics are commonly found elsewhere in *Begonia* and, therefore, offer little help in defining the section. Future years will undoubtedly witness the division of the section into smaller more natural groups.

Cultivated species: *B. acaulis, B. asperifolia, B. chloroneura, B. colorata, B. fenicis, B. fimbristipula, B. grandis*, B. hernandioides, B. josephii, B. labordei, B. luzonensis, B. modestiflora, B. morelii, B. nigritarum, B. ovatifolia, B. picta, B. ravenii*, B. sharpeana, B. subnummularifolia, B. taliensis, B. tayabensis**

section *Donaldia*

A section containing seven Brazilian species, one of which is commonly cultivated. This is a tall shrub that is easily identified by its leaves that are green on both sides, densely hairy, and either oblong-elliptic or almost obovate, with a rounded base and pinnate veins.

Cultivated species: *B. ulmifolia**

section *Doratometra*

A section of eight species from Central and South America. The four cultivated members are unusual in their annual life cycle and self-pollinating mechanism. *Begonia hirtella* and *B. humilis* are common weeds of glasshouses. A key to the cultivated members of the section is provided under *B. hirtella*.

Cultivated species: *B. filipes, B. hirtella*, B. humilis, B. wallichiana*

section *Erminea*

A Madagascan section with 12 species, only one of which is well known in cultivation, *Begonia bogneri*. It is easily distinguished by its linear leaves.

Cultivated species: *B. bogneri**

section *Eupetalum*

A predominantly Andean section containing about 27 tuberous species, many of which have large colorful flowers, which may be white, pink, red, orange, or yellow. The *Begonia* ×*tuberhybrida* group of cultivars largely resulted from hybridizing the species of this section. Despite the current popularity of this hybrid group the species themselves are uncommon in cultivation.

Cultivated species: *B. cinnabarina, B. froebelii, B. micranthera, B. novogranatae, B. octopetala, B. pearcei, B. tominana, B. veitchii**

section *Filicibegonia*

A section of eight species from tropical West Africa, one of which is rarely cultivated. It is easily identified by its combination of fern-like leaves, female flowers with two tepals, and kidney-shaped stigmas.

Cultivated species: *B. apleniifolia**

section *Gaerdtia*

A section of about 11 commonly cultivated species from eastern Brazil, the members of which are the only cane-like species to have axile placentae that are bifid but lack ovules on the inner surfaces of the placental branches. Two of the species deviate by either having bifid placentae with ovules on both sides of the branches or entire placentae. However, both are easily identified. They are *Begonia dichroa*, an orange-flowered species, and *B. edmundoi*, a species with distinct slender, black stems. A key to the cultivated cane-like members of the section is provided under *B. lubbersii*.

Cultivated species: *B. albo-picta**, *B. corallina, B. dichroa**, *B. edmundoi**, *B. lubbersii**, *B. maculata, B. pseudolubbersii, B. salicifolia, B. undulata*

section *Gireoudia*

A section of about 65 species largely restricted to Mexico and Central America. Many of the species are rhizomatous and almost all have two tepals in both the male and female flowers. The section is closely related to section *Weilbachia* but may be separated by its three-locular ovaries (two-locular in section *Weilbachia*) and its more erectly held fruit (in section *Weilbachia* the fruits nod toward the ground). Several of the species in section *Gireoudia* are common in cultivation (Plate 38). A key to the cultivated species endemic to Mexico is provided under *Begonia bowerae*. A key to those species naturally occurring in Central America or Central America and Mexico can be found in Burt-Utley (1985).

Cultivated species: *B. barkeri, B. bettinae, B. bowerae**, *B. breedlovei, B. cardiocarpa, B. carolineifolia, B. carrieae, B. conchifolia**, *B. crassicaulis**, *B. fusca, B. heracleifolia**, *B. hispidivillosa, B. huberti, B. hydrocotylifolia**, *B. involucrata**, *B. kellermanii**, *B. kenworthyae, B. lindleyana, B. lyman-smithii**, *B. manicata, B. mazae, B. multinervia**, *B. nelumbifolia**, *B. peltata, B. philodendroides, B. pinetorum, B. plebeja, B. polygonata, B. pringlei, B. pruinata, B. quaternata, B. sarcophylla, B. sericoneura, B. sousae, B. sparsipila, B. squarrosa, B. stigmosa, B. strigillosa**, *B. thiemei**, *B. urophylla*

section *Haagea*

This section contains a single commonly cultivated species from southern India and Sri Lanka. It is easily recognized by the combination of its flowers with two tepals, symmetrically arranged stamens, and ovaries with entire placentae and three equal wings that are usually rounded at both ends.

Cultivated species: *B. dipetala**

section *Hydristyles*

A predominantly Bolivian section containing about nine species of subshrubs, which can be distinguished from most other cultivated species by the combination of male flowers with two tepals, female flowers with five tepals, and styles that are multi-branched. *Begonia fissistyla* is the best known in cultivation, but none of the species are commonly grown.

Cultivated species: *B. andina, B. fissistyla, B. unilateralis*

section *Knesebeckia*

A section with about 50 species distributed from Mexico to the Andes. This section is often difficult to distinguish from section *Begonia* but can be separated by its members' often palmately lobed leaves (a characteristic never found in section *Begonia*) and anther connectives that do not project past the pollen sacs (in section *Begonia* they always project). Several of the species in this section are common in cultivation.

Cultivated species: *B. acerifolia, B. aconitifolia*, B. falciloba, B. incarnata*, B. kuhlmannii, B. leathermaniae, B. longimaculata, B. ludwigii, B. maynensis, B. michoacana, B. olbia, B. platanifolia, B. uniflora, B. viscida, B. wollnyi**

section *Leprosae*

A small Chinese section that is distinguished by its members' fleshy, club-shaped fruit.

Cultivated species: *B. leprosa**

section *Lepsia*

A section of two or perhaps more species from the northern Andes, one of which is commonly cultivated. This species is easily identified by the combination of its lack of rhizomes, often gracefully arching stems with numerous, small, symmetric, glossy green, elliptic leaves with pinnate venation, male flowers with four tepals and female flowers with five tepals.

Cultivated species: *B. foliosa**

section *Loasibegonia*

A section of 19 small to medium-sized rhizomatous species from Africa, which in cultivation are usually grown in terrariums or other enclosed containers. Most of the cultivated yellow-flowered begonias belong to this group. The section is distinguished from most other sections by the combination of its rhizomatous habit, male and female flowers each with two tepals, anthers that are widest at their apices, and ovaries with one placenta per locule. It is distinguished from the closely related section *Scutobegonia* by its ovary shape. In section *Loasibegonia* the ovary is narrowly oblong to very broadly obovate and in section *Scutobegonia* broadly obovate to very shallowly obtriangular or spindle-shaped. A key to the cultivated members of the section is provided under *Begonia quadrialata*.

Cultivated species: *B. duncan-thomasii, B. letouzeyi, B. microsperma, B. potamophila, B. prismatocarpa**, *B. quadrialata**, *B. scapigera, B. scutifolia, B. staudtii*

section *Mezierea*

A section of six species distributed throughout tropical Africa and in Madagascar, the Mascarene Islands, the Comores, and the Seychelles. It is identified by its combination of fleshy, wingless, indehiscent fruit and free styles. All six of its species are rarely cultivated. A key to the section is provided under *Begonia salaziensis*.

Cultivated species: *B. comorensis, B. humbertii, B. meyeri-johannis, B. oxyloba, B. salaziensis**, *B. seychellensis*

section *Monopteron*

A Himalayan section of two infrequently cultivated species that is distinguished by the combination of its members' lanceolate-ovate, glossy green leaf blades and two-locular ovaries with a single wing.

Cultivated species: *B. griffithiana, B. nepalensis*

section *Parietoplacentalia*

A section of two Central American species that is easily identified by the combination of its upright non-rhizomatous habit, distinctly beaked fruit with narrow wings, female flowers with three tepals, and ovaries that usually have at least some parietal placentation.

Cultivated species: *B. oaxacana**, *B. udisilvestris*

section *Parvibegonia*

A section containing roughly 30 tuberous or rhizomatous species from Asia. It is distinguished by its combination of non-peltate leaves, two-locular ovaries with three unequal wings, and anther connectives not projecting. Many of the species have tepals with distinctive red lines running along the main veins. None are common in cultivation.

Cultivated species: *B. crenata, B. phoeniogramma, B. tenuifolia, B. variabilis**

section *Peltaugustia*

A section of just two species, one of which is infrequently cultivated and easily identified by its unique combination of having bulb-like structures at the base of its stem; peltate, funnel-shaped leaves; and pink flowers with wedge-shaped bases.

Cultivated species: *B. socotrana**

section *Petermannia*

One of the largest sections of *Begonia*, but one that is nevertheless usually easy to recognize. Most of these Asian species have inflorescences that are often divided into a basal part that consists of a solitary or pair of female flowers and an apical part that is racemose and contains a few to several male flowers. The male flowers typically have two tepals and the female flowers have five. The ovaries are almost always three-locular and have bifid placentae and three more or less equal wings. Cultivated material of *B. amphioxus* often does not show all these characteristics but is nonetheless instantly identified by its leaves that are almost always peltate, pointed at both ends, and beautifully marked with red spots. Many species from the section are upright herbs that lack a rhizome or tuber, and several of them have attractively spotted leaves. This group of species is unusual in that on any given plant the female flowers will open before the male flowers—in most other *Begonia* sections the male flowers open first. The individual species of this section are often difficult to identify, as just more than 200 of them have been described but no treatment or key exists for the group as a whole. Furthermore, the list of cultivated species is constantly changing, with additional species being introduced and others being lost from cultivation.

Cultivated species: *B. aequata, B. amphioxus*, B. augustae, B. bipinnatifida, B. brevirimosa*, B. chlorosticta*, B. cummingii, B. isoptera, B. malachosticta, B. oligandra, B. polilloensis*, B. serratipetala, B. siccacaudata*

section *Pilderia*

The single northern Andean species classified in this section is doubtfully in cultivation. It is easily recognized by the combination of its terminal racemose inflorescence, leaves with pinnate venation, and ovaries with entire placentae.

Cultivated species: *B. buddleiifolia*

section *Platycentrum*

Another large Asian section, but again, one that is easily recognized. The species have characteristic ovaries that are two-locular and usually have bifid placentae (occasionally entire in *Begonia pavonina*). The fruits typically have two very short wings and one much longer wing. At maturity they are held in a nodding position so that the longest wing points toward the ground. In most species the stamens are arranged in a symmetric mass on top of a 2–4 mm-tall column, and the anthers usually have long projecting connectives. Many species have thick rhizomes and large, glossy, leathery leaves, but a few have thin leaves that are densely covered with long hairs (see Plate 89 for a selection). Vegetatively many species closely resemble those of section *Sphenanthera* with which they share a close evolutionary relationship. Though section *Platycentrum* is easily recognized, the approximately 100 and more species within it are often difficult to distinguish as no taxonomic treatment or key exists for the group as a whole. The late 1990s witnessed the introduction or reintroduction of several species into cultivation, some of which remain unidentified or perhaps even undescribed.

Cultivated species: *B. annulata, B. areolata, B. augustinei, B. beccariana, B. beddomei, B. cathayana**, *B. cathcartii, B. chitoensis, B. circumlobata, B. decora, B. deliciosa, B. diadema**, *B. digyna, B. emeiensis, B. formosana**, *B. hatacoa**, *B. hemsleyana**, *B. limprichtii, B. lowiana, B. megaptera, B. palmata, B. pavonina, B. pedatifida, B. rex**, *B. rockii, B. sizemoreae, B. teysmanniana, B. thomsonii, B. venusta, B. versicolor**, *B. xanthina*

section *Pritzelia*

With roughly 125 species centered in eastern Brazil this section is one of the largest. More than 50 of the species are cultivated (see Plates 21 and 74 for a selection), with many of them currently being grown as unidentified or misidentified plants. This is not surprising given the horticultural potential of the group and the absence of a comprehensive taxonomic treatment for these species.

Cultivated species: *B. acetosa**, *B. acida, B. angularis**, *B. arborescens* *, *B. bradei, B. capanemae**, *B. caraguatatubensis, B. coccinea**, *B. crispula, B. dichotoma**, *B. dietrichiana**, *B. echinosepala, B. epipsila**, *B. fernando-costae, B. friburgensis, B. gehrtii**, *B. hispida**, *B. hookeriana, B. huegelii, B. itaguassuensis, B. juliana**, *B. listada, B. longibarbata, B. metallica, B. obscura, B. odeteiantha, B. olsoniae**, *B. paranaënsis, B. parilis, B. paulensis, B. petasitifolia**, *B. piresiana, B. princeps, B. pulchella, B. ramentacea, B. reniformis, B. rigida, B. rufo-sericea, B. sanguinea, B. scabrida, B. scharffiana, B. scharffii**, *B. sementacea, B. soli-mutata**, *B. subacida, B. teuscheri, B. tomentosa, B. valdensium, B. valida*

section *Quadrilobaria*

A section of 19 Madagascan species. Its members are similar to those of sections *Rostrobegonia* and *Augustia*, but they differ from the former by being acaulescent or rhizomatous and having male flower with two tepals, and from the latter by having two placentae per ovary locule. Perhaps as many as five of the species are in cultivation, but none are common.

Cultivated species: *B. ankaranensis, B. francoisii, B. goudotii, B. mananjebensis, B. nossibea*

section *Quadriperigonia*

A section of about 17 Mexican species, whose cultivated members are often tuberous, unbranched herbs with terminal racemose inflorescences. Several species produce bulbils in their leaf axils and have tepals with toothed, ciliate margins. A key to the cultivated members of the section is provided under *Begonia gracilis*.

Cultivated species: *B. biserrata, B. boissieri, B. bulbillifera, B. gracilis*, B. pedata, B. sandtii*

section *Reichenheimia*

A section of about 50 rhizomatous or tuberous species distributed throughout Asia. All the cultivated representatives are rhizomatous. All the species have entire placentae, symmetric stamen masses, and non-projecting anther connectives. *Begonia goegoensis* and *B. rajah* are the most commonly cultivated members.

Cultivated species: *B. coriacea, B. floccifera, B. goegoensis*, B. morelii, B. muricata, B. rajah*, B. sudjanae*

section *Ridleyella*

A small section from Thailand and Peninsula Malaysia with one occasionally cultivated member that is easily identified by its creeping, rhizomatous habit, peltate leaves, asymmetric inflorescence, and two-locular ovaries with entire placentae.

Cultivated species: *B. kingiana**

section *Rostrobegonia*

A section of 10 African species that is closely related to section *Augustia*. It is most easily separated from that section by the presence of a ring of hairs at the junction of the petiole and blade, a feature that is found in only two easily identified members of section *Augustia*. A key to the cultivated members of the section is provided under *Begonia johnstonii*.

Cultivated species: *B. engleri, B. johnstonii*, B. keniensis, B. rostrata, B. sonderana*

section *Ruizopavonia*

A section of about 32 species that is largely restricted to Central America and the Andes. The cultivated members have tall stems, large elliptic leaves with pinnate venation and proportionally short petioles, and ovules with axil, bifid placentae.

Cultivated species: *B. alnifolia, B. carpinifolia, B. convallariodora*, B. cooperi, B. estrellensis, B. guaduensis*, B. holtonis, B. meridensis, B. peruviana, B. seemanniana*

section *Scheidweileria*

A small, predominantly Brazilian section whose cultivated members are easily identified by the combination of their tall upright stems, lack of a rhizome or tuber, palmate-compound leaves, and three-locular ovaries with entire placentae. A key to the cultivated species is provided under *Begonia luxurians*.

Cultivated species: *B. digitata, B. luxurians**, *B. semidigitata*

section *Scutobegonia*

A section of 21 species from Africa that are closely related to those of section *Loasibegonia*. For distinguishing features see that section. A key to the cultivated members of the section is provided under *Begonia quadrialata*.

Cultivated species: *B. ciliobracteata, B. clypeifolia, B. dewildei, B. ferramica, B. hirsutula, B. lacunosa, B. montis-elephantis, B. vittariifolia*

section *Solananthera*

A small section of three commonly cultivated species from eastern Brazil that are readily identified. They have a trailing-scandent habit and stamens that often dehisce via pore-like slits that extend to less than half the length of the anther. They also have three-winged ovaries with bifid placentae that lack ovules between the branches.

Cultivated species: *B. integerrima**, *B. radicans, B. solananthera*

section *Sphenanthera*

A widely distributed Asian section containing about 20 species. It is recognized by its combination of fleshy three- or four-locular ovaries with axile placentae, male flowers with four tepals, and anthers with projecting connectives. The female flowers of some species are pleasantly scented.

Cultivated species: *B. acetosella, B. handelii, B. longicarpa, B. longifolia**, *B. multangula, B. obovoidea, B. robusta**, *B. roxburghii**, *B. silletensis*

section *Squamibegonia*

A section of three infrequently cultivated species from Africa. It is easily identified by the unusual bract-like structures that persistently surround the inflorescence and by the female tepals, which are uniquely fused into a long, narrow tube at their base. A key to the section is provided under *Begonia ampla*.

Cultivated species: *B. ampla**, *B. bonus-henricus, B. poculifera*

section *Symbegonia*

The 13 described species of section *Symbegonia*, previously recognized as a distinct genus in the Begoniaceae, are now classified within the genus *Begonia*. Roughly another 12 species remain undescribed, one of which is in cultivation. The section is restricted to New Guinea and is easily distinguished by the combination of its female flowers with fused tepals, stamens fused into a column, and bifid placentae. In *B. symsanguinea* the tepals of the male flowers as well as the females are fused.

Cultivated species: *B. argenteomarginata, B. symsanguinea**, *B. sp. nov.*

section *Tetrachia*

A section with one frequently cultivated species from eastern Brazil that is readily identified by often having both peltate and non-peltate leaves on the same plant, a minutely bullate leaf surface, and ovaries with four wings and four locules.

Cultivated species: *B. egregia**

section *Tetraphila*

A section of 30 species from Africa (for a selection of the cultivated species see Plate 139). The cultivated members are easily identified by the combination of their more or less symmetric, thick leaf blades; male and female flowers with four tepals; and fruit that is sausage-shaped and wingless with parietal placentation. The majority of species have a trailing habit but *Begonia squamulosa, B. longipetiolata, B. rwandensis,* and *B. elaeagnifolia* have stems that are rooted in the substrate for most of their length. Keys to the cultivated members of the section are provided under *B. mannii* and *B. longipetiolata.*

Cultivated species: *B. capillipes, B. cavallyensis, B. ebolowensis, B. elaeagnifolia, B. eminii, B. furfuracea, B. fusialata, B. horticola, B. kisuluana, B. komoensis, B. longipetiolata**, *B. loranthoides, B. mannii**, *B. molleri, B. oxyanthera, B. polygonoides, B. rwandensis, B. squamulosa, B. subalpestris, B. subscutata*

section *Trachelocarpus*

A small, easily identified section from eastern Brazil whose members have leathery, often lance-shaped leaves that arise from short rhizomes. Solitary, stalk-less female flowers are borne close to the rhizome, and male inflorescences have stalks and few flowers. A key to the cultivated members of the section is provided under *Begonia herbacea.*

Cultivated species: *B. depauperata, B. fulvo-setulosa, B. herbacea**, *B. lanceolata*

section *Trendelenburgia*

A section with a single species from eastern Brazil that is doubtfully in cultivation and is easily distinguished by its woody gray stem and symmetric angular elliptic leaves, which are toothed only in their upper half.

Cultivated species: *B. fruticosa*

section *Wageneria*

A section of eight species from Central and South America, three of which are commonly cultivated (Plate 56). These species are readily distinguished because they are the only climbing begonias with entire, axile placentae. A key to the cultivated species is provided under *Begonia convolvulacea*.

Cultivated species: *B. convolvulacea**, *B. fagifolia*, *B. glabra*

section *Weilbachia*

A Central American section containing about 14 species that is distinguished by the combination of its female flowers with two to four (but never five) tepals and nodding, two-locular ovaries with bifid placentae and kidney-shaped stigmas. Most species are creeping-rhizomatous herbs, but *Begonia alice-clarkiae* and *B. purpusii* have upright, non-rhizomatous stems. Several species are commonly cultivated (Plate 120). A key to the cultivated members of the section is provided under *B. imperialis*.

Cultivated species: *B. alice-clarkiae*, *B. aridicaulis*, *B. imperialis**, *B. ludicra*, *B. popenoei*, *B. purpusii*, *B. pustulata*, *B. turrialbae*, *B. violifolia**

Begonia species not presently classified or section uncertain

*Begonia boisiana** (Vietnam), *B. halconensis* (Philippines; see *B. taiwaniana* in chapter five), *B. malabarica* (India; see *B. dipetala* in chapter five), *B. taiwaniana** (Taiwan), *B. thelmae** (Brazil)

5

Descriptions of 100 cultivated begonias

My choice of these 100 species includes those that are commonly cultivated, very distinct in appearance, or particularly interesting to gardeners. I have included almost all the species and many cultivars that are widely cultivated within North America and Europe. The emphasis on the species rather than the cultivar is deliberate—few previous horticultural works have included much information on the cultivated species, instead concentrating on the hybrids. This book is my attempt to redress this imbalance.

Species entries are arranged alphabetically by scientific name and include the authority, the name of the person or persons who first validly named and described the plant. Horticultural works often omit this part of the name, but I give it here to prevent confusion between species names that have been used more than once within *Begonia*. Directly beneath a species name are its botanical section and horticultural group. Beneath those is the publication in which the species was first validly named and described.

Next a list of synonyms appears, if any exist. As most gardeners know, the names of well-known garden plants sometimes change. The reasons for such name changes are varied and usually well founded—the division of a variable species into two or more species, the merging of two or more species, or the renaming of a species previously misidentified in cultivation. Names that are no longer accepted as the valid name for a species are termed synonyms. These synonymous names are often useful to know because they may once have been commonly used in the horticultural literature. The synonym lists presented in this book do not aim to be complete; instead, they include only the names commonly encountered in horticultural works. For a complete checklist of species and their synonyms see Golding and Wasshausen (2002). Unpublished names and American Begonia Society standardized codes for unidentified cultivated species, known as U-numbers, are listed along with the synonyms.

Next is a short description of the average appearance of the species as it is typically found in cultivation. Please bear in mind that growing conditions can affect the size and especially color of plant parts and as a result certain features, on occasion, may appear slightly outside the given ranges. To make the descriptions more accessible to a broad audience, I have attempted to keep botanical terms to a minimum while including all the essential information necessary to distinguish the members of this very large genus. When the scientific terms have no commonly used substitute (as usually they do not) they are explained and illustrated in the glossary. While using the descriptions please remember that organ lengths are measured from the apex of an organ to its point of attachment. Width is measured as the distance from one side of the organ to the other, at its widest part. All measurements should be based on a sample of mature plant parts.

Directly after the description, the species' chromosome number is given, when known. Following the description and chromosome number is an anecdotal account of the species in the wild and in cultivation. This may include such details as the species' discovery and subsequent introduction into cultivation, as well as brief notes on its natural history and cultivation. Along with each species, also, are lists of historically important or currently popular cultivars and naturally occurring variants of the species. I have mentioned closely related species when applicable and presented identification keys in some cases.

Begonia acaulis Merrill & Perry (PLATE 15)

section *Diploclinium*, tuberous group
Journal of the Arnold Arboretum 24: 43, pl. 1, l-q (1943)

Tuberous stemless perennial. **Stipules** usually obscured by the substrate, persistent, ovate 2.5–4 × ca. 1 mm. **Leaves: petiole** pink, sparsely hairy, 5–10 cm long, continuing straight into main vein of blade; **blade** thin, above green, often with pink bases to the main veins, with short soft white hairs, beneath paler green, often with pink bases to the main veins, sparsely hairy, asymmetric, circular-ovate, 4–7.5 × 5.2–8 cm, apex obtuse, base cordate, margin double short-toothed, veins palmate. **Inflorescence:** few-flowered, bisexual, cymose; **bracts** persistent, ovate to ovate-oblong, 3–6 × 1–3.5 mm, margin ciliate. **Male flowers: tepals** four, pink, outer pair broadly elliptic, 0.9–1.2 × 0.8–1.4 cm, apex rounded, hairy on the outer surface, inner pair narrowly obovate, 0.9–1.2 × 0.5–0.7 cm, apex distinctly notched; **stamens** about 50, arranged symmetrically, anther connectives not projecting. **Female flowers: bracteoles** absent; **tepals** four, pink, outer pair broadly elliptic to broadly obovate, 0.6–1.1 × 0.5–1 cm, apex rounded, inner pair narrowly obovate, 0.5–0.8 × 0.3–0.5 cm, apex distinctly notched; **ovary** pink, ellipsoid to ovoid or almost spherical, 0.2–0.5 × 0.2–0.5 cm, unequally three-winged, one wing much longer than the others, three-locular, **placentae** axile, bifid; **styles** three, shortly once-branched, stigmas in a band. **2n** = 28.

This exquisite species grows wild by the Laloki River near Port Moresby in southern Papua New Guinea and is said to be common there in the rain forest on lightly shaded, rocky slopes at an altitude of about 450 m. *Begonia acaulis* is easily recognized by the combination of its stemless habit, softly hairy green leaves, and pink flowers with distinctly notched inner tepals. The species has been cultivated in Europe and North America since 1968 but is a plant for the collector since it needs terrarium culture and is susceptible to fungal attack. Nevertheless, it is a highly desirable, free-flowering plant that is readily grown from seed. It prefers relatively low temperatures in the range of 62 to 65°F (16–18°C), as well as relatively high light levels. No hybrids with *B. acaulis* have been documented.

Six similar Asian species are also cultivated: *Begonia ravenii, B. fimbristipula, B. ovatifolia, B. josephii, B. luzonensis,* and *B. morelii.* Most of these plants are diminutive in stature and all have either small, round tubers or short, fleshy, underground rhizomes and require similar growing conditions to *B. acaulis. Begonia ravenii,* described in more detail later, is a native of Taiwan that is readily identified as the only cultivated species with stolons. *Begonia fimbristipula* is recognized by its slender, underground rhizomes, relatively large, asymmetric-ovate leaf blades with toothed and often lobed margins, and by its flowers that are white with a faint pink tinge. The species is famous in its native region of Guangdong Province, China, because it is used to make a popular commercial herbal tea (see chapter one for a photograph). Regarding this plant Woon-Young Chun and Faith Chun write in the journal *Sunyatensia* (vol. 4, p. 24, 1939):

> In stature, size of leaves and flowers it exhibits all gradations from large to small, and the inflorescence varies from a simple one-flowered, to a branched several-flowered scape. The diminutive form is invariably confined to rocky crevices on the higher slopes and, incidentally is reputed to have a more potent curative property therefore preferred and more highly valued by herbalists. Because it commands a higher price on the drug market herb collectors often risk their lives to climb high cliffs and precipices to gather it. In recent times only the large-leaved form is seen exposed for sale. The plant is employed for the treatment of tuberculosis.

Today *Begonia fimbristipula* is endangered in the wild and should, therefore, be carefully preserved in cultivation. *Begonia luzonensis* (Plate 16) is a native of the Philippines and has leaf blades that are green with silvery gray markings between the veins and flowers that are white with a pink tinge. Himalayan *B. ovatifolia* is represented in cultivation only by *B. ovatifolia* var. *cretacea*. This plant has short, fleshy, underground rhizomes, and produces a single small symmetric or slightly asymmetric-ovate leaf blade that is hairy on the veins beneath. Both the male and female flowers of this species are white or pink and have four tepals. *Begonia josephii* is also native to the Himalayas. It is readily distinguished from the other cultivated tuberous Asian begonias since it alone has peltate leaf blades. *Begonia morelii* has small, slightly asymmetric cordate leaves and white flowers that are faintly pink-tinged. It can be distinguished from the other species mentioned here by its entire placentae—all the others have ovaries with bifid placentae. *Begonia morelii* was described in 1975 based on a stowaway plant discovered at the Station Centrale de Physiologie Végétale in Versailles, France. Its natural habitat within Asia is still unknown.

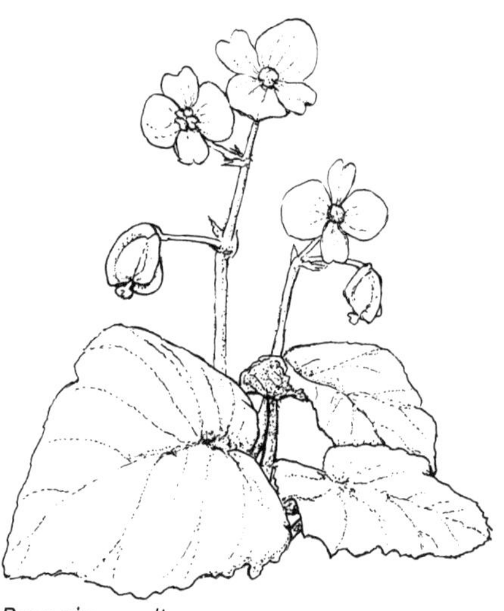

Begonia acaulis.

Begonia acetosa Vellozo (PLATE 17)

section *Pritzelia*, rhizomatous group

Florae Fluminensis, Icones 10: pl. 50 (1831)

Synonym: *B.* U254

Creeping rhizomatous perennial to about 1 m tall with numerous thick, horizontally spreading, pale green branches. **Stipules** persistent, triangular-ovate, 1.3–3.2 × 0.6–1.8 cm, main vein projecting. **Leaves: petiole** rust-brown to red, covered with short wooly hairs, 6–30 cm long, joining blade at an angle; **blade** above olive green, beneath bright red, both surfaces with a dense covering of short stiff white hairs, asymmetric, ovate to almost circular, 4–18 × 3.3–13 cm, apex abruptly short acuminate, base cordate, margin minutely toothed, veins palmate. **Inflorescence:** axillary, many-flowered, bisexual, cymose; **bracts** persistent, linear-lanceolate, 1–3 × ca. 0.3 mm. **Male flowers: tepals** four, white, outer pair elliptic, 10–12 × 5–8 mm, inner pair narrowly elliptic, 7–14 × 1.5–3 mm; **stamens** about 20–30, arranged in a symmetric mass on top of a column, anther connectives projecting. **Female flowers: bracteoles** persistent, linear, 1–2 × ca. 0.3 mm; **tepals** five, white, outer two narrowly elliptic, 6–10 × 1.5–2 mm, inner three elliptic, 10–13 × 4–5 mm; **ovary** white, ellipsoid, 6–11 × 3–5 mm, unequally three-winged, three-locular, **placentae** axile, entire; **styles** three, once-branched, stigmas in a spiraled band, completely covering style branches. **2n** = 38.

This Brazilian species is commonly grown for its distinctive leaves with wonderfully contrasting green upper and wine-red lower surfaces. *Begonia acetosa* has been cultivated in the United States since 1946, at which time Mulford B. Foster introduced it from the forested mountains near Rio de Janeiro. The species was first described in 1831 by a Portuguese-Brazilian clergyman-botanist José Mariano de Conceiçao Vellozo. It appears in his *Florae Fluminensis*, an ambitious work that included 1640 plates of botanical illustrations and descriptions. This work was plagued by troubles and remained unpublished for 70 years after its author's death, having been delayed because it was dedicated to Emperor Dom Pedro I, who had been forced to abdicate while the flora awaited publication. Once published the work fared little better. Shortly after its publication Joseph Hooker, who was then the director of Kew Gardens, described it as "equally remarkable for its pretentious character and the badness of its execution." True to Hooker's disparaging description, volume 10 includes an inaccurate description and dreadful illustration of *B. acetosa*, along with 21 other new begonias. The species name translated from Latin means "acid" or "sour" and refers to the taste of its leaves, which in common with most other begonias are rhubarb-like in flavor.

Begonia acetosa is readily grown in a greenhouse. The species requires relatively high humidity and should be kept slightly moist when actively growing, but during the winter months, when growth is slower, it should be watered only enough to prevent its leaves from wilting. To promote the natural deep red and green coloration of the leaves, position the plant in bright yet indirect light. Popular hybrids with *B. acetosa* parentage include: *B.* 'Art Hodes' (parentage unknown; Plate 18), *B.* 'Black Raspberry' (*B. acetosa* × *B. imperialis*), *B.* 'Carolina Moon' (*B.* 'Elda Haring' × *B. acetosa*), *B.* 'Christmas Theme' (*B.* 'Bill Brooks' × *B. acetosa*), *B.* 'Laura Jane' (*B. acetosa* × *B. acida*), and *B.* 'Old Woman' (*B. acetosa* × *B. heracleifolia*).

Begonia aconitifolia A. de Candolle (PLATES 19 AND 20)

section *Knesebeckia*, cane-like group

Annales des Sciences Naturelles Botanique (Paris) IV, 11: 127 (1859)

Synonyms: *B. sceptrum* Rodigas; *B. faureana* Garnier

Erect perennial to about 3 m tall. Stems green to brown or reddish brown with minute hairs when young, becoming hairless, usually few-branched, swollen at the base. **Stipules** deciduous, ovate, 1.9–3.3 × 1.1–1.5 cm. **Leaves: petiole** green with a red tinge, 4.5–10 cm long, joining blade at a slight to pronounced angle; **blade** above velvety green with dull reddish veins, often with few to several silvery white stripes between the veins, hairless, beneath pale green with yellowish to reddish veins, hairless, in outline more or less circular, palmate-lobed, 14–20 × 17–25 cm, lobes four to six, themselves lobed and minutely toothed, base cordate to truncate, veins palmate. **Inflorescence:** borne in upper leaf axils, few-flowered, bisexual, cymose; **bracts** soon falling, ovate, oblong or obovate-oblong, 0.5–1.1 × 0.7–1.5 cm. **Male flowers: tepals** usually two, white, ovate-cordate to broadly ovate, broadly elliptic, or circular, 1.2–2.2 × 1.5–1.9 cm; **stamens** about 35–50, arranged in a flattened, slightly asymmetric mass, anther connectives projecting. **Female flowers: bracteoles** one or two, staggered beneath ovary, linear, about 1 mm long; **tepals** five, white, broadly obovate to broadly elliptic, 0.5–1.4 × 0.5–1.1 cm, shallowly toothed toward their apex; **ovary** white, obovoid to ellipsoid, 0.3–0.8 × 0.1–0.2 cm, three-winged, wings equal, rounded at both ends, three-locular, **placentae** axile, bifid; **styles** three, once-branched, stigmas in a spiraled band. **2n** = 60.

Ludwig Riedel, director of the botanical section of Brazil's Museu Nacional, discovered this species near Rio de Janeiro in the mid 1800s. Soon afterward, botanist Alphonse de Candolle named it *Begonia aconitifolia* in reference to its palmate-lobed leaves, which resemble those of monkshood, or *Aconitum*. The species was brought into cultivation at William Bull's London nursery in 1884, at which time it was grown as *B. sceptrum*. *Begonia aconitifolia* is a tall, instantly recognized, cane-like species that flowers in the autumn. The species played a central role in the development of the ever-popular Superba group of hybrids, the first of which were created by Eva Gray in the 1920s by crossing *B. aconitifolia* with *B.* 'Lucerna'. Though few of Gray's original hybrids are grown today, several more recent cultivars in this group are popular. Examples include *B.* 'Irene Nuss', *B.* 'Lana', *B.* 'Pink Jade', and *B.* 'Sophie Cecile', all of which have the silver-splashed, palmate-lobed leaves so characteristic of *B. aconitifolia*. The species has curious swollen stem bases, which in the wild probably have a storage function, and along with the species' ability to periodically become dormant, most likely adapt it to life in a relatively dry, open forest habitat.

Begonia aconitifolia needs a great deal of space and frequent maintenance because it can grow up to 3 m tall, and if left to its own devices will develop an unsightly, leafless stem. Regular pruning in late winter will help keep the plant a manageable size and frequent pinching of growing points, starting at an early age, will result in a more compact, leafy plant. A bright, well-lit position and careful watering will also help. Water only when the surface of the plant's growing medium becomes dry; too frequent watering will lead to leaf drop. The species and many of the older *B. aconitifolia* hybrids become dormant in the winter as light levels and temperatures drop, and at that time will naturally shed many of their leaves. Stop fertilizing and reduce watering while plants are dormant.

Several related species are also cultivated, some of which, like *Begonia leathermaniae* and *B. platanifolia*, are classified by horticulturists as cane-like species and others, including *B. acerifolia* and *B. ludwigii*, as thick-stemmed species. *Begonia leathermaniae* and *B. platanifolia* are somewhat similar in appearance to *B. aconitifolia* and like that species have a swollen stem base. *Begonia leathermaniae*, a Bolivian species, is readily distinguished by its ruff-like collar of flattened hairs situated at the top of the petiole. *Begonia platanifolia*, from Brazil, is distinguished from *B. aconitifolia* by having slightly shorter ovate leaf lobes without silver markings. The thick-stemmed species, *B. acerifolia* and *B. ludwigii*, should be carefully maintained in cultivation because they are endangered in the wild due to the continuing destruction of their forest habitats. The latter is particularly attractive and has palmate leaves with long tapering lobes. Like *B. leathermaniae* its leaves have a ruff-like collar at the top of their petioles.

Begonia albo-picta W. Bull (PLATE 21A)

section *Gaerdtia*, cane-like group
Rare Plants Catalog, London 210: 13 (1885)

Perennial. Stems erect and resembling a bamboo cane to 1–1.5 m tall, branched toward the apex, green, sometimes tinged dark brown with narrow dull red rings just above the nodes and numerous small white lenticels, hairless, base of canes usually leafless or almost so. **Stipules** soon falling, lanceolate, concave, 1.8–2.5 × 0.5–0.6 cm. **Leaves:** distichous; **petiole** green with a red tinge, hairless, 0.6–0.8 mm long, continuing straight into main vein of blade; **blade** above green with several small (1–2 mm wide) silvery-white spots between veins, hairless, beneath pale green, hairless, asymmetric, ovate-lanceolate, 8.5–11.5 × 3–5 cm, apex acuminate, base shallowly cordate, margin wavy-toothed, veins pinnate. **Inflorescence:** axillary, many-flowered, cymose, bisexual with several male flowers and few female flowers; **bracts** deciduous, ovate, concave, 5–6 × ca. 3 mm. **Male flowers: tepals** four, white to pink, outer pair broadly ovate-cordate, 1–1.2 × 1.2–1.4 cm, inner pair elliptic to obovate-elliptic, 0.9–1 × ca. 0.4 cm; **stamens** about 20, arranged in a flattened symmetric mass, anther connectives rounded and shortly projecting. **Female flowers: bracteoles** paired directly beneath ovary, soon falling, ovate, 5 × 3 mm; **tepals** five, same color as males, outer pair broadly ovate, 0.8–1 × ca. 0.7 cm, inner three elliptic, 0.7–0.9 × 0.4–0.6 cm; **ovary** body pale green with pale pink wings, elliptic, 0.8 × 0.3 cm, three-winged, wings more or less equal, curved like propeller blades, three-locular, **placentae** axile, entire; **styles** three, once-branched, base flared, stigmas in a spiraled band. **2n** = 56.

This easy-to-grow Brazilian species was first introduced into cultivation in 1883 via William Bull's London nursery. The species name, *albo-picta*, refers to the numerous small, silvery white speckles that dot this plant's upper leaf surfaces. Similar spotted leaves are also common to the very closely related *Begonia maculata* var. *wrightii*, but in that plant the leaf blades are larger and the spots are less numerous and slightly larger. Nevertheless, the two are so similar that some authors have considered them variants of the same species. *Begonia maculata* var. *maculata* is at once recognized by its large white spots that often measure about 7 mm or more in width. Horticulturists classify *B. albo-picta* and *B. maculata* as cane-like begonias. Indeed, of the roughly 10–15 cane-like species and approximately 200 cane-like hybrids in cultivation, *B. maculata* is one of the closest in appearance to an actual bamboo cane since it has particularly tall, straight, green stems. Its flowers, however, are anything but bamboo-like; rather than being drab like those of a grass they are a dazzling white and quite showy. *Begonia maculata* is sometimes referred to as the "trout begonia" because of the silvery spots on its leaves, which resemble the markings on a freshly caught trout. The cultivar *B.* 'Medora', which also has spotted leaves, is sometimes also given this name. Most other cane-like begonias lack spots on their leaves. Of these the white-flowered *B. salicifolia* (Plate 23) and *B. undulata* are also very bamboo-like in appearance and common in cultivation. The former has glossy green, ovate-oblong leaves that are almost flat. *Begonia undulata* on the other hand has ovate-oblong leaves with undulate margins. Other bamboo-like begonias with red or orange flowers are discussed elsewhere under *B. coccinea* and *B. dichroa*. See Plate 21 for a comparison of begonias with bamboo-like stems.

Begonia albo-picta and its relatives are comparatively easy to grow because they are generally more accommodating to low atmospheric humidity than most other begonias. Perhaps the most important consideration with these cane-like begonias is to provide them with adequate light. They need to receive bright light year-round in order to flower and produce strong stems. These plants also need to dry out slightly between waterings or else they have a tendency to drop their leaves. Careful pruning can also help maintain a leafy appearance and keep these tall plants in bounds. Many growers cut down the older, woodier stems that have lost their lower leaves in order to promote the growth of newer leafier ones. Propagate via seed or cuttings made from young side branches and stem tips. *Begonia albo-picta* is a parent, along with *B. olbia*, of the trout leaf begonia, *B.* 'Argenteo Guttata', a commonly cultivated hybrid created in 1888 at Victor Lemoine's once famous nursery in France. It is probably also a parent of *B.* 'Medora' (Plate 22), one of the most frequently encountered of all the begonia hybrids, as well as one of the easiest to grow. Similarly, *B.* 'Lucerna' (Plate 22) is a popular hybrid, created in 1892 in Lucerne, Switzerland, with unknown parentage but which almost certainly includes one or more of the cane-like species. *Begonia* 'Flamingo' is a *B. dichroa* × *B. undulata* cross, and *B.* 'Flamingo Queen' is a *B. maculata* × *B.* 'Lenore Olivier' cross.

Begonia amphioxus M. J. S. Sands (PLATE 24)

section *Petermannia*, shrub-like group
Kew Magazine 7: 77, pl. 149 (1990)

Erect branching perennial to about 75 cm tall. Stems green, hairless. **Stipules** soon falling, ovate-lanceolate to oblong-lanceolate, 8–15 × 3–7 mm. **Leaves:** peltate; **petiole** pale green, hairless, 1–6 cm long; **blade** above glossy green with a burgundy spot where the petiole joins the blade and other burgundy spots scattered over the surface, margin with a thin red line, beneath pale green with pink spots corresponding to the burgundy spots above, angular-ovate, 4–15 × 0.8–2.8 cm, margin undulate and shallowly crenate. **Inflorescence:** axillary, unisexual, male inflorescences few-flowered, cymose, female flowers solitary; **bracts** soon falling, ovate, 2.2–3 × 1–1.5 mm. **Male flowers: tepals** four, greenish white, outer pair broadly ovate, 5–5.5 × 5.5–6 mm, inner pair obovate, apex rounded, 3.5–5 × 2–3 mm; **stamens** 50–60, arranged symmetrically, anther connectives not projecting. **Female flowers: bracteoles** absent; **tepals** three to five, often shortly fused at the base, greenish cream, ovate or ovate-elliptic, 8–10 × 4–5 mm; **ovary** pale green, ellipsoid, 8–12 × 4–6 mm, with two to three wings, two- to three-locular, **placentae** axile, bifid; **styles** two to three, once-branched, stigmas in a spiraled band.

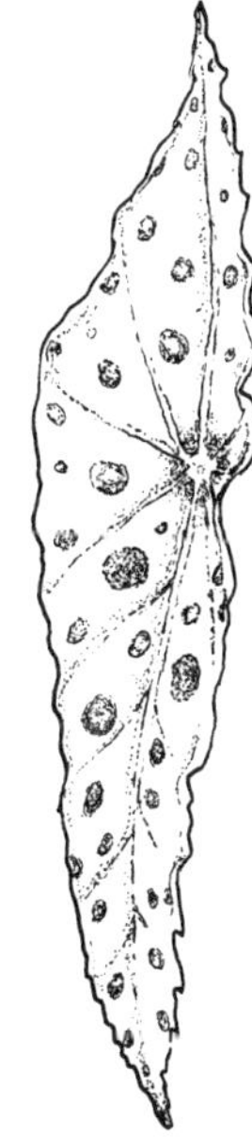
Leaf of *B. amphioxus*.

Begonia amphioxus is one of the most unusual of all the begonias. Not only are its leaves typically peltate and pointed at both ends, they are also covered with wine-red spots and rimmed with a thin line of the same color. The species name *amphioxus* means "sharp at both ends" in reference to the plant's strange leaf shape, a shape that is similar to the primitive marine, fish-like lancelet, or amphioxus. In the wild, *B. amphioxus* occurs only on two small, close, limestone outcrops in Sabah, Malaysia. There it grows in light shade at an altitude of 375–425 m, both upon the limestone crags and in the surrounding rain forest. It was introduced into cultivation in 1984 by Kew botanist Martin Sands, the person who also gave it its very appropriate name.

Begonia amphioxus is rare in cultivation but should be more widely grown, not only because it is an attractive species but also because it has such a limited natural distribution and is, consequently, of conservation concern. The species is best cultivated in a humid greenhouse or within a terrarium. It prefers an open, fibrous growing medium and at Kew is reported to grow well in a hanging basket. Propagation is usually via stem cuttings but, as is true of many of the Asian shrub-like begonias, the species can also be propagated from leaf cuttings. No artificial hybrids with this species have been documented.

Begonia ampla J. D. Hooker (PLATE 25)

section *Squamibegonia*, trailing-scandent group
in Oliver, *Flora of Tropical Africa* 2: 574 (1871)

Epiphytic or rock-dwelling, non-rhizomatous perennial. Stems branchless or few-branched, to 1 m long, becoming woody at base, pale gray to pale brown, youngest part densely covered with scale-like hairs. **Stipules** soon falling, narrowly ovate to triangular, concave, 2–5 × 1.5–2.5 cm. **Leaves: petiole** reddish with scale-like hairs, 5–22 cm long, joining blade at an angle; **blade** above glossy green, beneath paler green, both surfaces with tiny star-shaped hairs, asymmetric, ovate to broadly ovate, apex acuminate, base cordate, margin entire or short-toothed at vein endings, veins palmate. **Inflorescence:** axillary, few-flowered, bisexual, cymose, tightly enclosed by two large, thick, persistent, concave, bract-like structures. **Male flowers: tepals** two, white with red stripes along the veins, obovate to broadly obovate, 16–20 × 13–19 mm; **stamens** 25–55, arrangement resembling a bunch of bananas, anther connectives projecting shortly. **Female flowers: bracteoles** absent; **tepals** two, white with red stripes along the veins, base fused into a very narrow tube to about 5 mm long, free part obovate to almost circular, 17–27 × 14–20 mm; **ovary** pale green, covered with minute star-shaped hairs, barrel-shaped with four angles, 5.5–7.5 × 6–7 mm, wingless, four-locular, **placentae** parietal but superficially appearing axile, bifid; **styles** four, once-branched, stigmas in a spiraled band. **2n** = 36–40.

Begonia ampla and two other African species constitute the section *Squamibegonia*, which is at once recognized by its members' large, persistent bracts that form a cup-shaped structure that completely encloses all but the mature flowers of the inflorescence. These species also have very distinct but less easily observed female flowers. Unfortunately, the beautiful bract-like structure must be pulled apart and the inflorescence destroyed in order to see that the paired tepals of each female flower are fused at their base into narrow cylinders, a feature found in no other begonia. In the wild, all three species grow either upon tree trunks or rocks. Like the majority of other epiphytic African begonias, *B. ampla* and its relatives have particularly thick leaves. However, unlike several of those other species, they tend to live in very humid locations, and in the wild they often grow on trees overhanging rivers or swamps. None are commonly cultivated but *B. ampla* is perhaps the most frequently encountered in specialist collections. If any of these species can be acquired, they are best grown mounted on a piece of cork. They require a cool, humid greenhouse and benefit from being grown close to a pool or other water feature. In this manner, *B. ampla* has been successfully cultivated for several years next to a large waterfall in the cool-tropical section of the Princess of Wales Conservatory at Kew Gardens. No artificial hybrids involving *B. ampla* or its relatives have been documented. The identification key below is modified from: Wilde, J. J. F. E. de, and J. C. Arends, 1980. *Begonia* section *Squamibegonia* Warb.: a taxonomic revision. *Miscellaneous Papers Landbouwhogeschool Wageningen* 19: 377–421. This publication provides detailed descriptions and ecological notes for all three species.

Key to the species of section *Squamibegonia*

1 a. Stems 1–1.5 mm in diameter at their base; petiole continuing almost straight into leaf blade . . . . *B. bonus-henricus*
b. Stems 5–20 mm in diameter at their base; petiole joining leaf blade at a distinct angle 2
2 a. Main vein of leaf almost straight; base of leaf often deeply cordate . . . . . *B. ampla*
b. Main vein of leaf distinctly curved; base of leaf rarely deeply cordate . . *B. poculifera*

Begonia angularis Raddi (PLATE 26)
section *Pritzelia*, cane-like group
Memoriè di Matematica e di Fisica della Società Italiana della Scienze (Modena) 18: 407 (1820)
Synonyms: *B. compta* Bull; *B. zebrina* Klotzsch

Erect non-rhizomatous perennial to 2.5 m tall. Stems zigzagged toward apex, shortly branched, at maturity distinctly six-ribbed to six angled, green with narrow reddish bands above the nodes, or reddish throughout, hairless. **Stipules** persistent, soon drying out, ovate, margins often rolled inward, 0.9–2.5 × 0.9–1.6 cm. **Leaves:** distichous; **petiole** yellowish green to pink, hairless, 1.3–7 cm long, joining blade at an angle; **blade** above satiny green with grayish green veins or satiny green throughout, beneath paler green to purple, both surfaces hairless, asymmetric, narrowly ovate to ovate-oblong, 7–13 × 4–6.2 cm, apex acute, base cordate, margin undulate, shallowly toothed, veins palmate-pinnate. **Inflorescence:** in upper leaf axils, many-flowered, bisexual, cymose; **bracts** soon falling, obovate, 2–3 × 2–2.5 cm. **Male flowers: tepals** four, white to pink, outer pair almost circular, 5.5–6.2 × 5.5–5.7 mm, inner pair obovate-wedge-shaped, ca. 5.2 × 3 mm; **stamens** about 25, arranged symmetrically, anther connectives projecting. **Female flowers: bracteoles** usually solitary, soon falling; **tepals** five, same color as males, elliptic, 4–6 × 2.8–3.5 mm; **ovary** green, often with red-tinged wings, elliptic, ca. 4 × 2.2–2.7 mm, unequally three-winged, three-locular, **placentae** axile, entire; **styles** three, once-branched, stigmas in a spiraled band.

Begonia angularis is well worth growing for its foliage, which in good clones is an interesting satiny green with contrasting gray-green veins. Also striking are its angular or ribbed stems, a feature that is helpful in its identification, as highlighted by the scientific name *angularis*. Plants grown as *B. castanaefolia* also have this characteristic and appear to be identical to *B. angularis*. However, because *B. castanaefolia* is known only from a fragmentary botanical description and appears to lack a type specimen, knowing for certain how, or even if, the two can be separated is difficult. The name *B. stipulacea* is also commonly but incorrectly used for *B. angularis*. The true *B. stipulacea* is a distantly related species that I have not seen in cultivation.

Begonia angularis is native to steep, shady, moist areas in the central region of the Atlantic Coastal Forest of Brazil at an altitude of 600–1500 m. This forest is worth describing in some detail because more species of *Begonia* are cultivated from this area than from anywhere else in the world. The forest is home to almost 200 *Begonia* species, roughly half of which are in cultivation. In fact, almost all of Brazil's native begonias occur here, with only a handful of species being found in the considerably larger Amazonian rain forest; the probable reason for this discrepancy is that begonias generally prefer the relatively cool, moist upland climate of the eastern mountains to the lowland forests of the Amazon. The Atlantic Coastal Forest at one time covered Brazil's coastal mountains in an unbroken strip from the country's easternmost point in the state of Rio Grande do Norte southward to its southernmost borders where it spread out in a 600-km-wide swath in the far south of Brazil and northern Paraguay. Today, however, this region of Brazilian forests is subject to high human population density and only fragments now exist, with over 90 percent of the country's Atlantic Coastal Forest having been destroyed or drastically altered. Nevertheless, those pockets of forest protected as part of Brazil's National Park System still harbor an estimated 20,000 vascular plant species, more than are found in the entire continental United States. Because of its unusually high diversity the Atlantic Coastal Forest is considered one of the world's highest priority areas for conservation, especially as most of its species occur nowhere else in the world. Over 90 percent of the forest's *Begonia* species, for example, are endemic. The reason for this high level of endemism is due to the fact that the Atlantic Coastal Forests have long been isolated from the Amazonian and other forests by the dry uplands of the Planalto. This factor, coupled with the high climatic and geographic diversity of the area, has led to the local evolution of a large number of species, including many begonias. Examples of other species from this area that are commonly cultivated include: *B. coccinea*, *B. convolvulacea*, *B. cucullata*, *B. herbacea*, *B. luxurians*, and *B. venosa*.

Begonia angularis flowers from late winter to early spring and is readily cultivated in a greenhouse or on a windowsill. The species' growing points should be frequently pinched to produce a full plant. Bessie Buxton (1946) reports that the species is susceptible to root nematodes. *Begonia angularis* has been cultivated in Europe since 1845, at which time is was introduced to England from San Gabriel in the Sierra d'Estrella of Brazil. The species' gray-green leaves have been inherited in the cultivar, *B.* 'Grey Feather'.

Begonia arborescens Raddi (PLATE 27)

section *Pritzelia*, shrub-like group
Memoriè di Matematica e di Fisica della Società Italiana della Scienze (Modena) 18: 408 (1820)

Erect branched perennial to 2.5 m tall. Stems green infused with brownish purple for 0.3–1.5 cm above each node, hairless or hairy. **Stipules** deciduous, ovate-lanceolate, 0.6–1.2 × 0.3–0.4 cm. **Leaves:** distichous; **petiole** pale green with a reddish tinge on the upper surface to red throughout, covered with minute reddish brown hairs, 0.8–3.5 cm long, continuing straight into main vein of blade; **blade** above glossy green, hairless, beneath paler green to reddish, hairless or with dense hairs along the main veins, slightly asymmetric, narrowly elliptic to broadly elliptic, or broadly elliptic-oblong, 8–18 × 2.5–6 cm, apex abruptly acuminate, base shallowly cordate, margin shallowly toothed, veins pinnate, sunken above, raised beneath. **Inflorescence:** axillary, many-flowered, compact-branched, bisexual, cymose; **bracts** deciduous, small and inconspicuous. **Male flowers: tepals** four, white, outer pair elliptic, 3–6 × 2–3.5 mm, inner pair obovate-oblong, 2–4 × 1–1.5 mm; **stamens** numerous, arranged symmetrically, anther connectives shortly projecting. **Female flowers: bracteoles** deciduous, small and inconspicuous; **tepals** five, white, lanceolate to elliptic, 1.5–3 × 0.8–2 mm; **ovary** white or green, sometimes red tinged, broadly ovate to almost spherical, 1–4.5 × 0.5–4 mm, more or less equally three-winged, three-locular, **placentae** axile, entire; **styles** three, yellow, contrasting with the tiny white segments and as noticeable as they are, once-branched, stigmas in a spiraled band. **2n** = 56.

As the name suggests this begonia is tree-like and one of the tallest of all free-standing begonias. *Begonia arborescens* is native to the Atlantic Coastal Forest of Brazil, where it is common in humid, shady locations in the rain forest. After seeing this species in the wild, Marc Hachadourian, a horticulturist at New York Botanical Garden, has suggested that it may mimic certain species of *Cecropia*, which are common trees of the rain forests where *B. arborescens* lives. This hypothesis is intriguing since cecropias have an intricate relationship with ants that live inside their stems and protect them from herbivores. If this *Begonia* is indeed capable of fooling potential herbivores into thinking it is a *Cecropia* and therefore protected by ants, it is easy to see why this bluff may have evolved. Three readily distinguished varieties of *B. arborescens* have been described. The species, *B. arborescens* var. *arborescens*, as commonly found in nature, has large, very broad leaves and is almost hairless. The plant *B. arborescens* var. *confertiflora* inhabits a higher altitude and has dense, long, soft hairs along the main vein of its leaf blade and on its flower stalks. *Begonia arborescens* var. *oxyphylla* has relatively narrow leaf blades that measure no more than 6 cm across. This variant, while having the smallest natural distribution, is the one most often seen in cultivation.

Begonia arborescens needs a lot of space and for this reason is often grown in a bed within a greenhouse, rather than within a pot. The Atlanta Botanical Garden grows it in this way in their tropical house, and its large size helps produce the illusion that it is growing in a natural tropical rain forest. At that garden the species thrives in a very shady position with a high relative humidity. The species has seldom, if ever, been used in hybridization.

Begonia hookeriana (Plate 28) is a similar, very large-leaved, shrubby plant from Brazil. Unlike *B. arborescens*, it has a dense covering of minute, orange-brown hairs on its petioles, peduncles, and main veins on the undersurface of the leaves. It is only occasionally cultivated.

Begonia aspleniifolia A. de Candolle (PLATE 29)

section *Filicibegonia*, shrub-like group

Prodromus Systematis Naturalis Regni Vegetabilis 15 (1): 392 (1864)

Erect rhizomatous perennial to 20 cm tall, usually with several slender, green branches. **Stipules** persistent, linear, 0.5–0.6 × 0.5–0.8 cm. **Leaves: petiole** very short; **blade** green, symmetric, in outline ovate, 2.5–4 × 0.5–1.5 cm, margin pinnatisect, with five to seven linear-obovate divisions on each side of the midrib, these one- to five-toothed. **Inflorescence:** unisexual, male flowers in the uppermost leaf axils, solitary or in few-flowered cymes, female flowers solitary and positioned below male flowers, peduncles and pedicels very short; **bracts** persistent, lanceolate, 2–3 × ca. 0.5 mm. **Male flowers: tepals** two, white with a red flush on the base of the veins, ovate to almost circular, 0.3–0.5 × 0.2–0.3 cm; **stamens** about 9–11, arrangement resembling a bunch of bananas, anther connectives not projecting. **Female flowers: bracteoles** absent; **tepals** two, white with a red patch at the base of each segment, elliptic to broadly elliptic, 0.3–0.5 × ca. 0.3 cm; **ovary** white with a red stripe along the length of each locule, ellipsoid, ca. 3.5 × 1.5 mm, with three equal wings, wings rounded and narrowing at both ends, three-locular, **placentae** axile, entire; **styles** three, unbranched, stigmas kidney-shaped.

The deeply dissected leaves of this unusual West African species give it the appearance of a fern of the genus *Asplenium*, hence its scientific name. *Begonia aspleniifolia* is easily distinguished from the only other cultivated fern-like begonia—*B. bipinnatifida*, a rarely cultivated New Guinean species—because *B. aspleniifolia* alone has female flowers with two tepals, which are white with a red blotch at the base. I have seen *B. aspleniifolia* only in a few botanical collections and mention it here as a curiosity that would appeal to the collector if it were to become more widely available. In the wild it has a very restricted distribution in the Crystal Mountains of tropical West Africa.

Begonia aspleniifolia requires high humidity and is best grown either indoors in an enclosed terrarium under lights or in a greenhouse inside a partially open terrarium placed in a semi-shady position. This species prefers a chopped sphagnum moss–perlite mix and is said to be susceptible to over watering. No hybrids with *B. aspleniifolia* have been documented.

Begonia bogneri Ziesenhenne (PLATES 30 AND 31)

section *Erminea*, tuberous group
Begonian 40: 76 (1973)

Erect short stemmed tuberous perennial. Stem pink to yellowish green, to 4 cm tall. **Stipules** persistent, triangular, 2–4 × 1.5–2 mm. **Leaves:** crowded on the short stem; **petiole** pink to yellowish green, 0.3–3.5 cm long, continuing straight into main vein of blade; **blade** green, hairless to sparsely hairy, linear, tapering to an obtuse or acute tip, 4–15 cm × 1–2 mm, grooved on both surfaces. **Inflorescence:** axillary, cymose, with one or few male flowers and a single female flower; **bracts** soon falling, triangular-ovate, 2–4 × 1.3–2 mm. **Male flowers: tepals** four, outer pair pale pink, obovate, 5–10 × 3–6 mm, inner pair white suffused with pink, obovate, 7–8 × 2–3 mm; **stamens** 8–13, arranged in a more or less asymmetric cluster, anther connectives shortly projecting. **Female flowers: bracteoles** absent; **tepals** six, outer three pink, obovate, 5–7.5 × 2–4.5 mm, inner three white suffused with pink, obovate to broadly spatula-shaped, 6–9 × 2–6 mm; **ovary** pink to red, ovoid, 5–7 × 2–4 mm, with one wing, three-locular, **placentae** axile or parietal but superficially appearing axile, bifid; **styles** three, unbranched, stigmas crescent-shaped. **2n** = 38.

California nurseryman and gifted hybridizer Rudolf Ziesenhenne described this very unusual strap-leaved species in the April 1973 edition of the *Begonian*, naming it for Josef Bogner, curator of greenhouses at the Munich Botanic Garden. In 1969 Bogner had discovered the species growing in a remote, mountainous part of Madagascar. Indeed, he may well be the only person ever to have seen this species growing wild. He informs us that it grows in deep shade on moss-covered granite cliffs at an elevation of 50 m.

The begonias of Madagascar, as a whole, have great potential for the begonia collector, for on this island the genus has taken on some fascinating forms, as has much of the country's unusual plant and animal life. Unfortunately, few Madagascan begonias have ever been introduced into gardens, and those that have remain rare. One of them, *Begonia goudotii* (Plate 32), if it can be obtained, is particularly worth growing for its leaves that form bizarre plate-like structures pressed tight against the substrate. Other species yet to be cultivated, like *B. perpusilla*, are remarkable for their diminutive size—the species reaches no more than 1 cm in height, when not in flower. Another, *B. nana*, has curious ribbon-like leaves.

In cultivation, *Begonia bogneri* is usually grown in an enclosed glass container because it likes a very humid atmosphere. It also prefers a relatively cool position and performs best within a temperature range of 65 to 70°F (18–21°C). If grown in a greenhouse under natural light *B. bogneri* tends to become dormant in winter and will drop its leaves, but applying artificial lighting can prevent this resting period. *Begonia bogneri*'s tubers should be allowed to dry out between watering, which is the reason that it is often given an open mix containing lots of chopped sphagnum moss and perlite. The species is also occasionally grown in sphagnum moss mounted on a piece of cork. In fact, Bogner himself grew it this way. When using this method, never allow the sphagnum moss substrate to become saturated for this will cause the small tubers to rot. I have seen a few ingenious growers solve this problem by suspending the mounted plant over a large storage tank of water inside a greenhouse. This arrangement provides the plant with the necessary humidity without saturating the growing medium. Flowers are usually produced in early and mid summer. Propagation is typically achieved by dividing the plant or taking cuttings of whole leaves or sections of leaves. Place the cuttings in an open rooting mix, such as four parts sphagnum to one part perlite. A single hybrid involving *B. bogneri* has been documented, *B. bogneri* × *B. solananthera*. I have not seen this cultivar, but this unlikely parentage is reported to have created a plant with an appearance similar to *B. solananthera*.

Begonia boisiana Gagnepain (PLATE 33)

not yet classified, shrub-like group

Bulletin du Muséum National d'Histoire Naturelle (Paris) 25: 195 (1919)

Erect non-rhizomatous perennial to 60 cm tall. Stem brown, at least when mature, usually few-branched, the whole plant hairless. **Stipules** soon falling, ovate to elliptic, 0.6–1.3 × 4–5.5 mm. **Leaves:** distichous; **petiole** yellowish green to wine-red, 0.5–3.5 cm, continuing straight into main vein of blade or joining blade at an angle; **blade** above glossy green, beneath green with a burgundy tinge especially along the veins, asymmetric, narrowly ovate-lanceolate (one side of leaf distinctly less rounded than the other), 7.5–11.5 × 2–2.3 cm, apex acuminate, base rounded, margin shallowly angular-toothed, often undulate, veins palmate-pinnate. **Inflorescence:** axillary, 5–15-flowered, bisexual, cymose; **bracts** soon falling, ovate, 2–4 × 1–2.5 mm. **Male flowers: tepals** four, dull white with a pink tinge, especially on uppermost segment, outer pair broadly ovate to broadly elliptic, 7–8 × 6–9 mm, inner pair narrowly elliptic, 8–9 × 3–3.5 mm; **stamens** about 20, arrangement resembling a bunch of bananas, anther connectives projecting. **Female flowers: bracteoles** absent; **tepals** five, dull white with a pink tinge especially on margin, outermost segments broadly elliptic, 7–9 × 5–7 mm, innermost segment(s) narrowly elliptic, 8.5–9 × 3.5–4.5 mm; **ovary** white, often tinged pink, ovoid, three-winged, one wing longer than others, three-locular, **placentae** axile, entire; **styles** three, unbranched, stigmas crescent-shaped. **2n** = 30.

This Vietnamese species is something of a curiosity, as its unusual combination of vegetative and floral features do not fit within the existing botanical classification of *Begonia*. Ongoing research may well show that it deserves classifying in a new section. The species is readily distinguished by its unique combination of erect habit and pendulous, unequally winged ovaries with

Leaf of *B. boisiana*.

axile, unbranched placentae. In the wild I have seen it growing in shallow pockets of soil on limestone rock outcroppings in the lowland tropical rain forests of northern and central Vietnam.

Begonia boisiana is easily cultivated, flowers for much of the summer months, and should appeal to the collector of unusual begonias. Propagate via seed or stem cuttings. The American Begonia Society first offered *B. boisiana* as seed in 1975. No hybrids with this species have been documented.

Begonia boliviensis A. de Candolle (PLATE 34)

section *Barya*, tuberous group
Annales des Sciences Naturelles Botanique (Paris) IV, 11: 122 (1859)

Tuberous perennial to about 1 m tall. Stems branchless or few-branched, pale green with a white to pale pink powdery covering, hairless. **Stipules** persistent, triangular-ovate to oblong-lanceolate, 3.8–7 × 2–4 mm. **Leaves: petiole** green, hairless, 0.5–5 cm long, continuing more or less straight into the main vein of the blade; **blade** above green, beneath paler green, both surfaces with short hairs especially on the veins beneath, asymmetric, lanceolate to lanceolate-ovate, 4.2–17 × 1–5.5 cm, apex long acuminate, base cordate to more or less rounded-truncate, margin single- to double-toothed, veins palmate-pinnate. **Inflorescence:** axillary, few-flowered, bisexual, cymose; **bracts** persistent, triangular-ovate to broadly ovate or broadly elliptic, 2–10 × 2–8 mm, margin toothed. **Male flowers: tepals** four, held erect, bright red, outer pair elliptic to lanceolate, 1.9–5.5 × 0.5–1.4 cm, inner pair narrowly elliptic to elliptic, 2.1–4.6 × 0.3–0.7 cm; **stamens** numerous, attached to a fleshy column 1–2 cm tall, anther connectives not projecting. **Female flowers: bracteoles** absent; **tepals** five, held erect, bright red, lanceolate, 1.5–3.5 × 0.3–0.5 cm; **ovary** reddish tinged, ellipsoid, 0.4–0.9 × 0.2–0.6 cm, unequally three-winged, wings projecting over styles, three-locular, **placentae** axile, bifid; **styles** three, once-branched, branches long and erect, stigmas in a spiraled band. **2n** = 28.

Begonia boliviensis is at once recognized by its pendulous habit, long narrow leaf blades, and bright red flowers with long, lance-shaped tepals. In the wild, the species grows upon wet cliffs and other humid, shady places at the relatively high altitude of 1400–2400 m. Despite its name *B. boliviensis* is native to the Andean Mountains of Peru and Argentina in addition to Bolivia. German plant collector Hugh Weddell first discovered the species in the Andean mountains of Bolivia in 1857, hence the species name. Weddell did not introduce it into cultivation though; that was left for Richard Pearce to do in 1864 while collecting for the London nursery firm of James Veitch and Sons. When Veitch and Sons exhibited *B.*

boliviensis for the first time, at the 1867 International Horticultural Show in Paris, the plant is said to have attracted more attention than any other on display. Soon afterward the nursery started hybridizing the species with other tuberous Andean begonias, producing *B.* 'Sedenii' in 1867, shortly followed by other commercial successes. Once the Veitch nursery had established its lead in producing these showy-flowered hybrids, *B. boliviensis* itself was released commercially in 1870. Today, more than 130 years later, its influence shows in hundreds of cultivars classified in the *B.* ×*tuberhybrida* group (Plates 35 and 198–200). The species has been particularly important in producing pendulous members of this group. The history of the *B.* ×*tuberhybrida* group is discussed in more detail under *B. veitchii*.

Botanists classify *Begonia boliviensis* along with two other Andean species in the section *Barya*. These three species are unusual in having long, narrow tepals that never fully open and stamens that are attached to a fleshy, 1–2-cm-tall column. Interestingly, a similar stamen arrangement and half-open flowers are also found in the distantly related *B. symsanguinea* and its relatives from New Guinea. The two groups of plants appear to have independently evolved this characteristic in response to bird pollination. Given the enormous geographical separation of these plants, their pollinators naturally differ, with hummingbirds pollinating the Andean species and sunbirds the New Guinean ones. The bright red flowers of both *B. boliviensis* and *B. symsanguinea* are also indicative of bird-pollinated flowers.

Begonia boliviensis is one of the easiest tuberous species to cultivate but nevertheless can be a little temperamental. It needs excellent drainage and for this reason grows well in an open fibrous potting mix in a hanging basket. This method of cultivation is also esthetically pleasing because the species' drooping stems and flowers often cascade over the sides of the container. Because *B. boliviensis* is a native of relatively high altitudes it performs best in areas with cool climates, a cultural preference that it has passed on to its descendants in the *B.* ×*tuberhybrida* group.

Begonia bowerae Ziesenhenne (PLATE 36)

section *Gireoudia*, rhizomatous group
Begonian 17: 78 (1950)

Creeping rhizomatous perennial. Rhizome green to purple, branched. **Stipules** persistent, ovate to triangular-ovate, 0.5–1.2 × 0.5–0.9 cm. **Leaves: petiole** pale green with purple lenticels, sometimes purple throughout, hairy, 4–26 cm long, joining blade at an angle; **blade** above green or green with separate purple to almost black markings around margins and sometimes next to main veins, hairless, beneath paler green, sparsely hairy, asymmetric, ovate, 2–11.5 × 1.5–10 cm, apex acuminate, base cordate, margin wavy, short, angular-lobed, and minutely saw-toothed, with several long white cilia, veins palmate. **Inflorescence:** axillary, few-flowered, bisexual, cymose; **bracts** persistent, ovate to broadly elliptic, 1.5–13 × 1–14 mm, margin ciliate. **Male flowers: tepals** two, white, sometimes with a thin band of red encircling the base of the filaments, inner surface sometimes red-spotted, obovate to almost circular, 0.8–1.1 × 0.8–1.1 cm; **stamens** about 10–15, arrangement resembling a bunch of bananas, anther connectives not or slightly projecting. **Female flowers: bracteoles** absent or paired about 1 mm beneath ovary, persistent, elliptic, 1.2–3 × 0.5–1 mm; **tepals** two, white, obovate to almost circular, 5–9 × 0.5–8.5 mm; **ovary** green, sometimes with pink tinged wings, broadly ellipsoid to spherical, 4.5–5.5 × 4–5 mm, slightly unequally three-winged, three-locular, **placentae** axile, bifid; **styles** three, unbranched, stigmas crescent-shaped. **2n** = 28.

This Mexican species is often referred to as the eyelash begonia because the long white hairs on its leaf margin closely resemble eyelashes. Its scientific name honors Constance Bower, a begonia enthusiast who produced several popular begonia hybrids in the 1920s. *Begonia bowerae* is among the best species begonias; it is easy to grow, compact in habit, and has attractively patterned foliage. As a bonus, it produces numerous dainty white or pink flowers in late winter and early spring. Not surprisingly, *B. bowerae* is one of the most sought-after of all begonias and a parent of hundreds of hybrid cultivars. Rudolf Ziesenhenne, who described the species, lists 583 of its hybrids in the December 1981 volume of the *Begonian*. Ziesenhenne was also the first to commercially offer *B. bowerae* in 1950, having received seed of this plant a year or two earlier from Thomas MacDougall, who discovered the plant. MacDougall found *B. bowerae* in the state of Oaxaca in 1948 while exploring a ridge connecting the northern end of the Cerro Atravesado with the southern slopes of the Sierra Madre. It was growing in this area among rocks at an altitude of about 1220 m in what MacDougall describes as "cloud forest bordering on dry pine woods." The species is said to be locally common but restricted to a small area. Given its small distribution *B. bowerae* is remarkably variable in its flower color and leaf size and pattern. Three varieties have been described in addition to the typical plant, the most attractive of these being *B. bowerae* var. *nigramarga*, which has small green leaves with black bands bordering each of the main veins.

Begonia bowerae is classified in the section *Gireoudia*, which contains many other popular Mexican and Central American begonias, nine of which are described elsewhere in this book: *B. conchifolia*, *B. crassicaulis*, *B. heracleifolia*, *B. hydrocotylifolia*, *B. involucrata*, *B. kellermanii*, *B. multinervia*, *B. nelumbifolia*, and *B. strigillosa*. (See Plates 38–40 for a comparison of the leaves from many of the species in this section). The section *Gireoudia* is named after L. C. Gireoud who was the head gardener at Nauen's Gardens in Berlin. Kathleen Burt-Utley has published a taxonomic account of the Central American species of this section, which includes a useful key: Burt-Utley, K. 1985. A revision of the Central American species of *Begonia* section *Gireoudia* (Begoniaceae). *Tulane Studies in Zoology and Botany* 25 (1): 1–131. Since this work does not include the endemic Mexican species, such as *B. bowerae*, or the Central American *B. kellermanii* and its allies, I have included a key to the endemic Mexican species here, and a key to the *B. kellermanii* group under that species. These may be used in conjunction with Burt-Utley's key.

Begonia bowerae is commonly grown, but because this species is often of diminutive size and prefers reasonably high atmospheric humidity, it is often cultivated in a glass bowl or terrarium. *Begonia bowerae* needs a free-draining potting mix, which should be allowed to dry out slightly between waterings; otherwise, it is not demanding in its cultivation. The hybrid cultivars are nevertheless often easier to grow than the true species and will happily grow in a variety of situations (Plate 37). The species as well as its hybrids are readily propagated via leaf cuttings. Popular *B. bowerae* hybrids include *B.* 'Bow Nigra' (*B. bowerae* × a dark-leaved variant of *B. heracleifolia*), *B.* 'Maphil' (*B. bowerae* × unknown parent), *B.* 'Persian Brocade' (*B. bowerae* × *B.* 'Maphil'), *B.* 'Tiger Paws' (unknown parentage), and *B.* 'Virbob' (*B. bowerae* × unknown parent).

Key to the cultivated Mexican endemic species of section *Gireoudia*

1 a. Leaves palmately compound . . . . *B. carolineifolia*
b. Leaves not palmately compound 2
2 a. Leaves palmate-lobed to roughly half their width 3
b. Leaves entire, toothed, or shallowly lobed to considerably less than half their width 5
3 a. Stem a creeping rhizome growing beneath the surface of the substrate; petiole more or less continuing straight into main vein of blade . . . . . *B. philodendroides*
b. Stem erect, above ground; petiole joining blade at an angle 4
4 a. Stem about 2 cm in diameter at apex in mature plant; leaves stiff and fleshy, gray . . . . *B. kenworthyae*
b. Stem about 0.5 cm in diameter at apex in mature plant; leaves not stiff and fleshy, green . . . . *B. bettinae*
5 a. Plant lacking a creeping rhizome, stem erect and sometimes thick 6
b. Plant with a creeping rhizome 9

6 a. Leaf margin angular-lobed, irregularly toothed, not curved under, undulate . . . . *B. huberti*
b. Leaf margin unlobed, few-toothed, curved under, not or only slightly undulate . 7
7 a. Undersurface of leaf blade green . . . . *B. mazae* f. *viridis*
b. Undersurface of leaf blade red 8
8 a. Upper surface of leaf blade green near the center and along the veins, the rest of the blade with a brownish overcast . . . . *B. mazae* var. *mazae*
b. Upper surface of leaf blade green with the veins bordered with black . . . . *B. mazae* f. *nigricans*
9 a. Lowermost bract ovate-triangular with margins rolled backward . . . *B. breedlovei*
b. Lowermost bract not as above 10
10 a. Female flowers lacking bracteoles, with four or five tepals 11
b. Female flowers usually with bracteoles, with two tepals 12
11 a. Margin of leaf with a marginal dark red-brown border of hairs . . *B. lyman-smithii*
b. Margin of leaf without a marginal dark red-brown border of hairs . . *B. pinetorum*
12 a. Placentae entire . . . . *B. barkeri*
b. Placentae bifid 13
13 a. Petiole with flattened scale-like appendages 14
b. Petiole hairless or hairy, but lacking flattened scale-like appendages 16
14 a. Upper surface of leaf blade covered with short hairs . . . . *B. carrieae*
b. Upper surface of leaf blade hairless 15
15 a. Leaf blade large, about 21 cm across . . . . *B. stigmosa*
b. Leaf blade smaller, typically 4.5–8 cm across . . . . *B. squarrosa*
16 a. Margin of leaf blade with sharply pointed lobes, hairless . . . . *B. pringlei*
b. Margin of leaf blade unlobed, with very short or long hairs 17
17 a. Leaf blade 12–35 × 6–30 cm, with very short submarginal hairs . . . . *B. sousae*
b. Leaf blade 2–11.5 × 1.5–11 cm, with short to long marginal hairs 18
18 a. Petiole with red lenticels; flowers pink . . . . *B. bowerae* var. *roseiflora*
b. Petiole without red lenticels; flowers white 19
19 a. Main veins of leaf blade bordered by a black band . . .*B. bowerae* var. *nigramarga*
b. Main veins of leaf blade not bordered by a black band 20
20 a. Leaf blade 2–5 × 1.5–3 cm . . . . *B. bowerae* var. *bowerae*
b. Leaf blade 9–11.5 × 6.4–10 cm . . . . *B. bowerae* var. *major*

Begonia brevirimosa Irmscher (PLATES 41 AND 161)
section *Petermannia*, shrub-like group
Botanische Jahrbücher für Systematik, Pflanzengeshichte und Pflanzengeographie 50: 358 (1913)

Erect perennial to about 1 m tall, lacking a rhizome. Stems branched, green with red bands above the nodes. **Stipules** deciduous, lanceolate, 0.2–3.5 × 0.7–1.2 cm. **Leaves: petiole** yellowish green, pink, or red, sparsely hairy, 1–6 cm long, joining blade at an angle; **blade** above glossy green to glossy bronze-green with glossy purple or pink bands and sometimes additional smaller splotches between the veins or with spots only, sparsely hairy between the veins, beneath burgundy, sparsely hairy throughout, asymmetric, ovate or elliptic, 10–23 × 6–14.5 cm, apex gradually acuminate, base cordate, margin shallowly toothed, ciliate, veins palmate-pinnate. **Inflorescence:** unisexual, males in a terminal racemose structure consisting of several few-flowered cymes, female flowers axillary, paired, opening before the males; **bracts** soon falling, lanceolate-triangular, 0.7–2 × 0.3–0.7 cm. **Male flowers: tepals** two, bright pink, outer surface with short red hairs, broadly ovate with a convex bulge around androecium, base fused, truncate, 1–1.3 × 0.8–1.5 cm; **stamens** about 30, arranged symmetrically, anther connective not projecting. **Female flowers: bracteoles** absent; **tepals** five, bright pink, ovate or elliptic, 7–16 × 4–8 mm, base wedge-shaped to attenuate, shortly fused, margin with short glandular hairs toward the apex; **ovary** red, ovoid to ellipsoid, 1.6–1.7 × 0.7–0.8 cm, more or less equally three-winged, three-locular, **placentae** axile, bifid; **styles** three, once-branched, stigmas in a spiraled band. **2n** = 44.

Begonia brevirimosa as recognized here differs from Edgar Irmscher's original description of the species by the addition of material that was previously grown under the unpublished names *B. exotica*, *B. brevirimosa* 'Exotica', and *B. brevirimosa* 'Edinburgh'. Examination of both herbarium and cultivated material of these plants has led me to conclude that they are best recognized as a subspecies of *B. brevirimosa*, a change recently published (Tebbitt, 2005). *Begonia brevirimosa* subsp. *exotica* differs in that the leaf blades are ovate with gradually acuminate apices and on their upper surfaces have glossy purple or pink bands and sometimes additional smaller splotches between the veins. The leaf blades of *B. brevirimosa* subsp. *brevirimosa* are elliptic with often abruptly acuminate apices and on their upper surfaces have purple or pink spots or small blotches between the veins but no bands. A few other minor differences in leaf hairs and degree of serration of the leaf margins are found between the cultivated clones of these two subspecies but such distinctions do not stand up when additional wild collected herbarium specimens are examined.

These two subspecies both originate from northern Papua New Guinea but differ in their natural distributions. *Begonia brevirimosa* subsp. *brevirimosa* occurs along the coastal mountains and on the islands of Karkar and New Britain, while *B. brevirimosa* subsp. *exotica* occurs farther inland in the mountains of the Western Highlands in Pogera Province. Alfred B. Graf, author of the popular photo guides *Exotica* and *Tropica*, coined the name *B. exotica* in 1960 while he was in Australia on the way back from Papua New Guinea where his friend York Meridith was cultivating the plant. The name first appears in print in the 1963 edition of his *Exotica*. Graf intended the name to be an informal temporary label, but since it is become widely used for this popular plant I decided to validly publish it when describing the new subspecies. Graf evidently brought material of *B. brevirimosa* subsp. *exotica* to Australia. On page 157 of his first edition of *Tropica* is a photograph labeled "*Impatiens hawkeri* brought to Australia from New Guinea 1960" and next to the *Impatiens* is a potted specimen of *B. brevirimosa* subsp. *exotica*. However, I have been unable to locate any record of Graf having introduced the plant to the United States. Californian *Begonia* enthusiast Thelma O'Reilly informs me that she was once sent a leaf of this species by Anita Sickmon, who had acquired it in Australia in 1969. Perhaps this is how the plant was first introduced into the United States. *Begonia brevirimosa* subsp. *exotica* was also, however, collected in the wild by T. M. Reeve (collection number 142) in 1978 and introduced to cultivation at the Royal Botanic Garden Edinburgh. This clone was sent to the United States in November 1969 and distributed by nurseryman Rudolf Ziesenhenne. Today it is widely grown as *B. brevirimosa* 'Edinburgh'. It is uncertain as to exactly how long *B. brevirimosa* subsp. *brevirimosa* has been cultivated but it has been grown in the United States since at least 1974, when it was offered by Mike Kartuz's nursery.

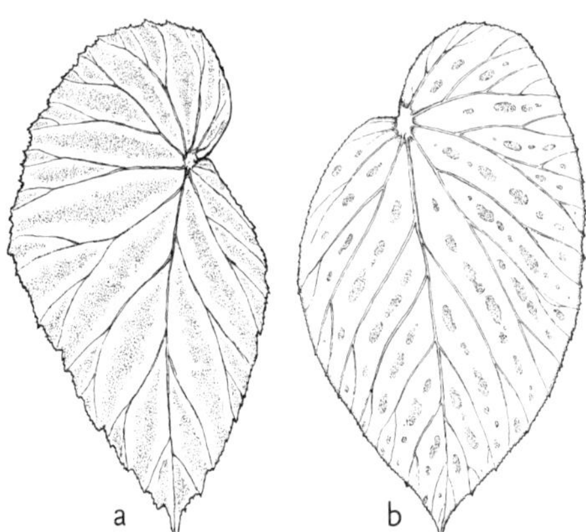

Comparison of the leaves of **a**) *B. brevirimosa* subsp. *exotica* and **b**) subsp. *brevirimosa*.

Both subspecies of *Begonia brevirimosa* need high atmospheric humidity but are not difficult to grow in a greenhouse or large terrarium. Propagation is usually via stem cuttings or seed. An alternative method of propagation may be achieved by laying a leaf lower-surface down on the potting mix and cutting a few of the main veins. New plantlets will develop from the cut veins in a few weeks. *Begonia* 'Tekla T' is a cross between *B. brevirimosa* subsp. *exotica* and *B. versicolor.*

Begonia capanemae Brade (PLATE 42)

section *Pritzelia*, shrub-like group

Archivos do Jardim Botânico do Rio de Janeiro 13: 73, pl. 2 (1954)

Erect non-rhizomatous subshrub to 1 m tall. Stem green but largely obscured by large deciduous scale-like appendages. **Stipules** persistent, transversely ovate, 2–3 × 3.5–4 cm. **Leaves: petiole** green, densely covered with large scale-like appendages, 3.5–20 cm long, continuing straight into main vein of blade or joining blade at an angle; **blade** above green, hairy, beneath paler green, hairy, asymmetric, broadly ovate, 11–22 × 10–35 cm, apex shortly acuminate, base cordate, margin wavy, with five to seven short triangular lobes, lobes toothed and ciliate, veins palmate. **Inflorescence:** axillary, compact, many-flowered, bisexual, cymose, much shorter than the leaves; **bracts** persistent, almost circular, 10–13 × 10–13 mm. **Male flowers: tepals** four, outer pair greenish white, outer surface densely covered with long greenish white or pinkish hairs, elliptic-circular, 0.8–1.4 × 0.7–1.4 cm, inner pair white, hairless, narrowly elliptic, to obovate-oblong, 0.7–1.2 × 0.4–0.5 cm; **stamens** about 40, arranged in a symmetric mass, anther connectives projecting. **Female flowers: bracteoles** paired at base of ovary, ovate, 6–7 × ca. 3 mm, margin toothed-ciliate; **tepals** five or occasionally six, greenish white, outer surface sparsely hairy, ovate or oblong, 4–5.5 × 8–9 mm, apical margin toothed-ciliate; **ovary** green, covered with rust-colored hairs, ellipsoid, 5–6 × 2–2.5 mm, unequally three-winged, three-locular, **placentae** axile, entire; **styles** three, once-branched, stigmas in a spiraled band. **2n** = 56.

Guilherm Schuech, Baron of Capanema, discovered this species on 4 January 1883 in Brazil's Atlantic Coastal Forest near Joinville. Unfortunately, most of the material he collected was lost soon afterward. Nevertheless, the few plants that did reach the Rio de Janeiro Botanical Garden were described as a new species by Alexandre Brade and given the name *Begonia capanemae* in honor of its discoverer. Remarkably this species was one of well more than 50 new *Begonia* species Brade was to name during his career as a botanist in Brazil. This was an especially impressive achievement considering that he started his career in Germany as an architect and for much of his life was forced by circumstance to consider botany a hobby, rather than a career. In fact, even when he did finally become employed full time at the botanical garden in Rio de Janeiro, Brade was more widely recognized as an expert on ferns and the flowering plant family Melastromataceae than on begonias. Nevertheless, his contribution to our knowledge of Brazilian begonias remains unequalled. In 1953 another great German *Begonia* taxonomist, Edgar Irmscher, named the Brazilian species *B. bradei* in his honor.

Begonia capanemae was introduced into the United States and Europe in 1966 via the American Begonia Society's seed list from seed collected by Ralph Spencer. Not until several years later, however, was the identity of the species determined. That this should be the case is somewhat surprising since *B. capanemae* is readily identified by the conspicuous covering of large, green, scale-like appendages on its stems and petioles and by its compact, many-flowered inflorescences of greenish white flowers that occur tucked beneath the leaves. *Begonia capanemae* can be a little tricky to cultivate since it requires excellent drainage and a humid atmosphere.

A number of the species' close relatives are cultivated and, like that species, have flattened, scale-like appendages on their petioles. Examples include *Begonia caraguatatubensis, B. huegelii, B. longibarbata, B. princeps,* and *B. ramentacea.* Of these *B. caraguatatubensis* and *B. ramentacea* are particularly attractive and deserve to be more widely cultivated. The former is a large-leaved plant with an erect stem to about 30 cm tall. It also has particularly large, semicircular, scale-like appendages toward the upper half of its petioles. Its large inflorescences bear numerous tiny white flowers. It was first collected at Caraguatatuba in Brazil's São Paulo State. *Begonia ramentacea* is a creeping rhizomatous species with larger white flowers and very many attractive, small, fringed, scale-like appendages running along the length of its petioles (Plate 43). It is definitely a species best appreciated up close. It is native to Brazil's Rio de Janeiro State. Another relative of *B. capanemae* is widely cultivated under the perhaps incorrect name of *B. paleata* (Plate 74a). The true identity of this cultivated plant is uncertain because whereas the cultivated plant reaches little more than 30 cm in height and has thin, more or less horizontally spreading stems, in the wild *B. paleata* is a robust and particularly tall shrub. Further studies are needed to determine the correct taxonomic status of the cultivated material. A species grown under the American Begonia Society code U304 also has scale-like appendages running along the length of its petioles. It also has particularly prominent marked veins and may be new to science. Whether this is the case or not also awaits further study.

Begonia cathayana Hemsley (PLATE 44)

section *Platycentrum*, rhizomatous group
Curtis's Botanical Magazine 134: pl. 8202 (1908)
Synonym: *B. bowringiana* nomen nudum

Rhizomatous perennial with erect, branched stems to 0.5–1 m tall. Stems green, becoming purple tinged at maturity. Stems, leaves, outer surfaces of tepals and ovaries covered with short, soft crimson hairs intermingled with longer white hairs. **Stipules** persistent, narrowly triangular, 1–2.5 × 0.3–0.6 cm. **Leaves: petiole** yellowish green, 4–25 cm, joining blade at an angle; **blade** above dark olive-green with crimson veins and a paler green ring about 1–2 cm from margin, beneath crimson, asymmetric, ovate, 8–20 × 5.5–16 cm, apex acute to acuminate, base cordate, margin shallowly lobed and minutely toothed, veins palmate-pinnate. **Inflorescence:** in upper leaf axils, 6–12-flowered, bisexual, cymose; **bracts** persistent, ovate-oblong or lanceolate, 4–9 × 1–2 mm. **Male flowers: tepals** four, salmon-orange, outer pair ovate or elliptic, 1.5–2 × 1–1.3 cm, inner pair narrowly ovate, 0.8–1.1 × 0.4–0.5 cm; **stamens** numerous, arranged in a symmetric mass on top of a column, anther connectives long projecting. **Female flowers: bracteoles** absent; **tepals** four to five, salmon-orange, ovate-oblong, outermost 1.3–1.5 × 1.3–1.4 cm, innermost 1.1–1.4 × 0.6–1.2 cm; **ovary** yellowish green, asymmetric-obovoid, 0.9–1.2 cm long, unequally three-winged, one wing much longer than the others, two-locular, **placentae** axile, bifid; **styles** two, once-branched, stigmas in a spiraled band. **2n** = 22.

Doctor Augustine Henry, an Irish medical officer and plant collector, discovered this distinct velvety-leaved, orange-flowered species in 1904 in "begonia-rich forests" close to the hill-town of Mengtse in southwestern China. The species was introduced into cultivation from seed he sent back to Arthur K. Bulley, founder of the English seed and nursery firm Bees Ltd. The name *cathayana* refers to "Cathay," an old name for China.

Begonia cathayana is sometimes temperamental in cultivation and desires terrarium culture, with a humidity of about 70 percent and a temperature of 72–75°F (22–24°C). For best leaf coloration, position the plant in bright, indirect light. Avoid splashing water on the hairy leaves, or they will quickly rot. *Begonia cathayana* does well in a sphagnum-perlite mix and roots easily from stem cuttings. It typically flowers from August to December. Shortly after being introduced into cultivation, *B. cathayana* was hybridized with members of the *B.* Rex-cultorum group (see *B. rex* for additional details). Examples of the results are *B.* 'Fireworks' and *B.* 'Witchcraft'. Other cultivars include *B.* 'China Curl' (*B. versicolor* × *B. cathayana*), *B.* 'Fantastic' (*B. cathayana* × *B. pustulata*), and *B.* 'Regalia' (*B. cathayana* × unknown parent).

Begonia venusta is a closely related Malaysian species that differs from *B. cathayana* by having leaves that are dark green throughout their upper surface and by its flowers that are white with a pink flush. It requires similar cultural conditions.

Begonia chlorosticta M. J. S. Sands (PLATE 45)

section *Petermannia*, shrub-like group
Curtis's Botanical Magazine, new series 183 (4): 134, pl. 827 (1982)
Synonyms: *B. ex* Kew species; *B.* U038

Erect non-rhizomatous perennial to 60 cm tall, usually with several branches, the whole plant hairless. **Stipules** soon falling, ovate-oblong, 14–21 × 6–9 mm, keeled, main vein projecting. **Leaves: petiole** pale green or flushed brownish red, 3.8–11.2 cm long, joining blade at an angle; **blade** above dark bronze-green with lighter green patches, up to 1.2 cm across, and with a mid to light green marginal band, 2–4 mm wide, beneath burgundy, later becoming green flushed red, asymmetric, ovate to ovate-oblong, 8–20 × 6–10.5 cm, apex acuminate, base cordate, margin toothed, veins palmate-pinnate. **Inflorescence:** either a bisexual terminal racemose structure with several male flowers on short cymose branches at the top and a few female flowers at the base, or a terminal inflorescence with only male flowers and the female flowers paired and axillary; female flowers opening before the males; **bracts** deciduous, broadly elliptic to almost circular, 5–8 × 5–8 mm. **Male flowers: tepals** two, greenish cream with red veining, ovate to circular, 4–7 × 3–6 mm; **stamens** about 35–40, symmetrically clustered on a raised receptacle, anther connectives not projecting. **Female flowers: bracteoles** soon falling, ovate or obovate, 3–4.3 × 1.7–2.5 mm; **tepals** five, crimson-pink to greenish white at the base, ovate to obovate-elliptic, 15–18 × 7.5–10 mm; **ovary** scarlet, ellipsoid, 16–20 × 7–8 mm, almost equally three-winged, wings broadly triangular, three-locular, **placentae** axile, bifid; **styles** three, once-branched, stigmas in a spiraled band.

Begonia chlorosticta is an uncommon species in cultivation that deserves to be more widely grown, because its mottled green leaves make it one of the most striking of all foliage begonias. The species has a very restricted wild distribution, occurring only on remote forested hills at the southeastern end of the Hose Mountains in Sarawak, Malaysia. In this region it is locally plentiful and grows on moist rocky slopes and damp cliffs. It was first collected in 1967 by Bill Burtt and Peter Martin and introduced into cultivation at the Royal Botanic Garden Edinburgh.

Begonia chlorosticta is challenging to cultivate since it prefers very humid conditions, semi-shade, and a temperature slightly above 70°F (21°C). It is usually happiest when grown in an open terrarium within a humid greenhouse, but I have seen it cultivated successfully in a research house at Kew on an open bench next to a humidifier. It requires a moist, porous soil mix and should not be allowed to dry out between waterings. Stem cuttings are best rooted in a relatively dry medium because they tend to rot if over watered. *Begonia chlorosticta* has contributed to the parentage of at least three commercially available cultivars: *B.* 'Aluminum' (*B. incarnata* × *B. chlorosticta*), *B.* 'Moon Maid' (*B. dregei* × *B. chlorosticta*), and *B.* 'Calico Kew' (*B. goegoensis* × *B. chlorosticta*; Plate 46). These cultivars are easier to grow than the species but unfortunately lack its bold leaf markings.

Begonia chlorosticta is classified in the section *Petermannia*, which is one of the largest in the genus, having roughly 200 described species and scores more yet to be named. The individual species of this section are frequently difficult to identify because not only do they often closely resemble each other, no taxonomic treatment exists for the group as a whole. The section itself is nevertheless usually easy to recognize. Most species in it have inflorescences that are divided into a basal part that consists of a solitary or pair of female flowers and an apical part that is racemose and contains a few to several male flowers. The male flowers typically have two tepals and the female flowers have five. The ovaries are almost always three-locular, have bifid placentae, and three more or less equal wings. *Begonia amphioxus*, which in cultivation is represented by aberrant plants, often does not show all the typical sectional characteristics; it, *B. brevirimosa*, and the newly described *B. polilloensis* I discuss separately. It is difficult to construct an accurate list of all the cultivated species from this section since this is constantly changing, with additional species being introduced and others being lost from cultivation. Furthermore, the identities of some cultivated members of the section remain unsure. At least 13 species are verified to be in cultivation: *B. aequata*, *B. amphioxus*, *B. augustae*, *B. bipinnatifida*, *B. brevirimosa*, *B. chlorosticta*, *B. cummingii*, *B. isoptera*, *B. malachosticta*, *B. oligandra*, *B. polilloensis*, *B. serratipetala*, and *B. siccacaudata*. Others are probably also present, however, and for this reason I have not attempted to construct a key. Of the verified species the ones most commonly encountered are *B. brevirimosa*, *B. malachosticta*, *B. serratipetala*, and *B. isoptera*.

Begonia malachosticta (Plate 47) like *B. chlorosticta* has a very limited wild distribution and spotted leaves. It can be readily distinguished from other cultivated begonias since its leaf blades are green with small but distinctive mauve-pink spots and a broken mauve-pink line that circles their margin. It is somewhat easier to cultivate than *B. chlorosticta* but is reported to suffer from leaf loss under low light conditions. It grows wild on a single, isolated limestone hill in southeast Sabah, Malaysia.

Begonia serratipetala (Plate 48) from Papua New Guinea is easily identified by its wine-red stems and its leaves with crinkled surfaces, that are glossy green above, with small, raised, pink dots, and bronze-green to wine-red beneath, and which have pinnately lobed, double-toothed margins. The species was first discovered by Rudolf Schlecter in 1909 "in the humus of the forests near Danip" but was not introduced into commercial cultivation until 1954 when Maurice Mason collected it near its original location and brought it to England. Today, *B. serratipetala* is widely grown in both Europe and North America. *Begonia serratipetala* has the reputation of being somewhat difficult to grow because it needs a high level of humidity and is susceptible to over watering. Nevertheless, good results can be obtained in a greenhouse by watering the plants until the water runs out of the bottom of the pot, and then leaving them un-watered until the top 1–2 cm of the growing medium becomes dry to the touch. If plants are over watered or if they become too dry they have a tendency to drop their leaves, a condition from which they are slow to recover. If this happens, cut the plants back to within several centimeters of the ground and wait for new growth to appear. In order to produce a densely branched plant, many growers pinch the tips of the branches to stimulate new branch growth. The species is best grown in a humus-rich medium and does well in a hanging basket.

An unidentified member of section *Petermannia*, which Scott Hoover introduced into cultivation from Mekale, Sulawesi, Indonesia, in 1998. Note the paired female flowers at the top of the plant (one partially hidden by a leaf), which are characteristic of this and several other species in section *Petermannia*. Drawing by Adèle Rossetti Morosini

Begonia isoptera (Plate 49) was reintroduced from Java by Scott Hoover and offered in the American Begonia Society's seed list in 1990. It is a shrubby plant to about 60 cm tall with ovate-oblong leaf blades that are glossy green with undulate margins and a purple spot above the apex of the petiole. It has small, greenish white flowers and is not particularly attractive. In its native land it has been reportedly used as a poultice to treat enlarged spleens. The closely related New Guinean *B. augustae* is similarly used to treat itching. The plant if mixed with hog feed will also, or so it is claimed, cure skin eruptions, but I am yet to try this for myself.

Begonia siccacaudata is also worth mentioning briefly because it is an intriguing stemless species with a short fleshy rhizome. The name *siccacaudata* refers to the axes of the inflorescence, which persist even when they are dry, a feature unique to this species. The sole living plant of *B. siccacaudata* that I have seen was growing at Wageningen Agricultural University several years ago. Nevertheless, I am told that a few enthusiasts in the United States now cultivate this interesting native of the Indonesian island of Sulawesi.

Begonia coccinea W. J. Hooker (PLATE 21C)

section *Pritzelia*, cane-like group
Curtis's Botanical Magazine 69: pl. 3990 (1843)
Synonym: *B. rubra* auct. non Blume: Irmscher

Erect perennial to about 3 m tall, stem green, sometimes reddish tinged, hairless, resembling a bamboo cane. **Stipules** soon falling, ovate-lanceolate to elliptic, strongly concave, 2.5–3.4 × 1.1–1.4 cm. **Leaves:** distichous; **petiole** green or yellowish green with a reddish tinge on the upper surface, hairless, 1–4 cm long, joining blade at an angle; **blade** above green, beneath paler green, both surfaces hairless, asymmetric, ovate-elliptic, 6.5–14 × 3–7 cm, apex acute to acuminate, base shallowly cordate, lowermost lobe extended backward for 4–5.5 cm, margin wavy-toothed, veins indistinct, palmate-pinnate. **Inflorescence:** axillary, large, 14–48-flowered, cymose, stalks bright red; **bracts** soon falling, ovate to broadly ovate or elliptic, concave, 6–9 × 4–9 mm. **Male flowers: tepals** four, red, outer pair ovate-cordate, 1.5–2 × 1.3–2.1 cm, inner pair ovate-elliptic to elliptic, concave, 0.8–1.7 × 0.4–0.5 cm; **stamens** 20–35, arranged in a flattened symmetric cluster, anther connectives rounded, not projecting. **Female flowers: bracteoles** paired beneath ovary, soon falling and easily overlooked, ovate, 5.5–6 × 4.5–5 mm; **tepals** five or six, ovate to oblong-ovate, more or less equal, 0.6–1.6 × 0.3–1.7 cm; **ovary** red throughout, ellipsoid or obovoid, 0.8–1.7 × 0.4–0.7 cm, with three almost equal rounded wings, three-locular, **placentae** axile, entire; **styles** three, once-branched, stigmas in a spiraled band. **2n** = 56.

Begonia coccinea is a native of the Organ Mountains of Brazil, a range of coastal mountains that are easily accessible from Rio de Janeiro and very rich in begonias. William Lobb discovered the species there in 1841 while collecting for Veitch and Sons nursery. Soon afterward he shipped a plant back to England, where it was exhibited, in flower, at the Royal Horticultural Society the following year. William Hooker described the plant as "Unquestionably the most beautiful of the many handsome species of Begonia now known to our collectors." But that was 1843, and better species were still to be discovered. Nevertheless, *B. coccinea* is a particularly graceful cane-like species with dazzling red flowers and attractive stiff green leaves. Hooker gave the species the name *B. coccinea* in reference to its characteristic bright red inflorescences; *coccineus* in Latin means "crimson." This is a particularly appropriate name since not only are the plant's tepals bright red, but so too are the ovaries and flower stalks. *Begonia coccinea* has been hybridized extensively, particularly with *B. maculata* and *B. undulata*, and along with these species has played an important role in the development of the modern-day cane-like hybrids.

Begonia coccinea is readily grown in a greenhouse under almost the same conditions as described for *B. albo-picta*, the only difference being that it needs slightly higher atmospheric humidity. *Begonia coccinea* may be propagated from cuttings made from young stem growth and by seed. Of the numerous hybrids produced using this species, the following are commercially available or at least widely grown: *B.* 'Annie Laurie' (*B. coccinea* seedling), *B.* 'Delores' (*B. glabra* × *B. coccinea*), *B.* 'Margaritacea' (*B.* 'Arthur Mallet' × *B. coccinea*) and *B.* 'President Carnot' (*B. coccinea* × *B. olbia*).

Begonia corallina is a similar-looking species that also has bamboo-like stems. Its flowers, however, are a reddish orange rather than the vivid scarlet of those of *B. coccinea*. My herbarium studies have found that *B. macduffiana* is identical to this species and should, therefore, be treated as a synonym of *B. corallina*. *Begonia corallina* is unusual among Brazilian begonias because, out of the roughly 200 species from this vast country, it is one of only a handful that are native to the lowland forests of the Amazon, all the other species being found in the forested mountains that run along the Atlantic coast.

Begonia conchifolia A. Dietrich (PLATE 50)

section *Gireoudia*, rhizomatous group
Allgemeine Gartenzeitung 19: 258 (1851)

Creeping rhizomatous perennial. Rhizome red to light green, hairless, usually branched, main rhizome 1.5–9 cm long. **Stipules** persistent, broadly to narrowly ovate-triangular, 6–15 × 2–9 mm. **Leaves:** peltate; **petiole** purple to pale green or pink, densely hairy, 0.5–16 cm long; **blade** above glossy green with a few short hairs, beneath paler green with short, sparse hairs, except along the principal veins, which are densely covered with wooly hairs, ovate to almost circular, 1–9 × 1–8 cm, apex acuminate, margin irregularly toothed to crenulate or undulate.

Inflorescence: axillary, asymmetric, 3–15-flowered, bisexual, cymose; flowers fragrant; **bracts** deciduous, broadly elliptic to ovate or obovate, 1.5–8 × ca. 2.9 mm. **Male flowers: tepals** two, or rarely three, white to deep pink, hairless, outer pair almost circular to elliptic, 3.5–6.5 × 2.8–6.5 mm, inner one when present oblanceolate, ca. 6 × 2.5 mm; **stamens** 6–13, arrangement resembling a bunch of bananas, anther connectives not projecting. **Female flowers: bracteoles** tardily deciduous, almost circular to broadly obovate or elliptic, 3–7 × 2.5–8 mm; **tepals** two or three, white to greenish white, outer pair broadly elliptic to obovate or almost circular, 2.5–7 × 2.2–6 mm, inner one when present oblanceolate, ca. 5 × 2 mm; **ovary** light green to white, frequently tinged pink, broadly ovoid to spherical, 4–6.5 × 4–5 mm, with three almost equal wings, three-locular, **placentae** axile, bifid; **styles** three, unbranched, stigmas crescent-shaped. **2n** = 28.

Begonia conchifolia is a small, attractive, rhizomatous species that is commonly cultivated and readily grown in a variety of situations. It is native to the rain forests of Costa Rica and Panama, where it grows upon tree trunks and steep, sparsely vegetated rock faces. Two distinct forms occur, *B. conchifolia* f. *rubrimacula*, which has a red dot on the leaf blade just above the petiole, and *B. conchifolia* f. *conchifolia*, which lacks the red dot. The first of these is particularly attractive and is found in the wild only in a small area of Costa Rica. These red-spotted plants were previously recognized as varieties but are now recognized as forms. I have made this change because plants with and without red dots occur together in mixed populations, and plants with red dots produce seedlings both with and without red dots when self-fertilized. The form with the red dot is also known under the cultivar name *B. conchifolia* 'Zip'. Interestingly, a similar red dot is also found in some individuals of the closely related *B. plebeja*.

Von Warszewicz first introduced *Begonia conchifolia* to Europe around 1850 from seed that he collected in Costa Rica. At that time the species was misidentified as *B. lindleyana*. In 1851 Dietrich described these plants as a new species. In his description he noted that this species' peltate leaves resembled "rounded shells," and for this reason named it *conchifolia*, after the conch shell.

Begonia conchifolia is easily cultivated under standard conditions and does well under lights. Propagation is by seed or rhizome cuttings. In particular *B. conchifolia* f. *rubrimacula* has been used as a parent of numerous popular hybrid cultivars. Examples include *B.* 'Boy Friend' (*B. conchifolia* f. *rubrimacula* × *B.* 'Dainty Lady'), *B.* 'Kiss Mark' (*B. conchifolia* f. *rubrimacula* × *B. bowerae* var. *nigramarga*), and *B.* 'Fairyland' (*B. conchifolia* f. *rubrimacula* × *B.* 'Bokit').

Begonia convallariodora C. de Candolle (PLATE 51)

section *Ruizopavonia*, shrub-like group
Botanical Gazette (London) 20: 538 (1895)

Erect many-branched subshrub to 4 m tall. Stems green with narrow red bands above the nodes to reddish pink throughout, hairless. **Stipules** soon falling, lanceolate, 3–4 × ca. 0.5 cm. **Leaves: petiole** reddish pink, hairless, 1–4 cm long, more or less continuing straight into main vein of blade; **blade** above green, beneath burgundy, both surfaces hairless, asymmetric, elliptic, 8–19 × 4–10 cm, apex acuminate, base cordate to obtuse, margin wavy, more or less toothed, veins pinnate. **Inflorescence:** in upper leaf axils, many-flowered, cymose, male flowers opening long before the female flowers appear; **bracts** soon falling, ovate, 2.5–6 × 1–1.5 mm. **Male flowers: tepals** two, white to pink, outer pair circular or ovate-cordate, 0.4–0.7 × 0.4–0.8 cm, inner one or two occasionally present, smaller; **stamens** numerous, arranged in a symmetric mass, anther connectives projecting. **Female flowers: bracteoles** paired beneath the ovary, deciduous, ovate, 4–5 × ca. 2 mm; **tepals** two, white to pink, circular or elliptic, 0.6–0.8 × 0.3–0.8 cm; **ovary** pink, ellipsoid, 2–4 × 2–4 mm, unequally three-winged, one wing much longer than the others, **placentae** axile, bifid; **styles** three, once-branched, stigmas in a spiraled band.

Casimir de Candolle named this species *Begonia convallariodora* because its floral scent reminded him of the lily-of-the-valley, *Convallaria majalis*, a garden plant whose flowers are employed in the perfume industry. This begonia has a large natural distribution that stretches from southern Mexico to Panama. Throughout its range it grows both on the forest floor and epiphytically on the trunks of rain forest trees, usually at an elevation of 600–2000 m. It is often found scrambling up surrounding vegetation, using the stems of its neighbors as props for its lanky stems—in cultivation it needs staking.

Begonia convallariodora is easily grown under standard conditions and appears to have been first introduced into the United States in the early 1960s. No hybrids of this species are recorded in the literature.

A handful of similar species also classified in the section *Ruizopavonia* are in cultivation. All have tall stems, large elliptic leaves with pinnate venation and proportionally short petioles, and ovules with bifid placentae (see Plate 51). A key is provided below for their identification. An additional member of this group is grown under the American Begonia Society code U199 and is shown in Plate 52.

Key to *Begonia convallariodora* and its cultivated relatives

1 a. Ovary with four ribs, one larger than the others . . . . *B. alnifolia*
  b. Ovary three-winged or with a single wing and two rib-like wings 2
2 a. Stem branches hairy; stipules persistent . . . . *B. cooperi*
  b. Stem branches hairless; stipules usually soon falling 3
3 a. Leaf blade 2–4 cm wide 4
  b. Leaf blade 4–10 cm wide 5
4 a. Leaf blade elliptic, apex gradually acuminate, base unequally obtuse *B. peruviana*
  b. Leaf blade asymmetric-ovate, apex abruptly acuminate, base unequally cordate . . . . *B. carpinifolia*
5 a. Teeth on margin of leaf blade ending in bristles . . . . *B. seemanniana*
  b. Teeth on margin of leaf blade not ending in bristles . . . . *B. convallariodora*

Begonia convolvulacea (Klotzsch) A. de Candolle (PLATES 53 AND 54)
section *Wageneria*, trailing-scandent group
in Martius, *Flora Brasiliensis* 4 (1): 367 (1861)
Synonyms: *B. geniculata* Vellozo; *B. repens* A. de Candolle; *B. rugosa* Klotzsch; *B. scandens* auct. non Swartz: Klotzsch; *B. unialata* C. de Candolle

Climbing perennial. Stems rooting at the nodes, to 5 m long, yellowish green to brown or sometimes pink when young, hairless. **Stipules** persistent, narrowly ovate, 1.3–2 × 0.7–0.9 cm. **Leaves:** distichous; **petiole** yellowish green with a red tinge at each end, or pink-tinged throughout, hairless, 1–14 cm long, continuing straight into main vein of blade, but joining it at a vertical 90° angle; **blade** above glossy dark green, beneath paler green, both surfaces hairless, rectangular-kidney-shaped to almost circular, 4–14 × 4–17 cm, apex indistinct, base cordate, margin angular with 6–13 short narrow acuminate lobes at the ends of the main veins. **Inflorescence:** axillary, many-flowered, 6-branched, bisexual, cymose; **bracts** soon falling, ovate, ca. 1 × 0.2 mm. **Male flowers: tepals** four, dull white, reflexed, outer pair obovate to elliptic, 4.5–7 × 3–4.3 mm, inner pair narrowly obovate, narrowly ovate or narrowly elliptic, 4–6 × 2–3 mm; **stamens** 15–25, arranged symmetrically, anther connectives usually projecting. **Female flowers: bracteoles** paired a short distance beneath ovary, easily overlooked and soon falling, ovate, 1–2 × ca. 0.3 mm; **tepals** five, dull white, reflexed, obovate to elliptic, 3.5–5.5 × 1.5–3 mm; **ovary** white becoming pale green with maturity, ovoid to ellipsoid, 4–7 × 2–5 mm, unequally three-winged, one wing longer than the others, three-locular, **placentae** axile, entire; **styles** three, once-branched, stigmas in a spiraled band. **2n** = 38.

Begonia convolvulacea is a commonly cultivated native of the Atlantic Coastal Forest of Brazil. The German naturalist Friedrich Sello first discovered the species there in 1853 and the following year introduced it to the gardens of Schoenbraun in Vienna. The name *convolvulacea* means "similar to *Convolvulus*," a genus of plants better known to gardeners as bindweeds on account of their ability to attach themselves to surrounding plants via their twining stems. The Latin root of the generic name is *convolvo* meaning "to twine around." While *B. convolvulacea* is also a climber it does not have twining stems; instead it climbs with the aid of adventitious roots that are produced at regular intervals along its stems. In the wild, *B. convolvulacea* climbs both dead and living trees, sometimes starting from ground level or occasionally from a convenient perch part way up the tree. Two close relatives, *B. fagifolia* and *B. glabra* (Plate 55), are also climbers, and like *B. convolvulacea* can eventually reach 5 m in height. All these plants are commonly cultivated. A key is provided here for their identification, and a comparison of their leaves is shown in Plate 56. *Begonia convolvulacea* has occasionally been recorded growing on limestone soils, but in cultivation it is not particularly choosy with regard to its growing medium.

Begonia convolvulacea and its two relatives are readily grown but perform best under relatively cool temperatures. Because of their long rope-like stems these species make excellent subjects for hanging baskets. They also look good grown in a pot in a greenhouse when their stems are allowed to cascade over the side of the bench. Propagation is via stem cuttings or seed. *Begonia* 'Rubacon' is a hybrid of *B. convolvulacea* × *B.* 'Orange Rubra'.

Key to the cultivated species of section *Wageneria*

1 a. Leaf blades covered with long hairs . . . . *B. fagifolia*
b. Leaf blades hairless 2
2 a. Leaf blades rectangular-kidney-shaped to almost circular, margin angular with 6–13 short, narrow, acuminate lobes . . . . *B. convolvulacea*
b. Leaf blades broadly ovate to elliptic, margin not angular- or acuminate-lobed . . . . *B. glabra*

Begonia crassicaulis Lindley (PLATES 57–59)
section *Gireoudia*, thick-stemmed group
Edward's Botanical Register 28: misc. 22, t. 44 (1842)
Synonym: *B.* U178

Rhizomatous perennial. Rhizome thick, green to orange-brown, densely hairy when young, erect or ascending and usually branched, 5–45 cm tall. **Stipules** tardily deciduous, orange-brown, asymmetric-ovate, 12–17 × 9–13 mm, keeled. **Leaves:** deciduous; **petiole** pink, 11–30 cm with dense rust-brown hairs when young but becoming hairless, continuing straight into main vein of blade; **blade** above glossy green with a red spot at the petiole junction and red vein bases, almost hairless, beneath paler green with pinkish brown veins, sparsely hairy with densely hairy veins, symmetric, in outline almost circular to broadly oblong-elliptic, 10–22 × 14–30 cm, palmate six- to eight-lobed, lobes often themselves lobed, apex indistinct, base cordate, margin toothed and ciliate, veins palmate. **Inflorescence:** in uppermost leaf axils but appearing in the spring before the leaves develop, strongly asymmetric to one-sided, few- to many-flowered, bisexual, cymose; **bracts** soon falling, broadly obovate, 9–19 × 8–12 mm. **Male flowers: tepals** two, white to pale pink, almost circular to broadly obovate, 6–19 × 5.5–14 mm; **stamens** 14–33, arrangement resembling a bunch of bananas, anther connectives not or slightly projecting. **Female flowers: bracteoles** obovate to almost circular, 5.5–10 × 6–9 mm; **tepals** two, same color as males, broadly obovate to almost circular, 5–15 × 5–14 mm; **ovary** green, almost spherical to broadly ellipsoid or obovoid, 0.7–1.5 × 0.4–0.6 cm, unequally three-winged, three-locular, **placentae** axile, bifid; **styles** three, entire, stigmas crescent-shaped. **2n** = 28.

Begonia crassicaulis is a native of Guatemala and southern Mexico, where it typically grows as an epiphyte in relatively sunny forest locations. It is remarkable for its unusual growth habit. It has short thick stems and sheds its leaves in the winter. Even more unusual is the fact that *B. crassicaulis* produces its flowers from January to March before the new season's leaves have developed. Together these features adapt it to the relatively dry and sunny niche it occupies on the trunks of trees. The species name means "thick-stemmed," and *B. crassicaulis* is perhaps the best of the species classified by horticulturists as the thick-stemmed group. The species was first introduced into cultivation in Europe in 1840 by Hartweg and distributed by the London Garden Association. However, it appears to have subsequently been lost from cultivation. The plants found in cultivation today probably stem from a collection made by Scott Hoover in 1979 from plants he found growing at 1095 m near the town of Salolá in southern Guatemala.

The natural dormancy of the species means that it should be watered relatively infrequently when it is resting during the winter. It also needs relatively high light intensities. Otherwise, it is not difficult to grow and is often seen in cultivation. Under lights the species does not go dormant, nor does it bloom. *Begonia* 'Bayberry Lane' is a little known hybrid from the cross *B. cardiocarpa* × *B. crassi-*

caulis. It also has the attractive glossy green, deeply divided leaves so characteristic of *B. crassicaulis*.

Begonia cubensis Hasskarl (PLATE 60)

section *Begonia*, shrub-like group

Hortus Bogoriensis Descriptus 342 (1858)

Synonyms: *B. cubincola* A. de Candolle; *B. plagioneura* Milne-Redhead

Erect several-branched perennial to about 1 m tall. Stem rust-brown, hairless, and woody at the base. **Stipules** persistent, ovate to ovate-oblong, 3–6 × 2–3 mm, main vein shortly projecting. **Leaves:** distichous; **petiole** green with a reddish tinge to red with short white hairs, 10–26 mm long, continuing straight into main vein of blade, sometimes joining blade at a more or less vertical 90° angle; **blade** bluish green on both surfaces, or beneath pale green, above hairless, beneath sparsely hairy, asymmetric, ovate to ovate-oblong, 3–7 × 1.2–3.5 cm, apex acute to acuminate, base rounded and very shallowly cordate, margin wavy, toothed, veins palmate-pinnate. **Inflorescence:** in upper leaf axils, four- to eight-flowered, bisexual, cymose, male flowers maturing long before the females; **bracts** deciduous, ovate to lanceolate, 3–4 × ca. 1 mm. **Male flowers: tepals** four, outer pair pink-tinged on outer surfaces, white on inner surfaces, broadly obovate to almost circular, base wedge-shaped to slightly cordate, 0.8–1.6 × 0.8–1.5 cm, inner pair white, obovate, base wedge-shaped, 0.7–1.1 × 0.3–0.6 cm; **stamens** about 15–20, arranged symmetrically, anther connectives projecting. **Female flowers: bracteoles** deciduous, paired beneath ovary, ovate to elliptic, 2.3–8 × 4–6 mm; **tepals** five, white, unequal, outermost ovate to elliptic, innermost narrowly obovate, 0.6–1.3 × 0.3–1.6 mm; **ovary** white to pinkish white, 0.5–1 × 0.5–0.8 cm, elliptic to almost spherical, three more or less equal to markedly unequal wings, three-locular, **placentae** axile, bifid; **styles** three, once-branched, stigmas in a spiraled band. **2n** = 52.

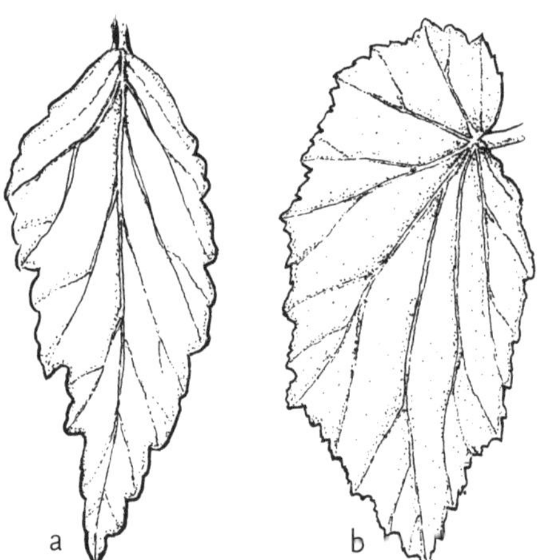

Comparison of the leaves of the often confused **a**) *B. cubensis* and **b**) *B. acutifolia*.

Like most of Cuba's other 9–10 endemic begonias, *Begonia cubensis* is restricted to the eastern end of the island, near the towns of Guantánamo and Santiago de Cuba. Here it is said to be abundant in the wet mountainous forests at an altitude of 400–1214 m. In cultivation, *B. cubensis* is often confused with *B. acutifolia* (syn. *B. acuminata*), a native of both Cuba and the nearby island of Jamaica. Why this confusion should exist is a bit of a mystery since they are quite distinct, most noticeably in terms of their leaves. Those of *B. cubensis* are blue-green with wavy, almost toothless margins and have petioles that continue straight into the main vein of the blade. In contrast, *B. acutifolia* has green leaves that are deeply toothed and petioles that join the blade at a distinct angle. Aside from *B. cubensis*, none of Cuba's other endemic begonias are widely cultivated. Indeed few even appear worth growing, with the possible exception of *B. linearifolia*, which is a shrub-like species with interesting linear-lanceolate leaves and white flowers. By a quirk of fate, *B. cubensis* was first described by German botanist Justus Hasskarl based on material cultivated at the Bogor Botanic Gardens in Java, Indonesia.

Begonia cubensis is readily grown under standard cultural conditions. *Begonia* 'Cubinfo' is the result of the cross *B. cubensis* × *B. foliosa*.

Begonia cucullata Willdenow (PLATE 61)

section *Begonia*, Semperflorens group
Species Plantarum 4: 414 (1805)
Synonyms: *B. semperflorens* Link & Otto; *B. hookeri* Sweet; *B. semperflorens* Link & Otto var. *hookeri* A. de Candolle

Erect non-rhizomatous, branched perennial to 1.3 m tall. Stem green to red, sparsely hairy when young, becoming hairless. **Stipules** tardily deciduous, rectangular-ovate, 1.4–2 × 0.8–1.2 cm. **Leaves: petiole** red to reddish green, sparsely hairy, almost absent to 5 cm long, continuing straight into main vein of blade or joining blade at an angle; **blade** glossy green above, paler green beneath, both surfaces hairless to sparsely hairy, asymmetric, broadly ovate or elliptic, 1–14 × 1.5–9 cm, apex acute to almost rounded, base more or less truncate and usually rolled inward or wedge-shaped, margin toothed, ciliate, sometimes very sparsely so, veins palmate but superficially appearing parallel. **Inflorescence:** axillary, few-flowered, bisexual, cymose; **bracts** persistent, ovate, 2–7 × 1–4.5 mm, margin fringed with long hairs. **Male flowers: tepals** four, white to rosy pink, outer pair almost circular, 8–15 × 8–15 mm, inner pair narrowly obovate, 0.9–1.1 × 0.4–0.6 cm; **stamens** 25–40, arranged symmetrically, anther connectives projecting. **Female flowers: bracteoles** three, situated about 2 mm beneath ovary, persistent, narrowly obovate to obovate, 0.6–1 × 0.2–0.5 cm, margin ciliate; **tepals** four or five, same color as males, ovate, elliptic or obovate, 4–14 × 2–8 mm; **ovary** white but becoming green to greenish red with maturity, ellipsoid, 0.6–1.2 × 0.4–0.8 cm, unequally three-winged, longest wing usually projecting above the styles, three-locular, **placentae** axile, bifid; **styles** three, once-branched, stigmas in a spiraled band. **2n** = 34.

Begonia cucullata was a founding parent of the *Begonia* Semperflorens-cultorum group, which includes thousands of hybrids commonly called wax- or Semperflorens begonias. The members of this group are among the most floriferous, easy-to-grow, and widely cultivated of all *Begonia* hybrids and since the late 1800s have been immensely popular subjects for outdoor bedding. *Begonia cucullata* itself, however, is a weedy, somewhat ungainly species that is native to Brazil's Atlantic Coastal Forest, where it is especially common in disturbed habitats. *Begonia cucullata* is reportedly used occasionally both as a diuretic and a spinach-like vegetable in its native land. In 1821 the species was accidentally introduced into cultivation at the Berlin Botanical Garden when stowaway seeds germinated in soil accompanying plants shipped from southern Brazil. The species was retained in cultivation but the first hybrids were not created until more than 50 years later, in 1878. At that time various hybridizers crossed the species with the shorter, more attractive *B. schmidtiana*, producing a range of easy-to-grow plants of medium stature, with glossy or sparsely hairy leaves and numerous pale pink flowers. For the next few years these early hybrids were intercrossed and the best plants selected. Then in 1881 a third species, *B. roezlii*, was included in the mix, leading to cultivars with deeper pink and red flowers. A further development occurred in 1891 when a bronze-leaved mutant that had arisen in a garden in France was used to produce a new series of bronze-leaved cultivars.

Hybrids with the compact habit and small, symmetric, waxy leaves typical of modern-day wax begonias appeared toward the end of the 1800s as these and other wax begonia hybrids were crossed with *Begonia foliosa* var. *miniata*, *B. gracilis*, and *B. schmidtiana*. Nurserymen Ernst Benary of Germany and Victor Lemoine of France were especially active at this time. Benary's crosses in particular were important because they led to the development of the first hybrid cultivars in the group that came true from seed. Today almost all the wax begonias are reproduced via seed. Other chance mutations in the late 1800s led to new cultivars with variegated leaves that collectively became known as calla-lily-begonias. Plants with white-blotched leaves appeared around 1886 (Plate 62), those with yellow-blotched leaves in 1892. Also worth mentioning at this point is *B.* 'Charm' (Plate 66), a 1948 introduction from Logee Greenhouses; its normally yellow leaf variegation turns pink in bright light. At the turn of the twentieth century, Eugene Vallerand introduced an important semi-double-flowered cultivar, *B.* 'Bijou de Jardin', which had been produced in his nursery in France by crossing *B. minor* with one of the existing hybrids. The first fully double-flowered cultivar, *B.* 'Gustav Lind', was introduced in Sweden in 1934 from crosses involving *B. foliosa* var. *miniata*. Around the same time the first picotee or bicolored flowers also arrived.

As each new variant appeared it was crossed with the existing hybrids so that hybrid cultivars were soon available with combinations of all the existing characteristics. Since the late 1800s thousands of cultivars have been developed and largely, with the whims of fashion, lost from cultivation. Six generations on, the Benary Nursery continues to be a major source of new high-quality Semperflorens begonias, although after World War II the company moved from Erfert in eastern Germany to Münden in western Germany. The Cocktail and Super Olympia (Plate 63) series of wax begonias were both bred at this nursery, for example, and have become immensely popular. Work still continues there on breeding improved wax begonias, as it does elsewhere in Europe and the United States. The very popular *B.* Dragon Wings released by PanAmerican Seeds in the 1990s, to the accompaniment of TV advertisements showing fire-breathing dragons, is also proof of the continued commercial power of the wax begonia. *Begonia* Dragon Wings was the result of a cross between a Semperflorens begonia and a cane-like begonia. It is easy to grow, relatively drought tolerant, and by virtue of its short cane-like stems, looks spectacular when grown in a planter or hanging basket (Plate 64). Since its release the plant has won numerous awards and is now one of the most widely grown of all begonias. The plant is currently available with pink or red flowers, but who knows what new characteristics will be introduced into this and other wax begonias in future years? For better or worse, it looks likely that several seed companies that employ transgenic techniques will soon be introducing plants with strikingly different features. Perhaps someday soon we will be able to buy that miniature wax begonia with fluorescent leaves and blue flowers that we have so long desired.

Apart from *Begonia cucullata*'s initial use in the Semperflorens-cultorum group, this species has not subsequently been used in the development of the hybrid group. However, the species is still occasionally cultivated and because of its naturally weedy nature has become naturalized in many tropical and subtropical areas, including northern Florida, where the United States Department of Agriculture considers it an invasive weed. Growers in this area, as well as in southern Georgia, are advised not to grow this or other wax begonias since additional plants could escape to become weeds.

Begonia cucullata and most of the Semperflorens-cultorum group are very easy to grow in a well-lit situation, either as bedding plants or in the home or greenhouse. Semperflorens begonias make particularly good bedding plants because, unlike many other garden plants, begonias are generally unpalatable to deer, which can be a major problem in some areas. Most cultivars should be grown in full sun in all but the hottest regions and will respond well to the early pinching of their stems and flower buds. If maintained for the first few weeks after planting, pinching will eventually result in neater, bushier plants with more numerous blooms. Many of the most commonly encountered Semperflorens begonia cultivars are arranged into series, the immensely popular Cocktail series being one such example. Its cultivars, all bronze-leaved, are best known under the trade names Whisky (flowers white), Brandy (flowers pale pink), Gin (flowers rose-pink), Vodka (flowers red), and Rum (flowers white, edged with red). Other series include Devil, Encore, Glamour, Inferno, Olympia, Party Mix, Prelude, Varsity, and Victory. Some, like the Olympia series, have flowers in pastel shades, but others like the Inferno series come in more saturated colors. Some series, including Victory, are available in both green and bronze-leaved versions, and others, as with the before-mentioned Cocktail series, come in just one leaf color. Not all the cultivars classified in the Semperflorens-cultorum group are arranged in series, such as *B.* 'Calla Queen', *B.* 'Lady Francis' (Plate 65), *B.* 'Nomo', *B.* 'Snowcap', and *B.* 'Richmondensis'. The last is a still-popular 1939 hybrid between a member of the Semperflorens-cultorum group and *B. foliosa* var. *miniata*.

Two naturally occurring varieties of *Begonia cucullata* are in cultivation, *B. cucullata* var. *cucullata* with ovate leaf blades having more or less truncate bases and *B. cucullata* var. *arenosicola* with elliptic leaf blades having wedge-shaped bases. The latter is reported to be frost-hardy. A once-recognized third variety, *B. cucullata* var. *hookeri*, is now treated as a synonym of *B. cucullata* var. *cucullata*. *Begonia cucullata* is sometimes confused in cultivation with *B. fischeri*, which differs by its often denser hair cover, oblique leaf bases, leaf blades that are wider than long (or at least as wide as long), and by its ovary wings, which are much more unequal in size so that one of them is much larger than the other two. *Begonia descoleana* is also very similar but is distinguished by its narrowly ovate leaf blades, its more readily deciduous stipules, and by the outer pair of tepals in the male flowers being much darker pink than the inner pair.

Further information on the *Begonia* Semperflorens-cultorum group may be found in Kraus (1947). The author, Helen Kraus, was the first to coin and define the name Semperflorens-cultorum group in 1945. The name *B. semperflorens* is a synonym of *B. cucullata* var. *cucullata*, the original variant of the species to be introduced into cultivation, and means "ever flowering."

1. The endangered *B. balansana* is restricted to the upper reaches of Mount Bavi in northern Vietnam.

3. Diseased and damaged *Begonia* leaves (clockwise from left): **a**) *Impatiens* necrotic spot virus on *B. cyathophora*, **b**) damage from low humidity on *B.* 'Otto Foster', **c**) damage from standing water droplets on *B. augustae*, **d**) powdery mildew on *B. masoniana*.

2. Remnant tropical rainforest on the relatively inaccessible ridges of Mount Bavi, home to *B. balansana* and several other rare begonias.

4. Leaf damage on *B. longifolia* caused by the begonia mite *Stenotarsonemus pallidus*.

5. Fungal damage on a leaf of *B. mannii*.

6. Cliff faces situated in the splash zones of waterfalls, such as this one in Ecuador, provide habitat for many different *Begonia* species around the world.

Photo by W. Scott Hoover

7. *Begonia fuchsiaflora* from Ecuador is unusual among begonias since it is hummingbird-pollinated, most being insect-pollinated. Photo by W. Scott Hoover

8. An unidentified species from *Begonia* section *Semibegoniella* showing the horned fruit characteristic of that section. Photo by W. Scott Hoover

9. *Begonia killipiana* is a very desirable but difficult-to-grow species from the montane cloud forests of Colombia. Photo by W. Scott Hoover

10. *Begonia*'s closest relative, *Hillebrandia sandwicensis*, on the Hawaiian island of Kauai.

11. Habitat of *Hillebrandia sandwicensis* and filming location for *Jurassic Park*, Hanalei Valley, Kauai.

13. *Datisca cannibina* and the author at the Beth Chatto Gardens in England. Photo by Laura Steger Tebbitt

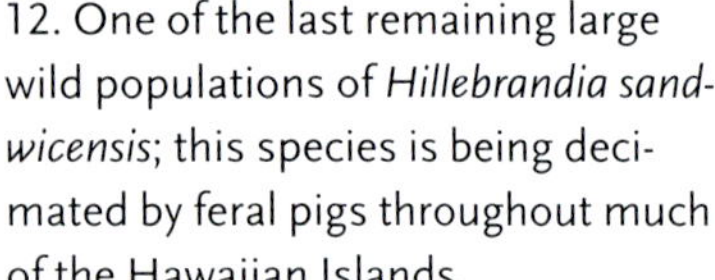

12. One of the last remaining large wild populations of *Hillebrandia sandwicensis*; this species is being decimated by feral pigs throughout much of the Hawaiian Islands.

14. The curious male flowers of *Datisca cannibina*; this genus contains just two species and is the begonia family's closest relative.

15. *Begonia acaulis*, showing the notched inner tepals of this pink-flowered New Guinean species; here growing with U074 from the Philippines.

16. *Begonia luzonensis* is a desirable plant for a humid terrarium.
Photo by Byron Martin, Logee's Greenhouses

17. *Begonia acetosa* is often shy to flower but is worth growing for its beautiful foliage with wine-red undersurfaces.

18. *Begonia* 'Art Hodes', a commonly grown hybrid cultivar with *B. acetosa* parentage.

20. Swollen stem base of *B. aconitifolia*; this is one of the few begonias to show this adaptation to a seasonally dry habitat.

19. *Begonia aconitifolia* with palmately lobed leaves, growing outdoors in a summer border in New Jersey. Photo by Jack Golding

21. A diverse selection of South American cane-like begonias: **a**) *B. albo-picta*, **b**) *B. maculata* var. *wrightii*, **c**) *B. coccinea*, **d**) *B. undulata*, **e**) *B. salicifolia*, **f**) *B. corallina*.

22. *Begonia* 'Lucerna' (left) and *B.* 'Medora' (right) are two of the most popular hybrid cultivars in the genus; both have *B. albo-picta* parentage.

23. Bamboo-like stems of *B. salicifolia*.

24. *Begonia amphioxus*, an unusual species from Borneo that deserves to be more widely cultivated.

25. The African *B. ampla*, showing the characteristic bract-like structures that obscure the lower portion of the plant's inflorescence.

26. *Begonia angularis*, a Brazilian species that is at once recognized by its angular or ribbed stems.

27. *Begonia arborescens* var. *oxyphylla* in the tropical house at Atlanta Botanical Garden.

28. *Begonia hookeriana* at the Montreal Botanical Garden.

29. *Begonia aspleniifolia*, a rarely cultivated begonia of tropical West Africa.

30. Madagascan *B. bogneri* is easily identified by its strap-like leaves.

31. *Begonia bogneri* requires high atmospheric humidity and is best cultivated in a glass bowl or similar container.

32. The intriguing, but rarely cultivated, Madagascan *B. goudotii* at the Royal Botanic Garden Edinburgh.

33. *Begonia boisiana* is an interesting species that grows on limestone outcrops in Vietnam.

34. *Begonia boliviensis*, a founding parent of the *B.* ×*tuberhybrida* cultivar group.

35. A pendulous-flowered member of the *Begonia* ×*tuberhybrida* cultivar group with *B. boliviensis* parentage.

36. *Begonia bowerae* var. *bowerae* on a bed of the leaves of *B. bowerae* var. *major*.

37. Hybrids of both *B. bowerae* and the *B.* Rex-cultorum group in a Hawaiian window box.

38. A selection of leaves belonging to species from the American section *Gireoudia*: **a**) *B. lyman-smithii*, **b**) *B. sericoneura*, **c**) *B. nelumbifolia*, **d**) *B. involucrata*, **e**) *B. fusca*, **f**) *B. bowerae* var. *bowerae*, **g**) *B. bowerae* var. *nigramarga*, **h**) *B. urophylla*, **i**) *B. multinervia*, **j**) *B. mazae* f. *nigricans*, **k**) *B. mazae* f. *viridis*.

39. Scale-like appendages on the petiole and lower leaf surface of *B. manicata*.

40. *Begonia plebeja*, a commonly cultivated native of Mexico and Central America.

41. *Begonia brevirimosa* subsp. *exotica* from Papua New Guinea is commonly grown but has been validly published only as recently as 2005.

43. *Begonia ramentacea* is best appreciated close up, here showing the beautiful fimbriate palea on the petiole.

42. The shrub-like *B. capanemae* and climbing *B. radicans*; Serra do Mar Atlantic Forest, São Paulo State, Brazil. Photo by Jacques Jangoux

44. *Begonia cathayana*, an orange- or occasionally pink-flowered species from the China-Vietnam border. Photo by Jack Golding

45. *Begonia chlorosticta* from Borneo has some of the most beautifully patterned leaves in the genus.

46. *Begonia* 'Calico Kew', a *B. chlorosticta* hybrid, growing at Logee's Greenhouses where it was bred and first released commercially.

47. In the wild *B. malachosticta* inhabits a narrow range on a single limestone hill on the island of Borneo; here showing its characteristic pink-polka-dotted leaves.

49. Introduced about 1995, *B. isoptera* at Gene and Anne Salisbury's greenhouse in Oklahoma.

48. *Begonia serratipetala*, like many of the species in section *Petermannia*, prefers high atmospheric humidity.

50. *Begonia conchifolia* f. *rubrimacula* differs from the typical *B. conchifolia* in having a red spot above the junction of the petiole and leaf blade.

51. *Begonia convallariodora* and its close relatives have distinct leaves with short petioles and pinnate veins.

52. This unidentified species, grown under the American Begonia Society code U199, is a close relative of *B. convallariodora*.

53. The easy to grow liana *B. convolvulacea* climbing metal pipes in the *Begonia* house at Montreal Botanical Garden.

54. Large pendulous dichasium of *B. convolvulacea*.

55. *Begonia glabra*, climbing a dead rainforest tree in Panama. Photo by W. Scott Hoover

56. Comparison of the leaves of (left to right) *B. fagifolia*, *B. glabra*, and *B. convolvulacea*.

57. *Begonia crassicaulis*, close-up of flowers.

58. The deciduous *B. crassicaulis* with summer foliage.

59. *Begonia crassicaulis* and *B. carolineifolia* flowering in January against a backdrop of snow; Institute of Ecosystems Studies, Millbrook, New York.

60. *Begonia cubensis*, often shy to flower, is widely grown for its unusual bluish green foliage.

61. *Begonia cucullata* in the aquatic house at Brooklyn Botanic Garden.

62. A white variegated "calla lily" Semperflorens begonia at an American Begonia Society convention. Photo by Jack Golding

63. *Begonia* Semperflorens-cultorum group cultivar series Super Olympia was released in 1998 from the Ernst Benary seed company based in Münden, Germany. Photo by Ernst Benary, Samenzucht GmbH

64. A popular hybrid of *B. cucullata* parentage, the dragon-wing begonia, photographed at Magnolia Plantation in South Carolina.

65. *Begonia* 'Lady Francis', a double pink-flowered Semperflorens begonia. Photo by Jack Golding

66. *Begonia* 'Charm', a yellow-variegated Semperflorens begonia whose yellow blotches turn pink in bright sunlight.
Photo by Jack Golding

67. *Begonia cyathophora*, from the Peruvian Andes, showing the characteristic red spots at the intersections of petioles and leaf blades.

68. Comparison of leaf shapes in *B. diadema* (left) and *B. deliciosa* (right).

69. *Begonia reniformis* at Brooklyn Botanic Garden.

70. *Begonia valida*, close-up of stem and leaves.

71. *Begonia scabrida*, a robust Venezuelan species.

72. *Begonia dichroa*, a parent of all the orange-flowered cane-like hybrids.

73. *Begonia dietrichiana*, an easily grown, shrubby, Brazilian species.

74. Small selection of commonly cultivated species from the diverse, predominantly Brazilian section *Pritzelia*: **a**) unidentified species widely grown as *B. paleata*, **b**) *B. friburgensis*, **c**) *B. parilis*, **d**) *B. scabrida*, **e**) *B. listada*, **f**) *B. acetosa*, **g**) *B. tomentosa*, **h**) *B. gehrtii*, **i**) *B. sanguinea*, **j**) unidentified species, **k**) *B. dietrichiana*.

75. Characteristic short spiky hairs on the tepals of *B. echinosepala*.

77. *Begonia obscura*, an obscure species.

76. *Begonia parilis*, showing the dense covering of rust-brown stem hairs characteristic of this Brazilian species.

78. *Begonia dipetala*, a common, easily grown species from the hills of southern India and Sri Lanka.

79. Comparison of the white- and pink-flowered cultivated variants of *B. dipetala*.

80. *Begonia floccifera*, an Indian species with stiff, fleshy leaves; recent molecular data indicates a close relationship with the largely dissimilar *B. dipetala*, also from India.

81. *Begonia dregei* in the wild in Natal Province, South Africa. Photo by Mark Hughes

82. *Begonia egregia*, a Brazilian species with interesting foliage.

83. *Begonia epipsila* from Brazil, in cultivation at Montreal Botanical Garden.

84. The young leaves of Brazilian *B. piresiana* have beautiful sinuate margins.

85. *Begonia foliosa*, the variant widely cultivated under the American Begonia Society code U010.

86. Comparison of typical *B. foliosa* var. *foliosa* (left) and the plant grown under the American Begonia Society code U010 (right).

87. *Begonia formosana* f. *albomaculata* (upper leaves and flowers) and *B. formosana* f. *formosana* (lower plant).

88. Streamside habitat of *Begonia* section *Platycentrum* in northern Vietnam.

89. A selection of leaves from species classified in the large Asian section *Platycentrum*: **a**) *B. sizemoreae*, **b**) *B. rex*, **c**) *B. decora*, **d**) *B. pavonina*, **e**) *B. xanthina*, **f**) *B. deliciosa*, **g**) *B. emeiensis*, **h**) *B. pedatifida*, **i**) *B. hemsleyana*.

90. *Begonia areolata* at Mount Pasiripis, Java, from where it was recently introduced into cultivation. Photo by W. Scott Hoover

91. The foothills of Mount Fan Si Pan in Vietnam close to the border with China, an area particularly rich in *Begonia* species belonging to sections *Platycentrum* and *Sphenanthera*.

92. *Begonia palmata* growing next to a waterfall close to Vietnam's border with China; this species' seeds are dispersed by falling water droplets.

93. *Begonia pavonina* from the Malay Peninsula develops iridescent blue leaves when grown in deep shade.

94. Male flower and leaf of the recently introduced Chinese *B. pedatifida*, which is marginally frost-hardy.

95. *Begonia emeiensis*, a recently introduced species endemic to Mount Emei in China's Sichuan province; note the bulbous petiole endings, which are characteristic of this marginally frost-hardy species.

96. *Begonia gehrtii* photographed at the United Kingdom's National Begonia Collection at the Glasgow Botanic Garden in Scotland.

98. *Begonia paulensis*, a close relative of *B. gehrtii*, distinguished by its peltate leaves.

97. *Begonia crispula* has a wonderful crinkled appearance, reminiscent of a piece of wax paper that has been crunched up and then spread out again. Photo by Johanna Zinn

99. *Begonia goegoensis*, from Sumatra, has beautifully patterned peltate leaves.

100. *Begonia coriacea* from Java is sometimes confused with the distantly related *B. conchifolia* from Central America, when not in flower.

102. *Begonia sandtii*, a choice tuberous species from western Mexico.

101. *Begonia gracilis* at an American Begonia Society convention. Photo by Jack Golding

103. *Begonia grandis* showing the species' racemose inflorescences.

104. Bulbils in a leaf axis of *B. grandis*.

105. The hardy begonia, *B. grandis*, emerging from the ground in early June, Brooklyn Botanic Garden.

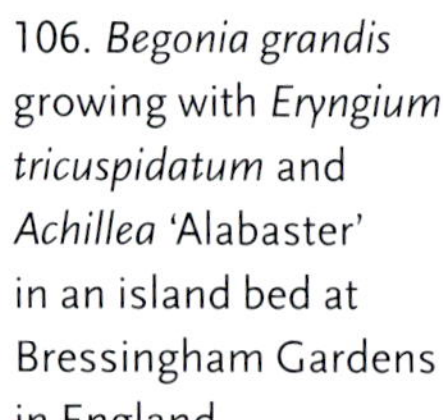

106. *Begonia grandis* growing with *Eryngium tricuspidatum* and *Achillea* 'Alabaster' in an island bed at Bressingham Gardens in England.

107. *Begonia taliensis* at Heronswood Nursery in the Pacific Northwest, where this species is winter-hardy.
Photo by Eric Hammond

109. *Begonia holtonis* is a rather coarse species from Colombia.

108. Comparison of leaf blades of (left to right) *B. holtonis*, *B. guaduensis*, and *B. meridensis*.

110. *Begonia meridensis*, a rarely grown Andean species.

111. Comparison of the leaves of typical *B. hatacoa* and *B. hatacoa* 'Spotted'.

112. A spotted variant of *B. hemsleyana*, which is usually grown under the American Begonia Society code U404.

113. *Begonia heracleifolia* growing on a pyramid at the ancient Mayan site of Palenque in southeastern Mexico.

114. The Brazilian epiphytic *B. lanceolata*, showing sessile female inflorescences and a stalked male inflorescence, a combination of features found only in the section *Trachelocarpus*.

115. *Begonia herbacea* at the 2004 Philadelphia Flower Show.

117. *Begonia hirtella* is self-pollinated; here showing male flowers positioned directly above the female flowers allowing pollen to fall onto the stigmas.

116. *Begonia fulvo-setulosa* at the 2004 Philadelphia Flower Show.

118. Bizarre adventitious leaflets are a distinguishing characteristic of *B. hispida* var. *cucullifera*.

119. *Begonia hydrocotylifolia* is readily grown under standard conditions and has long been a favorite of hybridizers.

121. *Begonia turrialbae* from Costa Rica being grown in a glass bowl at the home of Richard and Wanda Macnair.

120. Small selection of commonly cultivated species and hybrids from the Mexican–Central American section *Weilbachia*: **a**) *B. pustulata* (pale-leaved variant), **b**) *B. pustulata* (dark-leaved variant), **c**) *B.* 'Silver Jewel', **d**) *B.* 'Otto Foster', **e**) *B. aridicaulis*.

122. *Begonia alice-clarkiae*, from Mexico, has white flowers set against emerald green foliage. Photo by Jack Golding

123. *Begonia incarnata* in a park in Mexico City.

124. *Begonia* 'Phyllomaniaca', an old hybrid of *B. incarnata* × *B. manicata*.

125. *Begonia integerrima* is usually sold as *B. solananthera*; here showing the *Solanum*-like male stamens, after which *B. solananthera* and section *Solananthera* are named.

126. *Begonia integerrima* in a hanging basket at Montreal Botanical Garden.

127. The flowers of *B. radicans* are an unusual orangey red with white margins.

128. *Begonia* 'Fragrant Beauty' (*B. integerrima* × *B. radicans*) growing in a hanging basket at the New York Botanical Garden.

129. *Begonia engleri* is a close relative of the better known *B. johnstonii*; photographed in Tanzania. Photo by Mark Hughes

130. The Brazilian *Begonia kuhlmannii*.

131. *Begonia peltata* var. *peltata* at the Montreal Botanical Garden.

132. *Begonia leprosa* is easy to grow and widely distributed in southern China; curiously it remains rare in cultivation.

134. *Begonia longifolia*, showing its characteristic keeled fruit; photographed at Cuc Phuong National Park, Vietnam.

133. *Begonia listada* at the United States Botanic Garden in Washington, D.C.

135. *Begonia longipetiolata*, an epiphytic African species that in cultivation is often confused with its close relative *B. squamulosa*.

137. *Begonia lubbersii*, a sweetly scented Brazilian species and parent of numerous scented hybrid cultivars.

136. *Begonia luxurians* showing its characteristic cannabis-like leaves; here growing in the *Begonia* house at Montreal Botanical Garden.

138. *Begonia mannii* is the most commonly cultivated of the trailing-scandent African begonias. Photo by J. W. Mugge. Courtesy of National Herbarium Nederland: Wageningen branch, Biosystematics Group, Wageningen University, the Netherlands

140. *Begonia cavallyensis* is an epiphytic rainforest species from the Guineo-Congolian region of West Africa. Photo by J. W. Mugge. Courtesy of National Herbarium Nederland: Wageningen branch, Biosystematics Group, Wageningen University, the Netherlands

139. A selection of cultivated species from the large tropical African section *Tetraphila*: **a**) *B. mannii*, **b**) *B. fusialata*, **c**) *B. horticola*, **d**) *B. loranthoides* subsp. *loranthoides*, **e**) *B. loranthoides* subsp. *rhopalocarpa*, **f**) *B. komoensis*, **g**) *B. polygonoides*, **h**) *B. oxyanthera*, **i**) *B. molleri*.

141. *Begonia polygonoides*, an epiphytic African species; here growing attached to cork bark at the Montreal Botanical Garden.

143. Dehisced fruit of *B. loranthoides* subsp. *rhopalocarpa*; this species' seeds are thought to be dispersed by both ants and birds. Photo by B. Jansen. Courtesy of National Herbarium Nederland: Wageningen branch, Biosystematics Group, Wageningen University, the Netherlands

142. *Begonia loranthoides* subsp. *loranthoides* growing on a piece of cork in Montreal Botanical Garden's *Begonia* research collection.

144. The fruit of bird-dispersed *B. cavallyensis* has attractively colored placentae and inner walls that signal when the fruit is ripe and ready to be eaten. Photo by J. J. F. E. de Wilde. Courtesy of National Herbarium Nederland: Wageningen branch, Biosystematics Group, Wageningen University, the Netherlands

146. *Begonia masoniana* variants: **a**) 'Tricolor', **b**) var. *maculata*, **c**) var. *masoniana*.

145. The typical variant of the popular iron-cross begonia, *B. masoniana*.

147. *Begonia subvillosa* var. *leptotricha* is a somewhat weedy species that is classified in the Semperflorens-cultorum group; here showing its characteristically large bracteoles.

148. *Begonia multinervia*, a common species in Costa Rica, has interesting lanceolate to triangular-ovate stipules.

149. Dinner-plate-sized leaves of *B. nelumbifolia*, a common species from Mexico and Central America that in nature often grows in disturbed areas.

150. *Begonia obliqua*, the type species of the genus *Begonia*.

151. *Begonia oxysperma*, an orange-flowered epiphyte from the Philippines; here growing in a hanging basket at Montreal Botanical Garden with the epiphytic West African *B. komoensis* in the background.

152. *Begonia petasitifolia* from Brazil is commonly grown for its interesting frosted leaves.

153. Described only as recently as 2005, *B. polilloensis* is unusual among begonias in having palmately compound leaves.

154. The cheerful yellow flowers of the popular tropical West African *B. prismatocarpa*.

155. *Begonia dewildei* growing upon a sheer rock face in Gabon, West Africa. Photo by J. C. Arends. Courtesy of National Herbarium Nederland: Wageningen branch, Biosystematics Group, Wageningen University, the Netherlands

156. The beautifully patterned leaves of tropical West African *B. quadrialata* subsp. *nimbaensis* make this humidity-loving plant one of the best begonias for a glass bowl or similar container.

157. *Begonia quadrialata* subsp. *quadrialata* differs from subsp. *nimbaensis* in having concolorous, green leaf blades. Photo by H. C. D. de Wit. Courtesy of National Herbarium Nederland: Wageningen branch, Biosystematics Group, Wageningen University, the Netherlands

158. *Begonia scutifolia* from tropical West Africa. Photo by H. C. D. de Wit. Courtesy of National Herbarium Nederland: Wageningen branch, Biosystematics Group, Wageningen University, the Netherlands

159. *Begonia hirsutula*, a rarely cultivated species from tropical Africa.

160. *Begonia vittariifolia* growing on a moss-covered vertical cliff face in humid forest, Gabon, West Africa. Photo by M. S. M. Sosef. Courtesy of National Herbarium Nederland: Wageningen branch, Biosystematics Group, Wageningen University, the Netherlands

161. *Begonia rajah* (left) with other humidity-loving begonias in a glass bowl; also shown are *B. prismatocarpa* with yellow flowers (front) and *B. brevirimosa* subsp. *exotica* (right); 2004 Philadelphia Flower Show.

162. *Begonia* 'Merry Christmas', one of the best and most popular hybrids in the *B.* Rex-cultorum group. Photo by George Kalmbacker. Courtesy of Brooklyn Botanic Garden

163. Reintroduced into cultivation in about 2000, *B. robusta* is here growing on a volcanic mountain in western Java. Photo by W. Scott Hoover

164. *Begonia* 'Fireflush' showing its beautiful red hairs, a feature inherited from *B. robusta*.

165. The fleshy, keeled fruits of *B. multangula*, photographed in central Java. Photo by W. Scott Hoover

166. The female flowers of *B. roxburghii* are very sweetly scented; this Asian species is also remarkable for having horn-like projections on its ovaries.

167. The faintly scented male flowers of *B. roxburghii*, one of a relatively few dioecious begonias.

168. *Begonia silletensis* subsp. *mengyangensis*, showing its unusually large leaves; Kunming Botanic Garden, China.

169. *Begonia salaziensis*, a critically endangered species with brightly colored, animal-dispersed fruit.

170. *Begonia oxyloba*, an African species with unusual berry-like fruits.

171. *Begonia scharffii*, from Brazil, has been popular ever since it was first introduced to Europe in 1886.

173. *Begonia socotrana*, an important parent of the enormously popular hybrids in the winter-flowering Hiemalis and Rieger groups; here photographed on the island of Socotra. Photo by Mark Hughes

172. *Begonia schmidtiana*, an important parent, along with *B. cucullata*, of the *Begonia* Semperflorens-cultorum group.

174. Unusual bulb-like structures of *B. socotrana*, clustered at the plant's base. Photo by Tony Miller

175. *Begonia socotrana* growing in a crevice on a limestone cliff, Socotra. Photo by Mark Hughes

176. *Dracaena cinnabari* forest on Socotra, the island home of *B. socotrana*. Photo by Mark Hughes

177. *Begonia samhaensis* is a close relative of *B. socotrana* that was described in 2002 and is very rare in cultivation. Photo by Mark Hughes

179. *Begonia* 'Gloire de Sceaux', a hybrid of *B. socotrana* × *B. subpeltata* that was released commercially in 1884.

178. An arrangement of Rieger begonias showing the variety of flower colors available in this popular hybrid group. Photo by Derek Fell

180. *Begonia* 'Orococo', a popular hybrid of *B. glabra* × *B. soli-mutata* created by Patrick Worley.

181. The instant suntan begonia, *B. soli-mutata*, a species whose leaves change in a matter of minutes from dark green to brownish green with increased exposure to sunlight, a condition that is fully reversible.

182. The commonly cultivated *B. sutherlandii*, in the wild in South Africa. Photo by Mark Hughes

183. Natural habitat of *B. sutherlandii*, Rainbow Gorge, South Africa. Photo by Mark Hughes

184. Scarlet-flowered *B. symsanguinea*, the newly described *B. argenteomarginata* with white flowers, and a closely related undescribed species with distinct pink leaf margins; until recently these New Guinean species were classified in the genus *Symbegonia*.

185. *Begonia taiwaniana* var. *albomaculata* differs from the typical variety by its white-spotted, relatively broad leaf blades.

186. *Begonia halconensis*, introduced since 1995 from Mount Halcon in the Philippines.

187. *Begonia tayabensis* from the Philippines growing at Brooklyn Botanic Garden.

188. Close-up of the male and female flowers of *B. tayabensis*, showing the cleft inner female tepal typical of this species.

189. *Begonia hernandioides*, a commonly grown species that in cultivation is often misidentified as *B. tayabensis*.

190. White-flowered *B. fenicis* in the author's research collection at Brooklyn Botanic Garden.

191. *Begonia subnummularifolia* is a diminutive plant suitable for a terrarium.

192. *Begonia chloroneura* growing on a riverside cliff in the Sierra Madre mountains of Luzon Island in the Philippines; this species was first introduced in 1997. Photo by Peter Wilkie

193. *Begonia thelmae* is often considered tricky to grow because it desires high atmospheric humidity; here it is thriving in the aquatic house at Brooklyn Botanic Garden.

194. *Begonia carolineifolia* like its close relative *B. thiemei* has palmately compound leaves, but may be distinguished by its fleshy upright stems and more densely hairy petioles.

195. *Begonia ulmifolia*, showing its elm-like leaves.

196. The rarely cultivated Malaysian *B. phoeniogramma*, showing the beautifully striped tepals characteristic of this and closely related species.

197. An unidentified species from the section *Eupetalum*; this group of tuberous Andean species are important parents of the *B.* ×*tuberhybrida* group. Photo by W. Scott Hoover

198. The state of California is an important area for the commercial production of *B.* ×*tuberhybrida* plants; Golden State Bulb Growers' AmeriHybrid tuberous begonias offer a dazzling spectacle of color in the Monterey Bay area. Photo by Golden State Bulb Growers

199. *Begonia* Nonstop Mix of the *B.* ×*tuberhybrida* group. Photo by Ernst Benary, Samenzucht GmbH

201. The drought-tolerant *B. venosa* growing in the desert house at Glasgow Botanic Garden in Scotland.

200. *Begonia* Panorama Scarlet of the *B.* ×*tuberhybrida* group. Photo by Ernst Benary, Samenzucht GmbH

202. *Begonia venosa* showing its characteristic large, opaque stipules and beautiful silvery-white leaf hairs.

203. *Begonia versicolor* in a glass bubble. Photo by Chuck Tagg

204. *Begonia limprichtii* from China has attractive, long red hairs on its leaves and unusual scarlet roots.

205. *Begonia decora*, a relatively difficult-to-grow species from Peninsula Malaysia.

206. Cultivated plants of *B. wollnyi* are unusual in commonly having both peltate and non-peltate leaves on the same individuals. Photo by Jack Golding

207. The fuchsia-flowered begonia, *B. foliosa* var. *miniata* [tab. 4281, as *B. fuchsioides*]. Reproduced from *Curtis's Botanical Magazine*

208. *Begonia xanthina* [tab. 5102], a spectacular yellow-flowered species from the Himalayas. Reproduced from *Curtis's Botanical Magazine*

209. A tuberous Andean begonia, *B. veitchii* [tab. 5680, as *B. rosaeflora*]. Reproduced from *Curtis's Botanical Magazine*

210. A tuberous Andean begonia, *B. pearcei* [tab. 5545]. Reproduced A tuberous Andean begonia, from *Curtis's Botanical Magazine*

211. A tuberous Andean begonia, *B. cinnabarina* [tab. 4483]. Reproduced from *Curtis's Botanical Magazine*

212. A tuberous Andean begonia, *B. octopetala* [tab. 3559]. Reproduced from *Curtis's Botanical Magazine*

Begonia cyathophora Poeppig & Endlicher (PLATE 67)
section *Cyathocnemis*, shrub-like group
Nova Genera ac Species Plantarum 1: 7, pl. 11 (1835)
Synonyms: *B. obliqua* auct. non Linnaeus: Klotzsch; *B. roezlii* auct. non Regel: Lynch; *B. lynchiana* J. D. Hooker

Erect non-rhizomatous subshrub to about 2 m tall. Stem branched, thick, green with small white lenticels, hairless. **Stipules** soon falling, ovate, elliptic, or obovate, 2–6.2 × 1.5–3.5 cm. **Leaves: petiole** green with a red tinge at base and apex, hairless, 8–14 cm long, joining blade at an angle; **blade** above green with paler green veins, beneath paler green to red, both sides with a dark red spot where the petiole joins, both hairless, asymmetric, broadly ovate and somewhat funnel-shaped, 8–21 × 8–28 cm, apex short acuminate, base cordate, margin shallowly blunt-toothed, veins palmate. **Inflorescence:** axillary, many-flowered, bisexual, cymose; **bracts** deciduous, broadly ovate, 0.9–4 × 0.1–3.8 cm. **Male flowers: tepals** two, red, broadly ovate to almost circular, 0.8–1.8 × 0.8–1.8 cm; **stamens** about 25, arranged symmetrically, anther connectives projecting. **Female flowers: bracteoles** absent; **tepals** two, red, broadly elliptic to broadly obovate, 7–9 × 5–7 mm; **ovary** red, obovoid to ellipsoid, 0.8–1.1 × 0.4–0.7 cm, unequally three-winged, **placentae** axile, bifid; **styles** three, once-branched, stigmas in a spiraled band.

Begonia cyathophora is a rarely cultivated native of Bolivia and Peru, where it is found in primary or disturbed forest at an altitude of 500–2350 m. It is easily recognized by its large, broadly ovate and somewhat funnel-shaped leaves, which are green with a dark red spot at their point of attachment, and by the distinct cup of fused bracts that surround the first branching point of the inflorescence. *Begonia bracteosa* and *B. cryptocarpa* are related species that are even less frequently cultivated. The first is Peruvian and the second is a native of Colombia. *Begonia bracteosa* has leaf blades that are more narrowly ovate than those of *B. cyathophora* and that have abruptly acuminate apices and palmate-pinnate veins. *Begonia cryptocarpa* is distinguished by its fruits being hidden by large, toothed bracteoles and by its many-branched styles.

Begonia cyathophora is readily grown in a greenhouse, but since it is a large-leaved plant it needs lots of elbow-room. No hybrids with this species have been documented.

Begonia diadema Rodigas (PLATE 68)
section *Platycentrum*, rhizomatous group
Illustration Horticole 29: 43, pl. 446 (1882)

Erect perennial to 70 cm tall, young stems green with elongated white lenticels, mature stems gray-brown with brown lenticels. **Stipules** tardily deciduous, lanceolate, 1–2.5 × 0.5–0.8 cm. **Leaves: petiole** green to reddish brown, hairless, 3–7.5 cm long, joining the blade at an angle; **blade** above green with a reddish tinge along the margins and base of the leaf and prominent silver spots in rows on either side of the main vein of each lobe, beneath green with a red tinge on margin, in outline broadly ovate, 9–17 × 12–22 cm, palmate-lobed with five to six lobes that are sometimes secondarily lobed, apex of each lobe acute, margin irregularly toothed to double-toothed, base of blade cordate. **Inflorescence:** in upper leaf axils, few-flowered, bisexual, cymose; **bracts** soon falling, elliptic to obovate, 5–7 × 2.5–4 mm. **Male flowers: tepals** four, outer pair dull white and tinged pink on the margin, ovate-oblong, concave, 1.5–1.8 × ca. 1.2 cm, inner pair dull white, elliptic 1.4–1.5 × ca. 0.7 cm; **stamens** numerous, arranged in a spherical mass attached to a column, anther connectives long projecting and acute. **Female flowers: bracteoles** absent; **tepals** five, white with a pink flush along the margin and apex, outer two obovate, 1.8–2 × 1–1.6 cm, inner three obovate, 1.7–2 × 1.1–1.3 cm; **ovary** nodding, green with a red tinge, asymmetric-obovoid, 0.8–1 × 0.2–0.5 cm, very unequally three-winged with one long and two very short wings, two-locular, **placentae** axile, bifid; **styles** two, fan-shaped at base, stigmas in a spiraled band. **2n** = 22.

Sometimes, as with the case of *Begonia diadema*, it is difficult to determine whether a popular garden plant that has long been cultivated is actually a distinct species or an old artificial hybrid. Such a plant can either turn out to be a rare species that was collected just once from the wild and then never seen again except in cultivation, or it may represent a hybrid that has the appearance of a true species. Unfortunately, because not every plant collector or nursery keeps immaculate records, mix-ups do occur and can be difficult to straighten out afterward. In the case of *B. diadema*, the *Illustration Horticole* (1882, vol. 29, p. 43) reports that the plant was sent in 1881 to Belgian nurseryman Jean Linden together with some orchids from Borneo and that Linden commercialized it under its current name. However, this story appears unlikely since not only has this plant not been found in Borneo before or since that date, it is only distantly related to the other begonias from that area. In fact DNA sequence studies indicate that *B. diadema* is most closely related to the Himalayan begonias, particularly *B. rex*. Uncertainty remains, therefore, as to whether *B. diadema* is a distinct species native to either

Borneo or the Himalayas or an artificial hybrid, perhaps involving a cross with a Himalayan species. Regardless, *B. diadema* is very easily distinguished from most other cultivated begonias by the combination of its two-locular ovaries, erect stems that arise from short rhizomes, and palmate-lobed leaves with silver spots. The only begonia with which it could be confused is *B. deliciosa* (Plate 68), a plant that Linden is said to have received from either Borneo, India, Sri Lanka, or Bhutan, depending upon the author in question, and which likewise is possibly of hybrid origin. *Begonia deliciosa* can be distinguished from *B. diadema* by its less deeply divided leaves with ovate rather than oblong-ovate lobes and more pronounced silver spotting. Clearly, further taxonomic studies of both *B. diadema* and *B. deliciosa* are needed.

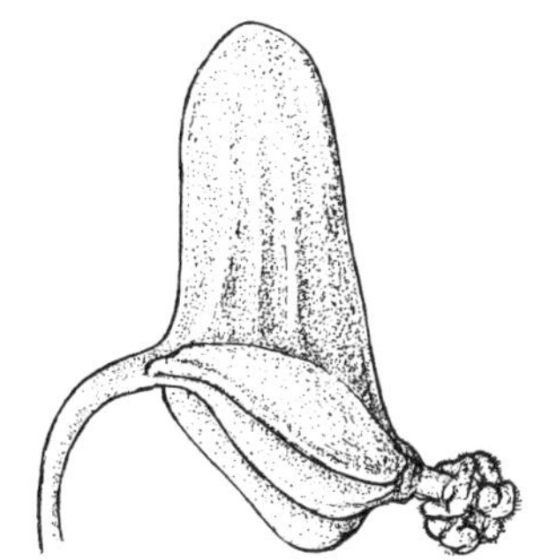

Fruit of *B. diadema*.

Begonia diadema and *B. deliciosa* can be grown under standard conditions as long as they are given a well-drained potting mix. They bloom from late summer to fall and in winter become semi-dormant. Propagation is usually by division and leaf cuttings. Both plants have been extensively hybridized with the *B.* Rex-cultorum group. Indeed they may even represent early hybrids of this group. Hybridizers have also occasionally crossed these species with other begonias outside the *B.* Rex-cultorum group, producing such results as *B.* 'Daniel Worley' (*B. dipetala* × *B. deliciosa*) and *B.* 'Red Reign' (*B. deliciosa* × *B. floccifera*).

Begonia dichotoma Jacquin

section *Pritzelia*, thick-stemmed group

Nicolai Josephi Jacquin Collectanea Botanicum, Chemiam, et Historiam Naturalem Spectantia 3: 250 (1790)

Synonyms: *B. sulcata* Scheidweiler; *B. sucrensis* L. B. Smith & B. G. Schubert

Erect non-rhizomatous subshrub to about 3.5 m tall. **Stipules** deciduous, lanceolate, 2–3.5 × 0.8–1.1 cm. **Leaves: petiole** green with medium to dense hairs, 10–20 cm long, joining blade at an oblique angle; **blade** above glossy green, hairless, beneath paler green, veins with medium to dense hairs especially toward the base of the blade, asymmetric, broadly kidney-shaped, 10–19 × 9–18 cm, apex acute, base cordate, margin often angular, unlobed, shallowly toothed, veins palmate. **Inflorescence:** axillary, large, many-flowered, bisexual, cymose; **bracts** persistent, lanceolate, 2–3.5 × 0.3–1 mm. **Male flowers: tepals** four, white, outer pair elliptic to oblong-elliptic, 5–7 × 2–7 mm, inner pair oblong to elliptic, 4–4.5 × 1–1.8 mm; **stamens** 30–40, arranged symmetrically, anther connectives projecting. **Female flowers: bracteoles** persistent, paired at base of ovary, lanceolate, 1.5–2 × ca. 0.3 mm; **tepals** five, white, elliptic or oblong, 4–8 × 1.5–3.5 mm; **ovary** white, ellipsoid, 4–6.5 × 1.5–4 mm, unequally three-winged, three-locular, **placentae** axile, entire; **styles** three, once-branched, stigmas in a spiraled band. **2n** = 68.

Begonia dichotoma is one of perhaps a handful of particularly tall, thick-stemmed species from South America that are in cultivation. Others include *B. scabrida*, *B. valida*, and *B. reniformis*. These tree-like species are closely related and the taxonomic boundaries between them are often difficult to delimit. As a result, certain of the species have been confused during the past 100 years or so. *Begonia dichotoma* is one of the most clearly demarcated of the species. It is native to Venezuela and Colombia and has angular, unlobed leaf blades that are noticeably longer than they are wide. The cultivated species most often confused with it is *B. reniformis* (Plate 69), a Brazilian species that has leaf blades that are approximately as long as they are wide and leaf margins with long triangular lobes.

Though *Begonia dichotoma* and *B. reniformis* can, with practice, be separated, the taxonomic boundaries of *B. reniformis* and certain other Brazilian species are far from certain. These days several previously recognized species are considered synonymous with *B. reniformis*, the most important of which, from a horticultural standpoint, is *B. vitifolia*. This commonly used name was originally meant to distinguish Brazilian plants that had asymmetrical, kidney-shaped, angular-lobed, hairy leaves and hairy flowers. Lyman Smith and Dieter Wasshausen synonymized *B. vitifolia* with *B. reniformis* in 1986, but I feel that this treatment perhaps makes for too variable a species. Based on the cultivated and herbarium material that I have seen, the two plants appear reasonably distinct and would seem to warrant recognition at some level, perhaps as varieties. Nevertheless, additional studies of these plants in the field are required before such variants are proposed formally.

Begonia valida (Plate 70) is a less commonly cultivated, relatively distinct, tree-like species, which can be distinguished by its shallowly lobed, broadly kidney-shaped leaves, its grooved petiole, and the presence of a collar-like outgrowth at the top of the petiole. Even more distinct and equally rarely grown is *B. scabrida* (Plate 71) with green leaf blades that are covered with short stiff hairs and are asymmetric-ovate with acute apices and truncate or very shallowly cordate bases. *Begonia parviflora* is also of a similar large size but is at once distinguished from the other tree-like species by its palmate-lobed leaf blades. It also is rarely cultivated. A detailed discussion of the tree-like group's taxonomic complexities appears in Doorenbos, J. (1979) *B. vitifolia* and other Elusive Tree-like Begonias. *Begonian* 46:

234–240. However, I must confess to being more confused about the identity of these plants after reading this article than I was before.

Begonia dichotoma and its relatives are readily cultivated under standard conditions. *Begonia reniformis* is also frequently planted outdoors as summer bedding in warm sheltered areas. Because the plants mentioned here are large they often perform well in a greenhouse when planted directly in a bed, rather than a pot. Grown this way I have seen plants of *B. valida* at the Montreal Botanical Garden reaching almost to the roof of their 25 ft tall display house. Hybrids involving *B. dichotoma* include *B.* 'Alpha Gere' (*B. dichotoma* × *B. glabra*) and *B.* 'Dieepa' (*B. dichotoma* × *B. epipsila*).

Begonia dichroa Sprague (PLATE 72)

section *Gaerdtia*, cane-like group

Bulletin of Miscellaneous Information, Royal Gardens, Kew 251 (1908)

Erect perennial to 60 cm tall. Stems brown, hairless, held more or less horizontally. **Stipules** deciduous, broadly ovate, 1.7–3 × 1–2 cm. **Leaves: petiole** green, 1.5–5 cm long, joining blade at an angle; **blade** above glossy green, young leaves sometimes silver spotted, beneath paler green, asymmetric, ovate-oblong, 10–20 × 6–11 cm, apex acuminate, base unequally cordate, margin wavy, entire to shallowly lobed, veins palmate-pinnate. **Inflorescence:** in uppermost leaf axils, bisexual, cymose; flowers sweetly scented; **bracts** persistent, ovate-cordate, decreasing in size up the inflorescence, basal-most 1.4–1.7 × 1.1–1.8 cm, uppermost 0.8–1.1 × 0.9–1.3 cm, strongly concave and overlapping along the short peduncles such that the inflorescence resembles a lobster's claw. **Male flowers: tepals** four, orange, outer pair broadly ovate, 1–1.9 × 1.7–1.9 cm, inner pair oblanceolate, 0.9–1 × 0.3–0.4 cm; **stamens** numerous, arranged symmetrically, anther connectives not projecting. **Female flowers: bracteoles** paired at top of pedicel, ovate-cordate, strongly concave, 0.9–1.3 × 0.9–1.5 cm; **tepals** five, orange, outer two broadly obovate, 1.3–1.6 × 1.1–1.4 cm, inner three obovate, elliptic or oblong, 0.6–1.6 × 0.4–1 mm; **ovary** white, ovoid, 1.6–2.1 × 0.5–0.7 cm, equally three-winged, wings strongly curved, three-locular, **placentae** axile, bifid; **styles** three, once-branched, stigmas in a spiraled band. **2n** = 56.

Begonia dichroa was introduced into cultivation by the German horticulturists Haage and Schmidt in 1907. From their nursery, flowering material was sent to Thomas Sprague at Kew Gardens who described it as a new species. The name he gave it means "two-colored" and refers to the bi-colored female flowers, which have orange tepals and contrasting white ovaries. Following its introduction *B.*

dichroa was hybridized with several other South American species and their cultivars to produce the many orange- and salmon-flowered cane-like cultivars grown today. Unfortunately, nowadays the pure species is seldom cultivated outside North America. *Begonia dichroa* is easily recognized by its combination of short, drooping, cane-like stems, glossy, green, ear-shaped leaves, and large, sweetly scented, orange flowers.

Begonia dichroa requires bright, indirect sunlight in order to flower and is happiest with temperatures between 60° and 70°F (16° and 21°C) and a relative humidity of 40–60 percent. Since even slight chilling will cause this species to drop its leaves and go dormant, position it well away from drafts. The species is particularly suited to greenhouse culture, but its slow growth rate means that it is one of the few cane-like species suitable for growing indoors under lights. Though naturally rather sparsely branched, *B. dichroa* can be encouraged to form additional side branches by pinching its main stems close to the ground. It is especially beautiful in a hanging basket when trained this way. If given proper attention, *B. dichroa* and many of its cultivars will remain in flower almost year-round. Commercially available cultivars of particular merit include *B.* 'Honeysuckle' (*B. dichroa* × unknown parent), *B.* 'Orange Rubra' (*B. dichroa* × 'Coral Rubra'), *B.* 'Ellen Dee' (*B. radicans* × *B. dichroa*), *B.* 'Di-Anna' (*B. dichroa* × *B.* 'Annie Laurie'), and *B.* 'Lenore Olivier' (*B. dichroa* × *B.* 'Elaine').

Begonia dietrichiana Irmscher (PLATE 73)

section *Pritzelia*, shrub-like group

Botanische Jahrbücher für Systematik, Pflanzengeshichte und Pflanzengeographie 76: 60 (1953)

Synonym: *B. fischeri* auct. non Scrank: Otto & A. Dietrich

Erect non-rhizomatous, branched perennial to 1.5 m tall. Stem glossy purple, hairless, zigzagged at apex. **Stipules** deciduous, ovate to ovate-lanceolate, 1–1.5 × 0.5–0.7 cm. **Leaves: petiole** glossy red, hairless, 1.2–3 cm long, joining blade at an angle; **blade** above green to bronze-green, hairless, beneath paler green with red flushing between veins or red with paler green veins, hairless, asymmetric, ovate, 5–8.5 × 2–4 cm, apex acuminate, base cordate, margin shallowly toothed, veins palmate-pinnate. **Inflorescence:** in upper leaf axils of branches, few-flowered, bisexual, cymose; **bracts** deciduous, narrowly elliptic, 1–5 × ca. 1 mm. **Male flowers: tepals** four, white, hairless, outer pair elliptic with a convex bulge around androecium, 5–6 × 2–4.5 mm, inner pair obovate, 5–6 × 2.5–3 mm; **stamens** about 15, arranged symmetrically, anther connectives projecting. **Female flowers: bracte-

oles deciduous, paired at base of ovary, insignificant and easily overlooked, linear, about 1 mm long; **tepals** five, white, subequal, ovate-lanceolate, 4–5 × 2–3 mm; **ovary** white with a pink tinge, ovoid, 2–5 × 1–2 mm, equally three-winged, three-locular, **placentae** axile, entire; **styles** three, once-branched, stigmas in a spiraled band. **2n** = 56.

Begonia dietrichiana is a native of Brazil's Atlantic Coastal Forest where it grows in the state of Rio de Janeiro. The species is widely cultivated and is available commercially. Its name honors Albert Dietrich, a former curator of the Berlin Botanical Garden. *Begonia dietrichiana* can be recognized from most other cultivated species by its hairless, thin stems with many zigzagged, purple branches and satiny green to bronze-green, hairless, ovate leaves. A smattering of small white flowers is produced from late summer to mid winter. When not in flower the species is easily confused with another commonly cultivated Brazilian species, *B. echinosepala* (Plate 75). Nonetheless, when in flower the two are instantly told apart since *B. dietrichiana* has hairless tepals, and those of *B. echinosepala* have short spiky hairs on their outer surfaces. Besides the typical variety, *B. echinosepala* var. *elongatifolia* is commonly grown. It has much narrower leaf blades that are about 1.5–2 cm wide compared to the 2–4 cm of *B. echinosepala* var. *echinosepala*.

Begonia dietrichiana and *B. echinosepala* are readily grown under standard conditions and may be propagated from stem cuttings and seed. *Begonia dietrichiana* has been little if ever used by hybridizers but *B. echinosepala* is a parent of several cultivars: *B.* 'Eunice Gray' (*B. echinosepala* × *B. venosa*), *B.* 'Ginny' (*B. echinosepala* × *B.* 'Margaritae'), and *B.* 'Paul Bee' (*B. paulensis* × *B. echinosepala*).

Within the section *Pritzelia* are a number of other Brazilian species that have a similar habit to *Begonia dietrichiana* as well as a distichous leaf arrangement. I discuss three of them here: *B. odeteiantha*, *B. parilis*, and *B. obscura*. *Begonia odeteiantha* is my favorite. This species has purple-green, pendant, rarely branched stems that have persistent dry brown stipules and can reach 60 cm in length. The leaves are closely arranged and have short petioles and blades that are glossy green and lanceolate with wedge-shaped bases and undulate, toothed margins. The flowers are rather modest and white. This species is best displayed in a hanging basket so that its pendant stems can spill gracefully over the sides. While few commercial nurseries offer *B. odeteiantha*, seed is often available from the American Begonia Society seed lists. *Begonia parilis* (Plate 76) is similar in its habit but has stems that are very conspicuously covered in orangey brown hairs, even when mature. Its leaves, like those of *B. odeteiantha*, are glossy green and lanceolate with wedge-shaped bases, but unlike those of the former species, they are not undulate along their margins. *Begonia parilis* grows readily under standard conditions and is available from several commercial sources. *Begonia obscura* (Plate 77) is also readily cultivated under standard conditions. It has erect green stems that are covered with orangey brown hairs when young, and its glossy green leaf blades are oblong with long acuminate apices, cordate bases, and double-toothed margins. The flowers are white and, like the rest of the plant, are not particularly showy. The species is nevertheless reasonably common in cultivation.

Begonia dipetala Graham (PLATES 78 AND 79)

section *Haagea*, thick-stemmed group
Curtis's Botanical Magazine 55: pl. 2849 (1828)
Synonyms: *B. hydrophila* Miquel; *B. malabarica* Lamarck var. *dipetala* Thwaites; *B.* 'Mrs. W. S. Kimball'; *B.* U044

Erect non-rhizomatous perennial, with a thick, few-branched, grayish brown stem to 1.5 m tall. **Stipules** tardily deciduous, lanceolate, 0.6–1.2 × 0.2–0.3 cm. **Leaves: petiole** yellowish green or red, sparsely hairy, 2–15 cm long, joining blade at an angle; **blade** above green with paler green or red veins, sometimes white spotted when young, beneath paler green or sometimes red-tinged, both surfaces densely covered with short, rough hairs, asymmetric, ovate to narrowly ovate, 5–17 × 3.5–11 cm, apex acute, base broadly cordate, margin double sharp-toothed or shallowly lobed and lobes with sharp teeth, veins palmate, prominently raised beneath. **Inflorescence:** axillary, pendulous, few-flowered, bisexual, cymose; flowers fragrant; **bracts** soon falling, small and inconspicuous. **Male flowers: tepals** two, white or pink, circular, 1.3–2 × 1.3–2 cm; **stamens** about 30–40, arrangement resembling a large bunch of bananas, anther connectives not projecting. **Female flowers: bracteoles** absent, one or two, situated about 3 mm beneath ovary, ovate to rectangular-ovate, 1–2.5 × 0.5–1.5 mm; **tepals** two, same color as males, circular, 1.5–2.1 × 1.7–2.2 cm; **ovary** white to pink, ellipsoid, 1–1.4 × 0.4–0.7 cm, equally three-winged, wings more or less rounded at each end, three-locular, **placentae** axile, entire; **styles** three, once-branched, stigmas in a spiraled band. **2n** = 30.

This easy to grow Asian species has been cultivated in England since 1826 and was introduced into the United States in 1913 under the erroneous name *Begonia* 'Mrs. W. S. Kimball'. *Begonia dipetala* may be recognized by its unique combination of erect, gray-brown stems, male and female flowers that each have two tepals, and its ovaries with three locules and entire placentae. In the wild, *B. dipetala* grows commonly on very shady, rocky slopes in Sri Lanka and the Nilgiri Hills of southern India. Several botanists and horticulturists have confused this species with *B. malabarica* (syn. *B. fallax*), which has a similar distribution and shares the unusual combination of an erect stem and ovaries with three locules and entire placentae. Despite the confusion, *B. malabarica* is very easily distinguished from *B. dipetala* by the more angular outline of its ovate leaf blade, its hairless leaves, its four-tepaled male flowers, and its ovary wings that are truncate rather than rounded at the apex. *Begonia malabarica* is only occasionally cultivated, but like *B. dipetala*, is amenable to standard growing conditions. *Begonia malabarica* was one of the earliest species of *Begonia* to have been discovered by Europeans. In 1689 Von Rheede tot Draakestein described it under the name *Tsjeria-narinampuli*, but it was evidently well known in India as early as 1650, some forty years before Plumier named the genus *Begonia*.

Begonia dipetala has long been used by hybridizers and as early as 1842 was crossed with both *B. manicata* and *B. hydrocotylifolia*. The species has also contributed its upright habit and ever-blooming nature to at least three cultivars in the *B.* Rex-cultorum group: *B.* 'Firmament', *B.* 'Heartthrob', and *B.* 'Mecca'. *Begonia* 'Amesbury's Dipetala' is a little known result of the cross *B. dipetala* × *B. grandis*.

Begonia floccifera (Plate 80) is a closely related but largely dissimilar species that also comes from southern India. It is rhizomatous and has thick, fleshy, almost circular leaf blades that are initially covered on both surfaces with white wooly hairs; they eventually become hairless above. The flowers are small and white; the males have two tepals and the females four. *Begonia floccifera* is only occasionally cultivated and needs a well-drained potting mix.

Begonia dregei Otto & A. Dietrich (PLATE 81)

section *Augustia*, semi-tuberous group

Allgemeine Gartenzeitung 45: 357 (1836)

Synonyms: *B. caffra* Meisner; *B. favargeri* Rechinger; *B. homonyma* Steudel; *B. macbethii* nomen nudum; *B. natalensis* W. J. Hooker; *B. partita* Irmscher; *B. parvifolia* Otto & A. Dietrich; *B. richardsiana* T. Moore; *B. richardsoniana* Houllet; *B. rubicunda* A. de Candolle; *B. rudatisii* Irmscher; *B. sinuata* Otto & A Dietrich; *B. sinuata* Graham; *B. suffruticosa* Meisner; *B. uncinata* Klotzsch

Erect perennial to 1 m tall (but usually to 40 cm tall in cultivation), typically with a swollen caudex. Stem pale green to reddish green or gray-brown, hairless, branched or branchless. **Stipules** persistent, linear-oblong to ovate-oblong, 3.5–13 × 1–6 mm. **Leaves: petiole** yellowish green to red, hairless, 0.8–9 cm long, joining blade at an angle; **blade** above green, often with reddish or purplish veins and margins, sometimes white-spotted, especially when young, hairless, beneath paler green, hairless, asymmetric, in outline ovate to ovate-lanceolate, 2.5–7 × 1.5–5 cm, apex acute to shortly acuminate, base deeply to very shallowly cordate, or almost truncate, margins entire, toothed, or with three to five short or long lobes, the lobes themselves sometimes lobed or toothed, veins palmate. **Inflorescence:** in upper leaf axils, few-flowered, bisexual, cymose; flowers fragrant; **bracts** deciduous, ovate to broadly ovate or oblong, 2.5–7 × 3–6.5 mm. **Male flowers: tepals** two, white, sometimes pink-tinged or pink, circular or kidney-shaped, 7–13 × 9–16 mm; **stamens** about 50, arranged in a flattened spherical mass, anther connectives projecting. **Female flowers: bracteoles** absent or rarely present and then small and insignificant; **tepals** five, same color as males, ovate, elliptic, almost circular, or obovate, 5–11 × 3–10 mm; **ovary** initially white but becoming green, oblong or narrowly ellipsoid to ellipsoid, 5–15 × 3–7 mm, three-winged, wings almost equal to unequal, **placentae** axile, entire; **styles** three, once-branched, stigmas in a spiraled band. **2n** = 56.

As is evident from the long list of synonyms, several previously recognized species are here included within *Begonia dregei*. The original separation of these species was based almost entirely on differences in the size and shape of their leaves. Tracy MacLellan has long been studying these plants and has concluded that they are best treated under the name *B. dregei*. I must concur with her because aside from having distinct leaf outlines they are otherwise very similar in appearance. In many cases, these distinct variants represent discreet populations that occur in isolated forest patches along the eastern coast of South Africa. These patches of forest appear to have been interconnected once and at that time the leaf outlines were probably less diverse. With the breakup of the forest it appears that the isolated populations are now in the process of evolving into distinct species. Nevertheless, since these identifiable populations are not yet as distinct as most other species recognized within the genus, I prefer to treat them as varieties of a single species. *Begonia dregei* as recognized here is the only African species with a swollen stem base, or caudex, and is, therefore, easily identifiable. Other caudiciform begonias, like *B. aconitifolia* and *B. leathermaniae*, are South American and have distinct, tall, cane-like stems arising from their swollen stem bases.

German plant collector F. J. Drège first discovered *Begonia dregei* in 1836 in South Africa near the coastal town of Port St. Johns and from there introduced it into cultivation in Europe, making it the first African begonia to be cultivated there. In the wild *B. dregei* grows on deeply shaded, south-facing slopes from the coast up to about 600 m in altitude. The species is well worth growing for its curious swollen caudex, which often gives it a somewhat gnarled appearance and makes it an excellent subject for a bonsai pot. I grow *B. dregei* and a number of other caudiciform plants this way on an east-facing windowsill where they receive bottom heat during the winter months via a hot water pipe situated two feet beneath their pots. During the winter, I keep watering to the barest minimum necessary to prevent the plant's fleshy caudex from shriveling. At this time *B. dregei* becomes semi-dormant and loses some of its stems and leaves. In the spring when growth resumes I water increasingly often, and in late spring place the plants upon a humidity tray. In the fall I remove the humidity tray and again gradually reduce watering, repeating the cycle. Others grow this species in a humid greenhouse, and that way the plants retain more of their foliage during the winter months; nevertheless the potting mix should be allowed to dry out between summer waterings and in the winter watering must be kept to a minimum. The species prefers a shallow pot and bright light. *Begonia dregei* is particularly prone to powdery mildew; a feature inherited by many of its hybrid cultivars. Propagation is usually via seed because *B. dregei*, like many other caudiciform plants, is slow or reluctant to develop a swollen base when grown from stem cuttings.

Since its introduction *Begonia dregei* has been widely hybridized. Particularly notable are the hybrid cultivars of the Cheimantha group, the first of which was produced in 1891 by crossing *B. socotrana* with *B. dregei*, as discussed under *B. socotrana*. *Begonia dregei* has also been important in the production of miniature hybrids in the Rex-cultorum group and in producing white-flowered hybrids in combination with a number of other begonias. Commonly cultivated examples include *B.* 'Dorothy Barton' (*B.* 'Lenore Olivier' × *B. dregei*), *B.* 'Weltonensis' (*B. dregei* × *B. sutherlandii*), and my own favorite *B.* 'Lubbergei' (*B. lubbersii* × *B. dregei*). All of the wild varieties of *B. dregei* are worth growing, but *B. dregei* var. *suffruticosa* and a plant widely grown under the erroneous name *B. dregei* var. *partita* have deeply dissected leaves and are particularly beautiful. *Begonia dregei* 'Glasgow' is also interesting for the white spots on its adult leaves, a trait normally seen only in juvenile plants of this species.

In its leaf shape and color *Begonia sonderana* is similar to certain individuals included here under *B. dregei*. It is identified by the combination of its erect stems that lack a swollen base, leaves with two to three short triangular lobes and a toothed margin, its few-flowered branched inflorescences, male flowers with four tepals, female flowers with five tepals, and ovaries with axile, bifid placentae. It is tuberous and usually has pink flowers. The German *Begonia* taxonomist Edgar Irmscher named the species in honor of W. Sonder, coauthor of an early South African flora. The species is rarely cultivated and those plants that I have seen were usually unnamed in cultivation.

A detailed taxonomic treatment of the *Begonia dregei* group and related species

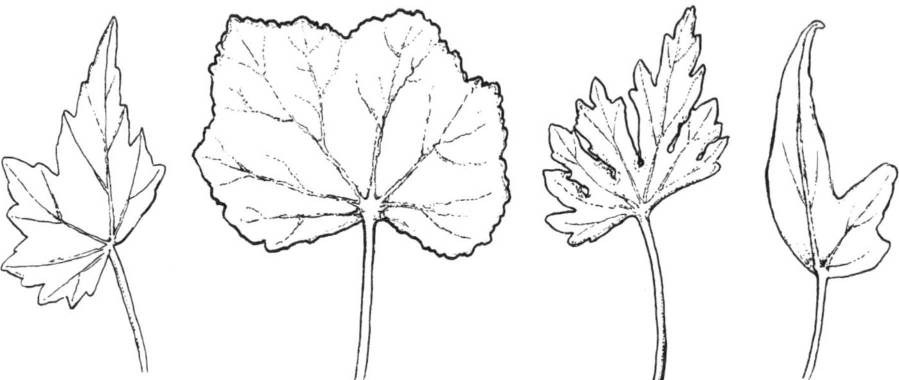

A selection of leaves drawn from plants of *B. dregei* in cultivation at the Montreal Botanical Garden, showing a small portion of the variation found in the species.

appears in: Irmscher, E. (1961) Monographische Revision der begoniaceen Afrikas 1. Sekt. *Augustia* und *Rostrobegonia* sowie einige neue Sippen aus anderen Sektionen. *Botanische Jahrbucher*, 81, 106–188. An English summary appears in: Karegeannes, K. (1974) The maple-leaved South African begonias. *Begonian* 41, 62–71. Another useful source of information is: McLelland, T. (1997) What is *Begonia partita*? *Begonian* 64: 88–90.

Begonia edmundoi Brade
section *Gaerdtia*, shrub-like group
Rodriquésia 18: 33, pl. 6 (1945)

Erect non-rhizomatous perennial to 70 cm tall. Stems slender, branched, and often only bearing leaves toward the apex, dark brown to black when mature, hairless. **Stipules** persistent, linear-lanceolate, 1–2.5 × 0.5–0.7 cm. **Leaves:** distichous; **petiole** pale green with a pink tinge, hairless, 3–6 mm long, continuing straight into main vein of blade; **blade** above dark green sometimes with numerous small round silvery white spots between the main veins, hairless, beneath burgundy, hairless, asymmetric, oblong-lanceolate to elliptic-lanceolate, 4–12 × 1.3–3.5 cm, apex acuminate, base very shallowly cordate, margin short wavy-toothed, veins pinnate. **Inflorescence:** axillary, few-flowered, bisexual, cymose; **bracts** soon falling to persistent, ovate, 7–16 × 5–9 mm. **Male flowers: tepals** four, white, outer pair ovate-cordate, 0.5–2.5 × 1.2–2.5 cm, inner pair obovate, 12–20 × 5.5–11 mm; **stamens** numerous, arranged more or less symmetrically, anther connectives not projecting. **Female flowers: bracteoles** paired 3–5 mm beneath ovary, soon falling to persistent, ovate, 8–14 × 5–11 mm; **tepals** five, white, unequal, obovate or oblong, 9–23 × 7–20 mm; **ovary** ellipsoid, equally three-winged, three-locular, **placentae** axile, bifid; **styles** three, unbranched, stigmas kidney-shaped. **2n** = 56.

Begonia edmundoi, though hardly a spectacular flowering plant, is interesting as it produces relatively short cane-like stems that are not only unusually thin but also dark brown to black, a stem color rarely found in the genus. The species is native to the Organ Mountains of Brazil, where it grows in the forest at an elevation of about 1400 m. *Begonia edmundoi* was named by Alexander Brade in honor of fellow botanist Edmundo Pereira who collected the species in 1944 at Córrego Beijaflor, a place where Brade had himself seen the plant a few years earlier.

Begonia edmundoi appears to have first entered cultivation at the New York Botanical Garden in 1951 from material sent by Brade. The species may be grown under standard conditions. Because *B. edmundoi* has a natural tendency to lose its lower leaves, its older stems periodically need cutting back to promote a leafier, more attractive plant. The only published record of a hybrid of this species appears to be *B.* 'Shinnecock' (*B. edmundoi* × unknown parent).

Begonia egregia N. E. Brown (PLATE 82)

section *Tetrachia*, thick-stemmed group
Gardener's Chronicle (London) III, 1: 346 (1887)
Synonym: *B. quadrilocularis* Brade

Erect branched subshrub to 1.2 m tall. Stem woody at base, dull olive-green to pale grayish brown, hairy. **Stipules** soon falling, narrowly ovate, 0.9–1.2 × ca. 0.4 cm. **Leaves:** both peltate and non-peltate on the same individual; **petiole** green with dense short white hairs, 2–7.5 cm long, continuing straight into main vein of blade; **blade** above green, minutely bullate with stiff hairs, beneath silvery green, hairy on veins, ovate-lanceolate to broadly oblong-lanceolate, 10–28 × 3.5–11 cm, apex acuminate, base peltate or obtusely cordate and lowest lobe rounded and pointing backward, margin crenate- or serrate-toothed, veins pinnate. **Inflorescence:** in upper leaf axils, many-flowered, bisexual, cymose, male flowers produced long before the females, main stalk pink, individual flower stalks white; flowers scented; **bracts** soon falling, lanceolate, 2–20 × 0.5–4 mm. **Male flowers: tepals** two, white, ovate, elliptic or obovate, 0.6–1.3 × 0.5–0.9 cm; **stamens** numerous, arranged symmetrically, anther connectives projecting. **Female flowers: bracteoles** paired about 3 mm beneath the ovary, deciduous, more or less rectangular-elliptic, 1–2 × ca. 0.5 mm; **tepals** six, white, narrowly obovate, 0.5–0.9 × 1.5–2.3 mm; **ovary** pale bluish green with white wings, broadly ellipsoid to almost spherical, 0.3–0.5 × 0.2–0.5 mm, more or less equally four-winged, four-locular, **placentae** axile, bifid; **styles** four, once-branched, stigmas in a spiraled band.

Begonia egregia was first introduced into cultivation via William Bull who in the 1800s operated a popular London nursery specializing in South American orchids and other tropical plants. Nicholas Brown, a Kew botanist and expert on Africa's succulents, described the species in 1887 based on plants grown at Bull's nursery. He must have liked it a great deal because the name he gave it is Latin for "excellent." *Begonia egregia* is an unusual species since its distinctive, minutely bullate leaves vary from peltate to non-peltate even on an individual plant. It also has unusual ovaries that are four-locular rather than two- or three-locular, as are typically found in *Begonia*. Partly for this reason *B. egregia* is classified in its own section, *Tetrachia*. Alexander Brade's synonymous name *B. quadrilocularis* also reflects this characteristic of the ovaries. *Begonia egregia* is native to the mountanous coastal forests of Brazil close to the city of Rio de Janeiro.

Begonia egregia is commonly cultivated and valued as an easy-to-grow, marginally frost-hardy garden plant, as well as a conservatory or greenhouse plant. In the open garden its tall stature and bold leaves make it a good choice for the mixed border. While *B. egregia* is easy to cultivate it is said to prefer less humidity and a larger root run than most begonias. The species must also have excellent drainage. Only two hybrid cultivars of *B. egregia* are documented: *B.* 'Egrelet' (*B.* 'Lettonica' × *B. egregia*) and *B.* 'Ernest Martin' (*B. egregia* × *B.* 'Tingley Mallet'). Neither is common.

Begonia epipsila Brade (PLATE 83)

section *Pritzelia*, shrub-like group

Archivos do Jardim Botânico do Rio de Janeiro 8: 227, pl. 1 (1948)

Erect non-rhizomatous subshrub to about 30 cm tall. **Stipules** persistent, ovate, 12–24 × 10–15 mm. **Leaves: petiole** pink to red with wooly rust-colored hairs, 2.5–8 cm long, joining blade at an angle; **blade** above glossy dark green with a white spot above the petiole, hairless, beneath red with a dense covering of short, wooly, rust-colored hairs, thick, asymmetric, ovate, 6–10 × 3–6 cm, apex shortly acuminate, base cordate, margin entire, undulate, veins indistinct, palmate-pinnate. **Inflorescence:** axillary, few- to several-flowered, bisexual, cymose, densely covered with rust-colored hairs; flowers fragrant; **bracts** soon falling, ovate, elliptic or obovate, 2.5–5 × 1–2 mm. **Male flowers: tepals** four, white, outer pair almost circular, 8–10 × 9–11 mm, outer surfaces with wooly hairs, inner pair oblong, 7–9 × 2–3 mm; **stamens** about 20–30, arranged symmetrically, anther connectives projecting. **Female flowers: bracteoles** absent; **tepals** five, white, almost circular to oblong,

7–8 × 3–6 mm, outermost sparsely wooly, hairy on their outer surfaces; **ovary** green with red wings, ovate, ca. 1.2 × 0.5 cm, unequally three-winged, three-locular, **placentae** axile, entire; **styles** three, once-branched, stigmas in a spiraled band. **2n** = 56.

Begonia epipsila is a low-growing Brazilian species that resides, like most of the begonias from that country, in the Atlantic Coastal Forest. Alexander Brade and Apparicio Pereira Duarte first discovered the plant in 1946 growing at Alto da Boa Vista, Furnas, near Rio de Janeiro. The name Brade gave it means "bare above" and refers to the species' glossy, dark green upper leaf surfaces, which contrast with the densely reddish brown felted lower surfaces. *Begonia epipsila* was introduced into the United States soon after it was described via seed imported by Florida nurseryman Mulford Foster. Today it is commonly grown in both North America and Europe. The species flowers during the winter and spring and is very floriferous. *Begonia sanguinea*, *B. friburgensis*, and *B. piresiana* are similar-looking plants that have a more upright habit than *B. epipsila*. The Brazilian *B. sanguinea* is distinguished by it leaves having gray-green upper surfaces and hairless undersurfaces. This species is commonly known as the "beefsteak begonia," or in German "Fleisch-blattler" (meat leaves), as the undersurfaces of the leaves are bright red. Even its scientific name, *sanguinea*, means "bloody." *Begonia friburgensis* shares *B. epipsila*'s densely reddish brown, felted lower leaf surfaces but can be readily distinguished by its broadly ovate to almost circular leaves that measure 12–16 cm across. It too is a native of Brazil. *Begonia piresiana* (Plate 84), also from Brazil, has leaves that are silver beneath.

Begonia epipsila is easy to grow as long as it is kept on the dry side during the winter months. It prefers a relative humidity of 60–70 percent and temperatures of 58–75°F (14–21°C). It requires a well-lit position but the leaves have a tendency to bleach if they receive too much light. It has been reported that *B. epipsila* looks especially good when planted in a hanging container because its stems will naturally cascade over the sides. It also looks good planted in rock crevices and is grown this way in the *Begonia* house at Montreal Botanical Garden. Propagation is via division, stem cuttings, or seed. Few *B. epipsila* hybrids are common, but some of the more popular ones include *B.* 'Venepi' (*B. venosa* × *B. epipsila*), *B.* 'Raythel' (*B. fernando-costae* × *B. epipsila*), and *B.* 'D'Artagnon' (*B. epipsila* × *B. scharffiana*). The last was bred by Marie Turner and named after one of the three musketeers because its leaves have the appearance of a musketeers' hat. The *B. sanguinea* hybrid cultivar *B.* 'Thurstonii' (*B. metallica* × *B. sanguinea*) is also very widely grown, while *B.* 'Olfri' is a rarely grown hybrid of *B. olsoniae* × *B. friburgensis*.

Begonia foliosa Kunth (PLATES 85 AND 86)

section *Lepsia*, shrub-like group

in Humboldt, Bonpland, and Kunth, *Nova Genera et Species Plantarum* 7: 183, pl. 642 (1825)

Synonyms: *B. foliosa* var. *australis* L. B. Smith & B. G. Schubert; *B. foliosa* var. *putzeysiana* (A. de Candolle) L. B. Smith & B. G. Schubert; *B. foliosa* var. *rotundata* L. B. Smith & B. G. Schubert; *B. jamesoniana* A. de Candolle; *B. microphylla* Klotzsch; *B.* U135; *B.* U260

Erect perennial, often with gracefully arching stems to about 4 m tall. Stems becoming tough and woody at base, hairless but sometimes with small bumps (papillae), main stem dark brownish red interspersed with white lenticels, side branches green or red. **Stipules** persistent, ovate, 3–10 × 2–5 mm. **Leaves: petiole** green or pink, hairless but sometimes with small bumps (papillae), 0.5–4 mm long, more or less continuing straight into main vein of blade; **blade** above glossy dark green, beneath paler green, sometimes with red veins, covered with numerous small white stomata, both surfaces hairless but sometimes with small bumps (papillae), slightly asymmetric, elliptic, 0.5–5 × 0.3–2 cm, apex acute to rounded, base very shallowly cordate, margin deeply toothed at apex, shallowly toothed along sides and entire at base, the teeth ending in short hairs, veins pinnate. **Inflorescence:** in upper leaf axils, 1–30-flowered, bisexual, cymose, but frequently with only a single male flower that is subtended by two female flowers; **bracts** persistent, ovate to ovate-lanceolate or ovate-elliptic, 1.5–6 × 0.3–5 mm. **Male flowers: tepals** four, white, pink or red, outer pair ovate to broadly ovate or elliptic, 5.5–8 × 5–5.5 mm, inner pair elliptic or obovate, 4.5–7 × 2.3–3 mm; **stamens** 25–30, arranged symmetrically, anther connectives long projecting. **Female flowers: bracteoles** paired about 1–3 mm beneath ovary, linear, 1.5–2 × ca. 0.5 mm; **tepals** five, white, pink, or red, outer pair ovate or elliptic, 3–10 × 2–5 mm, inner three elliptic to broadly elliptic, 4.5–8 × 2.5–4 mm; **ovary** pale green or whitish green, sometimes with a red tinge at base, ovoid, 3–6 × 1.5–5 mm, unequally three-winged, three-locular, **placentae** axile, entire or bifid; **styles** three, once-branched, stigmas in a spiraled band. **2n** = 60 and 84.

Begonia foliosa var. *foliosa* (Plate 86) is among the best cultivated begonias. It is easy to grow and almost continuously produces a smattering of dainty white flowers set against arching stems of fern-like foliage. The name *foliosa* means "with abundant leaves" and describes the plant accurately, for its stems are covered with numerous tiny leaves. Though a beautiful plant, the species is, from a taxonomic point of view, a mess. Taxonomists have proposed several different ways of delimiting *B. foliosa* and the other members of the northern Andean section *Lepsia*, and in doing so have, at various times, recognized between two and six species in this group. Nevertheless, I feel that Larry Dorr's taxonomic treatment clears up most of the confusion and have adopted his species concepts here. For more information consult: Dorr, L. J. (1999) Notes on *Begonia* (Begoniaceae) in the Venezuelan Andes. *Harvard Papers in Botany*, 4 (1): 253–264. This treatment builds upon earlier studies that regrettably had to change the names of two horticultural favorites. Thus the ever-popular *B. fuchsioides* is now named *B. foliosa* var. *miniata* and *B. foliosa* var. *amplifolia* is included in *B. holtonis* var. *holtonis*. The fuchsia-like *B. foliosa* var. *miniata* (Plate 207) has been of particular value to hybridizers and is a parent of several hybrid cultivars. It has pink or red flowers that are usually larger and grouped more numerously than those of *B. foliosa* var. *foliosa*, which has white flowers. The widely cultivated *B.* U010 (Plates 85 and 86) is either a variant of *B. foliosa* or an undescribed species. The plant's exact taxonomic status is difficult to establish because more field collections are needed, but the country from which *B.* U010 was collected is uncertain.

Begonia foliosa is native to Colombia, Venezuela, and Ecuador and in the wild is very common. It inhabits the interiors and margins of moist montane cloud forest at an altitude of 1200–3000 m, often growing as a liana, or vine, up into the forest canopy. In its native habitat mule drivers are said to pick the stems and chew them to alleviate fatigue and thirst. Interestingly, a similar practice has also been reported for *B. acetosella* and certain other Asian begonias, suggesting that there is a scientific basis for this practice. *Begonia foliosa* was originally discovered in Colombia by German geographer Alexander von Humboldt and French botanist Aimée Bonpland while on the first leg of their 1799–1804 expedition to the Americas. Plants were first introduced into cultivation in France, and from there reached England shortly afterward in 1868.

Begonia foliosa is a favorite for hanging baskets and planters because its arching stems look particularly graceful when seen at eye level. It requires more frequent watering than most species and likes to be slightly moist at all times. It also prefers a relatively cool, shady position with a relative humidity of 50–70 percent. Stem cuttings and seed are both ready means of propagation. Several *B. foliosa* var. *miniata* hybrids are commonly grown, including *B.* 'Fuchsifoliosa' (*B. foliosa* var. *miniata* × *B. foliosa* var. *foliosa*), *B.* 'Corbeille de Feu' (*B.* Semperflorens-cultorum group × *B. foliosa* var. *miniata*), *B.* 'Digswelliana' (*B. foliosa* var. *miniata* × *B.* Semperflorens-cultorum group), and *B.* 'Ingramii' (*B. minor* × *B. foliosa* var. *miniata*). *Begonia* 'Cascade' is a hybrid from *B. foliosa* var. *foliosa* × *B. holtonis*.

Begonia formosana (Hayata) Masamune (PLATE 87)
section *Platycentrum*, rhizomatous group
Journal of Geobotany 9 (3–4), pl. 41 (1961)
Synonyms: *B. laciniata* Roxburgh var. *formosana* Hayata; *B. laciniata* auct. non Roxburgh: Forbes & Hemsley; *B. laciniata* auct. non Roxburgh: Hayata

Creeping rhizomatous perennial with erect stems to 50 cm tall. **Stipules** tardily deciduous, ovate, 6.5–13 × 11–13 mm, main vein projecting. **Leaves: petiole** green, almost hairless to sparsely hairy, 10–30 cm long, joining blade at an angle; **blade** above glossy green, or glossy green with white spots, beneath paler green with red veins, both surfaces almost hairless to sparsely hairy, asymmetric, ovate, 8–15 × 6–11 cm, apex acuminate, base cordate, margin angular-lobed, lobes toothed, veins palmate. **Inflorescence:** axillary, three- to four-flowered, bisexual, cymose; **bracts** soon falling, ovate to ovate-lanceolate or ovate-elliptic, 1.5–6 × 0.3–5 mm. **Male flowers: tepals** four, outer pair pale pink, broadly oblong, 1.9–3 × 1.9–2.5 cm, inner pair white, obovate, 1.5–2.3 × 1–1.4 cm; **stamens** numerous, arranged symmetrically, attached to a column, anther connectives long projecting. **Female flowers: bracteoles** absent; **tepals** five, pale pink, ovate, 0.8–1.1 × 0.5–1.5 cm; **ovary** whitish green, asymmetric-obovoid, 7–11 × 3–4.5 mm, unequally three-winged, one wing longer than the others, two-locular, **placentae** axile, bifid; **styles** two, once-branched, stigmas in a spiraled band. **2n** = 60.

Begonia formosana, while not particularly attractive, is of horticultural value because it is one of only a few marginally frost-hardy species in the genus. Though less cold-hardy than the hardy begonia, *B. grandis*, this species may be grown outdoors in regions that experience relatively mild winters, like the Pacific Northwest, the Carolinas, and southwestern England. In the wild, *B. formosana* grows throughout Taiwan and the nearby Ryukyus Islands and is often very common at altitudes of 300–1000 m. Presumably at least some of the various clones found in cultivation were collected from the upper elevation range of the species since they are proving to be quite hardy. *Begonia formosana* may be recognized by its short hairless stems that arise from creeping rhizomes, laciniate leaf blades, and two-locular ovaries with one long, almost triangular wing and two much shorter rib-like wings. Two forms have been described, both of which are cultivated. *Begonia formosana* f. *formosana* (Plate 87, lower) has green leaves, and *B. formosana* f. *albomaculata* (Plate 87, upper) has leaves that are green with white spots on the upper surfaces.

Begonia formosana is readily grown under standard conditions. In the open garden the species is said to require a shaded position in moisture-retentive but well-drained soil. It will also perform well in a shaded container, to which a similar potting medium has been added. No hybrids with *B. formosana* have been documented.

Begonia formosana is one of a handful of marginally frost-hardy species that have been introduced or, as is the case with this species, reintroduced to our gardens in recent years. Dan Hinkley of Washington State's Heronswood Nursery has been particularly active in their introduction and promotion, but the Atlanta Botanical Garden and a few nurseries in the southeastern United States and the United Kingdom have also played a role. Three of these species are close relatives of *B. formosana* and I discuss them here. Others are mentioned under *B. grandis* and *B. veitchii*. Two of *B. formosana*'s frost-hardy relatives, *B. emeiensis* and *B. pedatifida*, were introduced by Dan Hinkley via Heronswood Nursery. A third, *B. palmata*, has been in cultivation much longer and is today represented by both frost-hardy and tender plants. *Begonia emeiensis* (Plates 89g and 95) is a particularly interesting and distinctive species. Many of its leaves produce a curious swelling at the junction of the petiole and the blade's upper surface, and from this area tiny adventitious plantlets are produced in late summer. The species has shallowly lobed leaf blades and large pink flowers produced on short, few-flowered inflorescences. In the wild it is restricted to Mount Emei in China's Sichuan Province. *Begonia pedatifida* (Plates 89h and 94) is another attractive species with palmately lobed leaves and large white flowers. It was recently collected on Mount Emei at about 915 m but has a much larger natural distribution than this, being found in China's Sichuan, Hubei, Hunan, and Guizhou provinces. Since this species has been recorded in the wild at elevation up to 1700 m, individuals considerably more cold-tolerant than those currently found in cultivation undoubtedly exist and could be introduced. *Begonia palmata* (syn. *B. laciniata*; Plate 92), as its name suggests, also has palmately lobed leaves. This species is native to much of tropical mainland Asia from northern India to eastern China. Throughout much of its range the species is common and is found at an altitude range of 100 to 3200 m, usually on dripping wet rock walls and other moist habitats. In recent years, Don Jacobs and the Atlanta Botanical Garden have been active in bringing some of the higher elevation plants into cultivation in the hope that they will prove winter-hardy in the southeastern United States. As would be expected from this species' large natural distribution, much variation exists and several varieties have been named. The typical variety has a broad white ring in the center of the leaf blade and hence is the most garden worthy. The species as a whole is recognized by the combination of its persistent stipules, upright stems that arise from short rhizomes, narrowly triangular leaf lobes, and two-locular ovaries.

Many species of section *Platycentrum*, including *Begonia formosana*, *B. rex*, and *B. hatacoa*, have evolved to disperse their seed in an ingenious manner. Their fruits typically have one long wing and two much shorter, rib-like wings. At maturity the fruit's peduncle becomes curved so that the capsule is inverted, with the longest wing pointing toward the ground. Simultaneously, small slits open next to the wings. Falling raindrops become trapped by the two small wings on the back of the inverted capsule and when enough water has accumulated it causes the capsule to nod up and down, thereby shaking out the seeds through the slits. Because these species need water for their seed dispersal, most are found along streams or rivers (Plate 88) or on wet cliff faces by waterfalls (Plate 92). The Himalayas and the China-Vietnam border region (Plate 91) are particularly rich in species from this section.

Begonia gehrtii Irmscher (PLATE 96)

section *Pritzelia*, rhizomatous group

Botanische Jarhbücher für Systematik, Pflanzengeshichte und Pflanzengeographie 78: 188–189 (1959)

Rhizomatous perennial with a short erect stem. **Stipules** persistent, obscuring much of stem, ovate or oblong, 3–3.5 × 1.7–1.8 cm. **Leaves: petiole** green, densely hairy when young, joining blade at an angle; **blade** puckered, above glossy green with whitish green main veins, when young with a covering of rust-colored hairs resembling a cobweb, beneath paler green with wooly hairs on the veins, asymmetric, ovate to elliptic, 8–21 × 8.5–21 cm, apex abruptly short acuminate, base cordate, margin shallowly toothed, veins palmate-pinnate. **Inflorescence:** in upper leaf axils, many-flowered, bisexual, cymose; **bracts** soon falling, ovate to broadly rectangular-ovate or elliptic, 0.9–1.5 × 0.4–1.5 cm. **Male flowers: tepals** four, white, outer pair obovate or elliptic, 16–19 × 9–13 mm, inner pair obovate-oblong, 11–17 × 4.5–7 mm; **stamens** numerous, arranged symmetrically, anther connectives projecting. **Female flowers: bracteoles** absent; **tepals** five or rarely six, white, ovate to elliptic, 7–16 × 5–9 mm; **ovary** green with a red tinge, especially on the wings, covered with cobweb-like hairs, oblong, 5–7.5 × 2–4.5 mm, unequally three-winged, three-locular, **placentae** axile, entire; **styles** three, once-branched, stigmas in a spiraled band.

The leaf blades of *Begonia gehrtii* have a wonderful crinkled appearance, reminiscent of a piece of wax paper that has been crunched up and then spread out again. Such leaves are found in only a few other cultivated begonias, all of which are from Brazil and closely related to *B. gehrtii*. The network of raised veins on one of them, the suitably named *B. crispula*, is even more finely textured than in *B. gehrtii*. I have provided a key to *B. gehrtii* and its relatives here. *Begonia gehrtii* appears to have entered cultivation in Europe prior to 1959, when German taxonomist Edgar Irmscher received it from Brazil as a new undescribed species. The material he received was previously cultivated at the São Paulo Botanical Garden. Irmscher named it after Dr. Gehrt, the botanist who had collected the dried herbarium specimens sent to him.

Begonia gehrtii and its closest relatives are usually only encountered in specialist collections since they are relatively challenging to grow. Nevertheless, *B. gehrtii*, *B. crispula* (Plate 97), and *B. paulensis* (Plate 98) are firmly established in cultivation and are periodically offered in the American Begonia Society seed lists. *Begonia moyesii* is much less frequently grown, if at all. The commonly encountered species all require similar growing conditions, with temperatures in the range of 65 to 75°F (18–24°C) and a relative humidity around 50–60 percent. They also need a shady position because bright sunlight will bleach and eventually burn their delicate leaves. Their growing medium should be well-drained yet moisture-retentive and must be allowed to dry out slightly between waterings. *Begonia crispula* needs slightly higher humidity than the other species and for this reason is best grown in a terrarium. Take care when handling these plants because their leaves are very brittle and easily damaged. It is recommended to repot them when they are slightly dry and wilted because in this state the leaves are less easily torn. Propagation is via seed or division of the rhizomes since leaf cuttings usually root but fail to produce new vegetative shoots. Only a few hybrid cultivars of *B. gehrtii* are reported in the literature. Examples include *B.* 'Alhambra' (*B. olsoniae* × *B. gehrtii*) and *B.* 'Jabberwocky' (*B. gehrtii* × unknown species). *Begonia* 'Crispie' is a hybrid of *B. dregei* × *B. crispula*, while *B.* 'Zuensis' has *B. paulensis* × *B.* 'Credneri' parentage.

Key to *Begonia gehrtii* and its close relatives

1 a. Leaves peltate . . . . *B. paulensis*
  b. Leaves not peltate 2
2 a. Leaf bases symmetric, surface of blade finely crinkled . . . . *B. crispula*
  b. Leaf bases asymmetric, surface of blade coarsely crinkled 3
3 a. Petiole circular in cross section, densely hairy when young . . . . *B. gehrtii*
  b. Petiole four-sided in cross section, hairless when young . . . . *B. moyesii*

Begonia goegoensis N. E. Brown (PLATE 99)
section *Reichenheimia*, rhizomatous group
Gardener's Chronicle (London) II: 71 (1882)

Creeping rhizomatous perennial. Stem brownish green, hairless, rooting at the nodes. **Stipules** persistent, triangular, 1.1–1.6 × 0.4–13.5 cm. **Leaves:** peltate; **petiole** four-sided, pale green, sometimes flushed red, hairless or almost so, 7.5–19 cm long; **blade** above bullate, dark green-bronze with pale green veins, margins purple-red, beneath red or purple-red, veins sparsely hairy, elsewhere hairless, broadly ovate to almost circular, 4.5–19 × 3–15.5 cm, margin crenate to finely toothed. **Inflorescence:** axillary, several-flowered, bisexual, cymose, male flowers produced long before the females; **bracts** persistent, narrowly elliptic, 5–6 × 1.5–1.8 mm. **Male flowers: tepals** four, outer pair pink on outer surface, off-white with a pink tinge on inner surface, circular-cordate, 6–10 × 6–10 mm, inner pair white, ovate to broadly obovate, 5–9.5 × 4–7.5 mm; **stamens** numerous, arranged symmetrically, anther connectives not projecting. **Female flowers: bracteoles** absent; **tepals** five, same color as males, outermost elliptic, 0.8–1.1 × 0.6–0.7 cm, innermost narrowly elliptic to narrowly rectangular, ca. 0.6 × 0.2–0.3 cm; **ovary** pink, broadly ellipsoid to spherical, ca. 5 × 4–5 mm, unequally three-winged, three-locular, **placentae** axile, entire; **styles** three, once-branched, stigmas in a spiraled band. **2n** = 34.

This species was discovered in Goego, Sumatra, by Charles Curtis, while plant collecting for the English nursery company of Veitch and Sons. It has remained in cultivation since its introduction in the late 1800s but has never been widely grown. Instead it is a collector's plant that is valued for its beautiful leaves that are more or less circular and attractively colored dark green-bronze with pale green veins and a purple-red margin.

Begonia goegoensis can be challenging to cultivate, which probably explains why it is not more commonly grown. It prefers relatively warm temperatures, 65–75°F (18–24°C), and an atmospheric humidity around 60 percent. In most areas it is best grown in a humid greenhouse or indoors under artificial lights in a large sealed terrarium. The growing medium should be rich and humusy, yet free draining. It benefits from the regular addition of fertilizer during the summer months. This species has been hybridized with a few other Asian species. Some of the more popular cultivars include *B.* 'Calico Kew' (*B. goegoensis* × *B. chlorosticta;* Plate 46), *B.* 'Freda Stevens' (*B.* 'Lenore Olivier' × *B. goegoensis*), *B.* 'Mumtaz' (*B. goegoensis* × *B. rajah*), and *B.* 'Sansouci' (*B. goegoensis* × *B. rajah*).

Three other cultivated species are somewhat similar to *Begonia goegoensis* in that they are rhizomatous and have peltate leaves and ovaries with entire placentae: *B. coriacea*, *B. kingiana*, and *B. sudjanae*. *Begonia sudjanae* is the closest in appearance to *B. goegoensis* but may easily be distinguished by its hairy green leaves. It also is a native of Sumatra. *Begonia coriacea* (Plate 100) from Java has relatively small green leaves and red flowers and is occasionally offered for sale. In cultivation it is sometimes confused with *B. conchifolia* from Central America, but the two are easily distinguished when in flower. *Begonia coriacea* has red flowers and ovaries with entire placentae, but *B. conchifolia* has white to deep pink flowers and ovaries with bifid placentae. The third species, *B. kingiana* has small leaves that shimmer with iridescent greens and purples. It has distinct one-sided inflorescences and hairless petioles. It is only rarely grown but is an interesting plant for the collector.

Begonia gracilis Kunth (PLATE 101)

section *Quadriperigonia*, tuberous group

in Humboldt, Bonpland, and Kunth, *Nova Genera et Species Plantarum* 7: 184 (1825)

Synonyms: *B. martiniana* Link & Otto; *B. gracilis* var. *martiniana* (Link & Otto) A. de Candolle; *B. diversifolia* Graham; *B. diversifolia* Knowles & Westcott

Erect tuberous perennial. Stem green to red, hairless to sparsely hairy, branchless, to about 1 m tall, often bearing clusters of small bulbils in the leaf axils. **Stipules** persistent, ovate, 4–7 × 2.5–10 mm. **Leaves: petiole** green to red, hairless, 0.4–9 cm long, joining blade at an angle; **blade** above green to bronze green, often with white flecks between the veins, hairless or almost so, beneath paler green, usually hairy on the veins, asymmetric, ovate to elliptic, 1.5–14 × 0.5–6.5 cm, gradually becoming smaller toward the apex of the plant, apex acute to acuminate, base cordate, margin coarsely double-toothed or crenate, veins palmate. **Inflorescence:** terminal, a racemose structure consisting of several few-flowered, bisexual cymes arranged on one side of the stem; **bracts** persistent, ovate, 2–6 × 2–4 mm, margin toothed. **Male flowers: tepals** four, white to deep pink, the outer pair broadly ovate, elliptic, or almost circular, 1.3–2.5 × 0.9–2.2 cm, the inner pair elliptic to obovate, 0.9–2 × 0.3–0.9 cm; **stamens** numerous, fused at the base into a column and arranged in a symmetric mass, anther connectives not projecting. **Female flowers: bracteoles** absent or one; **tepals** five, same color as males, elliptic, obovate, or broadly ovate to transversely elliptic, 0.8–2.5 × 0.3–2.2 cm; **ovary** green, ellipsoid, 0.5–1.7 × 0.3–0.7 cm, unequally three-winged, three-locular, **placentae** axile, bifid; **styles** three, once-branched, stigmas in a spiraled band. **2n** = 56.

The "hollyhock begonia" is a widespread native of Mexico, where it grows both on open steep hillsides and on shaded rocks and mossy banks under oaks and pines, usually at an altitude of 1000–2800 m. A particularly beautiful photograph of the species flowering on a mossy bank in southwestern Mexico appears on page 74, volume 2, of Phillips and Rix's *Indoor and Greenhouse Plants* (1997). *Begonia gracilis* has long been known to botanists and was first mentioned in 1651 by Francisco Hernandez, a Spaniard who has been dubbed the first naturalist of the Americas. He describes the plant in *Nova plantarum, animalium et mineralium Mexicanorum historia*, referring to it by the Nahautl name, the language of the Aztecs, as *Totoncaxoxo coyollin*. Hernandez reports that the plant was discovered before 1577, more than 100 years before the modern name for the genus *Begonia* was established. Other early European explorers also came across this species, most notably Alexander von Humboldt and Aimée Bonpland. Otto Kunth described the plants they collected on the last leg of their five-year expedition to the Americas under its currently accepted name, *B. gracilis*. The name *gracilis* means "slender" or "graceful" and is an apt description of this elegant plant. In cultivation *B. gracilis* is easily recognized by its erect, usually hairless, leafy stems that arise from underground tubers and by its racemose inflorescence with white to deep pink flowers. The species often has a striking resemblance to a hollyhock (*Alcea rosea*), hence its common name.

Though distinct among the cultivated species, *Begonia gracilis* is less easily identified in the wild. Kathleen Burt-Utley (2001a) in her account of the species in the *Flora Nova-Galiciana* writes:

> Although considered a variable species by some researchers, much of the perception of variability in *Begonia gracilis* has resulted from erroneous identification of other species as *B. gracilis*. Specimens treated herein as *B. fusibulba*, *B. gracilior*, *B. sandtii*, and *B. tapatia* were identified previously as *B. gracilis*. Further evaluation of *B. gracilis* from other parts of Mexico is in progress and may well result in the recognition of one or more additional distinct species, which will further reduce the variability reported for *B. gracilis*.

Nevertheless, most taxonomic confusion in cultivation stems not from the misidentification of this species, but from the continued use of the now synonymous names *B. martiniana* and *B. gracilis* var. *martiniana* for *B. gracilis*. These names were originally proposed for a variant that was almost completely hairless and which had crenate leaf margins. However, because wild material of *B. gracilis* cannot be divided discretely on the basis of these characteristics most modern-day botanists do not recognize such variants as named entities. That said, plants currently cultivated under the names *B. martiniana* and *B. gracilis* var. *martiniana* are often easier to grow than those long cultivated as *B. gracilis*. A key to *B. gracilis* and its cultivated relatives is provided here. One of these species, *B. sandtii*, is illustrated in Plate 102.

Begonia gracilis has been in cultivation since 1829 but is usually only grown by collectors because like many of the tuberous *Begonia* species it is a bit demanding. It does best when provided with relatively cool temperatures and high light levels. It should be grown in well-drained potting medium, and many growers recommend using a clay pot. The species is summer dormant. At the end of the summer the tubers require a minimum of water to start them into new growth. Once they have begun to sprout and grow they can then be watered increasingly freely. Plants achieve full growth and flower in early to mid winter. After the flowering season the leaves begin to yellow and die back to the storage tuber. As this occurs watering should be gradually reduced and finally withdrawn completely for the summer resting period. Propagation is usually via the clusters of tiny bulbils that form in the leaf axils. Seed is also a reliable method and is frequently offered in the American Begonia Society seed lists.

Racemose inflorescence of the hollyhock begonia, *B. gracilis*.

Begonia gracilis was hybridized with the early members of the Semperflorens-cultorum group from 1894 up until the early to mid 1900s (see *B. cucullata*). This way, German nurseryman Ernst Benary created a range of new hybrids with the small graceful leaves of *B. gracilis*, as well as its tolerance for direct sunlight, the legacy of which may be seen in many of the modern-day wax begonias. Leslie Woodriff, who from the late 1940s to late 1970s produced many notable hybrids, bred the tuberless *B.* 'Ivy Ever' (*B. gracilis* × *B. radicans*), as well as *B.* 'Winter Hollyhock' (*B. gracilis* × *B. socotrana*).

Key to the cultivated species of section *Quadriperigonia*

1 a. Leaf blade deeply palmate-lobed, base wedge-shaped, and the petiole apparently splitting into two parts 2

b. Leaf blade unlobed or very shallowly lobed, base usually cordate, the petiole never appearing to split into two parts 3

2 a. Lobes of leaf blade ovate-oblong, upper surface of blade hairless .... *B. pedata*
b. Lobes of leaf blade acuminate, upper surface of blade hairy .... *B. biserrata*
3 a. Plant covered with conspicuous stalked glandular hairs .... *B. sandtii*
b. Plant hairless or hairy but hairs lacking glands 4
4 a. Plant with a subterranean tuber; stipules persistent; inflorescence racemose .... *B. gracilis*
b. Plant lacking a subterranean tuber; stipules deciduous; inflorescence cymose .... *B. boissieri*

Begonia grandis Dryander (PLATES 103–106)
section *Diploclinium*, tuberous group
Transactions of the Linnean Society of London 1: 163 (1791)
Synonyms: *B. evansiana* Andrews; *B. grandis* subsp. *evansiana* (Andrews) Irmscher; *B. discolor* R. Brown

Erect tuberous perennial to about 75 cm tall, usually bearing bulbils in the leaf axils. Stem yellowish green with red nodes, hairless, unbranched or few-branched. **Stipules** deciduous, ovate-triangular, ovate, or elliptic, 1.5–2 × 0.6–1 cm. **Leaves: petiole** yellowish green with a red tinge, especially toward the two ends, hairless, 1–25 cm long, joining blade at an angle; **blade** above green to bronze-green, often with red veins, hairless to sparsely hairy, rarely densely hairy, beneath red to green, usually hairy only on the main veins, asymmetric, triangular-ovate to ovate or broadly ovate, 5–25 × 3–22 cm, apex acuminate, base cordate, margin slightly undulate, shallowly double-toothed, veins palmate-pinnate. **Inflorescence:** terminal, a leafy, one-sided racemose structure usually consisting of two to four few-flowered bisexual cymes; flowers fragrant; **bracts** deciduous, transversely ovate to transversely elliptic or almost circular, concave and cleft at the apex, 10–16 × 15–25 mm. **Male flowers: tepals** four, pink or occasionally white, outer pair oblong-ovate to broadly ovate, 0.8–2 × 0.7–1.9 cm, inner pair oblanceolate to obovate, 0.6–1.5 × 0.4–1.3 cm; **stamens** numerous, arranged in a symmetric or asymmetric mass on top of a column formed from the fused filaments, anther connectives not projecting. **Female flowers: bracteoles** absent; **tepals** usually three, rarely five, same color as males, outer two or four broadly ovate, 1.5–2 × 1.8–2.3 cm, inner one broadly obovate, 0.5–1.1 × 0.2–1 cm; **ovary** same color as tepals, narrowly ellipsoid, 0.7–1.6 × 0.4–0.7 cm, unequally three-winged and wings triangular, or occasionally with one long triangular wing and two rib-like wings, three-locular, **placentae** axile, bifid; **styles** three, once-branched and stigmas in a spiraled band, or styles unbranched and stigmas in a kidney- to crescent-shaped band. **2n** = 26.

In a genus that is almost entirely restricted to the tropical and subtropical regions of the world, *Begonia grandis* is an anomaly. It inhabits the temperate parts of China and is even found in the forested hills to the far north of Beijing. This unique distribution means that *B. grandis* is the only begonia adapted to live in areas experiencing prolonged periods below freezing. For that reason gardeners refer to it as the hardy begonia, an apt name, for at Brooklyn Botanic Garden it routinely survives winter temperatures down to 19°F (–7°C). The species' ability to survive the cold is due, at least in part, to the fact that it becomes dormant each winter, when it survives as resting tubers. Still it is not the only member of the genus to go dormant in winter and so must also have a further survival mechanism not found in other begonias. A few less hardy but still cold-tolerant begonias from high elevations in Asia and South America are also cultivated and may be grown in gardens experiencing only slight frosts. One from China, a relative of *B. grandis*, is poised to take the gardeneing world by storm. This is *B. taliensis* (Plate 107), which horticulturist Eric Hammond collected for Heronswood Nursery while in Sichuan Province. The species has sharply lobed leaves mottled with silver and dark purple and attractive pink flowers. I am told that it is hardy in Heronswood Nursery's display garden in the Pacific Northwest, an area noted for its mild climate. Discussions of other cold-tolerant begonias are under *B. formosana* and *B. veitchii*.

As the only truly frost-hardy member of its genus, *Begonia grandis* obviously has enormous horticultural potential. The ancient Chinese recognized this and first introduced it into cultivation several hundred years ago. They particularly valued the subtle beauty of the species' flowers and the fact that they are produced in the late summer and early autumn when relatively few other garden plants are at their best. In China the species is commonly known as Qiuhaitang, or "the autumn crab apple," and numerous folktales exist in which this plant is a symbol of virtue or forsaken love. One legend tells how the species first originated when a woman, deserted by her lover, watered the ground with her tears, and in response the plant grew up in order to console her. The beauty of this species has also been captured in several art forms, including pottery and banners dating back to at least the Ming Dynasty (1368–1644). *Begonia grandis* was introduced to Japanese gardens in 1641, where the first westerner saw it roughly fifty years later. That westerner was German physician Engelbert Kaempfer, whose observations of seventeenth-century Japan have given us one of the best snapsnots into the history of that country. The species was not introduced to Europe, however, until 1804, when it was sent to Kew Gardens.

Soon after its discovery by western gardeners and botanists, *Begonia grandis* was described under a plethora of scientific names, causing a great deal of subsequent confusion. These descriptions were based on plants collected in cultivation both in Japan (for example, *B. grandis*) and China (for example, *B. evansiana*, *B. grandis* subsp. *evansiana*, and *B. discolor*), as well as from the wild (for example, *B. sinensis* and *B. grandis* subsp. *sinensis*). The *Begonia* taxonomist Edgar Irmscher attempted to rectify this confusing situation when in 1939 he developed a new system of naming these plants, which was loosely based on the military system of ranks. The wider botanical community never adopted Irmscher's system, but later taxonomic treatments did accept a new subspecies that he recognized, *B. grandis* subsp. *holostyla*.

Clearly this confusion over the naming of these plants needs to be clarified. The most logical recourse seems to be the recognition of a single species composed of three subspecies: *Begonia grandis* subsp. *grandis* has long been cultivated in China and Japan and is known only from cultivation; *B. grandis* subsp. *sinensis* is the wild progenitor of the cultivated subspecies and grows wild in China from Yunnan to Hebei; and lastly *B. grandis* subsp. *holostyla* grows wild only in south and west Yunnan and southwest Sichuan and is a relatively recent introduction to western gardens. The names *B. evansiana*, *B. grandis* subsp. *evansiana*, and *B. discolor* should all be treated as synonyms of *B. grandis* subsp. *grandis* since they are more recent names for that plant.

Key to the subspecies of *Begonia grandis*

1 a. Stamens arranged in an asymmetric cluster; styles entire with the stigmas in a kidney- to crescent-shaped band at their apex ...... *B. grandis* subsp. *holostyla*

b. Stamens arranged in a symmetric cluster; styles branched with the stigmas arranged in a spiraled band around the two branches 2

2 a. Plant relatively stout, leaves broadly ovate, 9–25 × 8–22 cm, undersurfaces of blade usually red, male outer tepals 1.8–2 × 1.6–1.9 cm, stamen column 4–8 mm tall .... *B. grandis* subsp. *grandis*

b. Plant relatively slender, leaves triangular-ovate to ovate, 5–20 × 3–13 cm, undersurfaces of blade usually green, male outer tepals ca. 0.8 × 0.6 cm, stamen column 0.6–2 mm tall .... *B. grandis* subsp. *sinensis*

All three subspecies are in cultivation, but the plants most commonly seen in gardens belong to *Begonia grandis* subsp. *grandis*. This subspecies appears to have long ago been artificially selected in Chinese gardens from wild populations of *B. grandis* subsp. *sinensis* and differs from these wild plants in several characteristics, which are listed above in the key. These enhancements make for a more garden-worthy plant. Both pink- and white-flowered forms are in cultivation, but the pink-flowered ones are by far the most common.

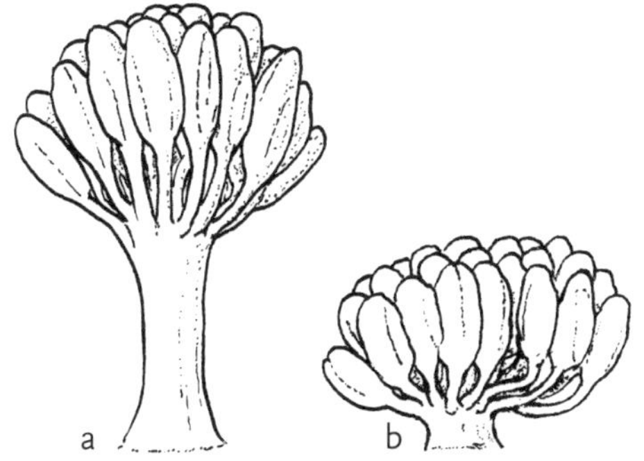

Comparison of stamen arrangements of **a**) *B. grandis* subsp. *grandis* and **b**) subsp. *holostyla*.

Begonia grandis is best planted in a well-drained position outdoors but can also be grown in a cool greenhouse. In most outdoor situations it should be planted in dappled light because its leaves can become scorched under the bright summer sun and will look messy by the time the flowers open. *Begonia grandis* looks its best in situations that allow the low autumn sun to shine through the backs of its leaves, causing them to glow red. The fragrant flowers of *B. grandis* subsp. *grandis* are likewise one of the joys of autumn.

Few hybrids involving *Begonia grandis* have been reported in the literature. This is surprising given that it is the only truly cold-tolerant member of its genus and could potentially be of enormous value in breeding cold-tolerant hybrid cultivars. Fotsch (1939) notes that a breeder by the name of Svahn made the cross *B. grandis* × *B. rex* in the 1870s to produce the still popular hybrid *B.* 'Abel Carriere'. *Begonia* 'Amesbury's Dipetala' is a little known *B. dipetala* × *B. grandis* subsp. *grandis* cross.

Begonia modestiflora (syn. *B. yunnanensis*) is a very closely related species to *B. grandis*, with a similar vegetative habit and racemose inflorescence, but with a more western distribution within Asia. It is only occasionally cultivated and is separated from *B. grandis* by its more compact inflorescence with peduncles that are shorter than their subtending bracts. Another close relative from China, *B. asperifolia*, was collected in 1999 and released commercially a few years later. It produces generous inflorescences of pink flowers.

Begonia guaduensis Kunth (PLATE 108)

section *Ruizopavonina*, shrub-like group

in Humboldt, Bonpland, and Kunth, *Nova Genera et Species Plantarum* 7: 178 (1825)

Erect subshrub with scrambling stems to 2 m tall. Stems branched, red to reddish brown or green, hairless. **Stipules** deciduous to persistent, ovate to oblong-ovate, 8–12 × 2.5–5 mm. **Leaves:** distichous; **petiole** red, hairless, 0.2–3 cm long, continuing straight into main vein of blade; **blade** above green, beneath paler green or burgundy, both surfaces hairless, asymmetric, oblong to elliptic-oblong, 5–11.5 × 2–4.5 cm, apex acuminate, base unequal, rounded, margin sharply toothed and ciliate, veins pinnate. **Inflorescence:** pseudo-terminal and axillary, many-flowered, bisexual, cymose; **bracts** deciduous to persistent, ovate to lanceolate, 0.4–1.6 × 0.2–0.8 cm. **Male flowers: tepals** two or four, white to pink, outer pair elliptic-ovate to elliptic, 1.1–1.6 × 0.7–1.3 cm, inner pair narrowly elliptic, 0.5–1.1 × 0.2–0.4 cm; **stamens** numerous, arranged symmetrically, anther connectives projecting. **Female flowers: bracteoles** paired at base of ovary, ovate to narrowly obovate, 2.5–6 × 1.5–3 mm; **tepals** five, same color as males, ovate to elliptic, outer pair slightly shorter than the others, 6–10 × 5–8 mm; **ovary** green, often with a red tinge especially on the wings, ovoid, ellipsoid, or obovoid, 0.4–0.9 × 0.2–0.5 cm, unequally three-winged, three-locular, **placentae** axile, bifid; **styles** three, twice-branched at base and each branch with three to four short branches, stigmas in a spiraled band. **2n** = ca. 104.

Begonia guaduensis is a common species in the wild that is widely distributed in Amazonian Brazil, Surinam, Guyana, Ecuador, Venezuela, Colombia, and possibly Panama. In the wild it occurs in a variety of habitats and has been reported growing on the forest floor, upon rocks in damp forests, upon sandstone cliffs, and in coffee plantations. Usually it is found scrambling up other vegetation at an altitude of 300–1800 m. The species is distinct from most other cultivated begonias but is easily confused with the closely related *B. holtonis* (Plate 109), *B. estrellensis*, and *B. meridensis* (Plate 110). Plate 108 shows a comparison of the leaves of these three species. *Begonia holtonis* is the most similar to *B. guaduensis*. The biggest difference between them is that the female flowers of *B. guaduensis* have many-branched styles and elliptic tepals, but the styles of *B. holtonis* are once-branched and its tepals narrowly obovate. Vegetatively the species are more difficult to distinguish, but they can usually be separated on the basis of their leaf outline. *Begonia holtonis* has elliptic leaf blades, and those of *B. guaduensis* are usually oblong. Furthermore, *B. guaduensis* usually has more hairs between the teeth on its leaf margin. *Begonia estrellensis* is distinguished by its leaf blades that are elliptic to ovate-elliptic and that have a long acuminate apex and entire, denticulate margins. Of these four species *B. estrellensis* alone has female flowers with two to three tepals. *Begonia meridensis* is identified by its leaf blades being broadly ovate with acute apices and by its usually more numerous-flowered inflorescences.

Begonia guaduensis and its relatives are readily cultivated under standard conditions. Nevertheless, none are widely grown, being largely restricted to specialist collections. No hybrids of *B. guaduensis* or its closest relatives have been reported in the literature.

Begonia hatacoa D. Don (PLATE 111)

section *Platycentrum*, rhizomatous group

Prodromus Florae Nepalensis 223 (1825)

Synonyms: *B. rubrovenia* W. J. Hooker; *B. rubronervia* Klotzsch

Rhizomatous perennial with a short, erect, leafy flowering-stem. Stem to 35 cm tall, pinkish green with white lenticels or reddish brown. **Stipules** persistent, triangular-lance-shaped, 1.5–2.2 × 0.8–1.5 cm. **Leaves:** often held upright; **petiole** green with a pink tinge, densely covered with minute rust-colored hairs, 1.5–21 cm long, continuing straight into main vein of blade; **blade** above green, green with silver spots, bronze-green, or silver, hairless, beneath pale green or burgundy with minute rust-colored hairs on veins, elsewhere hairless, asymmetric, narrowly ovate, 7.5–22 × 2–9 cm, apex acuminate, base shallowly cordate to almost truncate, margin with short sharp teeth at the end of the veins when young but often becoming entire with maturity, occasionally with very short lobes, veins palmate-pinnate. **Inflorescence:** terminal and axillary, produced on a short, erect, leafy shoot, few-flowered, bisexual or only male, short-branched, cymose; **bracts** deciduous, ovate, 0.5–1.8 × 1.3–1.4 cm. **Male flowers: tepals** four, upper segment of outer pair dull greenish white with red veins and a thin white margin, concave, thick, lower segment of outer pair pale green with red-flushed veins, thick, both ovate, 0.8–1 × 0.4–0.9 cm, inner pair dull white, thinner than outer segments, elliptic to obovate, 0.6–1.1 × 0.4–0.6 cm; **stamens** about 50–75, arranged symmetrically and attached to a short column, anther connectives projecting. **Female flowers: bracteoles** absent; **tepals** five, dull white with green or red-tinged veins, outermost segments red-tinged on veins, narrowly obovate to narrowly obovate-elliptic to narrowly rectangular-elliptic to narrowly rectangular-obovate, 0.7–1.2 × 0.4–0.7 cm, apex of outer segments rounded, apex of inner segments cleft; **ovary** nodding, pale green with red-tinged veins on lower two wings and lower portion of upper wing, asymmetric-obovoid, three-winged, one wing much longer than the others, two-locular, **placentae** axile, bifid; **styles** two, once-branched, stigmas in a spiraled band. **2n** = 22.

Thomas Booth collected *Begonia hatacoa* in Bhutan in the early 1850s and introduced it into cultivation in England via the nursery of his uncle, Thomas Nuttall. Shortly afterward, the plant was described and illustrated in tab. 4689 of *Curtis's Botanical Magazine* under the name *B. rubro-venia* W. J. Hooker, a name that is currently considered a synonym of *B. hatacoa*. The name *B. hatacoa* was first published by David Don in 1825 based on herbarium material collected in Nepal. *Begonia hatacoa* is readily identified by its combination of narrowly ovate leaves that are usually held upright, female flowers with two styles and two locular ovaries, and male and female flowers with tepals that are white with red veins. The species as originally described has green leaf blades, but variants exist with blades that are either green with white spots (*B. hatacoa* 'Spotted', Plate 111, right) or silver (*B. hatacoa* 'Silver'). All three variants are widely grown and available through commercial sources.

Begonia hatacoa is readily cultivated in a terrarium or humid greenhouse. Propagation is usually by division or by seed. *Begonia hatacoa* is the parent of a small number of named hybrid cultivars. Examples include *B.* 'Regal Minuet' (*B.* Rex-cultorum group × *B. hatacoa*) and *B.* 'Spanish Lace' (*B.* Rex-cultorum group × *B. hatacoa*).

The Himalayan *Begonia nepalensis* and *B. griffithiana* (syn. *B. episcopalis*) look similar to *B. hatacoa* but differ by having ovaries with a single wing. The former species is the more widely grown, but neither is common in cultivation. *Begonia nepalensis* has an unbranched stem, which is hairless in the upper part, and male flowers with two tepals; *B. griffithiana* has a branched stem, which is hairy in the upper part, and male flowers with four tepals. *Begonia pavonina* (Plate 93) is also somewhat similar to *B. hatacoa* and is well worth growing because its foliage can develop a beautiful iridescent sheen when the species is appropriately situated in a shady, humid position. In the wild variants with mid-green and very dark green leaves exist, both of which have a bluish sheen to their leaves. *Begonia pavonina* is very free flowering and has attractive pink tepals. When this Malaysian species was originally described it was said to differ from all the other members of the section *Platycentrum* in having entire placentae. However, plants of *B. pavonina* with bifid placentae also exist. In fact this is the case in all the cultivated examples that I have observed.

Begonia hemsleyana J. D. Hooker (PLATE 112)

section *Platycentrum*, rhizomatous group
Curtis's Botanical Magazine 125: pl. 7685 (1899)

Creeping rhizomatous perennial bearing erect, slender, leafy flowering-stems to about 25 cm tall. **Stipules** persistent, lanceolate to ovate, 12–17 × 5–7 mm. **Leaves: petiole** pink with short wooly hairs, 4–15 cm long; **blade** above glossy green, sparsely hairy between veins, beneath paler green with a burgundy tinge, sparsely hairy on veins, palmately compound, 5–10-lobed, lobes stalked, stalks 0.8–2.3 cm long, lobes angular-obovate, 3.5–13 × 1.2–4 cm, apex acute to acuminate, base wedge-shaped, margin toothed. **Inflorescence:** axillary, few-flowered, bisexual, cymose; flowers fragrant; **bracts** deciduous, ovate to obovate, 0.5–1.6 × 0.3–0.6 cm. **Male flowers: tepals** four, pink, outer pair ovate, 8–20 × 5–15 mm, inner pair obovate, 0.7–1.8 × 0.6–0.9 cm; **stamens** numerous, arranged in a symmetric mass on top of a column, anther connectives projecting. **Female flowers: bracteoles** absent; **tepals** five, pink, elliptic, 1.5–1.6 × 0.6–0.8 cm; **ovary** green with reddish tinged wings, asymmetric-obovoid, 6–8 × 3–5 mm, unequally three-winged, one wing much longer than the others, **placentae** axile, bifid; **styles** three, once-branched, stigmas in a spiraled band. **2n** = 22.

Begonia hemsleyana is one of only a few begonias with palmately compound leaves. It is also unusual in having ovaries with two locules and two styles, and consequently is readily identified. The species is distributed in the wild from northern Burma to the Chinese province of Yunnan. Throughout its range the species grows in moist upland forests. Ernest Henry first introduced *B. hemsleyana* to Kew Gardens in 1899 from seed he collected near the hill town of Mengtse, in southern Yunnan. Joseph Hooker, who was then the garden's director, named the species in honor of William Hemsley, who worked on Chinese plants at Kew. It was not named after its collector since Hemsley had already named a Chinese *Begonia* after him!

Begonia hemsleyana is an attractive, commonly grown species that can be a little tricky in cultivation. It naturally produces several short, closely spaced stems and as a result can suffer from botrytis and other diseases associated with poor air circulation. For this reason, a beneficial practice is to thin its inner stems to promote good air circulation within the plant. Because this species naturally grows at high elevations it prefers relatively cool temperatures in the range of 62 to 65°F (16–18°C). The potting mix should also be allowed to dry out slightly between watering. *Begonia hemsleyana* has been crossed with a few members of the closely related *B.* Rex-cultorum group. The most popular result is *B.* 'Raspberry Swirl'. A recently introduced spotted-leaved variant of *B. hemsleyana* (Plate 112) is currently being grown under the American Begonia Society's code U404.

Two relatives of *Begonia hemsleyana* with deeply palmate leaves are also occasionally cultivated. Dan Hinkley of Heronswood Nursery collected one of them, *B. pedatifida*, at 914 m on Emei Shan in China's Sichuan Province in 1998, and so far this species has proven hardy outdoors at this Washington State nursery. It has green leaves with narowly ovate to ovate-lanceolate lobes and white flowers. The other plant, *B. circumlobata*, has been in cultivation much longer, having been introduced in the 1940s. It was collected further south in China at an altitude of 365–518 m and is therefore not cold-hardy. Nevertheless, if this species can be obtained it is worth growing for its attractive leaves with large ovate-oblong lobes. Some have said, however, that it is a challenge.

Begonia heracleifolia Schlechtendal & Chamisso (PLATE 113)

section *Gireoudia*, rhizomatous group

Linnaea 5: 603 (1830)

Synonyms: *B. radiata* Graham; *B. tanacetifolia* Graham; *B. nigrescens* Otto; *B. jatrophifolia* Cels; *B. punctata* Link, Klotzsch & Otto; *B. trigonoptera* Sprague; *B. longipila* Lemaire; *B.* U039; *B.* U150

Creeping rhizomatous, branched perennial to 60 cm tall, internodes short, densely covered with long stiff white hairs and shorter, softer white hairs. **Stipules** persistent, asymmetric, ovate-triangular, 0.8–2 × 0.8–1.3 cm. **Leaves: petiole** green, sometimes tinged red with long dense hairs and a ring of hairs at the top of the petiole, 3.5–45 cm long, continuing straight into main vein of blade; **blade** above pale to dark green sometimes with black flecks, sometimes pale green along veins with sparse to dense long hairs, beneath dull burgundy, sometimes pale green along veins, hairy on the main veins, symmetric in flowering-sized plants, in outline almost circular, 4–26 × 3–24 cm, base broadly, shallowly cordate to broadly, deeply cordate, margin five- to nine-lobed, the lobes usually one-third to four-fifths the blade length, often secondarily lobed, margin of lobes toothed, ciliate, veins palmate. **Inflorescence:** axillary, many-flowered, asymmetric, bisexual, cymose; flowers fragrant; **bracts** persistent, ovate to narrowly ovate, 0.9–2.3 × 0.9–2.7 cm. **Male flowers: tepals** two, white to pale or deep pink, transversely elliptic to almost circular, or ovate to ovate-elliptic or oblong, 0.6–1.5 × 0.6–1.2 cm; **stamens** about 13–25, arrangement resembling a bunch of bananas, anther connectives not or shortly projecting. **Female flowers: bracteoles** absent or rarely present and paired beneath ovary, ovate to elliptic or obovate, 2–5 × 1.5–3 mm; **tepals** two, same color as males, ovate to broadly elliptic or almost circular, 5–12 × 5–12 mm; **ovary** green, ovoid to oblong or broadly ellipsoid, unequally three-winged, three-locular, **placentae** axile, bifid; **styles** three, once-branched, stigmas in a spiraled band. **2n** = 28.

Begonia heracleifolia was the first rhizomatous begonia with palmate-lobed leaves known to Europeans, having been discovered in the 1830s by plant hunter Ferdinand Deppe and physician C. J. Scheide near Mexico City. *Begonia heracleifolia* is widely distributed in the wild from the Mexican states of Durango and Tamaulipas south to Honduras. I have seen it in Mexico on several occasions, and it is particularly easy to observe in the vicinity of the Mayan pyramids at Palenque in the state of Chiapas, where it grows on the ground, on the pyramids, and on the trunks of trees. In the Mexican state of Puebla the species is reportedly grown in coffee plantations and the petioles harvested for food. *Begonia heracleifolia* is extremely variable in leaf size, shape, and color and a number of these variants have previously been described as distinct species or varieties. Several different collections have been brought into cultivation. A clone with particularly attractive leaf coloration is on display at the United States Botanic Garden in Washington, D.C. Following Kathleen Burt-Utley's taxonomic treatment of *B. heracleifolia*, these variants are considered here to be part of the general variation of the species. *Begonia heracleifolia* is easily recognized by its combination of creeping habit, petioles with long hairs, and symmetric, palmately lobed leaves. The species name refers to the fact that its leaves somewhat resemble those of certain European *Heracleum*, or hog-weed, species.

Begonia heracleifolia is commonly grown as a foliage plant and is readily cultivated under standard conditions but sometimes becomes dormant for long periods of time. The species usually flowers between November and April. Hybridizers have used *B. heracleifolia* ever since it was first introduced into cultivation in the early 1800s. The cultivar *B.* 'Ricinifolia' is a hybrid created in 1847 between *B. heracleifolia* and *B. barkeri* and appears to have been the earliest cultivar in the genus to be named. *Begonia* 'Pseudophyllomaniaca' is probably a cross between *B. heracleifolia* and *B. incarnata* and again is one of the older hybrids still grown. Other noteworthy cultivars include *B.* 'Bow Nigra' (*B. bowerae* × *B. heracleifolia*), *B.* 'Crestabruchii' (*B. manicata* 'Crispa' × *B. heracleifolia* 'Sunderbruchii'), and *B.* 'Fuscomaculata' (*B. heracleifolia* × *B. strigillosa*). The popular *B.* 'Texastar' also owes its star-shaped leaves to its *B. heracleifolia* parentage.

Begonia herbacea Vellozo (PLATE 115)

section *Trachelocarpus*, rhizomatous group
Florae Fluminensis Icones 10: t. 53 (1831)

Epiphytic perennial with a short, branched rhizome. **Stipules** persistent, ovate-triangular, 0.6–1.4 × 0.3–0.6 cm, margin ciliate, main vein projecting. **Leaves: petiole** absent to 2.5 cm long, when present green, hairless, continuing straight into main vein of blade; **blade** above glossy green, hairless, beneath paler green, hairless, symmetric, oblanceolate, 5–28 × 1–5 cm, apex acute to acuminate, base tapering gradually into the petiole when petiole present, margin slightly wavy, sparsely ciliate-toothed, veins pinnate. **Inflorescence:** axillary, unisexual; flowers fragrant; male inflorescence with a 2–5 cm long stalk, few-flowered, cymose; female flowers more or less stalkless, solitary; **bracts** of male and female flowers persistent, broadly ovate to almost circular, 3–5 × 2–3 mm, margin ciliate. **Male flowers: tepals** two, white, circular, 0.4–1 × 0.5–0.9 cm; **stamens** about 20–40, arranged in a symmetric mass on top of a column formed from the fused filaments, anther connectives projecting. **Female flowers: bracteoles** absent; **tepals** three, white, ovate, 7–12 × 4–8 mm; **ovary** narrowly ovoid, 7–11 × 2–5 mm, with a distinct beak to 1.5 cm long, equally three-winged, wings narrow, three-locular, **placentae** axile, entire; **styles** three, once-branched, stigmas in a spiraled band. **2n** = 56.

Begonia section *Trachelocarpus*, in which *B. herbacea* is classified, is one of the most distinctive and easily recognized sections in the genus. It is restricted to the montane forests of eastern Brazil and all of its included species are rhizomatous epiphytes with narrow, symmetric leaves and distinct inflorescences, the female flowers being more or less stalkless and solitary, while the male inflorescences are stalked and few-flowered. Despite few species having ever been classified in this section, the taxonomy of the group has been plagued with difficulties almost since the first species were described. Most of the problems stem from the fact that few adequate type specimens exist for the group. This problem is particularly prevalent with the cultivated members, which are largely typified by rather fanciful eighteenth-century artwork. Because of this problem, many authors have confused the two most commonly cultivated members of the section, *B. lanceolata* (Plate 114) and *B. herbacea* (Plate 115). Particularly misleading is that Vellozo's illustration of the type of *B. herbacea* is shown with scalloped leaf margins—this characteristic is more usually found in *B. lanceolata*. Nevertheless, the short descriptions that accompany the original type illustrations inform us that the species with elliptic leaves and sometimes-scalloped margins should be named *B. lanceolata*, and the plant with oblanceolate leaf blades and entire margins should be called *B. herbacea*. Unfortunately, just the opposite is how these species are currently recognized in most horticultural works. The former species was named *lanceolata* (rather than *elliptica*) because when it was described, the word *lanceolate* referred to the shape that we now call elliptic. Also somewhat confusing is the continued sporadic recognition of *B. attenuata* and *B. rhizocarpa* as distinct species; these names are synonymous with *B. lanceolata* and *B. depauperata*, respectively. Another member of the group, *B. fulvo-setulosa* (Plate 116), is often unnamed or wrongly named *B. olsoniae* in cultivation.

Begonia herbacea and its relatives require a humid environment and are best grown mounted on bark or cork in a greenhouse. Lacking a greenhouse I grow *B. herbacea* and *B. lanceolata* under bright artificial lights in a sealed terrarium, where they are planted in an open, fibrous mix and grown attached to a log. At the New

York Botanical Garden *B. lanceolata* is grown mounted on a large, dead tree branch in a particularly humid greenhouse and in this situation is very happy.

Key to the species of section *Trachelocarpus*

1 a. Leaves hairy on both surfaces . . . . *B. fulvo-setulosa*
   b. Leaves hairless on both surfaces 2
2 a. Leaves green, never with silver spots, oblanceolate, gradually merging into the petiole . . . . *B. herbacea*
   b. Leaves, blade green, often with silver spots, elliptic, base wedge-shaped to rounded; petiole distinct from blade 3
3 a. Leaf base wedge-shaped . . . . *B. lanceolata*
   b. Leaf base rounded . . . . *B. depauperata*

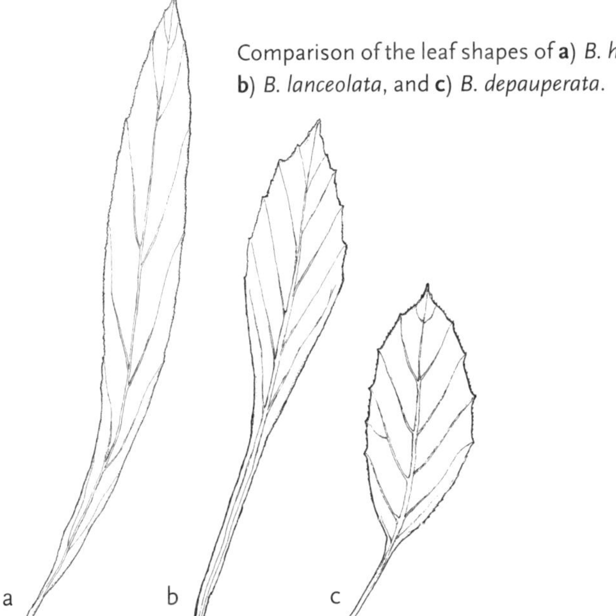

Comparison of the leaf shapes of **a**) *B. herbacea*, **b**) *B. lanceolata*, and **c**) *B. depauperata*.

Begonia hirtella Link (PLATE 117)

section *Duratometra*, Semperflorens group

Enumeratio Plantarum Horti Regii Berolinensis Altera 2: 396 (1822)

Erect branched annual 5–90 cm tall. Stem red with sparse to dense hairs, hairs up to 3 mm long. **Stipules** tardily deciduous, ovate, 0.6–1.5 × 0.2–0.6 mm. **Leaves:**

petiole pale pink with dense soft hairs, 1.4–8.5 cm long, joining blade at an angle; **blade** above green with a red spot where the petiole joins the blade, beneath paler green, sparsely hairy on veins or occasionally hairy throughout, asymmetric, ovate to transversely ovate, 3–10 × 1.5–8 cm, apex acute to acuminate, base shallowly cordate to almost truncate, veins palmate. **Inflorescence:** axillary, few-flowered, cymose; **bracts** persistent, linear to oblong or ovate, 1–3 × ca. 1 mm, margin laciniate. **Male flowers: tepals** four, white with a red tinge, outer pair ovate to almost circular, 2–8 × 2–6 mm, inner pair linear-oblong, 1–4 × 0.5–2 mm; **stamens** about 5–20, arranged asymmetrically, anther connectives projecting. **Female flowers: bracteoles** deciduous, elliptic to almost spatula-shaped, 3.5–4 mm long, margin ciliate; **tepals** five, same color as males, unequal, ovate to ovate-oblong, 2–4 × 1–2 mm; **ovary** whitish green, ovoid to ellipsoid, 4–8 × 2–5 mm, unequally three-winged, three-locular, **placentae** axile, bifid; **styles** three, once-branched, stigmas in a spiraled band. **2n** = 34.

Begonia hirtella is a widely distributed native of the West Indies and northern South America. It is commonly found in disturbed areas in a wide variety of habitats, from roadsides to tropical rain forests, and grows directly upon the ground, upon rocks, and as an epiphyte. The species was one of the first begonias to enter cultivation in Europe and was described from material cultivated at the Berlin Botanical Garden in 1822. Since this time it has unwittingly been introduced into several tropical areas as a garden escape. On Sri Lanka it has naturalized to such an extent that it has become the commonest species of *Begonia* on that island. It is equally common in Hawaii, an island group that has no native members of the genus *Begonia*, but which is home to the sole representative of the related genus *Hillebrandia*, as well as three introduced members of *Begonia*: *B. hirtella*, *B. foliosa*, and *B. reniformis*. I have seen it growing along a streamside on Oahu and it certainly looked at home there among the other introduced plant species, which have largely displaced the native flora of this tropical island. *Begonia hirtella* and other members of the section *Doratometra* are very unusual among begonias in that they are annuals. Other cultivated members of the section are: *B. filipes*, *B. humilis*, and *B. wallichiana*. One of these, *B. humilis*, has been in cultivation even longer than *B. hirtella*, having been introduced into cultivation at Kew Gardens around 1791, a time when gardeners knew of only a handful of begonias.

The members of the section *Doratometra* have a curious arrangement of flowers that facilitates self-pollination and enables them to succeed as annuals. The male flowers are positioned directly above the female flowers so that pollen can fall onto the stigmas of the female flowers and bring about seed set. Self-pollination is advantageous for these plants since it enables them to rapidly colonize newly disturbed habitats. Like other annuals, they produce lots of seed and have a quick life cycle, allowing them to grow and set a new batch of seed before their open habitats become overgrown by more aggressive, longer-lived yet slower to establish plants. As such, these weeds have evolved a colonist's lifestyle, constantly moving from place to place wherever bare or disturbed ground presents itself. They are, of course, doing well in these times of wide scale destruction of the world's rain forest. Nevertheless, they would have originally evolved this vagrant lifestyle to take advantage of gaps created in the forest by tropical storms and other similar phenomena.

Begonia hirtella and its close relatives are easy to grow under standard conditions and can even become a nuisance in a greenhouse if they are allowed to seed themselves into other potted plants. Because they are annuals they will need propagating from seed each year, although in my experience this is hardly necessary since it is usually easier to transplant rogue seedlings into their own pots. Few hybrid cultivars of these annuals have been produced. *Begonia* 'Bimpe', a *B. wallichiana* × *B.* 'Lucille Rolf' cross, may be the only one that is widely grown.

Key to the cultivated species of section *Doratometra*

1 a. Bracteoles absent; ovary wings equal, semicircular . . . . *B. wallichiana*
b. Bracteoles present, but deciduous; ovary wings usually unequal, more or less triangular 2
2 a. Stem sparsely to densely covered with long hairs; leaf blade often shallowly lobed and toothed, teeth more or less blunt . . . . *B. hirtella*
b. Stem hairless; leaf blade not shallowly lobed, teeth sharp and forward pointing 3
3 a. Male flowers with four tepals; largest ovary wing less than twice as tall as wide . . . . *B. humilis*
b. Male flowers with two tepals; largest ovary wing at least twice as tall as wide . . . . *B. filipes*

Begonia hispida Schott (PLATE 118)

section *Pritzelia*, shrub-like group
in Sprengel, *Systema Vegetabilium* 4: 407 (1827)

Erect branched subshrub to 2 m tall. Stem woody at the base, green to brown with short purple bands above each node, the whole plant with dense hairs. **Stipules** persistent, ovate, 0.6–2 × 0.4–1.4 cm. **Leaves: petiole** with dense matted hairs and sometimes a few small flattened hairs spaced along the petiole, particularly in the upper one-quarter, 4–19 cm long, joining blade at an angle; **blade** above green, hairy, and sometimes with small adventitious leaflets, beneath paler green to purple, hairs especially dense on main veins, asymmetric, ovate, 7–20 × 4–15 cm, apex abruptly short acuminate, base cordate, margin shallowly scallop-lobed, lobes shallowly toothed, veins palmate. **Inflorescence:** axillary, several- to many-flowered, bisexual, cymose; **bracts** persistent, ovate to ovate-lanceolate, 0.3–1.7 cm × 1.5–4 mm. **Male flowers: tepals** four, white or sometimes pink-tinged, outer pair broadly ovate, 6–7 × 4–7 mm, outer surface hairy, inner pair obovate, 5–7 × 3.5–5 mm; **stamens** numerous, arranged symmetrically, anther connectives projecting. **Female flowers: bracteoles** two, staggered beneath the ovary, and elliptic, 1–2 × ca. 1 mm, margin ciliate; **tepals** five, same color as males, ovate, elliptic or almost circular, outer surface hairy, slightly unequal, 4–10 × 4–8 mm; **ovary** hairy, ovoid to ellipsoid, 3–7 × 3–4.5 mm, unequally three-winged, one wing more than twice as long as the others, three-locular, **placentae** axile, entire; **styles** three, once-branched, stigmas in a spiraled band. **2n** = 56.

Begonia hispida is a native of the Atlantic Coastal Forests of Brazil, where it is common and widely distributed. It is reported to grow in particularly moist and shady areas in the forest. Two variants have been described: *B. hispida* var. *hispida*, which occurs in the wild and in cultivation, and *B. hispida* var. *cucullifera*, which is only known from cultivation. Edgar Irmscher described the latter in 1953 based on a plant cultivated at Hamburg Botanic Garden. Both varieties are large, densely hairy subshrubs with small white flowers. The name *hispida* means "with stiff hairs that are rough to the touch," a reference to the hairs that almost completely cover individuals of this species. *Begonia hispida* var. *cucullifera* is by far the most frequently cultivated of the two varieties. It is grown as a curiosity since it produces leaf-like appendages running along the upper surfaces of its leaf veins (Plate 118). These appendages differ from the true leaves in only minor details: they are usually cupped rather than flat, have pinnate rather than palmate veins, and they lack stipules. Unlike some *Begonia* species' true leaves they cannot be used to propagate new plants.

Both varieties of *Begonia hispida* are easily cultivated under standard conditions. Propagation is usually via stem cuttings. Two hybrids of *B. hispida* var. *cucullifera* are available commercially: *B.* 'Magic Carpet' (*B. metallica* × *B. hispida* var. *cucullifera*) and *B.* 'Quinebaug' (*B. scharffiana* × *B. hispida* var. *cucullifera*).

Begonia huegelii is a closely related species that is also from Brazil. It is similar in many respects to *B. hispida* var. *hispida*, but differs by its leaf blades, which by the time they are mature become almost hairless on their upper surfaces. The species is only occasionally cultivated. At least three named cultivars are grown: *B.*

'Rola-Y' is a *B. huegelii* × *B. metallica* cross, while *B.* 'Hugo' and *B.* 'Hugolette' are both said to be *B. huegelii* seedlings.

Begonia hydrocotylifolia W. J. Hooker (PLATE 119)

section *Gireoudia*, rhizomatous group
Curtis's Botanical Magazine 69: pl. 3968 (1843)

Creeping rhizomatous perennial to about 40 cm tall. Rhizome short and thick, pale brownish green with long wavy reddish brown hairs at the nodes. **Stipules** persistent, more or less triangular with the margins rolled inward, 0.8–1.1 × 0.9–1 cm. **Leaves: petiole** pale pink with sparse to dense, long, rust-colored, matted hairs, 1.8–11 cm long, joining blade at an angle; **blade** thick, above green, usually with a dark green border to the veins, in young leaves often covered with red hairs but becoming hairless, beneath pale red to green, sparsely hairy at base of veins to hairy throughout, symmetric, broadly kidney-shaped to almost circular, 2.5–7 × 3.3–8 cm, base cordate, margins shallowly angular-toothed with matted rust-colored hairs, veins palmate. **Inflorescence:** axillary, asymmetric, bisexual, cymose; **bracts** soon falling, obovoid-obtriangular, 0.8–1.1 × 0.8–1 cm, outer surface with long orangey brown hairs, margin toothed. **Male flowers: tepals** two, pale pink, broadly elliptic-obovate, 0.7–1 × 0.5–1 cm; **stamens** 15–20, arrangement resembling a bunch of bananas, anther connectives not projecting; **Female flowers: bracteoles** absent; **tepals** two, pale pink, elliptic to obovate, 0.5–0.9 × 0.6–1 cm; **ovary** pale green with pale pink wings, ellipsoid, 4–8 × 3–5.5 mm, almost equally three-winged, **placentae** axile, bifid; **styles** three, unbranched, widest at apex, stigmas crescent-shaped. **2n** = 28.

Begonia hydrocotylifolia appears to have been introduced into Berlin Botanical Garden from Mexico in the 1840s. Its name refers to the species' resemblance to pennywort (*Hydrocotyle vulgaris*), a native marshland plant of Europe and North Africa, although some American authors have instead likened this begonia to a miniature waterlily. *Begonia hydrocotylifolia* was crossed with *B. manicata* in Germany in 1845 producing *B.* 'Erythrophylla', the beefsteak begonia, one of the earliest hybrids still in cultivation. Karl Fotsch on page 236 of his book *Die Begonien* reports of this cultivar:

> In 1920, a Danish artist painted a picture of Paradise using among other plants *Begonia hydrocotylifolia* Hook. × *manicata* Brongn. (*Begonia* 'Feastii' [*B.* 'Erythrophylla']). This fact caused a florist to utter the following remark: "This begonia is from the new world." The artist, in answer to this remark, asked

whether the florist did not know where Paradise was situated, and whether it was not possible that the plants of all continents might grow there?

In the wild *Begonia hydrocotylifolia* grows on damp, steep rocks in rain forest in the Mexican state of Veracruz. Both pale- and dark-leaved variants exist in the wild and in cultivation.

Begonia hydrocotylifolia is readily grown under standard conditions. The species blooms mid winter and has long been a favorite of hybridizers. Commonly grown cultivars include *B.* 'Gertrude Nelson' (*B.* 'Lenore Olivier' × *B. hydrocotylifolia*), *B.* 'Question Mark' (*B. hydrocotylifolia* × *B.* 'Lenore Olivier'), and *B.* 'Rip van Winkle' (*B. hydrocotylifolia* × *B. carrieae*). *Begonia* 'Cathedral' is an unusual cultivar with leaves that resemble stained-glass windows. It arose as a seedling of *B.* 'Erythrophylla'. Steve Talnadge introduced this plant to the United States in the late 1960s from Australia, originally distributing it under the incorrect name of *B.* 'Cathedral Windows'. Though this mistake has since been corrected in the literature, plants are still occasionally grown under the incorrect name. *Begonia* 'Fiji Islands' is a curious mutation of *B.* 'Cathedral', which has smaller, crinkled leaves and flat, fused rhizomes.

Begonia imperialis Lemaire

section *Weilbachia*, rhizomatous group
Illustration Horticole 8: pl. 274 (1861)
Synonym: *B. imperialis* Lemaire var. *brunnea* Lemaire

Creeping rhizomatous perennial. Rhizomes shortly branched, brownish green, sparsely hairy. **Stipules** persistent, ovate to lanceolate-triangular, 0.9–1.3 × 0.5–0.8 cm. **Leaves: petiole** pale green to pale brown with dense short white hairs, 3.5–9 cm long, joining blade at an angle; **blade** above with numerous tiny cone-shaped protuberances each terminating in a small hair, velvet-green throughout, or green to olive-brown with paler green or pale-gray bands running along the main veins, beneath with small pits that correspond to the protuberances above, paler green, sometimes with darker green or brown markings corresponding to those above with dense short white hairs, asymmetric, ovate, 5–9 × 3.5–7.5 cm, apex abruptly short acuminate, base cordate, margin shallowly toothed and ciliate, veins palmate. **Inflorescence:** axillary, few-flowered, bisexual, cymose; **bracts** soon falling, elliptic, 2–9 × 0.5–7 mm. **Male flowers: tepals** two, white, hairy on outer or both surfaces, elliptic, 5–12 × 4–8 mm; **stamens** about 15–20, arrangement resembling a large bunch of bananas, anther connectives shortly projecting. **Female flowers: bracteoles** absent; **tepals** two, white, densely hairy on outer surface, elliptic, 5.5–13

× 0.3–10 mm; **ovary** green, asymmetric-oblong, 3–9 × 1.5–4 mm, unequally three-winged, two-locular, **placentae** axile, bifid; **styles** three, entire, stigmas crescent-shaped. **2n** = 28.

Begonia imperialis was first introduced into cultivation in Belgium in 1859. Its discoverer, M. Ghiesbreght, had found it growing wild in Mexico while on a collecting trip for Ambroise Verschaffelt's Nursery in Ghent. In the wild, the species occurs in limestone areas in the montane rain forests of the states of Oaxaca and Chiapas. The name *imperialis* means "showy" and refers to the beautifully variegated leaves that are characteristic of *B. imperialis* var. *imperialis*. The leaves of *B. imperialis* var. *smaragdina* lack variegation, but instead are a lush velvet-green throughout. This variety is less frequently cultivated than the typical species, possibly because it is slightly trickier to grow.

Begonia imperialis requires a humid atmosphere (85 percent humidity is ideal) and an open, fibrous growing medium. For this reason, it is often grown in an enclosed terrarium, but I have also frequently seen it happily growing in a humid greenhouse, suggesting that the species is not as difficult as some authors have suggested. Like several other very hairy begonias, this species resents water droplets on its leaves. *Begonia imperialis* has long been a favorite of hybridizers and has contributed its desirable leaf characteristics to more than 50 cultivars. The following outstanding cultivars are commercially available: *B.* 'Brown Jewel' (*B. pustulata* × *B. imperialis*), *B.* 'Emerald Jewel' (*B. imperialis* × *B. pustulata*), *B.* 'Meximperia' (*B. mexicana* × *B. imperialis*), *B.* 'Otto Foster (*B. imperialis* × *B.* Rex-cultorum group), and *B.* 'Silver Jewel' (*B. imperialis* × *B. pustulata*).

Begonia imperialis is classified in the Mexican and Central American section *Weilbachia* (Plates 120–122), which is distinguished by its combination of female flowers with two to four (but never five) tepals, and nodding, two-locular ovaries with bifid placentae and kidney-shaped stigmas. The section is unusual in that many of its members favor limestone habitats in the wild. It includes several cultivated species, of which *B. pustulata*, *B. turrialbae* (Plate 121), and *B. violifolia* are perhaps the most desirable. A key is provided here.

Key to the cultivated species of section *Weilbachia*

1 a. Plant non-rhizomatous, with an erect stem 2
  b. Plant with a creeping rhizome, lacking an erect stem 3
2 a. Margin of leaf blade with three to five deep-pointed lobes, upper surface of blade smooth . . . . *B. purpusii*
  b. Margin of leaf blade without lobes, upper surface of blade pustulate . . . . *B. alice-clarkiae*

3 a. Leaf blades pustulate 4
b. Leaf blades not pustulate 8
4 a. Tepals four in male flowers . . . . *B. turrialbae*
b. Tepals two in male flowers 5
5 a. Stamens 10–13 . . . . *B. violifolia*
b. Stamens 15–20 6
6 a. Leaf blade with large rounded pustules, hairy; flowers greenish white . . . . *B. pustulata*
b. Leaf blade with tiny conical pustules, densely hairy; flowers white 7
7 a. Leaf blade green to olive-brown with paler green or pale gray bands running along the main veins . . . . *B. imperialis* var. *imperialis*
b. Leaf blade velvety green . . . . *B. imperialis* var. *smaragdina*
8 a. Leaf blades lobed to deeply lobed . . . . *B. ludicra*
b. Leaf blades without lobes 9
9 a. Plant robust; leaf blade broadly ovate, more than 7 cm long . . . . *B. popenoei*
b. Plant diminutive; leaf blades narrowly ovate, less than 7 cm long . . *B. aridicaulis*

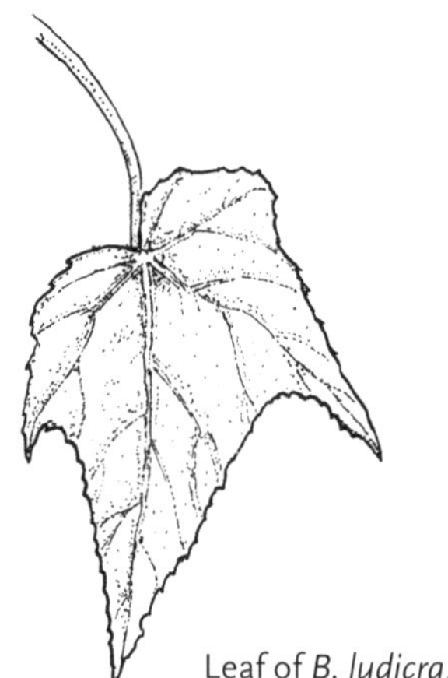

Leaf of *B. ludicra.*

Begonia incarnata Link & Otto (PLATE 123)
section *Knesebeckia*, shrub-like group
Icones Plantarum Rariorum 4: 37, pl. 19 (1829)

Erect branched perennial to 1 m tall. Stem mid green, tinged purple. **Stipules** persistent, narrowly triangular, 0.5–1.3 × 0.2–0.6 cm. **Leaves: petiole** mid green tinged purple, hairless, 1.5–6 cm long, joining blade at an angle; **blade** above mid to deep green with paler veins, hairless, beneath paler green with purple tinges between the veins, hairless, asymmetric, ovate, 3.5–14 × 1.5–6.5 cm, apex long acuminate, base cordate, margin sharply toothed with many small teeth and a few larger teeth, veins palmate. **Inflorescence:** axillary, few- to many-flowered, bisexual, cymose; flowers fragrant; **bracts** tardily deciduous, ovate, 0.8–1.2 × 0.3–0.6 cm. **Male flowers: tepals** four, pink, outer pair broadly ovate-cordate to broadly elliptic, 1.1–1.6 × 0.9–1.5 cm, inner pair narrowly obovate, 0.9–1.4 × 0.3–0.5 cm; **stamens** numerous, arranged symmetrically, filaments fused at base, anther connectives not projecting. **Female flowers: bracteoles** usually absent, when present paired beneath ovary, elliptic, 4–9 × 2–3 mm; **tepals** five, pink, ovate, slightly unequal, 0.6–1.1 × 0.3–0.9 cm; **ovary** pale green with a pink tinge, ellipsoid, 0.5–1.1 × 0.4–0.7 cm, unequally three-winged, three-locular, placentae axile, bifid; **styles** three, unbranched, stigmas in a horseshoe-shaped band.

Begonia incarnata is common in eastern Mexico, particularly in the state of Veracruz, where I have seen it on several occasions growing on moist, semi-shaded cliffs at an altitude of 1220–1370 m. In fact the species is so widespread in parts of Mexico that the petioles are collected and eaten as a vegetable. *Begonia incarnata* entered into cultivation when it was accidentally brought to Berlin Botanical Garden in soil attached to plants that Ferdinand Deppe had collected in Mexico. The garden's director, Heinrich Link, and its inspector, Friedrich Otto, jointly described it and a number of other begonias in 1829. The name *incarnata* means "flesh-colored" and probably refers to the species' pink flowers. *Begonia incarnata* produces copious blooms and is winter flowering.

Begonia incarnata can be grown under standard conditions and is readily propagated from stem cuttings or seed. Some horticulturists advise growing specimen plants anew from cuttings each spring. Hybridizers have long favored *B. incarnata*. Sometime prior to 1853 the species was crossed with *B. manicata* to produce *B.* 'Phyllomaniaca', one of the oldest cultivars still grown and an interesting plant with curious outgrowths erupting from its stems (Plate 124). Since the late 1800s *B. incarnata* has also been crossed with *B. socotrana* and members of the *Begonia* ×*tuberhybrida* group, but few of these are still grown and none are common. In 1884 M. Lionnet, while working for Arthur Mallet in France, crossed a member of the *B.* Rex-cultorum group with *B. incarnata* to produce the Mallet series of shrub-like hybrids, of which *B.* 'Arthur Mallet' and *B.* 'Tingley Mallet', two 1886 introductions, are popular more than 100 years later. Other commonly cultivated hybrids of *B. incarnata* include *B.* 'Florence Carrell' (*B. radicans* × *B. incarnata*), *B.* 'Inca Princess' (*B. incarnata* × *B. integerrima*), *B.* 'Luwalter' (*B. mazae* × *B. incarnata*), and the very popular *B.* 'Two Face' (*B. incarnata* × unknown parent).

Begonia integerrima Sprengel (PLATES 125 AND 126)
section *Solananthera*, trailing-scandent group
Neue Entdeckungen im Ganzen Umfang der Pflanzenkunde 2: 174 (1821)
Synonyms: *B. populnea* A. de Candolle; *B. solananthera* auct. non A. de Candolle

Climbing perennial with adventitious roots sometimes produced just below the nodes on the lowermost surface of stem. Stem usually branched to 1.5 m long, pale green or reddish green when young, becoming yellowish green with small elongated green lenticels at maturity, hairless. **Stipules** persistent, triangular-ovate, 1.8–2.2 × 0.9–1.2 cm. **Leaves: petiole** dull-pink, hairless, 1.5–11 cm long, more or less continuing straight into main vein of blade, but joining it at a vertical 90° angle; **blade** above dark green, hairless, beneath paler green, slightly asymmetric, broadly ovate, 4.5–7.5 × 3.7–7 cm, apex abruptly short acuminate, base truncate or obtuse, margin entire, veins palmate-pinnate. **Inflorescence:** in upper leaf axils, 3–16-flowered, bisexual or male only, cymose, hairless; flowers fragrant; **bracts** soon falling, ovate to elliptic, 1.2–1.6 × 0.7–1 cm. **Male flowers: tepals** four, white with a small red blotch at the base, hairless, outer pair ovate, 1.1–1.5 × 1–1.2 cm, inner pair obovate-oblong, 0.9–1.2 × 0.2–0.4 cm; **stamens** about 20, arranged symmetrically, anthers much longer than filaments, anther connectives slightly projecting. **Female flowers: bracteoles** absent; **tepals** five, white with a small red blotch at the base, hairless, outer pair ovate to broadly ovate, 1.3–1.7 × 1.1–1.3 cm, ovate or narrowly to broadly elliptic, 0.8–1.5 × 0.4–1.1 cm; **ovary** white, ovoid, unequally three-winged, three-locular, **placentae** axile, bifid, but ovules absent between placental branches; **styles** three, white with green bases, once-branched, stigmas in a spiraled band. **2n** = 56.

Despite the name *Begonia integerrima* being virtually unknown in horticultural circles, this is one of the most commonly cultivated of all the species of *Begonia*. For years *B. integerrima* has been incorrectly grown as *B. solananthera*, and in 2003 even received one of the Royal Horticultural Society's prestigious Awards of Garden Merit under that name. That this confusion should have occurred is not surprising as the two are remarkably similar. *Begonia integerrima* is hairless, and while I have not seen the true *B. solananthera* in cultivation, despite an extensive search, examination of herbarium specimens shows it to be virtually identical except for the dense hairs on its peduncles and the main veins of its lower leaf surfaces. Indeed, were it not for the fact that the name *B. solananthera* is so widely used in the literature, one might even consider treating it as a variety of *B. integerrima*. At the very least these plants are no more distinct than *B. arborescens* var. *arborescens* and its hairier variant, *B. arborescens* var. *confertiflora*, which have a similar natural distribution and were also considered to be distinct species at one time. Both *B. integerrima* and *B. solananthera* grow in the Organ Mountains of Brazil, while a third relative, *B. radicans* (Plates 42 and 127), has a slightly larger distribution within Brazil's Atlantic Coastal Forest. The last species is easily distinguished from *B. integerrima* and *B. solananthera* by its elliptic-lanceolate rather than ovate leaf blades. Furthermore, though *B. integerrima* is particularly free-blooming and has flowers that are white with a small red blotch at the base of the tepals, *B. radicans* can sometimes be a little shy to bloom and has orangey red flowers with white margins. *Begonia radicans* has also had a somewhat confusing taxonomic history and is frequently grown under the synonymous names *B. glaucophylla*, *B. limmingheana*, *B. limminghei*, or *B. procumbens*.

Begonia integerrima is readily grown in a humid greenhouse or outdoors in suitably warm, humid areas. It may also be grown as a houseplant but has a tendency to lose its lower leaves if humidity levels are too low. Between waterings, the potting mix should be allowed to dry out slightly as *B. integerrima* and its relatives resent being waterlogged. These species also require reasonably bright light but have a tendency to develop unnaturally pale leaves if they are exposed to excessive amounts of sunlight. As with other begonias, some experimentation is necessary in order to find a suitable light level. The members of this group look especially beautiful when grown in a hanging basket with their stems falling gracefully over the sides. *Begonia integerrima* has deliciously fragrant flowers.

Several excellent hybrids have *Begonia integerrima* parentage including *B.* 'Far Out', *B.* 'Inca Princess', *B.* 'Pink Chaser', *B.* 'Potpourri', *B.* 'Splotches', and *B.* 'Tiny Gem'. *Begonia* 'Fragrant Beauty' (Plate 128), a *B. integerrima* × *B. radicans* cross, is remarkably free flowering and my own personal favorite.

Begonia involucrata Liebmann (PLATE 38D)

section *Gireoudia*, thick-stemmed group

Videnskabelige Meddelelser fra Dansk Naturhistorik Forening i Kjøbenhavn 1852 15 (1853)

Erect branchless perennial to 1–2 m tall, densely covered with long wooly hairs. **Stipules** soon falling or deciduous, lanceolate-triangular to almost elliptic, 1.3–3.5 × 0.8–1.5 cm. **Leaves: petiole** pale green, densely hairy, 7–20 cm long, joining blade at an angle; **blade** above green, beneath paler green, both surfaces moderately to densely hairy, asymmetric, oblong, broadly elliptic, ovate or obovate, 8–27 × 8.5–17 cm, apex acuminate, base deeply and narrowly cordate, margin strongly wavy-lobed with two or three well-developed lobes, generally one on either side of the apex, the third, when present, on the side of the leaf opposite the petiole, lobes double-toothed, veins palmate. **Inflorescence:** axillary, dense, many-flowered, bisexual, cymose; flowers fragrant; **bracts** soon falling, broadly boat-shaped, broadly ovate to transversely elliptic, 1.5–3 × 1.6–2.5 cm. **Male flowers: tepals** two to four, white, outer pair ovate to broadly oblong-elliptic, 8–14 × 6.5–10 mm, inner segments absent or one to two, if present rudimentary or oblanceolate to narrowly obovate, 3–7 × 1–2 mm; **stamens** 20–41, arranged symmetrically, anther connectives projecting. **Female flowers: bracteoles** absent; **tepals** two or rarely three, white, outer pair broadly elliptic to transversely elliptic or almost circular 6–9 × 4–9 mm, inner segment usually absent, oblanceolate 3–4.5 × 0.6–1.2 mm; **ovary** white, ellipsoid, obovoid, or almost circular, 4–7.5 × 3–5.5 mm, unequally three-winged, three-locular, **placentae** axile, bifid; **styles** three, once-branched, stigmas in a spiraled band. **2n** = 28.

Begonia involucrata is native to Costa Rica and western Panama, where it grows in seasonally dry forests, usually at an altitude of 1400–2000 m. It is reported to often form large colonies on steep forested slopes and stream banks. It also occasionally grows as an epiphyte. Among cultivated begonias *B. involucrata* is easily recognized by its upright shrubby habit and green leaves with sunken veins and a medium to dense covering of soft white hairs. The species' scientific name highlights the unusual involucres, or rings of outer bracts that completely encircle the inner bracts of the inflorescence. *Begonia involucrata* was first discovered and named by Danish botanist Frederik Liebmann. It has been cultivated since 1946 and is frequently offered in the American Begonia Society seed lists. A key to this and related species is published in: Burt-Utley, K. 1985. A revision of the Central American species of *Begonia* section *Gireoudia* (Begoniaceae). *Tulane Studies in Zoology and Botany* 25 (1): 1–131.

Begonia involucrata is an intriguing but not particularly showy species that is usually grown only in specialist collections. The species flowers from late winter to spring, is fragrant, and is readily grown in a humid greenhouse. The cultivar *B.* 'Inzae' is a result of *B. involucrata* × *B. mazae.*

Begonia johnstonii J. D. Hooker

section *Rostrobegonia*, thick-stemmed group
Curtis's Botanical Magazine 112: t. 6899 (1886)

Erect non-rhizomatous perennial to about 1 m tall. Stem branched, thick, pale green, often with elongated purple lenticels, hairless. **Stipules** persistent, broadly ovate to oblong, 3–8 × 1.7–5 mm. **Leaves: petiole** yellowish green, often red-tinged at the base, with elongated purple lenticels, 3–16 cm long, joining blade at an angle, ring of bristles present at the top of the petiole; **blade** above dark green with a thin purple band circling the margin, hairless or rarely with short hairs, beneath paler green with soft, scattered hairs, asymmetric, ovate to elliptic, 3–12 × 1.8–9 cm, apex acute or shortly acuminate, base cordate, margin broadly crenate, veins palmate. **Inflorescence:** terminal and axillary, approximately four- to six-flowered, bisexual, cymose; **bracts** persistent, ovate or ovate-oblong, 2–4 × 1–2.5 mm. **Male flowers: tepals** four, white or rose-pink, outer pair elliptic, 0.8–1.5 × 0.5–1 cm, inner pair obovate–wedge-shaped, 0.9–1.9 × 0.6–1.3 cm; **stamens** numerous, arranged symmetrically, anther connectives projecting. **Female flowers: bracteoles** paired beneath ovary, small and insignificant; **tepals** five, white to rose-pink, outer pair elliptic, 7–11 × 5–8 mm, inner three obovate, 9–13 × 5.5–7 mm; **ovary** green, flushed red along veins of wings, ellipsoid or almost spherical, 7–8 × 5–8 mm; unequally three-winged, three-locular, **placentae** axile, bifid; **styles** three, once-branched, stigmas in a spiraled band. **2n** = 26.

In cultivation *Begonia johnstonii* is easily identified by its unique combination of erect pale green stems with elongated purple lenticels and thick fleshy leaves with crenate margins. The species name commemorates Harry Hamilton Johnston, a naturalist and British government official in Africa. Johnston collected a dried specimen of the then new species in 1885 while on an expedition to Mount Kilimanjaro. This specimen now resides in the herbarium at Kew Gardens and has been designated as the species' holotype—the particular herbarium specimen on which the scientific name *B. johnstonii* is based. In the wild, this unusual African species is most often found growing upon humid rocky cliff ledges in tropical forest. It occurs in Uganda, Kenya, and Tanzania. The species was probably first introduced into cultivation at Kew Gardens from seed provided by Bishop Hannington in the late 1800s. Nowadays, it is rather uncommon in cultivation.

Begonia johnstonii requires good drainage, bright light, and a relatively warm winter temperature. Stems should be pinched early in life in order to promote branching. The species is prone to mildew. Propagation is by stem or leaf cuttings or by seed. No artificial hybrids with this species have been reported in the literature.

Begonia johnstonii is a member of the section *Rostrobegonia* and is the most commonly encountered of the five cultivated species from that group. Most of these species are similar in appearance to *B. johnstonii* and like that species usually have a characteristic ruff of bristles at the top of their petioles. One of them, *B. engleri*, is illustrated in Plate 129. The following key was modified from: Irmscher, E., 1961. Monographische revision der Begoniaceen Afrikas I. Sekt. *Augustia* und

Rostrobegonia sowie einige neue Sippen aus anderen Sektionen. *Botanische Jahrbücher für Systematik, Pflanzengeshichte und Pflanzengeographie* 81: 106–188.

Key to the cultivated species of section *Rostrobegonia*

1 a. Leaves with two to three triangular lobes; apex of petiole hairless or with a few short bristles . . . . *B. sonderana*
b. Leaves not lobed; apex of petiole with a wreath of hairs and bristles, which in some species is collar-shaped 2
2 a. Stems covered with crimson-red shaggy hairs; bracteoles large and conspicuous . . . . *B. engleri*
b. Stems hairless or hairs present but not crimson-red; bracteoles very small and inconspicuous 3
3 a. Leaves thick and fleshy, margin crenate, with a purple border . . . . . *B. johnstonii*
b. Leaves not thick and fleshy, margin toothed, lacking a purple border 4
4 a. Inflorescences very short; styles forked once . . . . *B. rostrata*
b. Inflorescences not particularly short; styles forked twice . . . . *B. keniensis*

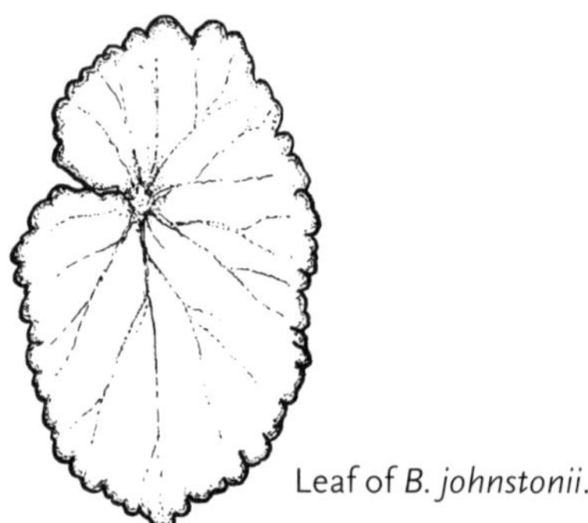

Leaf of *B. johnstonii*.

Begonia juliana Irmscher
section *Pritzelia*, shrub-like group
Botanische Jahrbücher für Systematik, Pflanzengeshichte und Pflanzengeographie 76: 62 (1953)
Synonyms: *B. peruviana* auct. non A. de Candolle: hort; *B.* U049

Erect non-rhizomatous subshrub with several stems to 1 m tall. Stems shortly branched, rusty brown with short rusty brown hairs. **Stipules** persistent, lanceolate-ovate, 1.2–1.8 × 0.6–0.8 cm. **Leaves:** distichous, pointing downward; **petiole** pink with rusty brown hairs, 2–5 cm long, joining blade at an angle; **blade** above green, beneath pinkish purple with a yellowish green main vein, both surfaces with short white hairs, asymmetric, lanceolate-ovate, 10–20 × 3–6 cm, apex acute, base cordate, margin shallowly toothed, ciliate, veins pinnate. **Inflorescence:** in upper leaf axils, many-flowered, bisexual, cymose; **bracts** persistent, lanceolate-ovate to ovate, 1–11 × 0.5–4.5 mm. **Male flowers: tepals** four, white, outer pair with dense long white hairs in the center, broadly ovate or broadly elliptic to almost circular, 1.1–1.4 × 1.3–1.4 cm, inner pair hairless, narrowly obovate, 0.9–1.1 × 0.3–0.4 cm, **stamens** about 25, arranged symmetrically, anther connectives long projecting. **Female flowers: bracteoles** absent; **tepals** four or five, white, curved inward, outer pair sparsely hairy on outer surface, ovate with a wedge-shaped base, 0.8–1.3 × 0.6–1.3 cm, margin toothed, inner two or three ovate to elliptic, base wedge-shaped, 1.1–1.3 × 0.4–1 cm, margin toothed; **ovary** white with a pale green tinge at the base, with pink wings, narrowly ovoid, 0.7–12 × 0.3–0.6 cm, unequally three-winged, three-locular, **placentae** axile, entire; **styles** three, once-branched, stigmas in a spiraled band.

Begonia juliana is an attractive, free-flowering, shrub-like species from the Atlantic Coastal Forest of Brazil. Like many of the begonias from this region, it belongs to the section *Pritzelia*. *Begonia juliana* is distinguished from its cultivated relatives by its combination of erect stems that are covered with short orangey brown hairs, its asymmetric, lanceolate leaf blades that are green above and burgundy beneath and covered with short stiff white hairs on both surfaces, and by its white tepals that have short hairs on their outer surfaces. Nevertheless, this commonly grown species is often unidentified in cultivation and is sometimes sold as *B. peruviana* or even as an unidentified Peruvian species. An account of the nomenclatural confusion previously surrounding this species is given in: O'Reilly, T. (1986) The pot of gold. *Begonian* 53: 42 and 47.

Begonia juliana is readily cultivated as long as it is grown in a humid atmosphere and the top 2–3 cm of its potting mix is allowed to dry out between waterings. The species flowers in late winter and spring. Since *B. juliana* is often unidentified in cultivation, the extent to which it has been used in hybridization is uncertain. Documented hybrids include *B.* 'Darlene Fuentes' (*B. echinosepala* × *B. juliana*) and *B.* 'Don Englund' (*B. juliana* × *B. venosa*).

Begonia kellermanii C. de Candolle

section *Gireoudia*, shrub-like group
Smithsonian Miscellaneous Collections 69 (12): 1 (1919)

Erect non-rhizomatous subshrub. Stem thick, branched, yellowish green or orangish brown, but obscured by short, wooly, silvery gray hairs. **Stipules** persistent, triangular-ovate to ovate, 0.5–0.9 × 0.6–1 cm. **Leaves:** peltate; **petiole** pink with short wooly hairs, 2.5–6 cm long; **blade** above green with short wooly hairs, beneath paler green but obscured by short hairs, ovate, 3–8.5 × 2.3–8.5 cm, apex shortly acuminate, margin wavy, entire. **Inflorescence:** in upper leaf axils, few-flowered, cymose; flowers fragrant; **bracts** soon falling, obovate-oblong, 1–1.5 × 1–1.5 cm. **Male flowers: tepals** four, white, sometimes with a hint of pink, outer pair elliptic to obovate, 1–1.6 × 1–1.1 cm, inner pair narrowly obovate to oblong-elliptic, 0.9–1.2 × 0.2–0.3 cm; **stamens** about 20, arranged asymmetrically, anther connectives projecting. **Female flowers: bracteoles** absent; **tepals** three, same color as males, outer two broadly obovate, 0.8–1.5 × 0.7–1.2 cm, inner segment narrowly obovate, 6–8.5 × 1.3–2.3 mm; **ovary** white to gray-green, wings often flushed pink, ellipsoid, 9–10 × 5–6 mm, three-winged, three-locular, **placentae** axile, bifid; **styles** three, twice-branched, stigmas in a spiraled band.

Begonia kellermanii is named in honor of William Kellerman, who was Professor of Botany at Ohio State University and an expert on Guatemalan fungi. He first discovered the species in southern Guatemala in 1906, and while botanizing in that region two years later, died of malarial fever. *Begonia kellermanii* is one of three widely cultivated species with thick, fleshy leaves that are densely covered with short hairs of either silvery gray or orangey brown; the other two are *B. kuhlmannii* (Plate 130) and *B. peltata* (Plate 131). A key is provided here for their identification.

Begonia kellermanii prefers to be kept drier than most begonias but is not difficult to cultivate and is widely grown. Propagation is usually via seeds because cuttings are prone to rot before roots are produced. *Begonia kellermanii* has been crossed with a number of other begonias, particularly those from within the same section. Only one of these hybrids appears to be commercially available: *B.* 'Notre Dame' (*B.* 'Zippo' × *B. kellermanii*). *Begonia* 'Hummel's Incana' is a *B. peltata* × *B. kellermanii* hybrid, and *B.* 'Tamo' is a result of *B. peltata* × *B. mazae.*

Key to *Begonia kellermanii* and similar species

1 a. Leaves non-peltate 2
b. Leaves peltate 3

2 a. Hairs toward apex of stem silvery gray; outer pair of tepals hairless on their outer surfaces . . . . *B. peltata* var. *auriformis*
b. Hairs toward apex of stem orangey brown; outer pair of tepals hairy on their outer surfaces . . . . *B. kuhlmannii*

3 a. Leaves usually ovate; outer surfaces of tepals hairless . . . . *B. kellermanii*
b. Leaves blade usually circular-ovate; outer surfaces of tepals hairy . . . . *B. peltata* var. *peltata*

Begonia leprosa Hance (PLATE 132)
section *Leprosae*, rhizomatous group
Journal of Botany, British and Foreign 21: 202 (1883)
Synonym: U033

Creeping rhizomatous perennial. **Stipules** persistent, broadly ovate, 8–12 × 2–2.5 mm. **Leaves:** rarely peltate; **petiole** pink, sparsely to densely long haired, 4–8.5 cm long, continuing straight into main vein of blade or joining blade at an angle; **blade** above dull green, hairless, beneath paler green with pink hairs on veins, circular, 4–8 × 4.5–11 cm, apex usually shortly acute, base slightly oblique, shallowly cordate, margin entire, ciliate, veins palmate. **Inflorescence:** axillary, short, four- to nine-flowered, typically bisexual, cymose; **bracts** soon falling, ovate, 2–7 × 2.5–3 mm, margin with long hairs. **Male flowers: tepals** four, white to pink, outer pair broadly ovate, 7–12 × 8–13 mm, inner pair narrowly ovate to narrowly elliptic or narrowly obovate, 5–12 × 2.5–6 mm; **stamens** about 75, arranged in a slightly flattened spherical mass, anther connectives short projecting at first but soon drying up. **Female flowers: bracteoles** absent; **tepals** four but one of the inner tepals often soon falling, or three, same color as males, outer pair broadly ovate to circular, 5.5–10 × 6–10 mm, inner one narrowly ovate to narrowly elliptic, 6–7 × ca. 1.5 mm; **ovary** pendulous, fleshy, pink, sausage-shaped, 4–10 × 2–3 mm, wingless, three-locular, **placentae** axile, entire to bifid; **styles** three, widening toward apex and shortly once-branched, stigmas in a spiraled band.

Englishman Reverend B. C. Henry first discovered *Begonia leprosa* in 1881 near the southern Chinese port city of Guangzhou, then known as Canton. Henry probably did not introduce the species into cultivation, but this was achieved sometime prior to 1914, when Liberty Hyde Bailey mentioned it in his *Standard Cyclopedia of Horticulture*. Regardless, the plants currently found in cultivation within the United States appear to have been introduced in the early 1980s, when the species was imported from a Japanese garden and distributed by American nurseryman Rudolf Ziesenhenne under the collection number RZ275. In the wild, *B. leprosa* is widely distributed throughout southern China in the provinces of Guangxi, Guangdong, and Yunnan. There it grows in moist shady areas among rocks or on moist cliffs in dense tropical forest at altitudes of 1200–1500 m. *Begonia leprosa* is easy to recognize, particularly when in fruit. It is the only cultivated species with pink, pendulous, sausage-shaped fruits with three locules and one to two axile placentae per locule. The species' almost circular leaf blades and bracts with eyelash-like hairs on their margins also help distinguish it. The name *leprosa* is Latin for "leprous" and refers to the crusty coating often found on the

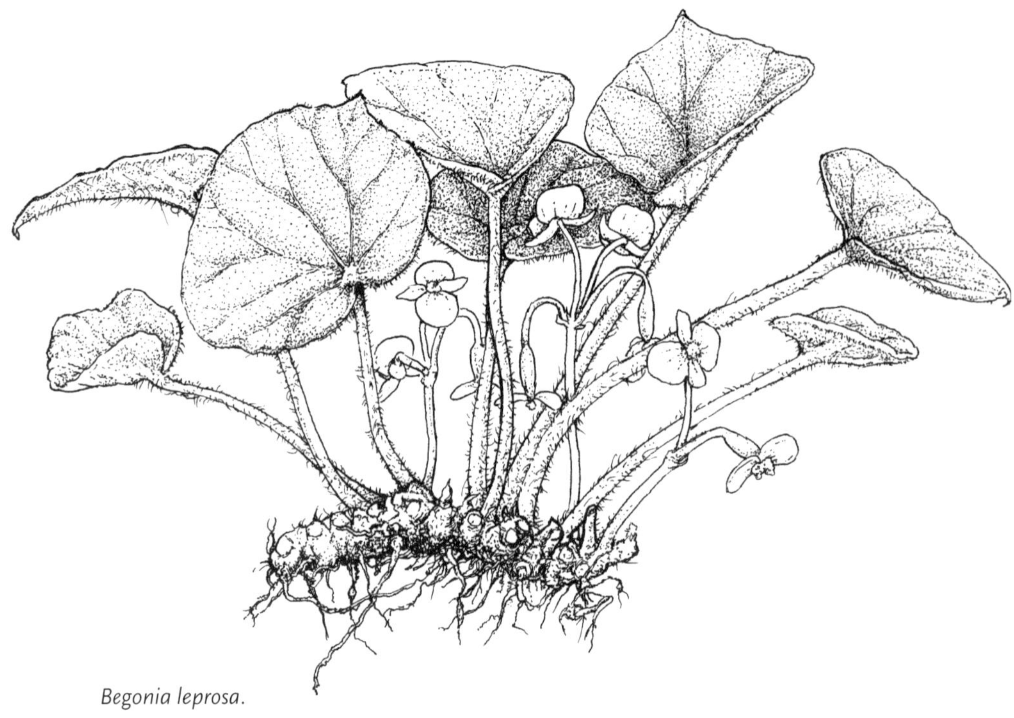

Begonia leprosa.

species' lower leaf surfaces after the plant has been pressed and dried. *Begonia leprosa* is a very desirable species that curiously is not cultivated as frequently as it deserves to be.

Begonia leprosa flowers from late summer to late winter and is readily cultivated in a humid terrarium under lights or in a greenhouse. No hybrids involving *B. leprosa* have been documented.

Begonia listada L. B. Smith & Wasshausen (PLATE 133)

section *Pritzelia*, shrub-like group
Begonian 49: 155 (1981)

Erect non-rhizomatous, branched subshrub to 1 m tall. Stem green to pinkish purple, hairy. **Stipules** persistent, of two distinct sizes on either side of stem, one side ovate-elliptic, 1.8–2.3 × 1.6–2 cm, main vein keeled, the other side ovate, 0.8–1.2 × 0.6–0.8 cm, lacking a keel. **Leaves: petiole** pale green to pink with short white hairs, 4.5–15 cm long, joining blade at an angle; **blade** above bronze with a pale yellowish green band 0.5–1 cm wide running down the main vein of the blade and the main vein of the basal lobe so that the band makes a wide-angled V, densely covered with soft, short hairs, beneath purple with two paler green veins, densely covered in short hairs, in outline usually angular-ovate, but occasional leaves may be hastate, 6–10 × 3.5–5 cm, apex acuminate, base very obliquely cordate, the left lobe acute and projecting almost directly backward, margin very shallowly toothed and ciliate, veins palmate-pinnate. **Inflorescence:** axillary, few-flowered, bisexual, cymose; **bracts** soon falling, ovate to elliptic, 6–7 × 3–4 mm. **Male flowers: tepals** four, white, outer pair covered with short red hairs, ovate-cordate to almost circular, 1.1–1.5 × 1.1–1.5 cm, inner pair narrowly obovate, 1–1.2 × 0.3–0.4 cm; **stamens** about 25–35, arranged symmetrically, anther connectives projecting. **Female flowers: bracteoles** absent; **tepals** five, white sometimes tinged red, narrowly to broadly elliptic, slightly unequal, 0.7–1.5 × 0.4–1 cm; **ovary** green with a pink tinge, especially on the wings, ellipsoid, 5–10 × 2.5–4.8 mm, almost spherical, unequally three-winged, three-locular, **placentae** axile, entire; **styles** three, once-branched, stigmas in a spiraled band. **2n** = 56.

Begonia listada is instantly recognized by its very oblique leaf blades that vary from angular-ovate to occasionally hastate, and that are dark green above with a prominent yellowish green stripe running along their main vein. The species is probably native to the far south of Brazil in the state of Rio Grande do Sol but the type specimen of the species was obtained from a gentleman in Argentina. The species name *listada* is derived from Spanish and means "striped," a reference to the plant's attractively striped leaves. The plant's name is occasionally mistakenly spelled "listida" because it was once offered as such in the American Begonia Society seed list of 1962. The species has been in cultivation in the United States since 1961, at which time it was introduced via the American Begonia Society's seed list. Details of how the species first reached the United States are discussed in the July 1981 volume of the *Begonian*; the same volume in which *B. listada* was originally published. Today, the species is widely grown throughout the world.

Begonia listada is readily grown under standard conditions, but prefers a relatively brightly lit position. Propagation is from stem or leaf cuttings. Several hybrids of this species are commercially available, including *B.* 'Mabel Corwin' (*B. listada* × *B.* 'Jill Adair'), *B.* 'Magdalene Madsen' (*B. listada* × *B. echinosepala*), *B.* 'Maxine Wilson' (*B.* 'Venetian Red' × *B. listada*), *B.* 'Murray Morrison' (*B. listada* × *B. paranaënsis*), *B.* 'Oh No' (*B. olsoniae* × *B. listada*), and *B.* 'Raymond George Nelson' (*B. listada* × *B.* 'Jack Golding'). Most of these have a similar leaf coloring to *B. listada*.

Begonia longifolia Blume (PLATE 134)

section *Sphenanthera*, shrub-like group

Catalogus 102 (1823)

Synonyms: *B. crassirostris* Irmscher; *B. inflata* C. B. Clarke; *B. tricornis* Ridley; *B.* U353; *B.* U429

Erect non-rhizomatous subshrub to 2 m tall. Stem green or reddish, usually hairless, occasionally sparsely hairy. **Stipules** deciduous, lanceolate, 6–17 × 1.3–3 mm. **Leaves: petiole** pale green, 0.7–14 cm long, joining blade at an angle; **blade** above green, beneath paler green, both surfaces usually hairless, asymmetric, lanceolate to elliptic-acuminate or broadly elliptic, 11–22 × 2.2–10.5 cm, apex long acuminate, base cordate, margin shallowly toothed to almost entire, often slightly wavy, ciliate, veins palmate. **Inflorescence:** axillary, very short, 5–10-flowered, bisexual or unisexual, cymose; **bracts** soon falling, lanceolate, 2.3–12 × 0.8–5 mm. **Male flowers: tepals** four, usually white, occasionally pale pink, outer pair broadly ovate or obovate to elliptic, strongly concave, 4–10 × 2.5–9 mm, inner pair broadly ovate to linear-obovate, 3.5–8.5 × 2–7.8 mm; **stamens** 30–60, arranged symmetrically, anther connectives projecting. **Female flowers: bracteoles** absent; **tepals** six, same color as males, elliptic, outer three 5–16 × 3.6–6 mm, inner three 4.7–13 × 2.6–4.6 mm; **ovary** berry-like, green but becoming reddish green at maturity, more or less spherical, 3–10 × 3–7 mm, three-lobed with three ribs, three-locular, **placentae** axile, bifid; **styles** three, once-branched, stigmas in a spiraled band. **2n** = 22.

Begonia longifolia has perhaps the largest natural distribution of any species in the genus and is common throughout an area of Asia stretching from northeastern India eastward to southeastern China, and southward to the Malay Peninsula and the Indonesian islands of Sumatra, Java, and Bali. Not surprisingly, it is found in a wide range of habitats from primary rain forest to degraded scrub and occurs both on acidic and basic substrates in full to half shade. It usually grows at elevations of 120–2000 m.

As would be expected with such a widely distributed species, *Begonia longifolia* is readily grown under standard conditions and is frequently cultivated. The species was reintroduced into cultivation in the 1990s, but is now represented by collections made in China, the Malay Peninsula, and Java. Nevertheless, plants of this species are often unidentified in cultivation. *Begonia longifolia* does not appear to have contributed to the parentage of any named hybrid cultivars, but at one time hybrids of *B. roxburghii* × *B. longifolia* were grown.

Begonia acetosella (syn. *B. tetragona*) is a closely related and very similar species that is readily distinguished from *B. longifolia* since it has ovaries with four rather than three locules. However, plants lacking fruit are easily confused. Nevertheless, with a little practice they can be separated since *B. acetosella* has a shallower leaf sinus than *B. longifolia* and stems that tend to be zigzagged toward their tips rather than straight. Two varieties are in cultivation, *B. acetosella* var. *acetosella*, with hairless or almost hairless leaves and petioles, and *B. acetosella* var. *hirtifolia* with hairy leaves and petioles. *Begonia acetosella* grows wild in an area stretching from southeastern Tibet south to northern Thailand. Here it prefers shady moist situations by streams in mixed or evergreen forest at an elevation of 400–2750 m. It is readily cultivated under standard conditions and like *B. longifolia* appears to have been introduced into cultivation in the 1990s. The leaves and stems of both *B. acetosella* and *B. longifolia* are eaten as a vegetable and occasionally used to treat fevers, coughs, and stomach complaints in parts of their natural range. A detailed taxonomic treatment of *B. longifolia* and *B. acetosella* is given in Tebbitt, M. C. (2003) Taxonomy of *Begonia longifolia* Blume (Begoniaceae) and related species. *Brittonia* 55 (1): 19–29.

Begonia longipetiolata Gilg (PLATE 135)

section *Tetraphila*, rhizomatous group

Botanische Jahrbücher für Systematik, Pflanzengeschichte und Pflanzengeographie 34: 92 (1904)

Synonyms: *B. graciliopetiolata* De Wildeman; *B. crassipes* Engler; *B. nicolai-hallei* Wilczek

Creeping rhizomatous perennial. Stems pale green to brown, rooting at nodes, to 40 cm long, with a dense covering of small brown scale-like appendages. **Stipules** persistent, narrowly triangular-lanceolate, 0.7–2.5 × 0.3–1.1 cm. **Leaves:** produced along the length of the rhizome; **petiole** green to dark red with scattered pale green elongated lenticels, 1–29 cm long, continuing straight into main vein of blade; **blade** above glossy, pale to dark green, beneath dull whitish green to red-purple, almost symmetric, lanceolate or narrowly elliptic to ovate-elliptic, 4–27 × 1–15 cm, apex acute to acuminate, base wedge-shaped, obtuse, or shallowly cordate, margin entire or with small teeth at the ends of the main veins, veins pinnate. **Inflorescence:** in upper leaf axils, unisexual, cymose; male inflorescence many-flowered, long-stalked; **bracts** triangular-ovate, 1–10 × 1–5 mm, often fused together; female inflorescence one- to three-flowered, almost stalkless; **bracts** narrowly triangular-ovate, to 1.2 × 0.3 mm, sometimes fused together. **Male flowers: tepals** four, white and dark pink variegated, rarely white throughout, outer pair fleshy, elliptic-obovate, 3–16 × 2–8 mm; inner pair thinner, elliptic-obovate, 2.5–8 × 1–2.5 mm; **sta-**

mens about 10–35, arrangement resembling a bunch of bananas, anther connectives not projecting. **Female flowers: bracteoles** absent; **tepals** four, same color as males, outer pair fleshy, elliptic-obovate, 7–10 × 5–7 mm, inner pair thinner, elliptic-obovate, 5–7 × 1.5–4 mm; **ovary** green to brown-red, shaped like a small banana, 10–20 × 2.5–5 mm, wingless, **placentae** parietal but sometimes superficially appearing axile, bifid; **styles** usually four, white to pink, once-branched, stigmas in a spiraled band. **2n** = 36, 38 (diploid) and 71, 72, 73 (polyploid).

Begonia longipetiolata is a beautiful picotee-flowered species that is best grown in a greenhouse or larger terrarium because it requires an atmospheric humidity of about 60 percent combined with good air circulation. In a greenhouse setting, plants can be grown attached to a piece of cork to simulate the species' natural preference to grow on tree trunks. More often, though, this species is cultivated in an open, fibrous soil mix in a clay pot or hanging basket. Given the species' rather exacting cultural preferences and unexciting appearance, not surprisingly only a few people grow it. In fact it was first brought into cultivation for its botanical rather than horticultural merits. (Look for the curious star-shaped, flattened trichomes on the stems, leaves, and ovaries). It was first introduced in the early 1980s by a team of botanists working at Wageningen Agricultural University in the Netherlands. From Wageningen, plants were distributed to other botanical collections and ultimately into private collections through the generosity of the late Jan Doorenbos. *Begonia longipetiolata* belongs to the moderately large African section *Tetraphila*, which is characterized by its species having an epiphytic habit; thick, leathery, almost symmetric leaves; male and female flowers with four tepals; and wingless, sausage-shaped ovaries with parietal placentation. *Begonia longipetiolata* is closely related and often confused with the very similar looking *B. squamulosa*. In fact, most plants that I have seen in cultivation labelled as *B. squamulosa* are actually *B. longipetiolata*. These two species, as well as *B. rwandensis* and *B. elaeagnifolia*, differ from the other cultivated members of the section *Tetraphila* since they have a creeping rhizomatous habit rather than a trailing-scandent one. A key to this subgroup is provided below. A larger key to the cultivated trailing-scandent species of section *Tetraphila* is provided under *B. mannii*. A detailed taxonomic account of *B. longipetiolata* and its closest relatives may be found in: Arends, J. C., 1992, The biosystematics of *Begonia squamulosa* Hook. f. and affiliated species in section *Tetraphila* A. DC. *Wageningen Agricultural University Papers* 91-6:1–223; and also in Wilde, J. J. F. E. de, 2002, *Begonia* section *Tetraphila* A. DC.: a taxonomic revision. *Wageningen Agricultural University Papers*. The key below is modified from the former publication.

No artificial hybrids involving either *B. longipetiolata* or *B. squamulosa* have been documented.

Key to the cultivated members of the *Begonia longipetiolata* group

1 a. Leaves peltate . . . . *B. rwandensis*
b. Leaves not peltate 2
2 a. Leaf blades on average less than five times as long as the internodes; male inflorescence up to three-flowered . . . . *B. elaeagnifolia*
b. Leaf blades on average more than five times as long as the internodes; male inflorescence usually more than five-flowered 3
3 a. Petiole usually distinctly grooved or flattened in cross section; male flower buds pendulous, flattened . . . . *B. longipetiolata*
b. Petiole circular to ovate in cross section; male flower buds erect, globose . . . . *B. squamulosa*

Begonia lubbersii Morren (PLATE 137)
section *Gaerdtia*, cane-like group
Belgique Horticole 33: 155 (1883)

Erect branched subshrub to 2 m tall. Stem brown, hairless. **Stipules** persistent, ovate to ovate-lanceolate, 1.8–2 × 0.8–1 cm. **Leaves:** distichous, peltate; **petiole** pink, hairless, 5.5–10 cm long; **blade** above velvety green with a white spot where blade joins petiole, beneath reddish purple, both surfaces hairless, angular-ovate, 8–16 × 3.5–7 cm, margin wavy, toothed. **Inflorescence:** axillary, drooping, few-flowered, bisexual, cymose; flowers very sweetly fragrant; **bracts** persistent, ovate to broadly ovate-cordate, 0.8–1.5 × 0.7–1.3 cm. **Male flowers: tepals** four, white, outer pair ovate-cordate to broadly ovate-cordate, 2.2–3.5 × 2–4 cm, inner pair narrowly obovate, 2.5–2.7 × 0.7–0.9 cm; **stamens** about 50, arranged symmetrically, anther connectives not projecting. **Female flowers: bracteoles** absent; **tepals** five, outer four broadly ovate to broadly elliptic, base wedge-shaped, 1.1–3.4 × 1.4–2.8 cm, the inner one sometimes smaller and then narrowly obovate to oblong-ovate; **ovary** very pale green, ellipsoid, 1.6–2 × 0.5–0.7 cm, more or less equally three-winged, wings rounded, three-locular, **placentae** axile, bifid but lacking ovules on the inner surfaces; **styles** three, shortly once-branched, stigmas in a spiraled band.

Louis Lubbers, while curator of the Brussels Botanic Garden, accidentally discovered this species in 1880 on the trunk of a tree fern that had been sent from Brazil by the plant collector Pedro Binot. He nursed the small plant back to a healthy condition, and when it eventually flowered, gave material to Édouar Morren of the University of Liége. Morren named it *B. lubbersii* in honor of its discoverer. Soon afterward Pynaert of Ghent introduced it commercially. However, it was not until after 1956, when it was first offered in the American Begonia Society seed fund, that *B. lubbersii* became widely grown.

Begonia lubbersii can be a little tricky to cultivate since it is susceptible to over watering. For this reason, it is easiest to grow in a hanging basket in a location with about 40–60 percent atmospheric humidity. If the species is grown in a pot, a well-drained potting mix and a pot just slightly larger than the root mass are important, otherwise excessive moisture in the medium may cause the roots to rot. Regular pinching of the young stems will result in a more attractively shaped plant. Since *B. lubbersii* is a desirable species with very fragrant flowers, it is well worth the extra attention necessary for its successful cultivation. *Begonia lubbersii* is a parent of numerous hybrid cultivars. Commercially available examples include: *B.* 'Apollo' (*B. lubbersii* × *B.* 'Laura Engelbert'), *B.* 'Bonanza' (*B.* 'Kentwood' × *B. lubbersii*), *B.* 'Florence Rita' (*B. lubbersii* × *B.* 'Orange Rubra'), *B.* 'Lubbergei' (*B. lubbersii* × *B. dregei*), *B.* 'Pink Jade' (*B.* 'Kentwood' × *B. lubbersii*), *B* 'Symphony' (*B.* 'Hannah Serr' × *B. lubbersii*), and *B.* 'Tom's Fantasy' (*B. lubbersii* × *B. dichroa*).

Begonia lubbersii is classified in the section *Gaerdtia*, the members of which are usually readily identified since they are the only cane-like species to have axile placentae that are bifid but lack ovules on the inner surfaces of the placental branches. Two of the lower growing species deviate by either having bifid placentae with ovules on both sides of the branches or entire placentae. Nevertheless, both are easily identified and are discussed elsewhere. They are *B. dichroa*, an orange-flowered species, and *B. edmundoi*, a species with unusual slender, black stems. Another member of the group *B. corallina* (syn. *B. macduffiana*) is of note because it is one of the few Brazilian species restricted to the Amazon, most being found in the Atlantic Coastal Forests. Comparison of the types of *B. corallina* and *B. macduffiana* show them to be the same species. *Begonia macduffiana* should, therefore, be treated as a synonym of the former species.

Key to the cultivated, tall, cane-like species of section *Gaerdtia*

1 a. Leaves peltate . . . . *B. lubbersii*
b. Leaves not peltate 2
2 a. Leaf blade spotted above; apex of anther hooded 3
b. Leaf blade not spotted above; apex of anther not hooded 4
3 a. Lower lobe of leaf blade projecting backward for up to 0.5 cm; upper leaf surface with numerous silver dots, each to 3 mm in diameter . . . . *B. albo-picta*
b. Lower lobe of leaf blade projecting backward for up to 5 cm; upper leaf surface with a few silver dots, each to 8 mm in diameter . . . . *B. maculata*

4 a. Flowers red to reddish orange . . . . *B. corallina*
b. Flowers white to pink 5
5 a. Lowermost lobe at base of leaf extended directly backward into a point; veins of leaf blade palmate-pinnate . . . . *B. pseudolubbersii*
b. Lowermost lobe at base of leaf not extended directly backward into a point; veins of leaf blade pinnate 6
6 a. Leaf blade 1–2 cm wide . . . . *B. salicifolia*
b. Leaf blade 2.7–35 cm wide . . . . *B. undulata*

Begonia luxurians Scheidweiler (PLATE 136)

section *Scheidweileria*, shrub-like group
Allgemeine Gartenzeitung 16: 131 (1848)

Erect subshrub to 4 m tall. Stem branched, becoming woody at the base, brownish red, hairless or covered with small white hairs. **Stipules** deciduous, lanceolate, 8–15 × 2.5–5 mm. **Leaves: petiole** pink, hairless or covered with small white hairs, 5–20 cm long, continuing straight into main vein of blade, junction of petiole and blade with a ring of hairs; **blade** above green with pink flushed veins at base, sparsely to densely covered with stiff hairs, beneath green with a pink tinge especially along the veins, stiff hairs largely restricted to the veins, sometimes almost hairless, palmate-compound, usually with 11–20 large narrowly elliptic lobes and a few to many smaller under-developed lobes where petiole joins blade, larger lobes 6–25 × 1–3 cm, occasionally themselves deeply split, margin with sharp forward-pointing teeth, apex acuminate, base wedge-shaped. **Inflorescence:** in upper leaf axils, large, many-flowered, bisexual, cymose, male flowers produced long before the females; flowers fragrant; **bracts** inconspicuous and soon falling, elliptic, 1–1.5 × ca. 0.5 mm. **Male flowers: tepals** four, creamy white, outer pair broadly obovate, hairless, 2.5–4 × 2–3.5 mm, inner pair broadly obovate, 2.5–3.5 × 2–3 mm, **stamens** numerous, arranged symmetrically, anther connectives shortly projecting. **Female flowers: bracteoles** paired beneath ovary, small and easily overlooked; **tepals** five, creamy white, slightly unequal, obovate to spatula-shaped, 3–5 × 1–2 mm; **ovary** pink but becoming green with maturity, broadly obovoid to spherical, 1–4 × 1–4 mm, **placentae** axile, entire; **styles** three, once-branched, stigmas in a spiraled band. **2n** = 56.

This robust subshrub with distinctive palmate-compound leaves and tiny, creamy white flowers is one of the easiest begonias to identify. Indeed, various authors have likened its appearance to that of a palm or large cannabis plant (*Cannabis sativa*). The name *luxurians* is certainly appropriate since this species, when happy, produces very luxuriant foliage and makes a great specimen plant. *Begonia luxurians* is native to the Brazilian states of Rio de Janeiro and São Paulo, where it is common and even, on occasion, grows by the roadside. In its native area, the species is sometimes used in the treatment of fevers. De Jonghe of Brussels is said to have been the first European to receive living plants of *B. luxurians* in 1848. A few years later, seeds were sent from Brazil to Germany. Miethe writes in the *Gartenwelt* 1915, p. 3, with regard to the accidental importation of *B. luxurians*:

> Whoever will take the trouble to sow the leftovers produced from the cleaning of imported Brazilian orchids will frequently see that a number of begonias germinate. It is true that seldom does anything really useful come from this —mostly it is small flowers of the pink and white sort—that have neither a commercial value as foliage or flowering plants. The only useful begonia I found after many sowings was *Begonia luxurians*, which at least on account of their unusually formed leaves and not unattractive flowers have ornamental value.

Indeed, *Begonia luxurians* is a very ornamental foliage plant, and nowadays is very popular in cultivation. The species is readily grown in a greenhouse, or in suitably warm areas, the outdoor garden. At the Central Park Zoo I have seen it used as a tender perennial in a planter, where it was grown to great effect alongside a palmate-leaved palm. *Begonia luxurians* was originally described by German-born Belgian botanist Michel Scheidweiler. The section *Scheidweileria*, in which this species is classified, is in turn named in Scheidweiler's honor. Two other members of this section are in cultivation, both of which like *B. luxurians* are unusual in having compound leaves. A key to the cultivated members of the section is provided here.

Begonia luxurians and its two close relatives are readily cultivated as long as they are kept slightly moist. All three species are best propagated via stem cuttings taken from near the base of the plant or by seed. The following hybrids of *B. luxurians* are among those widely grown: *B.* 'Benitochiba' (*B.* 'Filigree' × *B. luxurians*), *B.* 'Lady Clare' (*B. scharffiana* × *B. luxurians*), and *B.* 'Mrs. Fred T. Scripps' (*B. scharffiana* × *B. luxurians*). *Begonia* 'Rudy's Luxurians' and the very similar, if not identical, *B.* 'Lee's Luxurians' were both derived from wild seed collected by the late Sylvia Leatherman in Brazil in the 1950s. These plants differ from the typical *B. luxurians* in that their leaf blades are asymmetric with two to four shallow to deep lobes. They may be natural hybrids of *B. luxurians* and an unknown parent.

Key to the cultivated species of section *Scheidweileria*

1 a. Leaves with three to seven compound lobes, some of the lobes themselves deeply lobed . . . . *B. semidigitata*
b. Leaves with 7–18 compound lobes, lobes only occasionally secondarily lobed . . 2
2 a. Base of leaf blade usually with a few to many small under-developed lobes, main lobes 11–20, each about 1–3 cm wide . . . . *B. luxurians*
b. Base of leaf blade usually without small under-developed lobes, main lobes 7–12, each about 2–6 cm wide . . . . *B. digitata*

Begonia lyman-smithii Burt-Utley & Utley (PLATE 38A)

section *Gireoudia*, rhizomatous group
Brittonia 39: 59, pl. 1 (1987)

Creeping rhizomatous perennial. Rhizome green with very short internodes, nodes covered with flattened hairs, petiole base or leaf scar with a sparse band of scale-like appendages, elsewhere hairless. **Stipules** persistent, ovate, 1.2–2.2 × 0.7–1.3 cm. **Leaves: petiole** dark red with dense, rust-colored, wooly hairs, 7–27 cm long, joining blade at an angle; **blade** above dull dark green with a marginal dark red-brown border of hairs, otherwise hairless, beneath deep red with short wooly hairs, asymmetric, ovate to broadly elliptic, 5–17.7 × 6.5–13.2 cm, apex rounded to acute, base cordate, margin undulate to toothed at ends of major veins, veins palmate. **Inflorescence:** axillary, many-flowered, bisexual, cymose; **bracts** deciduous, ovate to ovate-elliptic, kidney-shaped, or broadly kidney-shaped, 4.5–15 × 6–14 mm. **Male flowers: tepals** two, outer surface dark pink, inner surface paler pink, ovate to almost circular or broadly transversely elliptic, 5.5–9 × 6–10 mm; **stamens** 20–31, filaments borne on a slightly raised column, arrangement resembling a bunch of bananas, anther connectives not projecting. **Female flowers: bracteoles** absent; **tepals** five, same color as males, asymmetric-ovate to elliptic, slightly unequal, 3–6 × 2.5–4.5 mm, reflexed; **ovary** greenish with pale pink wings, ovoid to ellipsoid, 7–9 × 7–9 mm, unequally three-winged, three-locular, **placentae** entire to bifid; **styles** three, fused to half their length, stigmas crescent-shaped.

Begonia lyman-smithii grows wild only in a small area of limestone hills in northern Oaxaca, Mexico. Here the species occupies an unusual habitat; it grows in crevices in the limestone, beneath the cover of seasonally deciduous forest, at an elevation of 160–300 m. The species is named after the late Lyman B. Smith, who worked for the Smithsonian Institution and published extensively on *Begonia* from 1941 to 1993. *Begonia lyman-smithii* is easy to recognize on account of the characteristic dark red-brown border of dense hairs found on its otherwise green upper leaf surfaces. It appears to have first been introduced into cultivation in the United States by cycad expert Loren Whitelock.

Begonia lyman-smithii is easily grown under standard conditions. It goes semi-dormant during the winter months. No artificial hybrids with this species have been documented, but Kathleen Burt-Utley and John Utley have reported what appear to be natural hybrids between it and *B. sericoneura*.

Begonia mannii W. J. Hooker (PLATE 138)

section *Tetraphila*, trailing-scandent group
Curtis's Botanical Magazine 90: pl. 5434 (1864)

Scrambling or pendulous non-rhizomatous perennial with few-branched, golden brown stems to 5 m long. Stem, leaves, and ovaries sparsely to densely covered with star-shaped hairs. **Stipules** tardily deciduous, lanceolate, 25–30 × 7–9 mm. **Leaves: petiole** brownish red, 1–7.5 cm long, continuing straight into main vein of blade; **blade** leathery, above glossy or dull mid- to dark-green, hairless or almost so, beneath paler green to silvery green with prominent brownish red veins, hairy along veins, almost symmetric, usually ovate, occasionally elliptic, 10–22 × 4–10.5 cm, apex acute to acuminate, base usually shallowly cordate, margins wavy-toothed to almost entire, veins pinnate, sunken above, raised beneath. **Inflorescence:** axillary, short, unisexual, cymose, male and female inflorescences usually found on separate branches; male inflorescences with 7–15 flowers; **bracts** soon falling, broadly ovate to triangular, 2–11 × 1–8 mm; female inflorescences with three to seven flowers; **bracts** soon falling, ovate to triangular, 2–20 × 1–15 mm. **Male flowers: tepals** four, outer surfaces glossy red, inner surfaces pinkish red with pink margins and a white patch at the base, outer pair elliptic to obovate, 7–12 × 4–8 mm, inner pair narrowly obovate, 7–12 × 2.5–3.5 mm; **stamens** 20–25, arranged in a symmetric cone-shaped mass, anther connectives not projecting. **Female flowers: bracteoles** absent; **tepals** four, same color as males, becoming reflexed, outer pair broadly ovate to elliptic, 11–16 × 8–10 mm, inner pair narrowly elliptic, 11–14 × 3.5–5 mm; **ovary** yellowish green, sometimes reddish tinged, narrowly cylindrical, often curved and resembling a small banana, wingless, 13–35 × 1.5–4 mm, four or rarely five-locular, **placentae** parietal but superficially appearing axile, bifid; **styles** four or rarely five, awl-shaped, dark red with a bright yellow base, stigmas on outer surface toward apex. **2n** = 36 and 38.

This species was discovered by Gustav Mann on the island of Bioko (formerly Fernando Póo) off the coast of tropical West Africa and introduced to Kew Gardens in 1862. Since then it has also been found growing wild on the mainland of tropical East Africa in several nearby areas bordering the Gulf of Guinea. *Begonia mannii* is readily cultivated in a greenhouse and looks spectacular when trailing from a hanging basket. No artificial hybrids involving *B. mannii* have been documented.

Begonia mannii is similar in appearance and easily confused with a number of other trailing-scandent African begonias (Plate 139). A key for their identification is provided on the next page. Most members of this group not only share *B. mannii*'s scrambling habit but also its thick, ovate, almost symmetric leaves, male and female flowers with four tepals, and ovaries that are wingless, sausage-shaped, and have parietal placentation. Most are epiphytic in the wild but often show different preferences for where they grow on a particular tree. *Begonia mannii, B. horticola*, and *B. komoensis* prefer relatively humid conditions and grow on fallen, decaying logs and branches close to the ground in forest gaps. *Begonia eminii* prefers to grow on the bases of trees, but again where the atmosphere is relatively humid. *Begonia kisuluana, B. oxyanthera* (syn. *B. jussiaeicarpa*), and *B. subalpestris* grow on the trunks of trees away from the ground where the atmospheric conditions are a little drier. Lastly, *B. cavallyensis* (Plates 140 and 144), *B. loranthoides* (Plates 142 and 143), *B. molleri*, and *B. polygonoides* (Plate 141) grow in the tree canopy where atmospheric conditions are usually much drier. These latter species have particularly leathery, drought-tolerant leaves. In cultivation mature fruits with viable seeds are obtained only if female flowers of these species are hand pollinated with pollen from male flowers of the same species. Pollen release from the anthers is optimal after the flowers have already shriveled, suggesting that these species are wind pollinated in the wild. *Begonia mannii* and its relatives are also unusual among begonias in having seeds that are dispersed by both birds and ants, with ants, most probably, only locally dispersing the seed and birds carrying them longer distances. A particularly fine collection of these unusual trailing-scandent African species can be seen in the *Begonia* house at Montreal Botanical Garden. In Europe, the

Begonia molleri.
Drawing by Ike Zewaldthe. Courtesy of National Herbarium Nederland: Wageningen branch, Biosystematics Group, Wageningen University, the Netherlands

Conservatoire du Begonia at Rochefort in France also hosts a collection of exceptionally well-cultivated and often rare species of this group. Four non-trailing-scandent members of the section *Tetraphila* are discussed under *B. longipetiolata*. Slightly less closely related, but still similar in appearance to *B. mannii*, are two other trailing-scandent African species: *B. ampla* and *B. salaziensis*, both of which are discussed elsewhere.

An authoritative treatment of *Begonia mannii* and its relatives can be found in Wilde, J. J. F. E. de, 2002, *Begonia* section *Tetraphila* A. DC.: a taxonomic revision. *Wageningen Agricultural University Papers*. The key provided here is modified from that work.

Key to the cultivated trailing-scandent species with fleshy, fusiform, sometimes berry-like fruit

1 a. Base of inflorescence enclosed with large persistent bract-like structures; female flowers with two tepals that are basally fused to form a short cylinder . . . . *B. ampla* and close relatives
b. Base of inflorescence not enclosed with large bract-like structures; female flowers with two or four tepals that are free at the base 2
2 a. Stem sparsely covered with minute, linear, glandular hairs and occasionally also with a few small star-shaped scales, but often appearing hairless to the naked eye; tepals rarely four in both male and female flowers; fruit indehiscent . . . . *B. salaziensis* and close relatives
b. Stem sparsely to densely covered with small star-shaped scales; tepals four in both male and female flowers; fruit dehiscent 3
3 a. Stamens arranged in a symmetric cluster that often resembles a pine cone . . 4
b. Stamens arranged in an asymmetric cluster that often resembles a bunch of bananas 12
4 a. Styles forked, stigmatic papillae coiled around the branches and continuous from one branch to the other 5
b. Styles awl-shaped, usually entire but sometimes shortly bifid at the apex; stigmatic papillae covering the apical part of each style 6
5 a. Leaf blades with a distinct red marginal band . . . . *B. subalpestris*
b. Leaf blades green throughout, lacking a red marginal band . . . . . *B. molleri*
6 a. Leaf undersurfaces completely covered with rusty red or gray scales . *B. subscutata*
b. Leaf undersurfaces pale green, often infused red, sometimes with scales but these never forming a dense mat 7

7 a. Leaves less than 2 cm wide; stamens 3–10 8
b. Leaves more than 2 cm wide; stamens 10–40 9
8 a. Stipules soon falling . . . . *B. capillipes*
b. Stipules long persistent, conspicuous . . . . *B. polygonoides*
9 a. Leaves early deciduous so that those that remain are clustered toward the ends of the stems; apex of leaf blade abruptly acuminate . . . . *B. oxyanthera*
b. Leaves long persisting and not clustered toward the ends of the stems; apex of leaf blade acute or gradually acuminate 10
10 a. Base of leaf blade asymmetric; outer tepals dark purple with a white edge . . . . *B. komoensis*
b. Base of leaf blade almost symmetric; outer tepals uniformly pink, red, or wine-red 11
11 a. Stipules persistent but soon becoming dry; primary veins three to five on either side of the midvein; flowers pale pink . . . . *B. horticola*
b. Stipules persistent and remaining fleshy for a long period; primary veins six to eight, rarely five, on either side of the midvein; flowers red, outer pair of tepals with a pale pink margin . . . . *B. mannii*
12 a. Young leaves with a purplish sheen and white stellate hairs . . . . *B. kisuluana*
b. Young leaves not as above 13
13 a. Upper surfaces of leaves green with red veins and a distinct purple marginal band . . . . *B. cavallyensis*
b. Upper surfaces of leaves green throughout 14
14 a. Inflorescences each with both male and female flowers . . . .*B. ebolowensis*
b. Inflorescences either male or female, never both 15
15 a. Leaf undersurfaces matted with rusty red or gray-fringed scales . .*B. furfuracea*
b. Leaf undersurfaces never completely covered, even if scales present 16
16 a. Peduncles of female inflorescences 1–8 mm long; ovary fusiform, usually three- or rarely two- or four-locular 17
b. Peduncles of female inflorescences 7–25 mm long; ovary club-shaped, four- to eight-locular 18
17 a. Leaf blades strongly asymmetric and strongly oblique at the base; ovary triangular in transverse section . . . . *B. fusialata*
b. Leaf blades slightly asymmetric and slightly oblique at the base; ovary round in transverse section . . . . *B. eminii*
18 a. Leaf blade strongly acuminate at the apex, midvein green; petiole of mature leaves typically more than 2 cm long . . . . . . *B. loranthoides* subsp. *loranthoides*
b. Leaf blade acute or obtuse at the apex, mid-vein brown-red; petiole of mature leaves typically less than 2 cm long . . . . . . *B. loranthoides* subsp. *rhopalocarpa*

Begonia masoniana Irmscher (PLATES 145 AND 146)
section *Coelocentrum*, rhizomatous group
Begonian 26: 202, 231 (1959)

Creeping rhizomatous perennial. Stems, leaves, and inflorescence glandular hairy. **Stipules** persistent, asymmetric-triangular, 0.8–1.5 × 0.7–1.1 cm. **Leaves: petiole** pink, 7–20 cm long, joining blade at an angle; **blade** above with cone-like projections bearing long stiff hairs, green, yellowish green, or white with bands of dark brown along main veins, these not usually reaching the margin, beneath with many depressions or cavities that correspond to the bases of the cone-like projections, paler, asymmetric, broadly ovate, 8–15 × 6.5–15 cm, apex abruptly short acuminate, base cordate, margin shallowly lobed, veins palmate. **Inflorescence:** axillary, 10–20-flowered, bisexual, cymose; flowers fragrant; **bracts** tardily deciduous, triangular-ovate, 2–5 × 2–5 mm, margin ciliate. **Male flowers: tepals** four, greenish white, outer pair broadly ovate, 8–9 × 9–10 mm, hairy on their outer surface, inner pair elliptic, 6–7 × 3–3.5 mm; **stamens** arranged symmetrically and attached to a short column, anther connectives not projecting. **Female flowers: bracteoles** absent; **tepals** three, outer pair greenish white infused with red on the outer surface, almost circular, 0.8–10 × 11–13 mm, inner one greenish white throughout, elliptic 5–7 × 3–4 mm; **ovary** pink, asymmetric-ovoid, 6–8 × 3–4 mm, unequally three-winged, one-locular, **placentae** parietal, bifid; **styles** three, once-branched, stigmas in a spiraled band. **2n** = 30.

British plant enthusiast Maurice Mason obtained this very distinct begonia from the Singapore Botanic Garden in 1952, dubbed it the "iron cross begonia," and distributed material to other begonia enthusiasts around the world. Mason is said to have given the plant its catchy name because the distinctive brown markings on its leaves reminded him of the German iron cross. Several years later, realizing that the iron cross begonia still did not have a scientific name, German *Begonia* expert Edgar Irmscher named the species after Mason. This was a fitting honor. Before Mason's death in 1993 his private greenhouse collection is said to have rivaled those of most botanical gardens and to have included hundreds of begonias. Today, the iron cross begonia is one of the most popular of all the cultivated begonias. In addition to its cross-like leaf markings, the species has interesting greenish white flowers that are slightly fragrant.

Begonia masoniana is classified in the section *Coelocentrum*, whose members typically occur on limestone rocks in southeastern China and northern Vietnam. In this group of about 12 species *B. masoniana* stands out as it is much larger and coarser than the others. Given this and the fact that it was originally described from a plant cultivated at the Singapore Botanic Garden, some authors have suggested that it may be of hybrid origin. However, in the *Flora Reipublicae Popularis Sinicae* of 1999, *B. masoniana* is recorded as a native of Guangxi Province, where it is said to grow in the wild close to China's border with Vietnam. Nonetheless, I have never seen any wild-collected specimens of *B. masoniana* and agree that the species deserves further study in order to ascertain whether or not it is a true species. Most other members of this section would also make good horticultural subjects and deserve to be introduced into cultivation.

Begonia masoniana usually looks its best when grown in a greenhouse or large enclosed terrarium but can be successfully raised on an east-facing windowsill if given a little extra humidity. Growing *B. masoniana* and a number of other plants close together will allow them to generate their own humid microclimate. Above all else though, *B. masoniana* requires a very well-drained potting mix, the surface 2–3 cm of which should be allowed to dry out between waterings. Plants should be positioned away from direct sunlight since this will very rapidly scorch their leaves. The species is easily propagated from leaf cuttings and seed. Cultivars include *B.* 'Goshe' (*B. dregei* × *B. masoniana*), *B.* 'Orphan Annie' (*B. goegoensis* × *B. masoniana*), and *B.* 'Wanda' (*B. versicolor* × *B. masoniana*). *Begonia masoniana* 'Tricolor' (Plate 146a) is a mutant with leaves with a brown cross, green fringe, and a whitish background. It was named by Mike Kartuz. In recent years a new color variant has been imported from China's Kunming Botanical Garden. This plant is named *B. masoniana* var. *maculata* (Plate 146b) and has leaves with a thin, purplish brown line around the margin and a brown cross set against a yellowish green background.

Begonia mollicaulis Irmscher

section *Begonia*, shrub-like group
Webbia 12: 507 (1957)

Erect branched perennial, densely covered with short soft hairs. Stem pale green, tinged red toward base of plant. **Stipules** persistent, narrowly ovate, 5–13 × 2–7 mm. **Leaves: petiole** pale green, tinged red at base, 3.5–16.5 cm long, joining blade at an angle; **blade** above pale green except for whitish green area at base, beneath paler green, asymmetric, broadly ovate, 6.5–12 × 4.5–11 cm, apex acuminate, base cordate, margin deeply triangular-toothed and ciliate, veins palmate. **Inflorescence:** in upper leaf axils, few- to many-flowered, bisexual, cymose; **bracts** persistent, oblong-ovate, circular or broadly ovate, 1–3 × ca. 1 cm, margin fringed with hairs. **Male flowers: tepals** four, white, outer pair hairy on the outer surface, broadly elliptic or almost circular, concave, 0.8–1.3 × 0.9–1.4 cm, inner pair hairless, narrowly obovate or obovate-oblong, 0.8–1.2 × 0.3–0.5 cm; **stamens** about 30, arranged symmetrically, anther connectives projecting. **Female flowers: bracteoles** two to three, spaced about 1 mm beneath ovary, obovate, 1.2–3 × 1–1.8 mm, margin ciliate; **tepals** five, white, sometimes tinged green, outer three hairy on the outer surface, elliptic to oblong-elliptic or obovate, 0.7–1.3 × 0.4–0.7 cm, inner two hairless, obovate, 1.2–1.3 × 0.3–0.5 cm; **ovary** pale green, obovoid to ellipsoid, 0.8–1.1 × 0.5–0.7 cm, with one wing to 1.4 cm tall and two rib-like wings, three-locular, **placentae** axile, bifid; **styles** three, once-branched, stigmas in a spiraled band. **2n** = 34.

This attractive free-flowering species is likely a native of Brazil's Atlantic Coastal Forest. However, it was originally described from cultivated material and I have not seen any wild collected material in the herbaria that I have visited. Certainly it is closely related to and often confused with *Begonia subvillosa* (Plate 147), a species that grows in the Atlantic Coastal Forests of Brazil and Paraguay and, therefore, could be expected to have a similar distribution. *Begonia mollicaulis* is distinguished from *B. subvillosa*, and most other cultivated species, by the dense, short, erect, soft, white hairs that cover the whole plant, including the outer surfaces of the tepals. *Begonia subvillosa* is also a somewhat hirsute species but is readily distinguished by its leaf blades, which are only sparsely hairy above and densely wooly haired beneath, hence the species name. Two varieties are in cultivation, *B. subvillosa* var. *subvillosa*, which has villous hairs on the stems, petioles, and leaf undersurfaces, and *B. subvillosa* var. *leptotricha* (also widely known as *B.* 'Wooly Bear') that differs by the stems, petioles, and leaf undersurfaces having matted wool-like hairs.

Begonia mollicaulis was published in 1957 and was one of more than 150 *Begonia* species that Edgar Irmscher described during his lifetime. In fact, Irmscher's contribution to our knowledge of begonias is without equal. Irmscher was born in Dresden, Germany, in 1887 and worked for more than 50 years in producing a monograph of the Begoniaceae until his death in 1968. Though this enormous task was never completed he published profusely. Not only did he describe an enormous number of new species, subspecies, and varieties, but he also worked on the sectional classification of *Begonia* and was one of very few botanists ever to gain an in-depth taxonomic knowledge of the whole family. During World War II Irmscher was also responsible for ensuring the safety of the vast collection of dried *Begonia* specimens now housed in the herbarium at the Botanical Garden and Museum in Berlin-Dahlem. While the War raged, Irmscher had on loan hundreds of specimens at the Hohenheim Agricultural College and in this rural area the priceless collection escaped the bombs that largely destroyed the important herbaria in Berlin and Hamburg. In 1955, *Begonia* taxonomists Lyman Smith and Bernice Schubert named a Colombian species in Irmscher's honor, *B. irmscheri*. This very beautiful plant is not in cultivation. However, many of the plants that Irmscher named himself now fill our homes and greenhouses. In addition to *B. mollicaulis*, examples include *B. brevirimosa*, *B. masoniana*, and *B. versicolor*.

Begonia mollicaulis is readily grown under standard conditions and is very free-flowering but needs regular pinching year-round to maintain a compact shape. The species is usually propagated from seed and has been in cultivation in Europe since the early 1900s. It was first offered in the American Begonia Society's seed list in 1962. No hybrids with *B. mollicaulis* parentage have been documented.

Begonia multinervia Liebmann (PLATE 148)

section *Gireoudia*, thick-stemmed group

Videnskabelige Meddelelser fra Dansk Naturhistorisk Forening i Kjøbenhavn 1852 18 (1853)

Synonyms: *B. glandulosa* auct. non W. J. Hooker: A. de Candolle; *B. cuspidata* C. de Candolle; *B.* U115

Erect or sprawling perennial, usually branchless, 1–3 m tall. **Stipules** persistent, lanceolate to triangular-ovate, 1–4 × 0.5–2 cm. **Leaves: petiole** reddish purple to pale green, sparsely hairy, 4–20 cm long, joining blade at an angle; **blade** above glossy dark green, hairless, beneath reddish purple or green, hairless or sparsely hairy on main veins, asymmetric, ovate to oblong-elliptic, 6–20 × 3–16 cm, apex acuminate, base cordate, margin entire to irregularly short-toothed, sometimes wavy, veins palmate. **Inflorescence:** axillary, few- to many-flowered, bisexual, cymose; **bracts** soon falling, boat-shaped, ovate, elliptic, or almost circular, 0.7–2.1 × 0.6 –1.7 cm. **Male flowers: tepals** two, white to pale or deep pink, almost circular to broadly elliptic or ovate, 4–9 × 4.5–10 mm; **stamens** 15–35, arrangement resembling a bunch of bananas, anther connectives projecting. **Female flowers: bracteoles** absent; **tepals** two, same color as males, almost circular, broadly elliptic or transversely elliptic, 4–8 × 3–9 mm; **ovary** greenish white with a pink tinge, more or less spherical, 0.2–0.5 × 0.2–0.5 cm, unequally three-winged, three-locular, **placentae** axile, bifid; **styles** three, either shallowly cleft and stigmas horseshoe-shaped or once-branched and stigmas in a spiraled band.

Begonia multinervia is a common species in Costa Rica and has occasionally also been recorded from neighbouring Nicaragua and Panama. In Costa Rica, *B. multinervia* grows in a variety of habitats including roadside banks and is unusual in that it inhabits open disturbed sites in full sun as well as deeply shaded undisturbed forests. It is found from sea level to around 900 m. *Begonia multinervia* is easily recognized by the combination of its thick, upright stem; unlobed, relatively thick leaves that are glossy dark green above and often reddish purple beneath; and male and female flowers with just two tepals. The species is commercially available and has been offered many times since 1979 in the American Begonia Society's seed list. It is easily cultivated under standard conditions, but being a large plant, needs a lot of space. No hybrids with *B. multinervia* parentage have been documented.

Begonia nelumbifolia Schlechtendal & Chamisso (PLATE 149)

section *Gireoudia*, rhizomatous group
Linnaea 5: 604 (1830)

Robust creeping rhizomatous perennial to about 1 m tall. **Stipules** persistent, triangular, 1–4 × 0.6–1.5 cm. **Leaves:** peltate; **petiole** green with dense short hairs but eventually becoming almost hairless, 11–63 cm long; **blade** above green, hairless, beneath paler green, hairless or with hairs on the main veins, asymmetric, broadly ovate, elliptic or almost circular, 6.5–40 × 6–32 cm, apex acuminate or acute, margin shallowly toothed. **Inflorescence:** axillary, many-flowered, bisexual, cymose; **bracts** soon falling, ovate to obovate, 1–15 × 1–6 mm. **Male flowers: tepals** two, white to pale pink, almost circular to broadly ovate or oblong-elliptic, 4–7 × 4–6.5 mm; **stamens** 15–20, arrangement resembling a bunch of bananas, anther connectives projecting. **Female flowers: bracteoles** absent; **tepals** two, white to pale pink, almost circular, ovate or obovate, 4–7 × 3.5–8 mm; **ovary** white to pale pink, ovoid, 4–7 × 2–5 mm, unequally three-winged, three-locular, **placentae** axile, bifid; **styles** three, once-branched, stigmas in a spiraled band. **2n** = 28.

The unusually large, peltate leaves of this commonly cultivated species make it one of the most easily recognized of all begonias. In fact the scientific name refers to the striking similarity between it and the water lotus, *Nelumbo*, a plant famous for its large umbrella-like leaves. In the wild, *Begonia nelumbifolia* is found in moist forests from central Mexico to Colombia. I have seen it at a number of locations in the Mexican state of Chiapas. It is particularly easily seen at Cascadas Agua Azul, where it grows in the splash zone of the waterfall and in the surrounding forest. In some parts of tropical Mexico the species is so common the petioles are eaten as a local vegetable. *Begonia nelumbifolia* has been brought into cultivation on several occasions, the first of which was in 1830, when Schiede collected it in Mexico.

Begonia nelumbifolia is easy to grow, but needs a lot of elbowroom and, for this reason, is best displayed in a bed in a greenhouse, rather than in a pot. *Begonia nelumbifolia* has been occasionally hybridized with other members of the section *Gireoudia*, but few of these plants are widely available. Examples include *B.* 'El Capitan' (*B.* 'Bokit' × *B. nelumbifolia*), *B.* 'Holley Moon' (*B. carriae* × *B. nelumbifolia*), and *B.* 'Lettonica' (*B. heracleifolia* × *B. nelumbifolia*).

Begonia oaxacana A. de Candolle

section *Parietoplacentalia*, shrub-like group

Annales des Sciences Naturelles Botanique (Paris) IV, 11: 127 (1859)

Synonyms: *B. candollei* Ziesenhenne; *B. luxii* C. de Candolle; *B. pubipedicella* C. de Candolle; *B. serrulatoala* C. de Candolle

Erect subshrub to 2 m tall. Stem green or red, hairless to hairy, becoming woody at base. **Stipules** soon falling, ovate to oblong, 0.8–1.5 × 0.4–1.2 cm. **Leaves: petiole** green or red, hairless to hairy, 7–20 cm long, usually joining blade at an angle; **blade** above green, beneath green to red, both surfaces sparsely to densely hairy, asymmetric, ovate to elliptic, 5–20 × 2–12 cm, apex long acuminate, base cordate, margin sharply toothed, teeth small and ending in short hairs, veins palmate-pinnate. **Inflorescence:** axillary, few-flowered, bisexual, cymose; **bracts** soon falling, ovate to elliptic, 0.7–1.5 × 0.2–1 cm. **Male flowers: tepals** four, white with a pink tinge to reddish pink, outer pair sometimes sparsely hairy on outer surfaces, broadly ovate to broadly elliptic, 0.6–1.7 × 0.7–1.7 cm, inner pair obovate, 0.7–1.4 × 0.4–1 cm; **stamens** numerous, arranged symmetrically, anther connectives not projecting. **Female flowers: bracteoles** absent; **tepals** three, same color as males, sometimes hairy on outer surfaces, outer pair broadly ovate-cordate to almost circular, 0.4–1.4 × 0.4–1.4 cm, inner one obovate, 0.3–0.7 × 0.2–0.5 cm; **ovary** fleshy, green and tinged red, ovoid to ellipsoid with a 1–5 mm long beak, 5–14 × 3–6 mm, with three almost equal to unequal narrow wings, two- to three-locular, **placentae** axile or parietal, bifid; **styles** three, once-branched, stigmas in a spiraled band.

Begonia oaxacana is one of about a dozen species that are highly desirable but constantly flit in and out of cultivation because the conditions found in their natural habitat are difficult to replicate. Other examples include *B. geminiflora*, *B. killipiana* (Plate 9), *B. urticae* and a handful of other, as yet unidentified, tubular-flowered members of the sections *Semibegoniella* (Plate 8) and *Casparya*. These plants are mostly native to the montane cloud forests of South America and as a result require very humid but somewhat cooler conditions than do most other begonias. *Begonia oaxacana* is the easiest to grow of these plants, and has a more northerly distribution. It occurs in the wild from southern Mexico to Panama and is com-

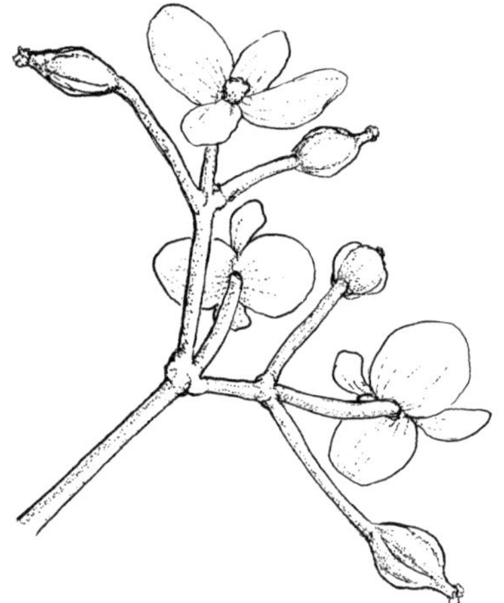

Inflorescence of *B. oaxacana*, showing the species' beaked fruit.

mon in moist montane cloud forests at an altitude of 1500–2700 m. The few examples of this species that I have seen in cultivation had a graceful habit and were covered in very attractive red berry-like fruit, making for a very desirable plant. The closely related *B. udisilvestris* is very similar and is also occasionally cultivated. It differs only by its completely hairless leaves and is probably best considered a variety of *B. oaxacana*. I have refrained from making this change, however, because I have not seen these plants in the wild.

Begonia oaxacana and the other montane cloud forest begonias are probably best cultivated under the same conditions as the orchid genera *Masdevallia*, *Dracula*, and *Pleurothallis*, with which they commonly grow in the wild. The cultivation of these orchids is a challenge but by no means impossible as can be witnessed at any large orchid show, where at least a few of them will be on exhibit. The most important factor in growing these plants is the provision of a nighttime temperature as close to 55–60°F (13–16°C) as possible, coupled with a relative humidity of about 80 percent. Daytime temperature is less critical but should be slightly higher than that of the night and must not exceed 75–80°F (24–27°C). In the daytime the humidity should be lowered to around 60 percent. Orchid growers have come up with a number of methods of achieving such conditions, some of which are commercially available, at a price. Most rely on a Wardian-case-type container provided with artificial lights, a humidifier, and an air conditioner or refrigeration unit. The efficiency and cost effectiveness of running these types of cases can be enhanced by locating them in an air-conditioned room or a cool basement so that cool temperatures can be maintained even during the hottest days of summer. If for any reason temperatures inside the case go over the desired level, keep the growing medium on the dry side but maintain a moderately high atmospheric humidity. This will help prevent fungal and bacterial diseases that cause rot to become established. The potting mix should be fibrous, very open, and free draining.

Begonia obliqua Linnaeus emended Golding (PLATE 150)

section *Begonia*, shrub-like group

Species Plantarum 2: 1056 (1753), excl. syn. Sloane

Synonyms: *B. suaveolens* auct. non Klotzsch: A. de Candolle; *B. suaveolens* auct. non Klotzsch: Loddiges; *B. macrophylla* Lamarck; *B. odorata* Willdenow; *B. dominicalis* Grisebach; *B. domingensis* auct. non A. de Candolle: Grisebach

Erect subshrub to 75 cm tall. Stem green to purplish with small, elongated, green lenticels, sometimes with narrow pink bands above the nodes, covered with wooly white hairs when young, eventually becoming hairless. **Stipules** persistent, triangular-ovate to elliptic, 0.5–1.5 × 0.3–1.1 cm. **Leaves: petiole** same color and pubescence as stems, 3–12 cm long, joining blade at an angle, **blade** above dark green with a dull pinkish red spot where petiole joins blade, hairless, beneath paler green or pale purple, veins often with white wooly hairs, elsewhere hairless, asymmetric, ovate to elliptic, 5–23 × 3.5–15 cm, apex shortly acuminate, base cordate, margin slightly wavy and short-toothed, veins palmate-pinnate. **Inflorescence:** in upper leaf axils, long-stalked, many-flowered, cymose; flowers fragrant; **bracts** persistent, ovate, 1.5–7.5 × 1–4 mm. **Male flowers: tepals** four, outer pair white with a pink flush or red on outer surfaces, white on inner surfaces, ovate to almost circular, 5–1.1 × 6–9 mm, inner pair white, elliptic to obovate, 6–9 × 2–4 mm; **stamens** about 20–30, arranged symmetrically, filaments much shorter than anthers, anther connectives projecting and rounded. **Female flowers: bracteoles** paired about 3 mm beneath ovary, deciduous, ovate, 1.5–2 × 1–1.5 mm; **tepals** four or five, same color as males, ovate, 0.6–1 × 0.5–0.9 cm, inner two or three elliptic or obovate, 0.8–1.2 × 0.5–0.8 cm; **ovary** white, tinged pink, with dark pink wings, ovoid, 0.3–0.5 × 0.2–0.5 cm, unequally three-winged, three-locular, **placentae** axile, bifid; **styles** three, once-branched, stigmas in a spiraled band. **2n** = 52.

In the past, some authors have split *Begonia obliqua*, as it is recognized here, into a number of species. The different species being recognized largely on the basis of slight differences in their bracteole and fruit wing shapes. Some of the resulting names, like *B. dominicaulis* and *B. odorata*, are frequently seen in cultivation. However, given the highly variable nature of bracteoles and fruit wings, I have followed Burt-Utley's 1991 treatment of the species in the *Flora of Dominica*, which recognizes a single variable species. As such, *B. obliqua* is a native of the Caribbean islands of Dominica, Guadeloupe, St. Lucia, St. Vincent, Grenada, and Martinique. On many of these islands, the species is very common in wet forests, particularly in the mountains. On some islands, it even grows along the roadsides. It should not be surprising then that this species was one of the first begonias to be discovered by Europeans and also one of a handful of species on which Plumier founded his genus *Begonia*, although Plumier did not call the species by its current Linnean binomial. More importantly, *B. obliqua* was the only *Begonia* species recognized by Carl Linnaeus in his *Species Plantarum* of 1753, a work that is used by modern-day botanists as a starting point for accepted botanical names. As a result *B. obliqua* is considered the type of the genus *Begonia*—the species to which the name *Begonia* is inseparably attached. An interesting discussion of why this should be appears in: Golding, J. (1980) *Phytologia* 45 (3): 221–254. *Begonia obliqua* was a good choice for the type species, as its oblique leaves and shrub-like habit are common to much of the genus. Indeed a great deal has been written about the symbolism of begonias' oblique leaf blades. John Ingram, for example, in his *Flora Symbolica* of 1869, on p. 345 mentions the asymmetric-leaved *Begonia* as a symbol of deformity.

Begonia obliqua is readily grown under standard conditions. The fragrant-flowered *B.* 'Tea Rose' is a result of *B. obliqua* × *B. dichroa* and is one of the few hybrids of this species commonly grown.

Begonia obliqua is classified in the section *Begonia*, a group of roughly 60 species mainly distributed in the West Indies and Brazil. Several of the included species are common in cultivation and are discussed separately in this book. They are *B. cubensis*, *B. cucullata*, *B. mollicaulis*, *B. rotundifolia*, *B. schmidtiana*, and *B. venosa*. Of these, *B. cucullata* is particularly noteworthy as it was a founding parent of the immensely popular Semperflorens- or wax begonias. *Begonia minor* is also from this section and is commonly cultivated. It is similar in its appearance to *B. obliqua* and like that species is a stout subshrub bearing large glossy green leaves. It is native to Jamaica and may be distinguished from *B. obliqua* by its hairless stems and petioles. In cultivation this species also tends to have paler stems and leaf blades, the latter of which have a white, rather than red, spot above where the petiole joins.

Begonia olsoniae L. B. Smith & B. G. Schubert

section *Pritzelia*, rhizomatous group
Phytologia 12: 250 (1965)
Synonym: *B. vellozoana* auct. non Walpers: Brade

Creeping rhizomatous perennial. Stem green, hairy. **Stipules** persistent, ovate, 0.9–1.3 × 0.7–0.9 cm. **Leaves: petiole** yellowish green, hairy, 2–7 cm long, joining blade at an angle; **blade** above dark green to brownish green with whitish yellow main veins, shortly hairy, beneath burgundy with pale green main veins, shortly hairy, asymmetric, ovate, 6.5–8 × 6–8 cm, apex acute, base cordate, margin minutely toothed, veins palmate-pinnate. **Inflorescence:** axillary, few-flowered, bisexual, cymose; **bracts** deciduous, lanceolate-ovate, 3–6 × 1–1.5 mm. **Male flowers: tepals** four, white, outer pair broadly elliptic, 1.3–1.9 × 1–1.5 cm, inner pair obovate, 1–1.3 × 0.5–0.8 cm; **stamens** about 35, arranged symmetrically, filaments very short, anther connectives projecting. **Female flowers: bracteoles** absent; **tepals** five, white with a pink flush on the outer surfaces of the outermost tepals, ovate to elliptic, 0.3–1.1 × 0.3–0.8 cm; **ovary** pale green with whitish green wings with a purple flush, ovoid, 0.5–0.6 × 0.3–0.4 cm, unequally three-winged, three-locular, **placentae** axile, entire; **styles** three, once-branched, stigmas in a spiraled band. **2n** = 56.

Begonia olsoniae is one of the most striking foliage plants in the genus. Its leaves are held at an attractive angle from the plant in a shield-like manner and are dark green to brownish green with contrasting whitish yellow main veins. The species has been in cultivation in the United States since at least 1956, when it was grown from Brazilian seed under the name *B. vellozoana* Brade. The name change occurred after begonia enthusiast Bee Olson pointed out to botanists Lyman Smith and Bernice Schubert that the name *B. velloziana* had already been used for a different Brazilian species, and since that species had been published earlier than Brade's species, it had priority over the name. Smith and Schubert fittingly renamed Brade's plant in honor of Olson. In the wild *B. olsoniae* has a narrow distribution, being found only in Brazil's Serro do Itatiaia National Park. It grows there on rocks in shady forest at an altitude of about 800 m.

Begonia olsoniae can be grown readily in a humid greenhouse or terrarium. The species looks particularly beautiful when grown in a hanging basket, as illustrated in Plate 11 of Mildred and Edward Thompson's *Begonias: The Complete Reference Guide*. *Begonia olsoniae* has been hybridized with several other, mostly Brazilian, begonias. Examples include *B.* 'Alva Graham' (*B. olsoniae* × unknown Brazilian species), *B.* 'Gwen Lowell' (*B. olsoniae* × *B. obscura*) and *B.* 'Jill Adair' (unknown African species × *B. olsoniae*).

Begonia oxysperma A. de Candolle (PLATE 151)

section *Baryandra*, trailing-scandent group
Annales des Sciences Naturelles Botanique (Paris) IV, 11: 122 (1859)
Synonyms: *B.* U020; *B.* U021; *B.* U073

Creeping rhizomatous perennial, which in the wild grows as an epiphyte. Rhizome thick, few-branched, ascending to 60 cm long, green with red flat hairs with laciniate apical margins. **Stipules** deciduous, ovate, 2–3 × 1.3–2.5 cm, main vein projecting. **Leaves: petiole** green with a reddish tinge on upper surface with hairs like those on the stems or almost hairless, 6.5–37 cm long, joining blade at an angle; **blade** above glossy green, red-tinged along base of veins, hairless, beneath paler green, main veins with few to several hairs like those on the stem and petioles, elsewhere hairless, ovate to broadly ovate, 11–23 × 5.5–21 cm, apex acuminate, base cordate, margin with tiny teeth, veins palmate. **Inflorescence:** axillary, long-stalked, many-flowered, bisexual, cymose, main stalk green with a red tinge, covered with hairs like those on stem or almost hairless, branches orange, hairless; **bracts** deciduous, broadly ovate, concave, 0.4–0.9 × 0.5–6.5 cm. **Male flowers: tepals** four, not opening fully, outer pair thick, orange on outer surfaces, whitish on inner surfaces, ovate-elliptic to oblong-elliptic, 0.8–1 × 0.6–0.7 cm, inner pair thinner, white and tinged pink on both surfaces, narrowly oblong-elliptic, 6–7 × 2–3 mm; **stamens** 25–30, filaments fused into a column, arranged symmetrically, anthers small, connectives not projecting. **Female flowers: bracteoles** absent; **tepals** four, outer pair orange, oblong-elliptic, 0.8–1.8 × 0.5–0.7 cm, inner pair white, oblong to oblong-elliptic, 5.5–8 × 2–3 mm; **ovary** orange throughout, ellipsoid, 0.5–0.9 × 0.4–0.7 cm, unequally three-winged, three-locular, **placentae** axile, bifid; **styles** three, once-branched, branches erect and long, stigmas in a spiraled band.

Begonia oxysperma is an interesting orange-flowered, climbing epiphyte from the Philippines. Martin Johnson appears to have first introduced it into cultivation in the United States from material he collected on Mount Banahao, a volcanic mountain located roughly fifty miles southeast of Manila. Martin Sands, who works on Asian begonias at Kew Gardens, informs me that the species occurs on several mountains in this vicinity and is always confined to a narrow altitudinal band, the lower limit of which coincides with the base of the clouds that swath these mountains. That this species needs humid atmospheric conditions for its survival is not surprising since it grows in an exposed environment, clinging to the trunks of trees. The name *oxysperma* means "with sharply pointed seeds." The seeds of this species are indeed unusual as they are equipped with air sacks that give them buoyancy and allow them to waft on the breeze. A distinct advantage for a plant that grows on tree trunks.

Begonia oxysperma needs a fibrous growing media and has a tendency to rot if over watered. The species needs excellent drainage, high atmospheric humidity, and does best in a hanging container or mounted on a piece of bark or cork. No hybrid cultivars of this species have been documented.

Begonia petasitifolia Brade (PLATE 152)

section *Pritzelia*, thick-stemmed group
Bradea 1: 37, pl. 1 (1971)

Creeping rhizomatous perennial. Rhizome thick, branched, orange-brown, hairless. **Stipules** persistent, broadly ovate, 1.1–3.5 × 0.8–2.5 cm, main vein keeled and projecting. **Leaves: petiole** pink with dense short, silvery gray star-shaped hairs, 7.5–18 cm long, continuing straight into main vein of blade, with a wedge of red scale-like appendages on lower side of petiole where it joins blade; **blade** green on both surfaces with small brownish white star-shaped hairs, the hairs especially dense on the veins, symmetric, kidney-shaped, 7–11 × 13–18 cm, apex indistinct, base symmetric, cordate, margin wavy and curled under, veins palmate. **Inflorescence:** in upper leaf axils, many-flowered, bisexual, cymose, to 1 m tall; **bracts** deciduous, linear, 1.5–4 × ca. 0.5 mm. **Male flowers: tepals** four, white, outer pair oblong ovate to almost circular, 5–9 × 5–9 mm, inner pair elliptic, 3.5–4.5 × 1.5–2 mm; **stamens** about 15–20, arranged symmetrically, anther connectives not projecting. **Female flowers: bracteoles** paired beneath ovary, linear, 1.5–1.8 × ca. 0.3 mm; **tepals** five, white with a pink tinge, hairless, outer pair oblong-ovate or elliptic, 7–10 × 2.5–5 mm, inner three narrowly spatula-shaped or ovate, 5–10 × 2–3 mm; **ovary** pale green or reddish with white wings, more or less oblong, 3–6 × 1.5–4 mm, almost equally to unequally three-winged, three-locular, **placentae** axile, entire; **styles** three, once-branched, stigmas in a spiraled band.

In the wild, the Brazilian *Begonia petasitifolia* is restricted to Morro do Chapéu, a distinct sandstone area about 200 miles northwest of the coastal city of Salvador. The species grows there upon sandstone outcrops in low woodland and occasionally along the streams that cross this areas' sandy soils. It is an attractive, easily recognized species with green leaves densely covered with small, brownish white, star-shaped hairs. When in flower the species' white tepals and ovary wings contrast beautifully with the pale green ovary bodies, making for a subtle but attractive display. The name *petasitifolia* highlights this species' resemblance to members of the genus *Petasites*, commonly known as butterburs. The species is occasionally sold under the incorrect name *petasifolia*.

Begonia petasitifolia is readily grown but requires good drainage. Like other species from relatively dry habitats, its potting medium must also be allowed to dry out slightly between waterings. *Begonia* 'Frostland' is a result of *B. petasitifolia* × *B. sanguinea*.

Begonia polilloensis M. C. Tebbitt (PLATE 153)

section *Petermannia*, shrub-like group
Edinburgh Journal of Botany (2005)
Synonym: *B.* U076

Erect branched perennial to about 30 cm tall. Stems pink, sparsely hairy, zigzagged toward the apex. **Stipules** persistent, ovate-lanceolate, 3–8 × 1.5–3 mm. **Leaves: petiole** pink, sparsely hairy, 0.7–2 cm long, joining blade at an angle; **blade** above green with red veins, sparsely hairy, beneath paler green with purple veins, hairy on veins, outline of blade asymmetric-ovate, 3.5–10.5 × 3–9 cm, palmately compound, five- to six-lobed, lobes themselves deeply lobed and their margin toothed. **Inflorescence:** unisexual, male inflorescence terminal, few-flowered, cymose; **bracts** deciduous to persistent, lanceolate, ca. 1 × 0.5 mm; female flowers solitary in upper leaf axils, occasionally hidden in the foliage; **bracts** persistent, lanceolate to ovate, ca. 2 × 1 mm. **Male flowers: tepals** two, white, tinged faint pink along veins, uppermost segment elliptic, 0.8–1 × ca. 0.6 cm, lowermost segment elliptic to oblong-elliptic, 0.8–1 × 0.6–0.8 cm; **stamens** 45–50, arranged symmetrically to slightly asymmetrically, filaments of the innermost stamens fused into a 1 mm tall column, anther connectives not projecting. **Female flowers: bracteoles** persistent, paired directly beneath ovary, linear, ca. 1.5 mm long; **tepals** five, pale pink with whitish pink apices, ovate, elliptic or obovate, 0.6–1.2 × 0.3–0.5 mm; **ovary** green with a pink tinge or reddish, ellipsoid to narrowly obovoid, 5–8 × 2.5–5.5 mm, more or less equally three-winged, three-locular, **placentae** axile, bifid; **styles** three, shortly once-branched, stigmas in a spiraled band.

Begonia polilloensis. Drawing by Adèle Rossetti Morosini

This small, choice, Philippine species was described only in 2005, despite having been introduced into cultivation in the United States in the early 1980s. At that time, Martin Johnson collected it as *Begonia* number 45. These days, however, it is usually grown under the American Begonia Society code U076 and is now cultivated in Europe as well as the United States. The plants in cultivation were collected as seed on the island of Polillo, but the species has also been collected in a location adjacent to this on the larger Philippine island of Luzon, near the town of Real, and on the Philippine island of Negros. In the past *B. polilloensis* was mistakenly identified as *B. incisa*, a name under which it is still commonly grown. *Begonia incisa* is a native of the Philippine island of Luzon and differs most noticeably from *B. polilloensis* by having deeply incised rather than palmately compound leaves. The palmately compound leaves of *B. polilloensis* coupled with its pink, two-tepaled male flowers that are borne in cymes and solitary female flowers with five tepals instantly distinguish it from all other widely cultivated begonias. A similar species from Papua New Guinea named *B. oligandra* is very rarely cultivated and is distinguished from *B. polilloensis* by being completely hairless and having white flowers.

Begonia polilloensis is readily grown as long as it is given a humid, lightly shaded position and a relatively low temperature in the vicinity of 65°F (18°C). It does well in a sealed terrarium but will grow equally well on a greenhouse bench. It produces attractive pink flowers in early spring. *Begonia polilloensis* is well established in cultivation but apparently is not yet available commercially. No hybrids with this species are recorded in the literature.

Begonia prismatocarpa W. J. Hooker (PLATES 154 AND 161)

section *Loasibegonia*, rhizomatous group
Curtis's Botanical Magazine 88: pl. 5307 (1862)

Creeping rhizomatous perennial to 11 cm tall. Rhizome slender, green, hairy. **Stipules** persistent, triangular-ovate, 0.8–3.5 × 1.5–2 mm. **Leaves: petiole** bronze-green, hairy, 1.7–7.5 cm long, continuing straight into main vein of blade; **blade** above glossy medium to dark green, sometimes tinged red, beneath paler dull silvery green, both surfaces hairless, asymmetric, ovate to broadly ovate, 1.3–4 × 0.6–3 cm, apex acute or sometimes obtuse, base rounded or cordate, margin usually unequally two- to three-lobed, distinctly shallowly toothed, veins palmate. **Inflorescence:** axillary, bisexual, cymose, with two to three male flowers and one to two terminal female flowers; **bracts** persistent, broadly elliptic to narrowly ovate, 0.9–2.5 × ca. 2 mm, margin toothed, ciliate. **Male flowers: tepals** two, outer surface of uppermost tepal orange-red with darker streaks, inner surface of uppermost tepal golden yellow with a red patch and red veins in the basal half, the lowermost tepal golden yellow on both surfaces, circular to broadly ovate or obovate, 5.7–13 × 6.1–12.5 mm; **stamens** 17–22, arrangement resembling a bunch of bananas attached to a short column, anther connectives not projecting. **Female flowers: bracteoles** absent; **tepals** two, same color as males, transversely ovate, 3.5–5.5 × 4.5–6 mm; **ovary** pale green, narrowly ellipsoid to narrowly obovoid, four-angular, 7–9 × 1.8–2 mm, with four narrow wings, four-locular, **placentae** axile, entire; **styles** four, fused at base, apex crescent- or V-shaped, stigmas in a non-spiraled band. **2n** = 32.

This yellow-flowered African begonia is an old favorite because its free-flowering nature and dwarf, creeping habit make it a perfect plant for an enclosed terrarium or bowl. Gustav Mann first collected *Begonia prismatocarpa* in 1861 in mountainous terrain on the West African island of Bioko (formerly Fernando Póo). Since Mann's discovery, it has also been found on nearby mainland Africa. Nevertheless, the cultivated material of this species must have been collected on Bioko since it has the lobed leaves and narrowly elliptic ovaries characteristic of the plants on this island. Whether the plants cultivated today are descended from material Mann sent to Kew Gardens, or if they represent a more recent collection, is not certain. What we do know is that the species was first introduced to the United States from England in 1969 and that these plants can be traced back to material sent to English plant enthusiast Maurice Mason around 1956. *Begonia prismatocarpa* has now become firmly established in cultivation and is available from several commercial mail order sources. The species is easily recognized by the combination of its small size, yellow flowers, and non-peltate, ovate leaves. Just a handful of other creeping rhizomatous yellow-flowered begonias are cultivated. These have peltate leaves and are discussed under *B. quadrialata*. Several other yellow-flowered African species deserve to be more widely grown. Paramount among these is the ribbon-leaved *B. vittarifolia* from Gabon (Plate 160). The rarely cultivated *B. iucunda* is also quite closely related to these other yellow-flowered species but is easily distinguished by its cordate leaf bases, underground tuberous rhizomes, and solitary yellow flowers that are wine-red in bud. *Begonia dewildei* (Plate 155) is likewise a rarely cultivated but highly desirable relative. It has tepals that are white to pale pink on the inner surface and leaf blades that are subpeltate and narrowly obovate to elliptic-obovate. *Begonia ciliobracteata* is a related species with usually peltate leaves, white or pale pink or very rarely yellow tepals, and obtriangular to very broadly obovate fruit to 2 × 3.8 cm.

Begonia dewildei. Drawing by Ike Zewaldthe. Courtesy of National Herbarium Nederland: Wageningen branch, Biosystematics Group, Wageningen University, the Netherlands

Begonia prismatocarpa is a deservedly popular species that is well worth the little extra attention necessary for its successful cultivation. The species requires high humidity and high light levels and is usually grown in an enclosed terrarium or glass bowl either on a windowsill or under lights. When grown under natural light, plants should be positioned away from direct sunlight since this can cause their containers to overheat. In the wild, *B. prismatocarpa* grows on rocks and decaying tree branches and accordingly in cultivation should be given an open soil mix. It is usually grown in a substrate of coarsely chopped sphagnum moss and perlite. The species is readily propagated from seed, rhizomes, or leaf cuttings and even, when several new plants are required, from small wedges taken from a single leaf. Even though *B. prismatocarpa* is perhaps the easiest of the yellow-flowered African species in cultivation, it is, nevertheless, temperamental and for this reason keeping a few small plants in reserve is prudent.

Begonia prismatocarpa has been crossed with two other yellow-flowered African begonias to produce two very popular cultivars: *B.* 'Buttercup' (*B. prismatocarpa* × *B. microsperma*) and *B.* 'Gold Coast' (*B. prismatocarpa* × *B. staudtii*). Other hybrids with *B. prismatocarpa* parentage include: *B.* 'Pink Chaser', *B.* 'Far Out', and *B.* 'Ona-Mae'. The last is an interesting, but rarely seen, cross between *B. violifolia* and *B. prismatocarpa*. *Begonia prismatocarpa* 'Variegation' is a sport with leaves that are almost white when young and later develop a green center and pinkish white margin.

Begonia quadrialata Warburg (PLATES 156 AND 157)

section *Loasibegonia*, rhizomatous group

Botanische Jahrbücher für Systematik, Pflanzengeschichte und Pflanzengeographie 22: 43 (1895)

Rhizomatous perennial to 25 cm tall. **Stipules** persistent, triangular-ovate or elliptic ovate, 1.7–6.1 × 5–6 mm. **Leaves:** peltate; **petiole** pale pinkish red to dark red, 2.5–18 cm long; **blade** above pale to medium green, or pale green with purplish brown bands along main veins, beneath pale green, sometimes reddish tinged or reddish brown, both surfaces hairless to hairy, asymmetric, broadly elliptic-ovate to more or less circular, sometimes elliptic-ovate, 2.5–12.5 × 2–9 cm, apex rounded to acuminate, margin entire to shallowly sinuate or sometimes denticulate toward the apex. **Inflorescence:** axillary, bisexual, cymose, with two to five male and one to two female flowers; **bracts** persistent, ovate to elliptic or elliptic-obovate, 1.2–3.8 mm long, margin toothed, ciliate. **Male flowers: tepals** two, outer surface of upper tepal reddish to orange, inner surface of upper tepal yellow with a red patch and veins, outer surface of lowermost tepal orange to yellow, inner surface of lowermost tepal yellow, both tepals broadly ovate to broadly elliptic, broadly elliptic-obovate to almost circular, or very broadly ovate, 0.5–1.2 × 0.5–1.1 cm; **stamens** 16–27, arrangement resembling a bunch of bananas, anther connectives not projecting. **Female flowers: bracteoles** absent; **tepals** similar to male; **ovary** green to brown, ellipsoid to broadly obovoid, 5–20 × 2–10 mm, almost equally four-winged, four-locular, **placentae** axile, entire; **styles** four, once-branched, stigmas in a straight or only slightly spiraled band. **2n** = 52.

A fascinating group of small yellow-flowered begonias grows in the wetter parts of tropical East Africa's lowland rain forest. One of these, *Begonia prismatocarpa* (Plates 154 and 161), is treated separately, along with *B. iucunda* and *B. vittariifolia*; the other ten cultivated species (for example, see Plates 156–160) are discussed here. These differ from *B. prismatocarpa*, *B. iucunda*, and *B. vittariifolia* in having peltate leaves, but otherwise all of them share several features reflecting their common ancestry. They occur in a variety of shady habitats, but most often grow close to streams or rivers and in many cases actually live in the spray zones of waterfalls. As would be expected, they require high atmospheric humidity in cultivation and do best when grown in enclosed glass or plastic bowls. The cultivation of begonias in bowls and terrariums is discussed in full in chapter two. If proper attention is given to their soil mix and the amount of light they receive, most are not difficult to grow. In fact, for those of us who must travel a great deal, these plants make excellent choices, since their sealed containers can be left unattended for many weeks. Care should, nevertheless, be taken to position the containers away from direct sunlight because these are naturally plants of the shady forest. A glass bowl positioned even a short time in sun will act as a cook pot and effectively stew the plant inside. In my experience placing the containers under artificial lights set on timers is usually safer than growing them under direct sunlight. *Begonia lacunosa*, *B. microsperma*, and *B. staudtii* grow in very deep shade in the wild and have evolved conical-shaped projections (bullae) on their leaf surfaces that serve to capture more efficiently light scattered by the forest canopy. All three also require relatively low light levels in cultivation. An identification key to the cultivated yellow-flowered African begonias is provided here. An interesting and authoritative account of these species is provided in: Sosef, M. S. M. (1994) Refuge begonias: taxonomy, phylogeny and historical biogeography of *Begonia* section *Loasibegonia* and section *Scutobegonia* in relation to glacial rain forest refuges in Africa. *Wageningen Agricultural University Papers*, Studies in Begoniaceae 5, 306 pp. Other less technical references are: Doorenbos, J. (1980) Yellow-flowering species from Africa. *Begonian* 47: 12–16 and Doorenbos, J. (1980) More of the Fascinating Yellow Flowerers. *Begonian* 47: 34–37.

Key to the cultivated yellow-flowered species of sections *Loasibegonia* and *Scutobegonia*

1 a. Leaves not peltate 2
b. Leaves peltate 3
2 a. Leaves ovate to broadly ovate, 1.3–4 cm long . . . . *B. prismatocarpa*
b. Leaves linear, 6.5–19 cm long . . . . *B. vittariifolia*
3 a. Upper surfaces of leaves bullate 4
b. Upper surfaces of leaves either smooth or hairy but never bullate 6
4 a. Leaves green in central part, purplish brown around the margins; tuft of hairs absent on upper leaf surface at position of petiole attachment; ovary hairy, almost as wide as long . . . . *B. lacunosa*
b. Leaves green throughout; a tuft of hairs usually present on upper leaf surface at position of petiole attachment; ovary hairless, more than twice as long as wide 5
5 a. Upper surfaces of leaves with large, solitary, conical bullae . . . . *B. microsperma*
b. Upper surfaces of leaves with groups of three to four small, rounded bullae . . . . *B. staudtii*
6 a. Rhizome creeping or only slightly ascending at apex; ovary more than 1.5 times as long as wide 7
b. Rhizome eventually forming a more or less distinct, erect, aerial stem; ovary almost as wide as long 11
7 a. Upper surfaces of leaves densely hairy . . . . *B. potamophila*
b. Upper surfaces of leaves hairless to sparsely hairy 8
8 a. Ovary with three short wings 9
b. Ovary lacking wings . . . . *B. scapigera*
9 a. Leaves broadly elliptic-ovate to more or less circular, sometimes elliptic-ovate, apex rounded to acuminate, 2.5–12.5 × 2–9 cm; ovary lacking a beak 10
b. Leaves very narrowly elliptic or elliptic-ovate to broadly elliptic or broadly ovate, 0.5–12 × 0.4–6.5 cm; ovary with a beak to 5 mm long . . . . *B. scutifolia*
10 a. Leaves pale to medium green . . . . *B. quadrialata* subsp. *quadrialata*
b. Leaves pale green with dark purple bands along the larger veins . . . .*B. quadrialata* subsp. *nimbaensis*
11 a. Leaves, blade hairless above; ovary with short wings 12
b. Leaves densely hairy above; ovary lacking wings . . . . *B. ferramica*
12 a. Petiole inserted 1 mm from nearest margin of blade . . . . . *B. montis-elephantis*
b. Petiole inserted 5–50 mm from nearest margin of blade . . . . *B. clypeifolia*

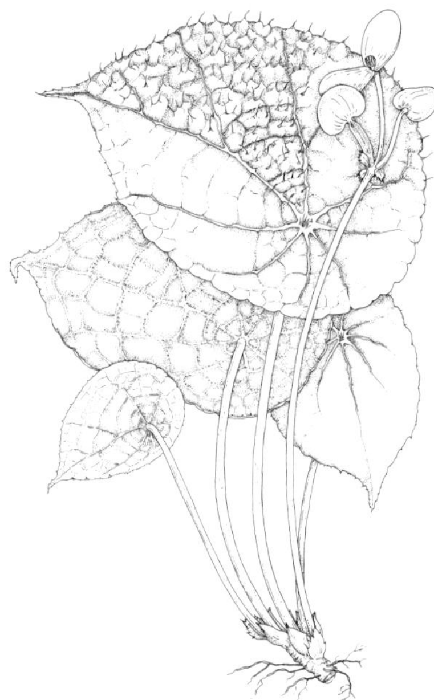

Begonia microsperma. Drawing by Wil Wessel. Courtesy of National Herbarium Nederland: Wageningen branch, Biosystematics Group, Wageningen University, the Netherlands

Of all the yellow-flowered species, *Begonia quadrialata* is my favorite. In fact, it must be many people's favorite as it is one of the most commonly cultivated of the yellow-flowered species. Two subspecies are cultivated, one with leaves that are green (the typical species) and one with leaves that have beautiful purplish brown bands along the main veins (*B. quadrialata* subsp. *nimbaensis*). The latter is a real gem and despite being described only in 1994, it has long been cultivated in both Europe and North America. It was previously grown under the unpublished name *B. leichtiana*. In the wild it grows on and around Mount Nimba at altitudes of 350–1600 m. Mark Sosef, an expert on the yellow-flowered begonias of Africa, reports that it often grows in drier forest conditions than the other yellow-flowered African species and is always found on rocks or cliff walls in semi-shaded to shaded locations. The typical species is found throughout much of tropical East Africa and is more variable than *B. quadrialata* subsp. *nimbaensis*. In the wild, this and other related species grow in acidic soils (pH 4.2 to 4.5) and for this reason need a soil mix containing sphagnum moss or peat. As with most of the other yellow-flowered African begonias hybridizers have largely ignored *B. quadrialata*.

Begonia rajah Ridley (PLATE 161)

section *Reichenheimia*, rhizomatous group
Gardener's Chronicle (London) 3. Ser. 16: 213, fig. 31 (1894)

Dwarf, creeping rhizomatous perennial. **Stipules** persistent, ovate, 1.5–11 × 5–6 mm. **Leaves: petiole** reddish pink with scattered hairs or hairless, 2–10 cm long, continuing straight into main vein of blade or joining at an angle; **blade** above bronze-green to purple-brown with yellowish green veins, interveinal area slightly raised, hairless throughout, beneath dull red, veins sometimes sparsely hairy, elsewhere hairless, circular or broadly kidney-shaped, angular, 4.5–9 × 3.5–14 cm, apex abruptly acuminate, base unequally cordate, margin shortly toothed, ciliate, shallowly angular-lobed, veins palmate. **Inflorescence:** axillary, few-flowered, bisexual, cymose, 10–20 cm tall; **bracts** persistent, circular, elliptic, or obovate, 2–7 × 1–4 mm, margin ciliate. **Male flowers: tepals** four, outer pair white with pink margins and veins, broadly ovate, 4–12 × 5–12 mm, outer surface hairless to moderately hairy, inner pair white with pink veins, narrowly obovate, 5–11 × 1.2–5 mm; **stamens** 20–100 or more, arranged in a spherical mass on top of a column, anther connectives not projecting. **Female flowers: bracteoles** absent; **tepals** usually three, but rarely four, pale pink, outer pair ovate, elliptic, or obovate-elliptic, base wedge-shaped, 6–11 × 5–8.5 mm, inner one to two narrowly oblong to narrowly obovate, base wedge-shaped, 4–10 × 1.2–3 mm; **ovary** white with a pink tinge, ovoid, 4–7 × 2–5 mm, almost equally three-winged, three-locular, **placentae** axile, entire; **styles** three, horseshoe-shaped, stigmas in a spiraled band. **2n** = 30.

Begonia rajah was first collected on the Malay Peninsula in Terengganu State and introduced into cultivation at Singapore Botanic Garden in 1892. From this important colonial garden, plants were sent to England. In 1894 one of them was exhibited at the Royal Horticultural Society by Sander and Company and received a coveted First Class Certificate. Eventually the species became widely cultivated, but no more has been seen of it in the wild. Furthermore, since much of its forest habitat has been destroyed it may well no longer exist as a natural plant. In 1989 *Begonia* taxonomist Ruth Kiew reported that she had relocated *B. rajah* growing in the foothills of Mount Lawit, presumably close to where this species had first been collected. However, upon closer study she discovered that these plants differ from *B. rajah* in their tepal number and several other important characteristics. Accordingly, in 2004 she published them as a new species—*B. reginula*. This species is obviously a close relative of *B. rajah* and is not currently in cultivation.

Because *Begonia rajah* is known only from cultivated material the species is considered critically endangered. For this reason, we must strive to conserve it in cultivation. Luckily *B. rajah* is widely cultivated and available from several commercial sources. However, the entire group of cultivated plants stem from the few plants introduced to England in the late 1800s, and it is, therefore, not very genetically diverse.

With its distinctive undulated leaf surfaces that shimmer with bronze-green or purple-brown tints, *Begonia rajah* is one of the most attractive of the begonias suitable for a humid, enclosed terrarium. To produce its attractive, brightly colored leaves *B. rajah* needs a cool temperature, in the range of 62 to 65°F (16–18°C), and a relatively low intensity of light. It is also said to benefit from the regular application of fertilizer. *Begonia rajah* is readily propagated from leaf cuttings or fresh seed. Commercially available hybrid cultivars include *B.* 'Butterscotch' (*B.*

subnummularifolia × *B. rajah*), *B.* 'Mumtaz' (*B. goegoensis* × *B. rajah*), *B.* 'Rajkumari' (*B. sudjanae* × *B. rajah*), and *B.* 'Sansouci' (*B. goegoensis* × *B. rajah*).

Begonia ravenii C.-I. Peng & Y.-K. Chen

section *Diploclinium*, tuberous group

Botanical Bulletin of Academia Sinica 29: 217, pls. 1–2 (1988)

Tuberous, stoloniferous perennial to 50 cm tall. **Stipules** deciduous, ovate, 5–7 × 2–4 mm, main vein projecting at apex, margin ciliate. **Leaves: petiole** pink, hairless, 2.5–16 cm long, continuing straight into main vein of blade; **blade** green on both surfaces, hairless, almost symmetric, ovate, 3.5–27 × 2.2–18 cm, apex almost acute to acuminate, base cordate, margin irregularly toothed, veins palmate-pinnate. **Inflorescence:** axillary, drooping, few-flowered, bisexual, cymose; **bracts** deciduous, narrowly ovate or elliptic, 8.5–12 × 5–7 mm, margin finely toothed. **Male flowers: tepals** two, pink, ovate-cordate, 1–2.2 × 1.4–2.1 cm; **stamens** about 20–40, arranged asymmetrically, anther connective not projecting. **Female flowers: bracteoles** absent; **tepals** two or rarely three, pink to pale purple, almost circular, 12–15 × 12–15 mm; **ovary** white, becoming pink to red with maturity, obovoid, 0.7–0.8 × 0.5–0.6 cm, almost equally three-winged, three-locular, **placentae** axile, bifid; **styles** three, once-branched, stigmas in a spiraled band. **2n** = 36.

Begonia ravenii, showing its unusual stolons, which arise from small tubers. Drawing by Wanling Peng, Institute of Botany, Academica Sinica, Taiwan

Begonia ravenii is notable for having thread-like stolons that are produced from small tubers, a feature that is otherwise very rare in the genus. Along with its deciduous leaves the stolons and tubers adapt it to grow and disperse on the shallow soils that accumulate on steep, shady rock faces in the seasonally dry mountains of west-central Taiwan. It is found there at an altitude of 350–1000 m. It is remarkable, but by no means unprecedented, that such a distinct species remained undescribed until 1988. Soon after its discovery, *B.*

ravenii was introduced to the United States via Missouri Botanical Garden. The name *ravenii* commemorates that garden's director, Peter Raven.

Begonia ravenii can be a little tricky in cultivation, especially during the winter when it sometimes becomes dormant and survives as underground tubers. At that time it needs less frequent watering. It is best grown in a terrarium or humid greenhouse and prefers relatively cool temperatures in the range of 62 to 65°F (16–18°C). The species is best grown in a slightly heavier mix than other terrarium species, with a little light potting soil added to the typical chopped sphagnum–perlite mix. It produces its flowers from late spring through autumn. Propagation is by seed, division, or by potting up the small plants that form at the ends of the stolons. No hybrids with *B. ravenii* have been documented.

Begonia rex Putzeys (PLATE 89B)

section *Platycentrum*, Rex-cultorum group

Flores des Serres et des Jardins de l'Europe II, 2: 141, pls. 1255–1258 (1857)

Creeping rhizomatous perennial. Rhizome rooting at nodes, reddish brown, sparsely hairy. **Stipules** persistent, triangular, main vein projecting, 1.8–2.5 × 1.1–1.5 cm. **Leaves: petiole** yellowish green or pink with long white hairs, 5.5–25 cm long, joining blade at an angle; **blade** above dark velvety gray-brown with a 2–5-cm-wide silver-gray band 1–3 cm from the margin, base of veins yellowish green with a few scattered long hairs, beneath burgundy, hairy on the main veins, asymmetric, ovate, 7–20 × 5.5–17 cm, apex shortly acuminate, base obtusely cordate, margin with short blunt irregular teeth, ciliate, veins palmate. **Inflorescence:** axillary, few-flowered, unisexual or bisexual, cymose; **bracts** soon falling, ovate, concave, 9–16 × 5–7 mm. **Male flowers: tepals** four, outer pair white with pink and pale green tinges, ovate, 1.4–2.3 × 1.3–2 cm, concave, inner pair white, broadly obovate to broadly elliptic, 1.2–2 × 0.9–1.2 cm; **stamens** numerous, arranged symmetrically and attached to a column, anther connectives long projecting and pointed. **Female flowers: bracteoles** absent; **tepals** five, white with a pink tinge, outer pair ovate to elliptic, 1.5–2 × 1.1–1.3 cm, inner three obovate-elliptic to obovate, 1.5–1.9 × 1.1–1.4 cm; **ovary** pale green, sometimes tinged pink, asymmetric-obovoid, 0.8–1.3 × 0.3–0.6 cm, unequally three-winged, one wing much longer than the others, two-locular, **placentae** axile, bifid; **styles** two, once-branched, stigmas in a spiraled band. **2n** = 22.

Begonia rex is an attractive plant with large, velvety, gray-brown leaves that are ringed with a prominent silver-gray band. The species, though currently rare in cultivation, is important because it has played a prominant role in the development of the Rex-cultorum group, a large, diverse group of hybrids, whose members are famed for their particularly beautiful foliage. Belgian horticulturist Jean Linden was the first to commercialize the species in 1858. Records conflict on whether he received his original plant directly from the collector, Charles Simons, who had discovered it in northeast India, or if, in a more arresting but less likely version of the story, he discovered it himself at a London auction growing in the leaf axil of an orchid Simons had collected.

Regardless of how the species arrived in cultivation, *Begonia rex* has proven to be one of the most commercially important of all *Begonia* species. Ever since it came to the attention of Europe's hybridizers it has been crossed with numerous other begonias to form thousands of hybrid cultivars, a few hundred of which are still grown today. Often, *B. rex*'s closest relatives were used in the initial crosses, not only because many of them are beautiful foliage plants in their own right, but also because they readily produce hybrids with *B. rex*. They hybridize easily because they share the same chromosome number, 2n = 22. Prominent examples include *B. annulata*, *B. cathayana*, *B. decora*, *B. diadema*, *B. hatacoa*, *B. palmata*, and *B. xanthina*. In addition, more distantly related species were hybridized with *B. rex* soon afterward. Examples include *B. grandis* and *B. robusta* from Asia, *B. dregei* from southern Africa, *B. socotrana* from the Yemeni island of Socotra, and *B. imperialis* from Mexico. Each of these species introduced new characteristics into the group. The use of *B. cathayana*, for example, led to a range of hybrids covered with lush, velvety hairs, and *B. decora* gave rise to plants having colorful, often reddish foliage with a metallic sheen. *Begonia diadema* gave rise to plants with lobed leaves, and *B. dregei* produced the first miniature-leaved hybrids. Not surprisingly the Rex-cultorum group contains an incredibly diverse mix of plants now at the start of the twenty-first century. The hybrids often differ strikingly in habit and size, as well as in the coloration, pubescence, and shape of their leaves. Strictly speaking the Rex-cultorum group is defined as containing only those hybrids with *B. rex* parentage, which have showy foliage. The appearance of some of the hybrids in the group, however, suggests that they may not have received any *B. rex* parentage at all. From a practical standpoint, this matters little, though, since most people, whether they realize it or not, use the name Rex-cultorum group to provide a convenient label under which can be grouped the showiest of the hybrid foliage begonias, whether they have in their parentage *B. rex* or another closely related species from the section *Platycentrum*.

Much of the groundwork that produced the Rex-cultorum group was carried out in the mid to late 1800s, a time when foliage plants were particularly fashionable and many of the parent species were first entering into cultivation. Indeed, one of the early hybrids important in subsequent *Begonia rex* crosses was produced prior to *B. rex*'s introduction in 1853. Benedict Roezl produced it by crossing *B. xanthina* (Plates 89e and 208), a striking foliage plant, with a form of *B. hatacoa* with silver-spotted leaves. The resulting hybrid inherited the large attractive leaves of *B. xanthina* and the silver color of *B. hatacoa*. Almost as soon as Linden acquired *B. rex* in 1857 he crossed it with this hybrid. However, the early *B. rex* hybrids were produced not only at Jean Linden's nursery in Belgium, but elsewhere in continental Europe and in England. Springfield Nursery, situated in what is now the London district of Upper Tooting, was a particularly important source of early hybrids since the nursery's owner, William Rollinson, bought a portion of Linden's stock plants in 1857 along with the exclusive rights to distribute the species in England. In continental Europe prominent nurseries, like those owned by Louise Van Houtte and Ambroise Verscheffelt, must also have purchased plants of *B. rex* from Linden soon after the species appeared in cultivation, because they too were commercially producing hybrids a year or two after the species' introduction. Perhaps the earliest of the *B. rex* hybrids that still survives in our gardens is *B.* 'Fireflush' (Plate 164), an 1866 French introduction that is covered with beautiful long red hairs that were inherited from the parental species *B. robusta*. This hybrid remains one of the most beautiful members available from the Rex-cultorum group. In 1883 Nemeczek, a gardener for the Erdody family of Hungary, produced *B.* 'Comtesse Louise Erdody', which was probably the first of the spiral-leaved hybrids. In this and subsequent spiral-leaved cultivars the lowermost of the two basal leaf lobes is spiraled and projects above the rest of the leaf blade.

Further selection and hybridization of this and other members of the Rex-cultorum group has continued into the twenty-first century. One continuing trend has been the production of plants more amenable to use as outdoor foliage plants for mixed containers (Plate 37). Another interesting direction that artificial selection has taken has been the production of cultivars with flowers that are hidden beneath the leaves, a distinct advantage in a group of plants grown almost exclusively for their beautiful foliage. Two modern cultivars that are now in high favor include *Begonia* 'Purple Petticoats' with spiral leaves fringed in pastel purple, a 1968 release, and my own favorite, *B.* 'Merry Christmas' (Plate 162), which has multicolored leaves, and which first appeared in 1974.

Despite the long-standing popularity of the Rex-cultorum group, few but the serious collector grow the true species today. Indeed, even by the early 1900s *Begonia rex*, had become rare in cultivation. This is not too surprising given that the species is somewhat demanding in its cultural requirements. *Begonia rex* is native to the monsoon-drenched mountains that occupy the remote, and currently largely inaccessible, far northeast corner of India. As a result of its cloudy, rain-soaked habitat *B. rex* requires more protection from direct sunlight and more humidity than most other begonias. Despite the species' aversion to direct sunlight, best leaf coloration in many of the hybrids results when they are grown in a bright location. For these reasons such members of the Rex-cultorum group are often grown commercially in a humid, shaded greenhouse, under lights. Typically with a daytime temperature range of 70 to 85°F (21–29°C) and slightly lower nighttime temperatures. At Brooklyn Botanic Garden the species is cultivated in a shady position on the floor next to a wet pad where the atmosphere is particularly humid and the temperature relatively cool. Growers at the garden have tried a variety of soil mixes and the species has thrived in all, even flowering profusely when grown in no more than wet sand.

Further detailed information on the history and cultivation of *Begonia rex* and the Rex-cultorum group is available in the March 1980 edition of the *Begonian*, which is devoted to this subject. Krauss (1947) also provides descriptions of several of the older cultivars.

Recently a closely related species, *Begonia sizemoreae*, with leaf markings similar to *B. rex*, has entered cultivation and is starting to become widely distributed. Mary Sizemore originally collected this species in 1996 in Vietnam on a bank of a river near Hanoi; it was previously cultivated under the American Begonia Society code U388 and is sometimes grown under the incorrect name *B. longiciliata*. This newly described species is certainly a very beautiful foliage plant and in my experience is somewhat easier to grow than *B. rex*. It can be distinguished from *B. rex* by its greener leaf blades that have a greenish gray band 1–3 cm from the margin, and a few long hairs upon their upper surface. The species also has attractive pink flowers. Plate 89 shows a comparison of the leaf blades of this species and a number of other members of the section *Platycentrum*, including *B. rex*.

Begonia robusta Blume (PLATE 163)

section *Sphenanthera*, rhizomatous group
Enumeratio Plantarum Javae 1: 96 (1827)
Synonym: *B. splendida* K. Koch

Erect shortly rhizomatous subshrub to 2 m tall. Stems, leaves, and outer surfaces of tepals with a dense covering of long red or white hairs. **Stipules** persistent, lanceolate to ovate, 1–3.7 × 0.9–2.4 cm. **Leaves: petiole** green, 10–40 cm long, joining blade at an angle; **blade** above green, beneath grayish green, in outline ovate to almost circular, 10–25 × 10–35 cm, usually irregularly five- to eight-lobed, sometimes almost entire, especially in young plants, lobes narrowly to broadly triangular, to 7 cm long, margin of lobes entire, base cordate, veins palmate. **Inflorescence:** axillary, short, 12–22-flowered, bisexual, cymose; **bracts** soon falling, broadly elliptic to obovate, 0.6–2.5 × 0.2–1 cm. **Male flowers: tepals** four, white to pink, outer pair broadly elliptic, 0.8–1.6 × 0.7–1.2 cm, inner pair elliptic, 0.7–1.7 × 0.5–0.9 cm; **stamens** 65–75, arranged symmetrically, anther connectives projecting. **Female flowers: bracteoles** absent; **tepals** five, white to pink, elliptic to obovate, 0.9–2 × 6.5–1.1 cm; **ovary** fleshy, green, almost spherical, 0.7–1.5 cm in diameter, unequally three-winged, one wing much longer than others, three-locular, **placentae** axile, bifid; **styles** three, once-branched, stigmas in a spiraled band. **2n** = 88.

Many begonias are covered in interesting hairs, but those of *Begonia robusta* are among the most beautiful. In the best individuals they are bright red and very long, giving the whole plant a vibrant glow when hit by the light. In the wild, *B. robusta* is restricted to the rain forests of western Java, where it occurs on the volcanic mountain slopes at an elevation of 1100–2195 m. In this area, it often grows alongside its closest relative, *B. multangula* (Plate 165), which has a distribution that extends considerably farther east than *B. robusta*'s, eventually reaching Bali and the Lesser Sunda Islands. The two species are very much alike, particularly in the area where their distributions overlap. However, *B. robusta* has less angularly lobed leaves, longer peduncles, and more distinctly winged fruit. *Begonia multangula* is also a less hairy plant, particularly as one moves eastward, where its upper leaf surfaces are almost always a glossy green.

Begonia robusta has been cultivated on and off since the late 1850s, but does not appear to have ever been common. Scott Hoover reintroduced both it and *B. multangula* in the 1990s via numerous seed collections, which were distributed by the American Begonia Society. Since much of this seed was unnamed at the time of its introduction many of the resulting plants are currently unidentified in cultivation. Nevertheless, both *B. robusta* and *B. multangula* are easily recognized by the combination of their tall upright stems, large leaves that typically hide the relatively short inflorescences, three-locular ovaries with axile, bifid placentae, and their fleshy fruits that remain attached to the plant for several months without releasing their seed. The only species with which they could be confused vegetatively is *B. areolata* (Plate 90), which Scott Hoover also introduced from Java at the same time. Nevertheless this species differs by having bullate leaf surfaces and ovaries with two locules.

Both *Begonia robusta* and *B. multangula* are tricky to grow because they are intolerant of high temperatures. They need to be grown around 62–65°F (16–18°C), but otherwise they may be cultivated under standard conditions. In the mid to late

1800s *B. robusta* was hybridized with members of the Rex-cultorum group and species of the section *Platycentrum*, producing several cultivars bearing its striking red leaf hairs. *Begonia* 'Fireflush' (Plate 164) is undoubtedly the best of these, but others probably include *B.* 'Baby Rainbow', *B.* 'Child's Spotted', *B.* 'Damon', and *B.* 'King Henry VII'.

Begonia rotundifolia Lamarck

section *Begonia*, rhizomatous group
Encyclopédie Méthodique Botanique 1: 394 (1783)

Creeping rhizomatous perennial. Rhizome greenish brown, hairless, branched to about 10 cm long. **Stipules** persistent, broadly ovate, concave, 0.7–1 × 0.5–0.7 cm. **Leaves: petiole** reddish, hairless, 8–20 cm long, almost continuing straight into main vein of blade or joining it at a distinct angle; **blade** above green, hairless, beneath paler green, hairless, slightly asymmetric, circular, 2–8 × 3–9.5 cm, apex indistinct, base cordate, margin crenate, veins palmate. **Inflorescence:** in upper leaf axils, few-flowered, bisexual, cymose; **bracts** obovate, concave, 1–1.5 × 0.7–1.2 cm. **Male flowers:** not opening fully; **tepals** four, white or occasionally pink to red, sometimes faintly tinged green at base, outer pair ovate to elliptic, 0.7–1.4 × 0.6–0.9 cm, inner pair elliptic to obovate, 5–11 × 3–6 mm, apex cleft; **stamens** about 8–15, arranged symmetrically, anthers much longer than filaments, anther connectives projecting. **Female flowers: bracteoles** paired about 2 mm beneath ovary, obovate, 3–5 × 1–2.5 mm; **tepals** five, same color as males, elliptic, 5–10 × 3–7 mm; **ovary** white to pale green, ellipsoid to broadly obovoid, 3–8 × 1.8–6 mm, unequally three-winged, one wing longer than the others and usually curved over the styles, three-locular, **placentae** axile, bifid; **styles** three, once-branched, stigmas in a spiraled band. **2n** = 52.

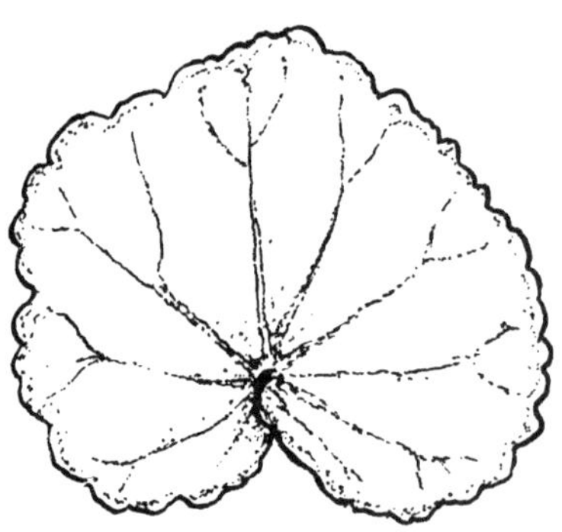

Leaf of *B. rotundifolia*.

Begonia rotundifolia is native to Haiti, where it grows on steep, inaccessible slopes and clay cliffs in the mountains at an altitude of 325–1000 m. The species is easily recognized by its creeping rhizomatous habit and small, circular leaves with crenate margins. *Begonia rotundifolia* was one of the first begonias known to European botanists, having been discovered by Charles Plumier in 1690. Plumier gave it its pre-Linnaean name of *Begonia roseo flore, folio orbiculari* in reference to its (sometimes) pink flowers and circular leaves. He does not, however, appear to have introduced it into cultivation. This species was probably first introduced into cultivation at the New York Botanical Garden from seeds that a Mr. Nash collected on Haiti's Mount Maleuvre in 1903. However, Helen Krauss on page 146 of her 1947 *Begonias for American Homes and Gardens* states that:

> Our plants came from Haiti where they grew in rosettelike clusters in the perpendicular walls of the citadel at three thousand feet altitude. A charming subject for the window garden, rockwork in the conservatory or in rock walls where the climate permits.

Begonia rotundifolia is commercially available and since 1963 has frequently been offered in the American Begonia Society seed lists. It is easy to cultivate under standard conditions and by virtue of its small size is a good plant to grow indoors under lights. However, the species is susceptible to scale and mealy bugs, which can disfigure the leaves and flowers. *Begonia* 'Kirinomegami' is a little-grown hybrid of *B. rotundifolia* and an unknown parent.

Begonia roxburghii (Miquel) A. de Candolle (PLATES 166 AND 167)

section *Sphenanthera*, rhizomatous group

Prodromus Systematis Naturalis Regni Vegetabilis 15 (1): 398 (1864)

Erect subshrub to 1.2 m tall. Stems green or burgundy with numerous red elongated lenticels. **Stipules** soon falling, narrowly ovate, 1.5–2 × 0.8–1 cm. **Leaves: petiole** green with red elongated lenticels, 7–30 cm long, joining blade at an angle; **blade** green with minute hairs, asymmetric, broadly ovate, 16–25 × 10–23 cm, apex acuminate, base cordate, margin with small widely spaced teeth, veins palmate. **Inflorescence:** axillary, few-flowered, cymose, usually not exceeding 2 cm and hidden by the leaves; male and female flowers on different plants, female flowers very sweetly fragrant; **bracts** soon falling, lanceolate, ca. 0.5 × 2.5 mm. **Male flowers: tepals** four, white or sometimes pink-tinged, outer pair ovate, deeply concave, 1–1.7 × 1–1.1 cm, the outer surfaces covered with minute hairs, inner pair obovate, 1.1–1.2 × 0.7–0.8 cm; **stamens** 25–50, arranged symmetrically, anther connectives projecting. **Female flowers: bracteoles** absent; **tepals** four, same color as males, outer pair obovate to oblong, 0.6–1.8 × 0.6–1.8 mm, outer surfaces covered with minute hairs, inner pair oblong, 0.7–1.4 × 0.5–0.8 mm; **ovary** succulent, green with red lenticels, spinning-top-shaped with a short horn at each of the four corners, four-locular, wingless, **placentae** axile, bifid; **styles** four, once-branched, stigmas in a spiraled band. **2n** = 22.

This unusual species is easily recognized by its erect green stems with red lenticels and large leathery leaves with broadly cordate bases. It is also the only cultivated species with four-locular, fleshy fruits that bear small horn-like structures. Furthermore, *Begonia roxburghii* is one of only a relatively few begonias that produce their male and female flowers on separate plants, a condition known as dioecy. The female flowers are largely hidden by the foliage, but produce a powerful spicy fragrance, which perhaps represents the strongest floral scent found in the genus. The male flowers on the other hand are only slightly fragrant. In the wild, *B. roxburghii* grows from sea level to 760 m in northeastern India, Bhutan, Bangladesh, Burma, and western Thailand. The species name commemorates William Roxburgh, who was the surgeon and superintendent of the Royal Botanical Garden of Calcutta from 1793 to 1813.

Begonia roxburghii is readily grown under standard conditions and produces its flowers freely during the spring and summer. It may also be grown as a houseplant but grows less vigorously under low humidity. At one time unnamed hybrids of *B. roxburghii* × *B. longifolia* were grown but these appear to have been lost from cultivation. No other hybrids are recorded in the literature.

Begonia handelii is a similar species that differs from *B. roxburghii* most noticeably by having a creeping, rather than erect, stem. Two varieties are recognized, differing most consistently in the size and shape of the outer tepals of their male flowers. Those of *B. handelii* var. *handelii* are an astonishing 3–6.5 cm long and have acute apices. Those of the other variety, *B. handelii* var. *prostrata*, are a more modest 1.5–2.1 cm long and have rounded apices. *Begonia handelii* var. *prostrata* was until recently recognized as a distinct species and is usually cultivated under Bob Cherry's collection number BC15. Both varieties are uncommon in cultivation and like *B. roxburghii* have fragrant flowers. *Begonia silletensis* subsp. *mengyangensis* (Plate 168) is another close relative that I introduced into cultivation in the United Kingdom in 1995 and which Bob Cherry independently introduced to Australia slightly before that (*Begonian* [1994] 61: 200–201). It is a spectacular, easy-to-grow foliage plant with creeping stems and large broadly ovate leaves measuring up to 27 × 27 cm. It too has fragrant flowers.

Slightly more distantly related is *Begonia longicarpa* from the border region of China and Vietnam, which I have only seen cultivated in the United Kingdom. It may be distinguished by its combination of creeping rhizomes; broadly ovate, glossy green leaf blades that measure 9–15 × 5–13 cm; male flowers with four tepals; female flowers with three tepals; and its white, club-shaped ovaries. The flowers are white and are produced close to the rhizome beneath the leaves.

Begonia salaziensis (Gaudichaud) Warburg (PLATE 169)
section *Mezierea*, trailing-scandent group
in Engler and Prantl, *Die Natürlichen Pflanzenfamilien* 3 (6A): 139 (1894)

Shrub with arching or erect branches to 2.4 m long. Stem branched, green when young becoming silvery brown and woody at maturity, hairless. **Stipules** deciduous, lanceolate to ovate, 1.5–4.5 × 0.5–1 cm. **Leaves: petiole** green, hairless, 2.5–11 cm long, joining blade at an angle; **blade** green on both surfaces, hairless, asymmetric, ovate, 7–16 × 3.5–10.5 cm, apex acute to acuminate, base cordate, margin entire, veins palmate. **Inflorescence:** axillary, bisexual, cymose, with up to 15 flowers; **bracts** deciduous, ovate, 10–15 × 6–10 mm. **Male flowers: tepals** four, or rarely two or three, white, outer pair almost circular, 4–8 × 5–7 mm, inner pair, when present, obovate to elliptic, 3.5–5 × 1–2 mm; **stamens** 15–18, arranged symmetrically, filaments fused at base, anther connectives not projecting. **Female flowers: bracteoles** absent; **tepals** four, white, broadly ovate to almost circular, 7–12 × 3–5 mm; **ovary** yellowish green but becoming orange in fruit, ovoid-ellipsoid, 5–10 × 2.5–6 mm, wingless, three-locular, **placentae** parietal, bifid; **styles** three, once-branched, stigmas in a spiraled band.

Begonia salaziensis is on the brink of extinction as its wild populations are restricted to a few forest fragments on the islands of Réunion and Mauritius in the Indian Ocean, and in cultivation it is found in just a handful of collections. The species was first introduced into cultivation by Wendy Strahm, who in 1986 sent seed from Mauritius to the horticultural staff of the Wageningen Agricultural University in the Netherlands. From there seed was distributed in 1987 to a few other begonia collections in Europe and North America. *Begonia salaziensis* is easily distinguished from all other begonias by its combination of long arching stems, glossy green leaves, and bright orange berry-like fruit. In the wild, it grows on moist rocks and in rock crevices in montane rain forest.

Begonia salaziensis requires plenty of room in cultivation, but it is otherwise not difficult to grow and should be more widely distributed in cultivation if it is to be preserved. No hybrids with *B. salaziensis* have been documented.

In addition to *Begonia salaziensis*, the other five members of the section *Mezierea* are very rarely cultivated: *B. comorensis*, *B. humbertii*, *B. meyeri-johannis*, *B. oxyloba*, and *B. seychellensis*. All have indehiscent, berry-like fruits that differ from those of other begonias in containing a much higher percentage of parietal placentation (over 60 percent). *Begonia comorensis* is found only on the Comoro Islands, where it grows in mist forests at altitudes above 500 m. *Begonia humber-*

tii is a little known native of Madagascar. *Begonia meyeri-johannis* occurs in a large area of tropical East Africa and grows within tropical montane forests rooted both in the soil and on fallen tree trunks. Unlike most other African begonias, it is sweetly fragrant. *Begonia oxyloba* (Plate 170) grows wild throughout the montane rain forests of tropical Africa and is the only begonia native to both continental Africa and Madagascar. In nature it grows upon fallen tree trunks within tropical montane forests. *Begonia seychellensis* is an endemic of the Seychelles' granitic islands. A detailed taxonomic treatment of the section is provided by Klazenga, N., J. J. F. E. de Wilde, and R. J. Quené, 1994, *Begonia* sect. *Mezierea* (Gaud.) Warb., a taxonomic revision. *Bull. Jard. Bot. Nat. Belg.* 63: 263–312. The key here is modified from that work.

Key to the species of section *Mezierea*

1 a. Plant with woody, vine-like stems; inflorescences unisexual . . *B. meyeri-johannis*
b. Plant with fleshy, erect, or ascending stems; inflorescences bisexual 2
2 a. Female flowers with two tepals 3
b. Female flowers with four tepals 5
3 a. Individual female flowers not surrounded by a pair of bracts, instead each pair of bracts surrounding a group of one male and two female flowers . . *B. oxyloba*
b. Individual female flowers each surrounded by a pair of bracts 4
4 a. Ovary and axis of inflorescence hairless . . . . *B. comorensis*
b. Ovary and axis of inflorescence with fine, short glandular hairs . . *B. seychellensis*
5 a. Male flowers with two tepals . . . . *B. humbertii*
b. Male flowers with four tepals . . . . *B. salaziensis*

Begonia scharffii J. D. Hooker (PLATE 171)
section *Pritzelia*, shrub-like group
Curtis's Botanical Magazine 114: pl. 7028 (1888)
Synonym: *B. haageana* Watson

Erect non-rhizomatous perennial to about 50 cm tall, the whole plant densely covered with long soft white hairs. Stem branched, pale green with short purple bands above each node. **Stipules** persistent, ovate, 1.2–2.8 × 0.9–1.9 cm. **Leaves: petiole** pale green to pale pink, 2.5–15 cm long, joining blade at an angle; **blade** above green, beneath paler green, tinged pink, asymmetric, ovate, 8–16 × 6–14 cm, apex abruptly long narrow acuminate, base cordate, margin wavy-crenate-lobed and irregularly toothed, ciliate, veins palmate-pinnate. **Inflorescence:** in upper leaf axils, many-flowered, bisexual, cymose; **bracts** deciduous, ovate, 0.3–1.6 cm × 0.5–7.5 mm. **Male flowers: tepals** four, pale pink, outer pair hairy on outer surfaces, broadly ovate to almost circular, 1.4–3 × 1.4–3 cm, inner pair obovate, 1.4–1.7 × 0.4–0.5 cm; **stamens** numerous, arranged symmetrically, anther connectives projecting. **Female flowers: bracteoles** paired beneath ovary, ovate to lanceolate-ovate, 3–5 × ca. 1 mm; **tepals** five, same color as males, outer pair hairy on outer surfaces, ovate-oblong to obovate-oblong, 0.5–2.9 × 0.3–2.8 cm, inner three elliptic, 0.6–1.4 × 0.5–0.9 cm; **ovary** pinkish white with red hairs, almost spherical, 0.3–0.7 × 0.2–0.5 cm, unequally three-winged, three-locular, **placentae** axile, bifid; **styles** three, once-branched, stigmas in a spiraled band.

Begonia scharffii is a short shrub-like species from Brazil with a dense coat of soft white hairs on its stems, leaves, and flowers. The species has been in cultivation since at least 1884, when it was first grown at Kew Gardens. The species name honors its discoverer, Scharff, as does that of another Brazilian species, the close related *B. scharffiana*. The two plants are very much alike, but *B. scharffiana* is said to have leaf bases with backward pointing lower lobes and only shallowly indented leaf veins, while *B. scharffii* has a shorter, more rounded lower lobe and much more deeply sunken veins. Of the two species, *B. scharffii* is today the one most often seen in cultivation. That said it is sometimes encountered under the incorrect name of *B. haageana*. This now synonymous name was given to it in 1889 because the plant's correct name was deemed too similar to *B. scharffiana*. However, since the current rules of botanical nomenclature do not allow this kind of name change, the older name, *B. scharffii*, still stands. Another very similar plant is *B. tomentosa*, which can be distinguished by its leaf blades having rust-colored, wool-like hairs on their undersurfaces. It also is from Brazil.

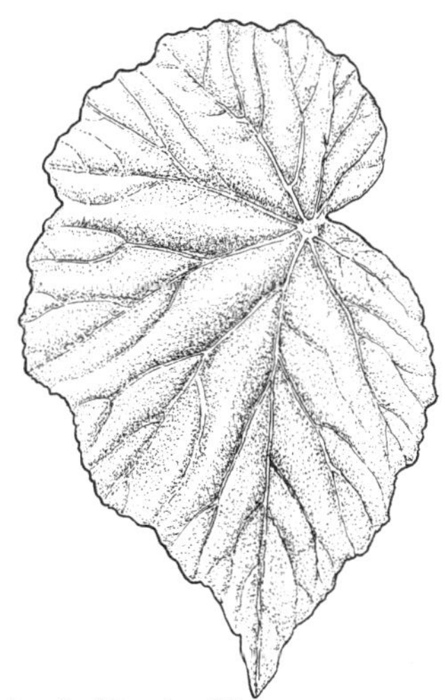
Leaf of *B. scharffii*.

Begonia scharffii, *B. scharffiana*, and *B. tomentosa* are very readily cultivated under standard conditions, as long as their growing medium is allowed to dry out slightly between waterings. *Begonia scharffii* and *B. scharffiana* are said to prefer relatively cool temperatures. Propagation is via stem cuttings or seed. *Begonia* 'Braemar' (*B. scharffii* × *B. metallica*) appears to be the only commercially available *B. scharffii* cross. *Begonia scharffiana* on the other hand is reportedly the parent of many popular hybrid cultivars, including *B.* 'Alto Scharff' (*B. scharffiana* × *B.* 'Indian Maid'), *B.* 'Credneri' (*B.*

scharffiana × *B. metallica*), *B.* 'Lady Clare' (*B. scharffiana* × *B. luxurians*), *B.* 'Ramirez' (*B. scharffiana* × *B. bradei*), and *B.* 'San Miquel' (*B. venosa* × *B. scharffiana*).

Begonia schmidtiana Regel (PLATE 172)

section *Begonia*, Semperflorens group
Gartenflora 28: 321, pl. 990 (1879)

Erect non-rhizomatous perennial with brownish red stems to 60 cm tall. Stems, leaves, and inflorescences densely covered with short white hairs. **Stipules** persistent, ovate, 0.6–1 × 0.2–0.5 cm. **Leaves: petiole** yellowish brown to pinkish brown, 1–8 cm long, attached to blade at an angle; **blade** above dull olive-green, beneath dull burgundy-red with a paler green marginal area, asymmetric, ovate, 2–6.5 × 2–5.5 cm, apex acute, base shallowly cordate to truncate, margin wavy, shallowly triangular-lobed and triangular-toothed, ciliate, veins palmate. **Inflorescence:** terminal and axillary in upper leaf axils, few-flowered, bisexual, cymose; **bracts** persistent, transversely obovate, ca. 1.5 × 1 mm, margin ciliate. **Male flowers: tepals** four, outer surfaces of outer pair white with a reddish tinge turning to pink at base, inner surfaces white, sometimes pink-tinged along veins, outer pair broadly elliptic, 1–1.5 × 0.7–1.4 cm, inner pair white, rectangular-obovate to spatula-shaped, 7–10.5 × 3–4 mm; **stamens** about 15–20, arranged symmetrically, anther connectives projecting. **Female flowers: bracteoles** three, at base of ovary, ovate, 7–10 × 2.5–4 mm, margin ciliate; **tepals** five, white with a pink tinge, elliptic, almost equal in size, 2.5–3 × 1.8–2.5 mm, **ovary** green to pink, ellipsoid, 5–6.5 × 0.4–0.5 cm, uequally or almost equally three-winged, uppermost wing longer and triangular with a hook-shaped apex projecting above the style, lowermost wings shorter, rounded, three-locular, **placentae** axile, bifid; **styles** three, once-branched, stigmas in a spiraled band. **2n** = 34.

Begonia schmidtiana was one of three very hairy species discovered in Brazil by Scharff and Haage of the German nursery firm Haage and Schmidt (the other two being *B. scharffii* and *B. scharffiana*). This species, however, occupies a particularly prominent position in the "begonia hall of fame" because soon after it was introduced in 1878 it was crossed with *B. cucullata* resulting in the first of the modern-day Semperflorens or wax begonia hybrids (see *B. cucullata* for more details). Despite being less commonly grown than the wax begonia hybrids, *B. schmidtiana* is a more attractive plant, which when happily situated will produce large numbers of attractive pinkish white flowers almost year-round.

Begonia schmidtiana should be grown in a warm, well-lit position out of direct sunlight in a greenhouse or in the home under lights. The main consideration with this species is to be careful only to water it when the top 2–3 cm of potting medium feels dry to the touch, otherwise the roots have a tendency to rot. The species is readily propagated from stem cuttings placed in a well-drained rooting mix. Aside from the numerous Semperflorens begonia hybrids, *B. schmidtiana* has contributed to the parentage of the following cultivars: *B.* 'Mandiana' (*B. subvillosa* var. *leptotricha* × *B. schmidtiana*), *B.* 'Mark Thornton' (*B. schmidtiana* × *B.* U014), *B.* 'Toe' (*B.* 'Evening Nymph' × *B. schmidtiana*), and *B.* 'Wichita Falls' (*B. schmidtiana* × *B. subvillosa* var. *leptotricha*).

Begonia socotrana J. D. Hooker (PLATES 173–175)

section *Peltaugustia*, tuberous group

Gardener's Chronicle (London) 8, fig. 1 (1881)

Erect thick-stemmed perennial to 20–45 cm tall, base of stem surrounded by a cluster of bulb-like structures encased in papery bracts. **Stipules** persistent, broadly ovate, 5.5–9 × 5–8 mm. **Leaves:** peltate and funnel-shaped; **petiole** green, sparsely hairy, 4–20 cm long; **blade** above glossy green, hairless, beneath paler green with short glandular hairs especially on the veins, circular, 4–13 cm in diameter, margin crenate. **Inflorescence:** axillary and terminal, two- to three-flowered, bisexual, cymose; **bracts** persistent, broadly ovate, 5–7 × 4–5 mm. **Male flowers: tepals** four, rose-pink, outer pair almost elliptic or broadly obovate, wedge-shaped at base, 16–24 × 13–21 mm, inner pair broadly obovate, 17–27 × 13–17 mm; **stamens** 25–35, arranged symmetrically, anther connectives not projecting. **Female flowers: bracteoles** paired beneath ovary, linear or linear-oblong, small and insignificant; **tepals** six, rose-pink, obovate or obovate-elliptic, 11–17 × 7–10 mm, persisting in fruit; **ovary** green, almost spherical, unequally three-winged, three-locular, **placentae** axile, entire; **styles** three, once-branched, stigmas in a spiraled band. **2n** = 28.

Begonia socotrana, as its name suggests, is a native of the Yemeni island of Socotra. This island is situated roughly 155 miles off the Somalian coast in the Indian Ocean and unlike most islands has retained a wonderfully rich native flora. The reason for this is that the often treacherous seas that surround Socotra render it inaccessible for much of the year. Glasgow University's Isaac Bailey Balfour discovered the species there in 1880 while he was writing a flora of the island. That a begonia was found on Socotra is remarkable since the location was thousands of miles from where the nearest begonias had previously been collected. Furthermore, much of Socotra receives very little rainfall and, as such, is an unlikely place to find this usually humidity-loving genus. More typical of such conditions are the stands of dragon's blood trees, *Dracaena cinnabari*, which are common on the island above 500 m in elevation (Plate 176). That *B. socotrana* manages to grow in this largely arid land is in part due to the fact that it inhabits the cloud-swathed mountains and high plateaus in the northeast of the island. There it grows upon cliffs and in other rocky places at an altitude of 700–1500 m, both upon granitic and limestone substrates. Another factor that allows the species to survive in a seemingly inhospitable environment is its ability to go dormant during the dry summer. To do this it produces bulb-like structures at the base of its stem (Plate 174) that store water and nutrients and tide it over until the winter rains arrive.

Until recently such structures were known in no other begonias. Then in 1996 Vanessa Plana, of the Royal Botanic Garden Edinburgh, discovered a new *Begonia* species on the nearby island of Samha that produces the same bulb-like structures. This species, which has been named *B. samhaensis* (Plate 177), differs from *B. socotrana* by only minor characteristics, such as an ovate rather than circular leaf blade, and is obviously a close relative. Both species have been the subject of studies by scientists at the Royal Botanic Garden Edinburgh. Their findings are fascinating and suggest that the two species are relicts that were "left behind" in the midst of the Indian Ocean as the early begonias migrated into Asia from Africa.

Since its discovery in the early 1880s *Begonia socotrana* has been the subject of intensive hybridization work that has resulted in what, from a commercial standpoint, are the most important of all the indoor "flowering" begonias. The early work on these hybrids was carried out at the now disbanded nursery of Veitch and Sons in London. Before *B. socotrana*'s arrival this large nursery had been active in breeding summer-flowering tuberous begonias, but when *B. socotrana* came into cultivation the company's resources were redirected to produce crosses between it and the existing tuberous hybrids. The aim was to produce a new range of cultivars with the large flowers of the *B.* ×*tuberhybrida* group, but that like *B. socotrana* flowered during the potentially lucrative winter months. John Heal, one of the hybridists employed with this task, succeeded in producing the first hybrid, which the Veitch family named in his honor, *B.* 'John Heal'. This cultivar was soon followed by additional Veitch introductions and shortly afterward by introductions from other horticultural firms, notable among which were Clibran of England and the Dutch firm of Barardse. Such was the interest in these hybrids that in 1933 Karl Fotsch coined the name *B. hiemalis* for what was then a sizable hybrid group derived from *B. socotrana* and the tuberous hybrids. Today they are correctly known as the *B.* Hiemalis group. The name *hiemalis* means "winterly" and refers to the time of year when these plants flower. Somewhat confusingly, this same group of hybrids has also in the past been referred to as the Elatior group, after one of Veitch and Sons' best releases, *B.* 'Elatior'. Other examples of cultivars in the *B.*

Hiemalis group available today include *B.* 'Altrincham Pink', *B.* 'Emily Clibran', and *B.* 'Nelly Visser'. Due to the difficulties associated with growing many of the earliest hybrids of this group their commercial success did not become fully realized until after 1955. At that time, German nurseryman Otto Rieger developed a vastly improved race that was relatively easy to grow, more disease resistant, and produced more flowers. These today are known as the *B.* Rieger group and are of immense commercial importance as winter-flowering houseplants (Plate 178). Many of the commercially available members of this hybrid group do not have cultivar names. Those with names include *B.* 'Aphrodite Joy' (a member of Rieger Nursery's Aphrodite series), *B.* 'Baluga', *B.* 'Lido', *B.* 'Northern Sunset', and *B.* 'Whisper O'Pink'.

Another historically important cross was made in 1891 at the then large nursery of Victor Lemoine in Nancy, France. At that time, Lemoine crossed *Begonia socotrana* with *B. dregei* to produce *B.* 'Gloire de Lorraine'. This cultivar, though still grown, has always been of little commercial value since it is difficult to cultivate. Nevertheless, after it was commercially released, more amenable plants were produced, both by self-pollinating *B.* 'Gloire de Lorraine' and as bud sports. These plants were perpetuated under new cultivar names and collectively became known either as Lorraine or Christmas begonias. In 1940 Thomas Everett, who was then the director of horticulture at the New York Botanical Garden, formally described all the seedlings, bud sports, and hybrids of *B.* 'Gloire de Lorraine' under the scientific name *B. cheimantha*. According to the rules of nomenclature these plants are now collectively called the *B.* Cheimantha group. A few of these cultivars are probably still in specialist collections. Examples are *B.* 'Melior', *B.* 'Marjorie Gibbs', and *B.* 'Lady Mac'. *Begonia socotrana* has also been hybridized with a few other species, the results of which have not been classified in cultivar groups. One such example is *B.* 'Gloire de Sceaux' (*B. socotrana* × *B. subpeltata*; Plate 179).

Begonia socotrana is currently rare in cultivation, because it is somewhat needy in its growing requirements. It must have a well-drained potting medium in a bright, humid environment. Most growers recommend the use of a clay pot. The species is summer dormant. In late summer or early fall the clusters of bulbils require a minimum of water to start them into new growth. Once they have begun to sprout and grow they can then be watered increasingly freely. Plants achieve full growth and flower in mid winter. After the flowering season the leaves begin to yellow and die back to the storage bulbils. As this occurs, watering should be gradually reduced and finally withdrawn completely for the summer resting period. Propagation is usually via division of clusters of bulbils.

Like *Begonia socotrana*, the many hybrids derived from this species have also frequently been considered difficult to grow. Though this is certainly true for the older cultivars many of the newer Rieger begonias are much easier to please. Nevertheless, they do need a well-drained growing medium and careful watering, for they too are prone to rot when given excess water. To prevent over watering, allow the growing medium to dry out slightly between each watering. The optimum temperature for these plants is around 65°F (18°C). Atmospheric humidity should be less than for most other begonias, somewhere in the range of 35 to 45 percent. Good air circulation should also be provided since these hybrids, when crowded, are prone to powdery mildew, a characteristic inherited from *B. dregei*. Spent flowers should likewise be removed to prevent this fungal disease from gaining a toehold. To promote flower production, give these plants bright light during the winter. Propagation is usually via leaf cuttings, but stem cuttings also work well for some cultivars. Many growers treat the Reiger hybrids as temporary display plants and buy new ones each year. They can, nevertheless, be coaxed through the summer by keeping them in a cool, lightly shaded position and by reducing watering to a minimum. Since these hybrids require a lower atmospheric humidity than most begonias they make good houseplants and can be grown, at least temporarily, on a well-lit windowsill. During the winter months a south- or east-facing window will provide optimum light exposure and promote flower production.

Begonia geranioides is quite closely related to *B. socotrana* but quite different in its appearance. It is instantly recognized from all other cultivated begonias by the combination of its tuberous habit, short stems, symmetric and almost circular (but non-peltate) hairy leaves, long-stalked white flowers, and ovaries with three almost equal wedge-shaped wings and entire placentae. It is occasionally offered in the American Begonia Society seed lists. In the wild it grows in shady, moist forests in South Africa. *Begonia geranioides* has been in cultivation since at least 1864, when it was first grown at Kew Gardens.

Begonia soli-mutata L. B. Smith & Wasshausen (PLATE 181)

section *Pritzelia*, rhizomatous group
Begonian 57: 217 (1990)
Synonyms: *B. glaziovii* nomen nudum; *B.* U003

Creeping perennial with several short, horizontally spreading stems. **Stipules** persistent, ovate-oblong, 0.7–2.6 × 0.8–2 cm. **Leaves: petiole** green, often with a pink tinge, covered with wooly hairs, 4.5–15 cm long, joining blade at an angle; **blade** above dark green or dark brownish green with lighter yellowish green areas along the main veins, pustulate, the pustule covered with short erect or spreading hairs, beneath pinkish when plant is well grown, otherwise pale whitish green, densely hairy, asymmetric, circular, 3–13 × 5–21 cm, apex indistinct, base cordate, margin shallowly angular-lobed, veins palmate. **Inflorescence:** axillary, several-flowered, bisexual, four-branched, cymose; **bracts** persistent, ovate-lanceolate to lanceolate, 1–10 × 0.3–1.5 mm. **Male flowers: tepals** four, white, outer pair elliptic, broadly elliptic, or broadly obovate, 7–10.5 × 4–8 mm, inner pair narrowly elliptic, 3–6 × 1–2 mm; **stamens** about 20–25, arranged symmetrically, attached to a columnar receptacle, anther connectives projecting. **Female flowers: bracteoles** paired directly beneath ovary, linear-lanceolate, 2–3 × 0.3–1 mm; **tepals** five, white, oblong to ovate, slightly unequal, 4–5 × 1–2 mm; **ovary** pale green, often with white wings, ellipsoid, 3–4 × 3–3.5 mm, unequally three-winged, three-locular, **placentae** axile, entire; **styles** three, once-branched, stigmas in a spiral band, completely covering style branches.

Owners of this plant can try an interesting experiment that was first conducted by Jacques Jangoux of Brazil. Place a piece of thick card over one side of a leaf that has been kept in full sun, hold it in place for a few minutes so that the sunlight is obscured, then remove the card and observe the leaf. You will find that the shaded portion of the leaf is dark green while the portion left in the sun remains a brownish green color. This curious change in color is fully reversible and is due to the leaves' microscopic, disc-shaped chloroplasts switching their orientation from a vertical to a horizontal position as the sunlight decreases (and back to a vertical position as the sunlight increases), a behavior which enables them to continually photosynthesize at a maximum rate, regardless of the weather. Jacques Jangoux originally purchased the plants he experimented with in the Amazonian market town of Belém and in 1989 sent a dried specimen to Lyman Smith and Dieter Wasshausen of the Smithsonian Museum. It was described as a new species and given the name *Begonia soli-mutata* to reflect its unusual response to differing intensities of sunlight. Interestingly, plants of *B. soli-mutata* were already in cultivation within the United States and were being grown under the American Begonia Society's unidentified species code U003. The species is native to the forests of Rio Grongogy Basin in the Brazilian state of Bahia at an altitude of 100–500 m.

Begonia soli-mutata is readily cultivated but likes to be kept slightly moist and has a tendency to develop crispy leaf edges in low humidity. It is available from several commercial sources, sometimes being sold in the United States under the unpublished name *B. glaziovii*. Hybrids include *B.* 'Jabberwocky' (*B. gehrtii* × *B. soli-mutata*), *B.* 'Midnight Sun' (*B.* 'Jill Adair' × *B. soli-mutata*), *B.* 'Orococo' (*B. glabra* × *B. soli-mutata*; Plate 180), and *B.* 'Spellbound' (*B.* 'Lospe-tu' × *B. soli-mutata*).

Begonia acida is a related species with a somewhat similar appearance. It may be distinguished from *B. soli-mutata* by its completely green, symmetric, almost circular leaves that have a markedly puckered appearance, since even the smallest veinlets are deeply sunken. It is a native of eastern Brazil and is currently available from at least one commercial source. It prefers relatively high temperatures and plenty of moisture.

Begonia strigillosa A. Dietrich

section *Gireoudia*, rhizomatous group
Allgemeine Gartenzeitung 19: 330 (1851)
Synonyms: *B. daedalea* Lemaire; *B. barbana* C. de Candolle; *B. tinctoria* L. B. Smith & B. G. Schubert

Creeping rhizomatous perennial. Rhizome branching at maturity, to 39 cm long. **Stipules** persistent, ovate-triangular, 1.2–1.7 × 0.7–1.2 cm. **Leaves: petiole** yellowish green and red-spotted, covered with long white hairs at point of contact with blade, 6.3–18 cm long, joining blade at an angle; **blade** above dark green, often sparingly to densely brown-spotted, beneath light green often with deep red primary veins and reddish brown spotting, hairless to hairy, asymmetric, narrowly to broadly ovate, oblong or almost elliptic, 3.8–18.5 × 2–9.3 cm, apex acuminate, base cordate, margin ciliate and usually broadly shallowly toothed at the ends of the major veins, occasionally with a broad, shallow, obtuse to acuminate lobe opposite the petiole insertion, veins palmate. **Inflorescence:** axillary, 10–25-flowered, asymmetric, bisexual, cymose; **bracts** deciduous, narrowly elliptic to ovate, 1.1–1.5 × 0.7–0.9 cm, margin ciliate. **Male flowers: tepals** two, white to pale or dark pink, broadly elliptic to almost circular to angular-ovate to elliptic, 6–10 × 5.5–10 mm; **stamens** 6–17, arrangement resembling a bunch of bananas, filaments fused at base, anther connectives not projecting. **Female flowers: bracteoles** absent; **tepals** two, same color as males, elliptic, almost circular to obovate, 5–9 × 5–7 mm; **ovary** greenish white and pink-tinged, ovoid to oblong, 7.5–11 × ca. 5 mm long, almost equally to unequally three-winged, three-locular, **placentae** axile, bifid; **styles** three, entire, stigmas crescent-shaped. **2n** = 28.

Begonia strigillosa is a commonly cultivated and very beautiful species, which in the wild is distributed from southern Mexico to western Panama. The species usually grows upon the bases of tree trunks and on steep, rocky, moss-covered banks in forests, but it can, on occasion, be seen growing on shady roadside banks. It typically grows at an elevation of 1400–2600 m. In the wild *B. strigillosa* usually flowers during the latter part of the rainy season from August to December and only occasionally during other times of the year. In cultivation, however, it usually flowers in late winter to early spring. Most cultivated plants have beautifully spotted leaves, but this characteristic is variable in the wild, with plants from Mexico and Guatemala having spots on their leaf blades and those from lower Central America lacking spots.

Begonia strigillosa can be grown under standard conditions and is usually propagated by division of the rhizome or by seed. It is the parent of several hybrids including *B.* 'Fuscomaculata' (*B. heracleifolia* × *B. strigillosa*), *B.* 'Golden Goddess' (*B. strigillosa* × unknown parent), *B.* 'Norah Bedson' (*B. bowerae* × *B. strigillosa*), and *B.* 'Whirlwind' (*B. strigillosa* × *B.* 'Bokit').

Begonia sutherlandii J. D. Hooker (PLATE 182)

section *Augustia*, tuberous group
Curtis's Botanical Magazine 94, pl. 5689 (1868)

Erect tuberous perennial with one or more stems arising from the tuber. Stem green or pinkish red, hairless to sparsely hairy, slender, usually branched, zigzagged toward the apex, 5–75 cm tall. **Stipules** persistent, ovate to lanceolate-oblong, margin ciliate, 3–15 × 1.5–10 mm. **Leaves: petiole** pinkish red, hairless or sparsely hairy, 1.5–15 cm long, joining blade at an angle; **blade** above pale green, sometimes with red veins, beneath paler green, sometimes red-tinged especially along veins, asymmetric, elliptic to ovate-lanceolate, 2.5–17 × 1–13 cm, apex acute to long acuminate, base cordate to almost truncate, margin sharply double-toothed and often shallowly lobed, veins palmate. **Inflorescence:** axillary and terminal, few-flowered, bisexual or male only, cymose; **bracts** persistent, ovate to broadly ovate or oblong, 2.5–12 × 1–10 mm. **Male flowers: tepals** four, pale pinkish orange to deep orange or occasionally brick-red, outer pair almost circular, elliptic or broadly ovate, 10–18 × 6.5–15 mm, inner pair obovate-wedge-shaped, 9–18 × 6–12 mm; **stamens** about 50, arranged symmetrically, anther connective surrounding top of locules and shortly projecting above them. **Female flowers: bracteoles** absent or small and insignificant; **tepals** five, same color as males, outer pair elliptic or broadly ovate, 8–16 × 3.5–11 mm, inner three obovate, 9–17 × 3.5–9 mm; **ovary** green, wings sometimes tinged red, broadly ovoid to narrowly ellipsoid, 4.5–9 × 2–5 mm, slightly unequally three-winged, three-locular, **placentae** axile, entire; **styles** three, once-branched, stigmas in a spiraled band. **2n** = 26.

This African species is deservedly among the most popular in the genus. It is elegant in stature, has beautiful clear orange flowers, and is easy to grow, at least in areas with cool summers. It is also one of the hardiest begonias and will happily grow outdoors in many colder regions right up until the first hard frosts arrive. The species name honors Peter Sutherland, Surveyor-General of Natal, who first discovered the species in 1864 growing in the South African province of Natal. Here and elsewhere in the forests of southern Africa, in a region stretching from the eastern cape of South Africa to Malawi, the species commonly grows along shady stream banks and other moist woodland habitats (Plate 183). Backhouse Nurseries in England introduced *B. sutherlandii* into cultivation in 1867. In 1885 it was listed in John Saul's catalog from his Washington, D.C., nursery and sold for 25 cents. Joseph Hooker, who published the original description of the species, called it "by far the most elegant" of the South African begonias, a position with which I heartily agree.

Begonia sutherlandii is commonly grown both as a greenhouse plant and outdoors as a tender container plant. It is not suitable for a terrarium since in this situation it has a tendency to get leggy. The species grows best outdoors in humid regions that experience relatively cool summer temperatures such as occur in North America's Pacific Northwest or in Great Britain. In these areas it is easy to grow and very free-flowering. In warmer climates it often sulks and only starts to improve when temperatures get cooler in the autumn. Occasionally though even in warmer climates if the summer has been cool and the fall not too wet *B. sutherlandii* can produce the wonderful displays seen in areas with climates more amenable to it. The species can be propagated from seed, cuttings, or the small bulbils that form in the leaf axils in late summer. *Begonia sutherlandii* is the parent of several hybrid cultivars. Commercially available examples include *B.* 'Tamborine' (*B.* Rex-cultorum group × *B. sutherlandii*), *B.* 'Victoria Kartack' (*B. sutherlandii* × *B. olsoniae*), and *B.* 'Weltonensis' (*B. dregei* × *B. sutherlandii*).

Begonia symsanguinea (Warburg) L. L. Forrest & Hollingsworth (PLATE 184)

section *Symbegonia*, shrub-like group
Plant Systematics and Evolution 241: 208 (2003)
Synonym: U013

Erect non-rhizomatous perennial 30–50 cm tall. Stem branched, dull pink with pink glandular hairs. **Stipules** persistent, ovate-lanceolate, 1–1.5 × 0.5–0.8 cm, main-vein projecting. **Leaves: petiole** pink with pink hairs, 6–8 mm long, joining blade at an angle; **blade** above brownish green, with purplish red hairs when young, hairs eventually becoming brown, intervenal areas pustulate and veins deeply sunken, beneath burgundy with pink hairs on the veins, asymmetric, ovate, 5–12 × 3.5–7 cm, apex acuminate, base cordate, margin toothed and ciliate, veins palmate-pinnate. **Inflorescence:** terminal, short-stalked, unisexual, few-flowered, cymose; **bracts** persistent, ovate to ovate-lanceolate, 0.2–1.5 × 0.2–0.8 cm. **Male flowers: tepals** two, crimson, margins fused together into a tube for about half their length, tube more or less angular-ovate with an acute triangular apex and a wedge-shaped base, 1–1.3 × 0.7–0.9 cm, outer surface with dense crimson hairs; **stamens** about 15, filaments fused into a 1.5 mm tall column on which the stamens are arranged symmetrically, anther connectives not projecting. **Female flowers: bracteoles** absent; **tepals** five, fused for most of their length into a vase-shaped tube with five lobes, tube 0.8–2.1 cm long, lobes 2–4 mm long, crimson with red hairs on the outer surface; **ovary** crimson, obovoid-ellipsoid, 0.9–1.4 × 0.4–0.6 cm, more or less equally three-winged, three-locular, **placentae** axile, bifid; **styles** three, once-branched, branches erect, long, stigmas in a spiraled band.

This New Guinean species was originally described in 1905 by German taxonomist Otto Warburg, who classified it in the genus *Symbegonia*. At that time the species was named *Symbegonia sanguinea*. By 1953 a total of 12 species had been described and classified in the genus *Symbegonia*, all of them native to the Pacific island of New Guinea and all with distinct tubular female flowers. Recently, however, this group of species has been reclassified and merged with the genus *Begonia*, where it is recognized as a section. This taxonomic change followed an intensive study carried out by Laura Forrest and Peter Hollingsworth of the Royal Botanic Garden Edinburgh. Forrest and Hollingsworth examined the DNA from several different species of *Begonia* and three species of *Symbegonia*. In 2003 they published their finding that the *Symbegonia* species appear to have evolved directly from New Guinean species of *Begonia* and should therefore be included in the same genus (a summary is reprinted in the *Begonian* 71: 94–99). Since the name *Begonia* was published before that of *Symbegonia* all the species of the latter group had to be renamed *Begonia* according to the rules of botanical nomenclature. However, because *Begonia* already contained a Brazilian species named *Begonia sanguinea* a new name had to be penned for the more recently published New Guinean species originally described as *Symbegonia sanguinea*. It was renamed *Begonia symsanguinea*, a name that recognizes its previous allegiance to the genus *Symbegonia*, as well as its current membership in *Begonia* section *Symbegonia*.

No members of section *Symbegonia* have ever been common in cultivation, being only rarely seen outside specialist collections. Nevertheless, at least three species are grown. *Begonia symsanguinea* is distinguished by its brownish green leaf blades and scarlet tepals that are tubular in the male as well as the female flowers. I have recently described a second species as *B. argenteomarginata* (Plate 184). It has white flowers and green leaf blades with silver markings along their margins and was previously cultivated under the incorrect name *Symbegonia fulvo-villosa*. The third member of the group is still undescribed and has green leaves with pink margins (Plate 184). Currently, it is cultivated as U012. I have yet to see this species in flower, despite observing it at Glasgow Botanic Garden over the course of 10 years, so have, therefore, refrained from publishing it as a new species.

Begonia symsanguinea and its relatives all require greenhouse or terrarium care and are a challenge to grow. They require relatively low to moderate temperatures and high atmospheric humidity and resent transplanting or the taking of large numbers of cuttings at any one time. Propagation is via stem cuttings. No artificial hybrids involving *B. symsanguinea* or its relatives have been documented.

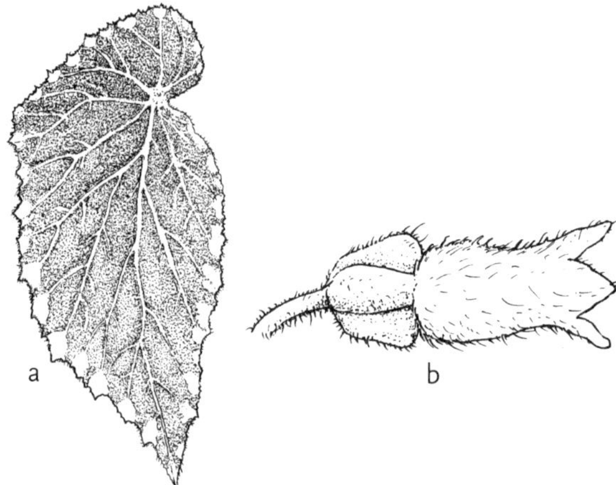

Begonia argenteomarginata: **a**) leaf, **b**) female flower.

Begonia taiwaniana Hayata (PLATE 185)

section uncertain, shrub-like group

Journal of the College of Science, Imperial University of Tokyo 30: 125 (1911)

Erect perennial with branched stems to about 1 m tall. **Stipules** deciduous, lanceolate, 1.1–1.6 × 0.6–0.8 cm, main vein projecting. **Leaves: petiole** brown with white lenticels or pink throughout, hairless, 4.5–12.5 cm long, continuing straight into main vein of blade; **blade** above dark velvety green, sometimes spotted white, beneath burgundy, both surfaces hairless, asymmetric, narrowly ovate, 6.5–14.5 × 2–8.5 cm, apex acute, base cordate, margin minutely toothed, shallowly angular-lobed toward the base, veins palmate-pinnate. **Inflorescence:** axillary, few-flowered, bisexual, cymose; **bracts** deciduous, ovate, 0.5–0.9 × 0.2–0.4 cm. **Male flowers: tepals** four, white to pink, outer pair broadly elliptic, concave, 0.9–1.1 × 0.8–1 cm, inner pair narrowly elliptic, 1–1.3 × 0.5–0.6 cm; **stamens** numerous, arranged in a symmetric mass attached to a column, anther connectives projecting. **Female flowers: bracteoles** paired 3–10 mm beneath ovary, deciduous, narrowly rectangular, 5–6 × 2–3 mm; **tepals** five, same color as males, outermost obovate-oblong, 1–1.6 × 0.6–1 cm, innermost narrowly angular-elliptic to narrowly obovate, 0.9–1.6 × 0.5–1 cm; **ovary** white, asymmetric-obovoid to ellipsoid, 4.3–8 × 4.5–6 mm, unequally three-winged, one wing sometimes much longer than the other two, three-locular, **placentae** axile, bifid; **styles** three, once-branched, stigmas in a spiraled band. **2n** = 38.

Two distinct varieties of this Taiwanese endemic are found in cultivation, the typical variety with narrow green leaves and *Begonia taiwaniana* var. *albomaculata* (Plate 185), which has broader leaves with white spots. The latter is undoubtably the more attractive of the two. Both varieties were introduced into cultivation in the United States in 1984, via seed sent to nurserywoman Mildred Thompson from Taiwan. *Begonia taiwaniana* occurs on the southern half of this island, an area that is home to an interesting mix of coniferous and broadleaved trees, as well as many garden-worthy herbs.

Begonia taiwaniana is readily cultivated in a humid environment and *B. taiwaniana* var. *albomaculata* is starting to become widely grown. No artificial hybrids involving the species have been documented.

Begonia halconensis (Plate 186) is a similar, closely related species from the Philippines, which I have seen only in cultivation in the United Kingdom. It can be distinguished from *B. taiwaniana* by its ovaries, which have fleshy wings that are slightly concave on the side facing the styles (rather than straight or rounded). These ovaries are interesting to watch mature, as they start off bright white and slowly turn green. This species is also readily cultivated.

Begonia tayabensis Merrill (PLATES 187 AND 188)

section *Diploclinium*, rhizomatous group
Philippine Journal of Science 13: 38 (1918)

Creeping rhizomatous perennial to 30 cm tall. Rhizome few-branched, bearing leaves along its length, reddish purple with small white lenticels, sparsely covered with minute hairs. **Stipules** persistent, asymmetric, triangular-ovate, 1.3–1.8 × 0.5–0.8 mm, main vein strongly keeled, keel laciniate. **Leaves:** peltate; **petiole** pale yellowish green, tinged purplish red in basal half, hairless to sparsely hairy, 5–25 cm long; **blade** above glossy green, hairless or with short hairs, beneath paler green with short hairs on main veins to hairy throughout, almost symmetric, ovate to oblong-ovate, 6.5–15 × 4–11 cm, apex acuminate, margin irregularly toothed, veins palmate-pinnate. **Inflorescence:** axillary, few-flowered, bisexual, cymose; **bracts** deciduous, broadly ovate, 5–8 × 5–8 mm. **Male flowers: tepals** four, white, often with a faint pink tinge, hairless, outer pair broadly elliptic-ovate to broadly obovate or almost circular, 1–1.7 × 0.8–1.6 cm, inner pair obovate, 0.9–1.8 × 0.4–0.8 cm; **stamens** 40–45, arranged symmetrically, anther connectives rounded at apex and shortly projecting. **Female flowers: bracteoles** absent; **tepals** four but superficially appearing to be five as one of the inner segments is cleft for up to half its length, or five and all tepals free, white, hairless, outer pair obovate, 1.1–1.7 × 0.9–1.2 cm, inner pair narrowly obovate, the free tepals 1.3–1.6 × ca. 0.6 cm, the cleft tepal 1.4–1.6 cm long, each lobe 0.5–0.9 cm wide; **ovary** white with green wings to pink throughout, ovoid to ellipsoid, 0.4–0.6 × 0.2–0.4 cm, unequally three-winged, **placentae** axile, bifid; **styles** three, once-branched, stigmas in a spiraled band.

Begonia tayabensis is a species with an identity crisis. It is frequently grown misidentified as the very dissimilar *B. rizalensis*, and plants that I have seen labeled *B. tayabensis* have usually turned out to be the closely related and quite similar *B. hernandioides*. In fact, *B. hernandioides* (Plate 189) is an altogether more commonly cultivated plant. Even so, this species is rarely mentioned in the literature, which is not surprising since it is usually misidentified as *B. tayabensis*! The two plants are, nonetheless, readily identified by the shapes of their peltate leaf blades, with the blades of *B. tayabensis* being much more drawn out at their apices than those of *B. hernandioides*, which are almost circular. *Begonia tayabensis* also lacks a ring of hairs at the top of its petiole, a feature that is always present in *B. hernandioides*, along with a row of red hairs on the veins of the leaf undersurfaces. Both species are native to the Philippine island of Luzon, with *B. tayabensis* coming from Tayabas Province and *B. hernandioides* coming from Cagayan Province. Both grow in similar habitats, by the sides of streams and rivers on steep rocky slopes in the forest. An interesting feature of *B. tayabensis* and some other members of the section *Diploclinium*, such as *B. chloroneura* (more on these follows), is that one of the inner tepals of its female flowers is often deeply cleft, giving the appearance of two rather than a single tepal (Plate 188). *Begonia*

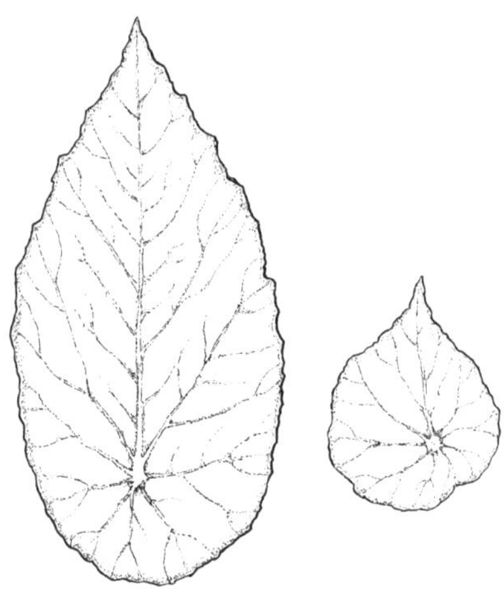

Comparison of leaf blades of *B. tayabensis* (left) and *B. hernandioides* (right).

tayabensis was first offered in the American Begonia Society's seed fund in 1986 as *B. rizalensis,* hence the confusion with this distantly related species. *Begonia hernandioides* was introduced in 1984.

Begonia tayabensis and *B. hernandioides* are readily grown under standard conditions, but I find that they prefer a relatively cool, shady location if they are to look their best. No hybrids involving either of these species have been reported in the literature.

A number of other species from the section *Diploclinium* are also in cultivation. Those species with underground tuberous or semi-tuberous rhizomes are discussed under *Begonia acaulis* and *B. grandis.* Those with non-tuberous, creeping rhizomes are discussed here. They include *B. fenicis, B. chloroneura, B. sharpeana, B. nigritarum,* and *B. subnummularifolia. Begonia fenicis* (Plate 190) is a native of the Philippines and the Ryukyus Islands, where it grows upon elevated coral rocks by the sea and in woodland in subtropical river valleys. It has non-peltate, glossy green, hairless, very broadly ovate leaf blades that measure 6.5–18 × 7–20 cm and white flowers, which are produced in about 30–50-cm-tall bisexual cymes. The species is widely cultivated. *Begonia subnummularifolia* (Plate 191) is a choice little species from Banggi Island, Sabah, Malaysia, where it is said to grow on forested slopes at an altitude of about 150 m. It has slender, creeping, almost hairless rhizomes and small, bright green, slightly asymmetric, cordate to almost circular leaf blades. Its small white flowers are produced freely in spring and early summer. The species is an excellent choice for a terrarium. *Begonia chloroneura* (Plate 192) is less commonly cultivated since it has only very recently been described and introduced into cultivation. Nevertheless, it is a very beautiful plant that is bound to become popular in the future. *Begonia chloroneura* hails from Isabela Province on the Philippine island of Luzon, where it grows in an unusual habitat, on riverbanks below the flood line. The species has thick, fleshy, creeping rhizomes that grasp the fissures in the rocky riverbanks, allowing it to survive periodic flooding even though its large leaves may be broken off. *Begonia chloroneura* is instantly recognizable by virtue of its attractively colored leaf blades, which are covered with stout dark red hairs. They are purple-brown above with light green veins, and purplish red beneath. The species is described in the September 1999 edition of the *New Plantsman. Begonia sharpeana* is also an attractive foliage plant. The species' petioles are densely hairy, but its leaf blades are large, glossy green when mature, slightly asymmetric, and elliptic to almost circular with deeply sunken veins above. The male flowers have two pairs of tepals, the outer pair are red on their outside and pale pink on their inner surfaces, and the inner pair are pale pink on both surfaces. *Begonia sharpeana* is a native of Papua

New Guinea, where it grows on limestone rocks by the Omati and Kikori Rivers. It was first introduced to Europe in 1977 via seed sent to Jan Doorenbos at the Wageningen Agricultural University in the Netherlands. From there seed was further distributed to begonia enthusiasts around the world. *Begonia nigritarum* is a native of the Philippines where it is common and shows a great deal of natural variation in terms of its leaf shape, size, and coloration. Several different clones are in cultivation. In the better clones the green leaves are attractively patterened with silvery white blotches. That said, the species is very responsive to differing light levels and the same clone will often look markedly different under different light levels.

Begonia thelmae L. B. Smith & Wasshausen (PLATE 193)

not yet classified, trailing-scandent group
Begonian 49: 114 (1981)
Synonym: *B.* U009

Trailing non-rhizomatous perennial, rooting at nodes. Stems few- to many-branched, eventually to about 1 m long, very pale green with brown hairs, almost completely covered by large stipules. **Stipules** persistent, ovate with the basal lobes directed downward, 0.8–1.2 × 0.7–0.9 cm, margin ciliate. **Leaves:** distichous; **petiole** orange-green, hairy, 2–5 mm long, almost continuing straight into main vein of blade; **blade** above brownish green with pale green veins, beneath burgundy with pale green veins, both surfaces covered with soft reddish hairs, oblong-elliptic, 2.5–4 × 1.7–3 cm, apex rounded to acute, base cordate, margin bluntly toothed, veins palmate-pinnate. **Inflorescence:** axillary, few-flowered, bisexual; **bracts** deciduous, ovate, ca. 0.8 × 0.5 mm. **Male flowers: tepals** four, white, hairless, outer pair ovate-cordate, 6–8 × 5–6.5 mm, inner pair obovate-elliptic to obovate, 5.5–6 × ca. 3 mm; **stamens** about 10, arranged symmetrically, anther connectives shortly projecting and rounded. **Female flowers: bracteoles** paired at base of ovary, elliptic, 1–2 × 0.5–1 mm; **tepals** five, white, hairless, outermost narrowly elliptic, 0.7–1 × 0.3–0.5 cm, innermost narrowly elliptic to narrowly obovate, 0.8–1 × 0.4–0.5 cm; **ovary** white but becoming green at maturity, hairless, body broadly ovoid to ellipsoid, ca. 0.7 × 0.4 cm, slightly unequal three-winged, three-locular, **placentae** axile, entire; **styles** three, once-branched, stigmatic papillae completely covering surfaces of style branches.

Begonia thelmae was first introduced into the United States in January 1974 by the then president of the American Horticultural Society, Gilbert Daniels. Daniels's plants came from the Brazilian garden of the late, great landscape architect Roberto Burle Marx. What is not known is where the species was collected prior to entering Burle Marx's garden. Presumably it like many other cultivated begonias is a native of Brazil's Atlantic Coastal Forest. I have not, however, seen any wild-collected herbarium specimens of this distinct species, nor have I seen any published records of it in the wild. Presumably it has a localized distribution in nature, since the species' creeping stems, distichous leaves, inflorescences with usually three male flowers and a single female flower, and entire placentae very clearly distinguish it from other begonias. Indeed it is so distinct, it has not yet been classified in a botanical section and may well require its own new section. Whether this is the case awaits the results of an ongoing molecular study. The species is named after begonia enthusiast Thelma O'Reilly who brought the species to the attention of the botanists who named it. The original description and a discussion of the species appears in the May 1981 issue of the *Begonian*.

Begonia thelmae is widely cultivated and available from several commercial sources. The species requires a shady, humid environment and grows well either in a greenhouse or in a terrarium. For best effect it should be positioned where its creeping stems and overlapping leaves can create a dense mat across the soil. Growing new specimens from cuttings each year is prudent since plants usually lose all but their uppermost leaves in the winter giving them a straggly appearance. Cuttings should be taken in the fall before this happens and positioned several to a pot in order to produce an attractively shaped plant. Hybrids of this species include *B.* 'Manaus' (*B. thelmae* × *B. soli-mutata*), *B.* 'Satin Robe' (*B. thelmae* × *B. olsoniae*), and *B.* 'Withlacoochee' (*B. thelmae* × *B. juliana*).

Begonia thiemei C. de Candolle

section *Gireoudia*, rhizomatous group
Botanical Gazette (London) 20: 542 (1895)
Synonym: *B. macdougallii* Ziesenhenne

Creeping rhizomatous perennial. Rhizome thick, sometimes branched, green to brown, hairless, to 30 cm long. **Stipules** deciduous, asymmetric, broadly ovate to triangular, 1.1–2 × 0.5–2 cm. **Leaves: petiole** pink to purple, hairless or almost so, 9–50 cm long; **blade** above glossy green to purple, hairless to sparsely hairy, beneath paler green to purple, sparsely hairy on veins, in outline broadly ovate to almost circular, 14–54 × 20–30 cm, palmately compound with 7–10 leaflets, leaflets lanceolate, narrowly elliptic or obovate oblanceolate, 7–13 × 3–6 cm, margin often acutely lobed toward the apex, irregularly toothed and sometimes ciliate, veins of leaflets pinnate. **Inflorescence:** axillary, tall, few- to many-flowered, asymmetric, bisexual, cymose; **bracts** soon falling, broadly obovate to ovate-elliptic, 5–9 × 4.5–6 mm. **Male flowers: tepals** two, white to greenish white or yellow, hairless, broadly ovate to almost circular or transversely broadly elliptic, 7–13 × 8–14 mm; **stamens** 21–30, arrangement resembling a large bunch of bananas, anther connectives projecting. **Female flowers: bracteoles** absent; **tepals** two, same color as males, ovate or obovate, 5–7 × 6–7 mm; **ovary** ellipsoid, 6–10 × 6–10 mm, unequally three-winged, the largest triangular, the two smaller linear, narrow, three-locular, **placentae** axile, bifid; **styles** three, stigmas broadly crescent-shaped. **2n** = 28.

Begonia thiemei was named in honour of C. Thieme whose dried specimens of this species were used by Casmir de Candolle to describe the species. They curiously remain the only collection of the species known from Honduras. The species is otherwise widely distributed in the southern Mexican states of Veracruz and Chiapas and in Guatemala. Throughout its range *B. thiemei* grows in moist forests on steep, rocky slopes at an altitude of 50–495 m. In certains parts of southern Mexico a few populations can be found containing plants with either purple or green leaves. Both variants are in cultivation and the elegant purple-leaved plants have been named *B. thiemei* 'Purpurea'. *Begonia thiemei* is easily identified by the combination of its creeping rhizome and large palmately compound leaves that are completely or almost hairless. Nonetheless, it is sometimes confused with the closely related *B. carolineifolia*, which also has large, palmately compound leaves. *Begonia carolineifolia* (Plates 59 and 194) nevertheless differs in having an erect or ascending rhizome and male flowers with only 13–19 stamens. Its distribution overlaps with that of *B. thiemei* but it is restricted to the Mexican states of Oaxaca and Veracruz. *Begonia macdougallii* was, at one time, also recognized as a distinct species closely related to these two. However, examination of the type specimen of this species, which is housed at Kew, shows that it is identical to the earlier-published *B. thiemei*. *Begonia macdougallii* should, therefore, be treated as a synonym of *B. thiemei*.

Begonia thiemei and *B. carolineifolia* are readily grown under standard conditions, although they may be slow to establish. Both species also make interesting subjects for containers in areas with warm humid summers. *Begonia thiemei* has occasionally been used by hybridizers, examples include *B.* 'Aussie Star' (*B. wollnyi* × *B. thiemei*) and *B.* 'Max' (*B. nelumbifolia* [red-veined variant] × *B. thiemei*). *Begonia carolineifolia* hybrids include *B.* 'Palmgarten' (*B. carolineifolia* × *B.* 'Leslie Lynn), *B.* 'Star Frost' (*B. carolineifolia* × *B. wollnyi*), and *B.* 'Verschaffeltii' (*B. manicata* × *B. carolineifolia*).

Begonia ulmifolia Willdenow (PLATE 195)
section *Donaldia*, thick-stemmed group
Species Plantarum 4: 418 (1805)

Erect, slightly woody subshrub to about 3 m tall. Stems green with whitish lenticels or red, densely hairy especially when young, bluntly angular in cross section and longitudinally grooved, main stem with several short branches. **Stipules** persistent, rectangular-ovate, 1.2–1.6 × 0.5–0.6 cm. **Leaves: petiole** pink, densely hairy, 0.3–1.1 cm long, continuing straight into main vein of blade; **blade** above green, beneath paler green, densely hairy on both sides, oblong-elliptic or almost obovate, 4–20 × 1.5–7 cm, apex acuminate, base unequal, rounded, margin sharply toothed and ciliate, veins pinnate. **Inflorescence:** in upper leaf axils, 15–60-flowered, cymose, some inflorescences with only female flowers, others with several male flowers and a few female flowers that develop after the males have fallen; **bracts** persistent, lower ones narrowly lanceolate, 1–1.4 × 0.2–0.4 cm, upper ones linear, 4–10 × 1–2 mm. **Male flowers: tepals** two, white, broadly ovate to almost circular, 8–11 × 8–13 mm, sparsely hairy on outer surface; **stamens** 30–50, arranged symmetrically, anther connectives projecting. **Female flowers: bracteoles** paired at base of ovary, lanceolate-triangular, 2–4 × ca. 1 mm; **tepals** five, white, outer pair ovate to lanceolate, 4–6.5 × 2–3 mm, inner three elliptic, concave, 8–9.5 × 4.5–5 mm; **ovary** pale green, ellipsoid, 8–9 × 5–5.5 mm, unequally three-winged, three-locular, **placentae** axile, bifid; **styles** three, once-branched, stigmas completely covering surfaces of style branches. **2n** = 30.

Begonia ulmifolia is commercially available, frequently offered in the American Begonia Society seed lists, and commonly seen in cultivation, yet almost nothing has been written previously about this species. This is especially surprising given that it has been cultivated in Europe since at least 1920, at which time Lodiges of London offered it for sale. Perhaps its absence from the literature is due to the species' large size and lack of showy flowers, or maybe it is so easy to grow under standard greenhouse conditions that enthusiasts have not needed to swap information. The species is native to Guyana, Brazil, Venezuela, and the neighboring islands of Trinidad and Tobago. However, *B. ulmifolia* has escaped from cultivation on numerous occasions and is now found as a weed in many tropical areas of the world. The name *ulmifolia* means "elm-leaved"; *Ulmus* is the scientific name for the elms. This species' leaves are indeed reminiscent of some elms and in well-grown plants are colored an attractive shade of green. Like many elms they also have a dense covering of short stiff hairs. Among the cultivated begonias, the

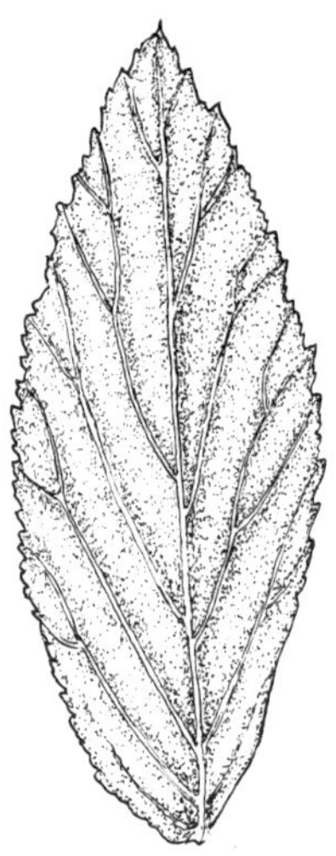
Leaf of *B. ulmifolia*.

species' erect habit and distinctly shaped, hairy leaves easily identify it. In its native range, *B. ulmifolia* grows in forests or thickets in moist or wet areas, and like other weedy species is often found in disturbed habitats. It has occasionally been recorded growing on limestone. *Begonia ulmifolia* is the only cultivated member of the section *Donaldia*, which also contains six other species of similar appearance.

Begonia ulmifolia is readily grown under standard conditions but should be given a position in dappled shade since its leaves are easily bleached by strong light. The stems need to be periodically pinched or they have a tendency to become a bit gangly. Propagation is usually via seed or stem cuttings, the latter of which are very easily rooted. No hybrids with this species have been documented.

Begonia variabilis Ridley

section *Parvibegonia*, tuberous group
Journal of the Straits Branch of the Royal Asiatic Society 57: 50 (1911)

Erect single-stemmed tuberous perennial to 30 cm tall. Stems slender, sometimes with a few short branches, occasionally falling over and forming roots and tubers at nodes, pale green, often with a pink tinge, hairless. **Stipules** tardily deciduous, oblong-lanceolate, 8–11 × 2–2.5 mm. **Leaves: petiole** pale green, hairless, 2.5–10 cm long, lower leaves with longer petioles than the upper ones, joining blade at an angle; **blade** thin, above green with a rosy-purple margin and pink-tinged veins, covered with numerous small dull white spots, sparsely hairy, beneath pinkish red with paler green veins, sparsely hairy, asymmetric, variable in outline even on an individual plant, broadly ovate to lance-shaped, 8–23 × 2–9 cm, apex short to long acuminate, base cordate, margin with very short wavy lobes, veins palmate. **Inflorescence:** axillary but superficially appearing terminal as they are usually borne in the axils of side branches that are longer than the main stem, a few-flowered raceme-like cyme, bisexual with male flowers basal and the uppermost flower female; **bracts** deciduous to persistent, oblong, 8–10 × 3–3.5 mm. **Male flowers: tepals** four, white to pink-tinged, veins pink-striped, outer pair broadly ovate to elliptic, 4–12 × 1.5–9 mm, inner pair narrowly elliptic to narrowly obovate, 5–10 × 2.5–5 mm, **stamens** numerous, arranged in a spherical cluster on top of a column, anther connectives not projecting. **Female flowers: bracteoles** absent; **tepals** white to very pale pink, pink striped along veins, five to seven but usually six, elliptic, 5–12 × 2–5 mm; **ovary** nodding, green with pink stripes, asymmetric-obovoid, 4–4.5 × 1.5–4.5 mm, three-winged, one wing becoming longer than the others at maturity, two-locular, **placentae** axile, bifid; **styles** two, fan-shaped, stigmas in a wavy band.

This species was previously misidentified in cultivation as *Begonia guttata,* a closely related species that differs most noticeably by its broader leaf blades. Henry Ridley chose the name *variabilis* because the species exhibits considerable variation in the shape and color of its leaves. *Begonia variabilis* is rare in cultivation and uncommon in the wild, and is found only on the Malay Peninsula. It was introduced into cultivation from a single plant collected by Don Miller and Scott Hoover in Perak State in 1990. This plant was growing above a highway at the base of a small cliff at 457 m. *Begonia variabilis* belongs to the Asian section *Parvibegonia,* which is also represented in cultivation by *B. crenata, B. phoeniogramma* (Plate 196), and *B. tenuifolia,* all three of which are also very rarely grown. *Begonia variabilis* has curious axillary inflorescences that appear to be terminal as they are borne in the axils of side branches that are longer than the main stem.

I vividly recall a plant of *Begonia variabilis* at the 2003 annual meeting of the American Begonia Society that had been grown to perfection. Its exhibitor, Johanna Zinn, informs me that it had been grown in a cool basement in a sealed terrarium with grow lights placed 15–20 cm above the plant. The lights were set to come on for 12 hours each day and the plant experienced a temperature ranging from a minimum of 55°F (12°C) in the winter to a maximum of 78°F (25°C) in the summer. During the hotter summer months a fan was used to remove excess heat produced by the lights. The potting medium consisted of a layer of long fibered sphagnum moss over a thin layer of commercial potting soil over a thin layer of horticultural charcoal over a thin layer of perlite. In mid winter this species will often become dormant and rest below ground as tubers. It will usually remain in that state for two to four months. Needless to say, this species is not one for the uninitiated.

Begonia veitchii J. D. Hooker (PLATE 209)

section *Eupetalum*, tuberous group
Gardener's Chronicle (London) I, 734 (1867)
Synonym: *B. rosiflora* J. D. Hooker

Tuberous, very short-stemmed perennial, bearing only a few leaves. **Stipules** persistent, triangular-ovate, 0.8–1 × 0.7–0.9 cm. **Leaves: petiole** green, tinged red, especially toward the blade, hairy, 1–6.5 cm long, continuing straight into the main vein of the blade; **blade** above green with a red margin, hairless, beneath paler green, hairy on the veins, symmetric, broadly ovate to circular, somewhat funnel-shaped, 4–8.5 × 4.5–13.5 cm, apex indistinct, base cordate, margin more or less shallowly crenate-lobed and crenate-toothed, ciliate, veins palmate. **Inflorescence:** axillary, few-flowered, bisexual, cymose; flowers sweetly scented; **bracts** persistent, oblong to broadly elliptic, 0.8–2 × 0.6–1.4 cm, margin ciliate. **Male flowers: tepals** four, pink, red, or pale purple, outer pair broadly elliptic to broadly obovate, 2.5–3 × 1.5–2.1 cm, inner pair broadly obovate, 1.8–4 × 1.3–2.8 cm; **stamens** numerous, arranged symmetrically, anther connectives not projecting. **Female flowers: bracteoles** absent; **tepals** five, same color as males, broadly elliptic to broadly obovate, 1.1–2.3 × 0.8–2.3 cm; **ovary** green, broadly obovate to broadly elliptic or almost spherical, unequally three-winged, three-locular, **placentae** axile, bifid; **styles** three, once-branched, stigmas in a spiraled band. **2n** = 28.

Begonia veitchii is a native of the Andean Mountains of Bolivia where it grows along the rocky margins of streams and in other shady places at 2550–4000 m, an unusually high elevation for a begonia. It is an attractive species with a short thick stem, large flowers, and leaves that are more reminiscent of a bergenia than a begonia. Plant collector Richard Pierce discovered the species in 1865 near the ancient Inca capitol of Cuzco and sent plants back to his employer, Veitch Nursery, in England. *Begonia veitchii* was not the first tuberous species to be introduced from the Andes, but the species is notable because along with two of Pierce's earlier introductions, *B. boliviensis* (Plate 34) and *B. pearcei* (Plate 210), it sparked an intense interest in the hybridization of the showy-flowered Andean begonias, which ultimately led to the development of a vast hybrid group formally known as *B.* ×*tuberhybrida* Siebert & Voss.

That the horticultural potential of these plants was recognized so soon after their introduction is owed to a large extent to the Veitch Nursery. This firm no longer exists, but at the time of the species' introduction it was one of England's largest nurseries and was famous worldwide. The basis for the initial hybridization work was carried out by Veitch's foreman, John Seden, and largely involved the three species introduced by Pierce and *Begonia cinnabarina* and *B. clarkei*, which had been commercialized by Henderson's Nursery. The first of the resulting hybrids to be exhibited and sold was fittingly named *B.* 'Sedenii', in honor of its hybridizer. In the James Veitch and Sons *Catalogue of New and Beautiful Plants for 1870* this hybrid is described as having large flowers of the richest magenta color. It was the result of a cross between *B. boliviensis* and an unidentified Andean tuberous species. *Begonia* 'Sedenii' was an immense success, being used in many of Seden's later crosses and by several other hybridizers once it had been released for sale.

Indeed, once the Veitch nursery commercialized *Begonia* 'Sedenii' and its holding of Andean *Begonia* species, many growers throughout Europe took up the challenge of hybridizing and developing the group. Intense efforts led to the first true white-flowered tuberous begonia hybrid, *B.* 'White Queen', around 1874, a cultivar developed by Henderson's Nursery in London by crossing *B.* 'Sedenii' with a white-flowered South African species, *B. dregei*. Another prominent early hybridizer, Victor Lemoine, was based in France, where he produced a number of improved hybrids including the first yellow-flowered cultivar. His work was largely based on crossing *B.* 'Sedenii', *B. veitchii*, and *B. pearcei*. Lemoine is also to be remembered as one of the first breeders in the 1870s to develop a double-flowered tuberous begonia. Around this period many of Europe's other leading nurseries, such as Van Houtte in Belgium, Crousse in France, and William Bull, John Laing, and Sutton and Sons in England, had also entered the intense competition to develop additional new and improved hybrid cultivars. The work continued at such a pace that by 1880 few of the wild species were being used any longer for hybridization; instead, most of the work on the group involved the further selection of the existing hybrids. Today, the gradual improvement of the hybrids continues at a slightly less frantic pace, but with work now being carried out in California and New Zealand as well as in Europe. Somewhat surprisingly, commercial work on the *B.* ×*tuberhybrida* group did not commence in the United States until 1919, when the U.S. Plant Quarantine Act forced American growers into the market by prohibiting the importation of further plants from Europe. Nevertheless, California is now the world's second largest commercial producer of begonia tubers after Belgium (Plate 198).

Intense selection on this hybrid group since the late 1800s has led to the development of a number of distinct named lineages within the *Begonia* ×*tuberhybrida* group. Examples include the Fimbriata group, with large double male flowers that have ruffled, fringed tepals; the Pendula group, with pendulous stems and flowers; the Multiflora group, with many small double male flowers; and the descriptively named Large-Flowered Double group, with large double flowers that are not otherwise distinctly marked or shaped. In total, 17 groups are recognized. Useful detailed descriptions of each are provided in Haegeman (1979) and Thompson and Thompson (1981). Though commercial growers have tended to recognize their plants as belonging to one of these groups, a parallel trend has been the commercial production of unnamed hybrids. The English nursery firm of Blackmore and Langdon stands out, however, because shortly after the firm's establishment in 1901 it became the world's leading producer of high-quality, named cultivars. Even today its tuberous begonia cultivars are world renowned for their high quality.

The years since 1875 have also witnessed a switch in the manner in which the tuberous Andean species and their hybrids are cultivated. Early on in the group's development, prominent nurserymen, like Veitch and Lemoine, considered the tuberous species to be suitable only for the hothouse. Only later did they realize that these high altitude species performed better under cooler conditions. In fact, because of *Begonia veitchii*'s natural high altitude origin, it is winter-hardy in the southwest of England and parts of the United States with a similar climate. Joseph Hooker must have realized this as, when he described this species in 1867, he wrote that the species "promises to be one of the greatest acquisitions to our gardens that has been procured for many years." Nevertheless, the use of tuberous hybrids as outdoor bedding plants did not become widely practiced until about 1875 when *B.* 'Sedenii' was first used as a bedding plant. Just one year later, however, these begonias were as popular as the nineteenth-century-gardener's stalwarts, *Pelargonium* and *Fuchsia*. Today in many cool temperate parts of the world the *B.* ×*tuberhybrida* group still ranks among the most cherished of all bedding plants. Nonetheless, many growers intent on producing high-quality plants for the show bench still continue to grow their plants in greenhouses.

A further important commercial development that occurred in the late 1800s was the introduction of tuberous hybrid cultivars that could be propagated true to type from seed. In 1879 Vallerand of France produced the first of these, *Begonia* 'Erecta Superba'. Such was its commercial success that by 1900 named cultivars were available as seed in a wide range of colors. With the exception of the Multiflora group and a few large-flowered, double cultivars that are raised from stem cuttings, propagation by seed is now the rule for members of the *B.* ×*tuberhybrida* group. Nevertheless to this day, tubers have still remained important. Indeed, it is no coincidence that these commercially successful plants are tuberous, for tubers are much easier to transport than whole plants, making their shipment easier and hence more economical.

Despite the continued prominence of the *Begonia* ×*tuberhybrida* group in gardens, none of the original parent species are common in cultivation, with many of them having been lost fairly soon after their introduction due to the difficulty of their cultivation. *Begonia boliviensis* is by far the most frequently grown and is described elsewhere in this book. Others that are occasionally encountered in cultivation include the orange-flowered, erect-stemmed *B. cinnabarina* (Plate 211), the scarlet-flowered *B. froebelii*, the yellow-flowered *B. pearcei* (Plate 210), and the white-flowered *B. octopetala* (Plate 212). It is fascinating to look for the distinct characteristics of each of these species in the modern-day hybrids. In some hybrids, for example, one can see the long, red-pointed tepals and pendulous flowers of *B. boliviensis*, and in others are found the large beautifully shaped flowers characteristic of *B. veitchii*, or the yellow flowers and dark, velvety green leaves of

B. pearcei. It is a shame that the true species, with few exceptions, are now so rare in cultivation. We must do our best to conserve those that remain, particularly as some like *B. froebelii* have become very rare in the wild.

Much has been written about the cultivation of the tuberous Andean species and their hybrids, so I will only describe the basics here. Further information can be found, for example, in Haegeman (1979), Langdon (1969), and Stevens (2002). *Begonia veitchii* and the other tuberous Andean species are usually a challenge to cultivate, but members of the *B.* ×*tuberhybrida* group are typically much easier to grow. Because the species come from the high mountains (Plate 197) both they and their hybrids need above all else to be grown under cool temperatures, ideally in the range of 55 to 86°F (12–30°C). Understandably these plants are easiest to grow in places like the San Francisco Bay area, New Zealand, and northern Great Britain, which naturally experience relatively cool summer temperatures and high atmospheric humidity. Good air circulation is also important, because when these plants are crowded, fungal diseases such as botrytis and powdery mildew can attack, damaging the leaves. Plants also benefit from bright indirect light, a reasonably humid atmosphere, and careful watering when they are in or entering their dormant winter phase or resuming growth in the spring. Many of the most commonly encountered cultivars are arranged into series—for example, the immensely popular Nonstop series (Plate 199). Its included cultivars have flowers of bright red, yellow, and white, respectively. Other popular series include Cascade, Clips, Illumination, Panorama (Plate 200), and Pin-Up. Some *B.* ×*tuberhybrida* group cultivars are available directly from the breeders as tubers, and others are sold as F1 hybrid seed. A few of the numerous individually named cultivars include *B.* 'Falstaff' (a Blackmore and Langdon cultivar with bright red double flowers), *B.* 'Firedance' (a Blackmore and Langdon cultivar with double, clear orange flowers), *B.* 'Fred Martin' (picotee with cream ground and pink edges), *B.* 'Midas' (yellow flowers with slightly wavy tepals), *B.* 'Roy Hartley' (large flowers, pink with a salmon tinge), *B.* 'Tamakihada' (*B.* 'Orange Rubra' × *B. pearcei*), and *B.* 'Thelma's Pet' (*B.* 'Yellow Sweety' × *B.* ×*tuberhybrida* group).

Begonia venosa J. D. Hooker (PLATES 201 AND 202)
section *Begonia*, shrub-like group
Curtis's Botanical Magazine 125: pl. 7657 (1899)

Erect thick-stemmed perennial to about 1 m tall, vegetative parts densely covered with short silver-gray felt-like hairs. **Stipules** persistent and very conspicuous, opaque with darker net veins, ovate to obovate, 4–6 × 2.5–4.3 cm. **Leaves: petiole**

3–10 cm long; **blade** both surfaces covered with white felt-like hairs but more densely so beneath, asymmetric, kidney-shaped, 6–12 × 8–12 cm, apex abruptly short acuminate, base cordate, margin very shallowly angular-lobed, wavy, veins palmate. **Inflorescence:** axillary, long-stalked, few- to many-flowered, compact, bisexual, cymose, stalks densely covered with short felt-like hairs; flowers fragrant; **bracts** soon falling, ovate to ovate-oblong or linear-oblong, 0.8–1.4 × 0.3–0.6 cm. **Male flowers: tepals** four, white, outer pair obovate to broadly obovate, elliptic or transversely ovate, 0.8–1.5 × 0.6–2.1 cm, often hairy on base of outer surfaces, inner pair narrowly obovate, 0.8–1.4 × 0.3–0.5 cm; **stamens** about 8–15, arranged symmetrically, anthers much longer than filaments, anther connectives projecting. **Female flowers: bracteoles** paired beneath ovary, elliptic, 6–7 × 3–4 mm; **tepals** five, white, broadly to narrowly obovate or circular, slightly unequal, outermost 0.9–1.3 × 0.9–1.1 cm, innermost 0.8–1.2 × 0.5–0.9 cm; **ovary** green, hairy, ellipsoid with three angles, 0.7–1.2 × 0.4–0.8 cm, wingless, three-locular, **placentae** axile, bifid; **styles** three, once-branched, stigmas in a spiraled band.

Swedish-born botanist, Albert Lofgren discovered this species in Brazil, and probably suspecting that he had found a new species, had dried specimens and a living plant sent to Kew Gardens in 1899. Records of exactly where the plants had been collected do not appear to have accompanied the specimens, for when Joseph Hooker described the species in *Curtis's Botanical Magazine* he wrote:

> The native country of *Begonia venosa* is not satisfactorily known. Mr. Thos. Christy F.L.S., who sent to Kew Herbarium the specimen here figured, together with the living plant for the Royal Gardens (which has already flowered), informs me that it was discovered by Professor Lofgren, head of the Botany Dept. of the state of Sao Paolo, in an island off the coast of Brazil, but whether off Para, or off the mouth of the river Santos (Prov. Sao Paulo), Mr. Christy cannot inform me.

Despite extensive searching, I have only managed to locate one herbarium sheet bearing collection data, a specimen housed in the Smithsonian Institution's herbarium. This plant had been collected in the coastal hills of the state of São Paulo. Presumably the islands that Hooker mentions are those that lie offshore of this location. This would certainly make sense, for Lofgren was director of the São Paulo Botanical Garden at the time he collected *Begonia venosa*. Within the state of São Paulo *B. venosa* must be very localized since it has so rarely been collected, yet with its conspicuously white-felted leaves, it is a highly visible species. Furthermore, *B. venosa* probably grows naturally in exposed localities in full sun. Certainly *B. venosa*'s close relative *B. umbraculifera* grows in such situations, and at least in cultivation *B. venosa* requires a relatively brightly lit situation in order to develop its distinctive coating of white felt-like hairs. The name *venosa* means, "prominently veined," and refers to the species' conspicuous veined stipules. All the material of this species currently in cultivation appears to be descended from Lofgren's collection sent to Kew Gardens in 1899.

Begonia venosa is widely grown but is considered somewhat of a challenge since it needs different growing conditions than most other begonias. For a number of years I grew this species in a well-lit bathroom where it thrived on neglect, only requiring infrequent watering. Then, when I moved house I decided to give my plant a "better" location and more frequent care. Needless to say, it died soon afterward. The secret seems to be that this species should be treated more like a succulent than a typical begonia, and given excellent drainage and a brightly lit position. At the United Kingdom's National Begonia Collection at Glasgow Botanic Garden it grows in a cactus and succulent potting mix away from the rest of the begonias and is thriving under somewhat dry conditions. *Begonia venosa* is worth cultivating for its spice-scented flowers as well as its beautiful felted leaves. Care must be taken when handling the plant as the attractive felt-like hairs are easily dusted off. Commercially available hybrid cultivars include *B.* 'Don Englund' (*B. juliana* × *B. venosa*), *B.* 'Eunice Gray' (*B. echinosepala* × *B. venosa*), *B.* 'San Miquel' (*B. venosa* × *B. scharffiana*), and *B.* 'Venepi' (*B. venosa* × *B. epipsila*).

Begonia versicolor Irmscher (PLATE 203)

section *Platycentrum*, rhizomatous group
Mitteilungen aus dem Institut für Allgemeine Botanik in Hamburg 10: 546 (1939)

Dwarf creeping rhizomatous perennial to about 25 cm tall. Vegetative parts densely covered with long soft hairs. **Stipules** persistent, ovate to broadly triangular, 8–9 × 5.6–8 mm. **Leaves: petiole** densely covered with red hairs, 9–12 cm long, joining leaf at an angle; **blade** pitted so that it has a crinkled appearance, above pale green with white highlights and a purplish brown border along the veins, hairs mostly translucent, beneath also pitted, paler with dense red hairs, asymmetric, broadly ovate or almost elliptic, 7.5–14 × 7–13 cm, apex abruptly very short acuminate, base cordate, margin entire, wavy, with red cilia, veins palmate. **Inflorescence**: axillary, few-flowered, bisexual, cymose; **bracts** deciduous, ovate, 4–7 × 2–2.5 mm, margin ciliate. **Male flowers: tepals** usually four, rarely five, outer pair rose pink, broadly ovate, 1.4–1.9 × 1.5–1.8 cm, outer surface with red hairs, inner two or three segments white, obovate, 0.9–1.1 × 0.5–0.7 cm; **stamens** numerous, arranged in a symmetric mass on top of a short column, anther connectives shortly projecting. **Female flowers: bracteoles** absent; **tepals** five, rose-pink, unequal, outer segments broadly obovate to almost circular, 9–12 × 3–9 mm, outer surface hairy, inner segments broadly to narrowly obovate, 6.5–11 × 2–6 mm; **ovary** nodding, red, oblong, 4.5–8 × 2.5–4.5 mm, three-winged, one wing slightly longer than others, two-locular, **placentae** axile, bifid; **styles** two or three, shortly once-branched, stigmas in a band. **2n** = 22.

Begonia versicolor is a very choice but somewhat demanding species suitable for a terrarium or similar container. Its scientific name means "variously colored," a reference to the plant's stunning leaves, which are pale green with white highlights and purplish brown borders to the veins. As if this were not enough, the leaf margins have red ciliate hairs, and the upper surfaces are covered with soft white hairs, giving them a velvet-like texture. The species is a native of southwestern China and in the wild is reasonably common in Yunnan Province's damp forests at an altitude of 1280–2135 m. *Begonia versicolor* was introduced to the United States from China in the late 1940s via the nursery of the talented hybridizer Leslie Woodriff.

Begonia versicolor requires high atmospheric humidity and even within a greenhouse setting is often grown in an enclosed terrarium or similar container. The species should be kept slightly moist at all times and is liable to wilt suddenly if its roots dry out. It prefers relatively low temperatures in the range of 60 to 65°F (16–18°C). Bright light will promote the species' naturally beautiful leaf coloration. Propagation is usually via rhizome, leaf, or leaf wedge cuttings. Seed is also periodically available from the American Begonia Society seed lists and offers another

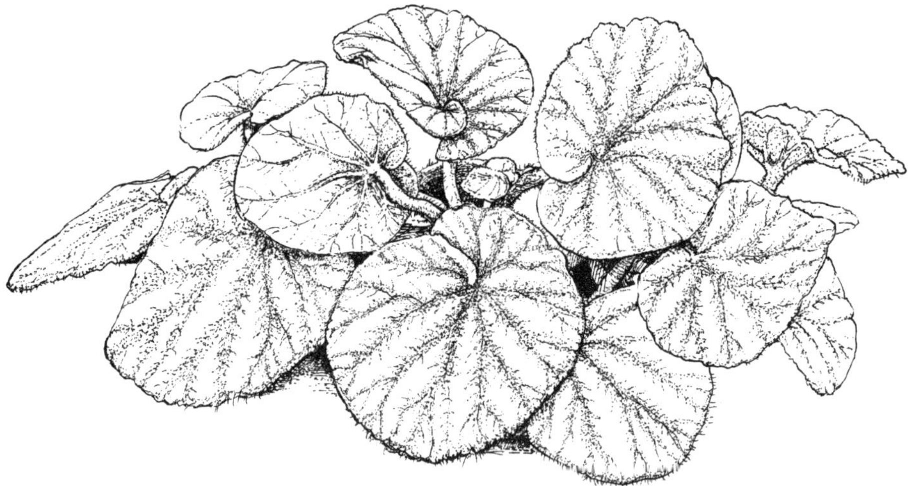

Begonia versicolor.

means of propagation. Unlike most other challenging begonias, *B. versicolor* is commercially available and has been widely hybridized. Commonly grown cultivars include *B.* 'China Curl' (*B. versicolor* × *B. cathayana*), *B.* 'Millie Thompson' (*B. versicolor* × *B.* 'John Blair'), and *B.* 'Wanda' (*B. versicolor* × *B. masoniana*).

Three other Asian species are similar to *Begonia versicolor* in their general appearance and cultural requirements. *Begonia limprichtii* (Plate 204) is a closely related species from China's Sichuan Province. It has small green leaves with prominent red hairs spaced over their surfaces, and is particularly unusual in having red roots. Though it needs terrarium culture, this species is not as demanding as *B. versicolor*. Nonetheless, it is less often seen in cultivation. *Begonia decora* (Plate 205) from the Malay Peninsula has leaves that are coppery red with yellowish veins and a covering of hairy papillae. Like *B. versicolor* it is available commercially. *Begonia picta* is a particularly common and widespread native of the Himalayas that is surprisingly rare in cultivation. The species is tuberous and produces only a few leaves, which are attractively blotched with shades of purple, brown, white, and green. This is a particularly fine species that I would dearly love to grow.

Begonia violifolia A. de Candolle

section *Weilbachia*, rhizomatous group

Annales des Sciences Naturelles Botanique IV, 11: 134 (1859)

Dwarf creeping perennial with slender rhizomes. Stems greenish brown to dark brown often with pale green lenticels, slender. **Stipules** persistent, triangular to lanceolate, 0.7–1 × 0.4–0.6 cm. **Leaves: petiole** pinkish brown, densely covered with forward-pointing white hairs, 2.5–9.5 cm long, attached to blade at an angle; **blade** above green, pustulate, covered with short, white hairs, beneath paler green, densely hairy on veins, sparsely hairy elsewhere, 2.5–5.5 × 2.5–5 cm, asymmetric, ovate, apex acute to long acuminate, base cordate, margin ciliate, veins palmate. **Inflorescence:** axillary, few-flowered, bisexual, cymose; **bracts** persistent, lowermost ovate, uppermost elliptic, 0.7–1 × 0.4–0.6 cm. **Male flowers: tepals** two, white with several short red hairs on the center of outer surfaces, inner surfaces white, transversely ovate to transversely elliptic to circular, 0.5–0.7 × 0.5–0.7 cm; **stamens** 10–15, arrangement resembling a bunch of bananas, filaments fused at their base into a column, apex of anther hooded. **Female flowers: bracteoles** absent; **tepals** two or rarely three, similar to males; **ovary** green with red hairs, asymmetric-obovoid, 4–5.5 × 2–3 mm, unequally three-winged, two-locular, **placentae** axile, entire; **styles** three, entire, stigmas crescent-shaped. **2n** = 28.

Begonia violifolia is a dainty plant with small white tepals that sport striking red hairs on their outer surfaces. The species name refers to the resemblance of the leaves to those of a violet. In the wild, the species grows among calcareous rocks in the Mexican state of Tabasco.

Begonia violifolia requires high atmospheric humidity and performs best in a terrarium. It is only infrequently grown and flowers in late spring. The species has been hybridized with at least two others, both of which are also diminutive in stature, resulting in *B.* 'Abu Dahbi' (*B. bowerae* var. *nigramarga* × *B. violifolia*) and *B.* 'Ona-mae' (*B. violifolia* × *B. prismatocarpa*).

Begonia wollnyi Herzog (PLATE 206)

section *Knesebeckia*, thick-stemmed group
Repertorium Novarum Specierum Regni Vegetabilis 7: 63 (1909)
Synonyms: *B. williamsii* Rusby & Nash; *B. williamsii* B. S. Williams; *B. acrensis* Irmscher

Erect perennial with a thick, pale green, hairless, few-branched stem to about 50 cm tall, leaves often clustered toward the end of the branches in older plants. **Stipules** persistent, ovate, ovate-oblong, or oblong, 1.2–1.6 × 0.4–0.8 cm. **Leaves:** peltate or non-peltate, even on same individual; **petiole** pale pink, hairless, 7–16 cm long, joining blade at an angle, junction of petiole and blade with an inconspicuous ring of hairs; **blade** above pale green with elongated white spots between the secondary veins, especially when young, base of veins sometimes flushed purple, the entire surface with scattered white hairs, beneath pale green, hairless or almost so, in outline almost circular, 8–16 × 8–20 cm, palmate-lobed to about half the length of the blade, lobes ovate-triangular, 1.5–11 cm long, apex of lobes acute or acuminate, margin toothed, ciliate, base of blade cordate, veins palmate. **Inflorescence:** axillary, several-flowered, bisexual, cymose, male flowers produced long before the females; **bracts** deciduous, linear-oblong, 6–13 × 1.4–4.8 mm. **Male flowers: tepals** two to four, creamy white to greenish yellow, outer pair broadly ovate-cordate to almost circular, 6–16 × 7–15 mm, inner one or two obovate, 8–11 × 2.5–4 mm; **stamens** numerous, arranged symmetrically, anther connectives projecting and rounded. **Female flowers: bracteoles** paired beneath ovary, linear or linear-lanceolate, 2.8–3.5 × 0.2–1 mm; **tepals** five, same color as males, ovate to broadly ovate, 6–12 × 4–8 mm wide; **ovary** green, ovoid to oblong-ovoid or ellipsoid, ca. 0.8 × 0.3–0.5 cm, slightly unequally three-winged, wings deltoid, three-locular, **placentae** axile, bifid; **styles** three, once-branched, stigmas in a spiraled band. **2n** = 28.

With their fleshy, gangly stems sporting tufts of white-striped leaves at their very tips, mature specimens of *Begonia wollnyi* are reminiscent of a fanciful plant illustration from Dr. Seuss. Needless to say, these features make *B. wollnyi* an easily identified species. It is also unusual in commonly producing a mixture of peltate and non-peltate leaves on the same plant and in having a variable tepal number. In the wild *B. wollnyi* usually has male flowers with two tepals, but occasionally individuals exhibit three or four tepals; by chance, those with four tepals predominate in cultivation. *Begonia wollnyi* is native to the remote mountainous region where Bolivia, Peru, and Brazil meet. The species grows there in dry or moist areas in upland forests at an altitude of 475–1550 m. *Begonia wollnyi* was introduced into cultivation at the New York Botanical Garden from seeds secured from capsules on the herbarium specimens collected by Williams, after whom *B. williamsii*, a synonym of *B. wollnyi*, is named.

In cultivation, *Begonia wollnyi* requires good drainage and bright light and will only develop thickened stems when mature. Several hybrids with this species have been produced, including *B.* 'Aussie Star' (*B. wollnyi* × *B. thiemei*), *B.* 'Jelly Roll Morton' (*B.* 'Erythrophylla Helix' × *B. wollnyi*), *B.* 'Peppermint BonBon' (*B. integerrima* × *B. wollnyi*), and *B.* 'Star Frost' (*B. carolineifolia* × *B. wollnyi*).

Appendix A

Useful addresses

Specialist societies

American Begonia Society
157 Monument Road
Rio Dell, California 95562
United States
www.begonias.org

Association of Australian Begonia Societies
Carmel Browne, Chairperson
"Paradise"
Browns Road
Belli Park, Queensland 4562
Australia

Canadian Begonia Society
190 Julia Cresent
Orillia, Ontario L3V 7W9
Canada

Canterbury Begonia Circle
Mike Stevens
47 Burnside Crescent
Christchurch 8005
New Zealand

National Begonia Society
John Taylor, Membership Secretary
3 Rose Close, North Luffenham
Oakham, Rutland LE15 8JJ
United Kingdom

Scottish Begonia Society
John Hamilton, Secretary
262 Bellfield Road
Coalburn ML11 0NQ
United Kingdom

Commercial sources of begonias

Antonelli Brothers Begonia Gardens
2545 Capitola Road
Santa Cruz, California 95062
United States
Phone: 1-831-475-5222
Toll-free phone: 1-888-423-4664
Fax: 1-831-475-7066

Blackmore and Langdon
Pensford, Bristol, Avon
England BS39 4JL
Phone: 011-44-12-7533-2300
Fax: 011-44-12-7533-1207

Cloudy Valley Nursery
8005 Rowell Creek Road
Willamina, Oregon 97396
United States
Phone: 1-503-879-5652
Fax: 1-541-258-8694

Glasshouse Works
Church Street, P.O. Box 97
Stewart, Ohio 45778
United States
Phone: 1-740-662-2142

Hi-Mark Nursery
1635 Cravens Lane
Carpinteria, California 93013
United States
Phone: 1-805-684-4462
Fax: 1-805-684-8132

Kartuz Greenhouses
Sunset Island Exotics
1408 Sunset Drive
P.O. Box 790
Vista, California 92085
United States
Phone: 1-760-941-3613
Fax: 1-760-941-1123

Lauray of Salisbury
423 Undermountain Road, Route 41
Salisbury, Connecticut 06068
United States
Phone: 1-860-435-2263

Logee's Greenhouses
141 North Street
Danielson, Connecticut 06239
United States
Phone: 1-860-774-8038
Toll-free phone: 1-888-330-8038
Toll-free fax: 1-888-774-9932

McClure and Zimmerman
108 W. Winnebago Street
Freisland, Wisconsin 53935
United States
Toll-free phone: 1-800-883-6998
Toll-free fax: 1-800-374-6120

Palm Hammock Orchid Estate
9995 S.W. 66th Street
Miami, Florida 33173
United States
Phone: 1-305-274-9813

Rhodes and Rockliffe
2 Nursery Road
Nazeing, Essex
England EN9 2JE
Phone: 011-44-19-9245-1598
(open by appointment only)

Notable public collections

Fort Worth Botanic Garden
3220 Botanic Garden Blvd
Fort Worth, Texas 76107
United States

Montreal Botanical Garden
4101 Sherbrooke East
Montréal, Québec H1X 2B2
Canada

Glasgow Botanic Garden
730 Great Western Road at
Queen Margaret Drive
Glasgow, Strathclyde
Scotland G12 OUE

Royal Botanic Gardens Kew
Richmond, Surrey
England TW9 3AB

Conservatoire du Begonia
"La Prée Horticole"
1, rue Charles Plumier
F-17300 Rochefort
France

Royal Botanic Gardens Sydney
Mrs. Macquaries Road
Sydney
New South Wales 2000
Australia

Appendix B
Begonias recommended for beginners

Cane-like

B. albo-picta
B. angularis
B. coccinea
B. maculata

Shrub-like

B. acutifolia
B. cubensis
B. dietrichiana
B. echinosepala
B. sanguinea
B. scharffii

Thick-stemmed

B. multinervia
B. parilis
B. ulmifolia

Rhizomatous

B. fenicis
B. heracleifolia and hybrids

Tuberous

B. dregei
B. grandis

Trailing-scandent

B. convolvulacea
B. fagifolia
B. glabra
B. radicans

Appendix C

Begonias recommended for terrariums

Rhizomatous

B. bowerae
B. cathayana
B. conchifolia
B. crispula
B. decora
B. dewildei
B. hatacoa
B. herbacea
B. imperialis
B. lanceolata
B. microsperma
B. nigritarum
B. pavonina
B. prismatocarpa
B. pustulata
B. quadrialata
B. rajah
B. subnummularifolia
B. sudjanae
B. turrialbae
B. venusta
B. versicolor
B. violifolia
B. xanthina

Shrub-like

B. alice-clarkiae
B. amphioxus
B. aspleniifolia
B. bipinnatifida
B. chlorosticta
B. polilloensis
B. symsanguinea

Tuberous

B. acaulis
B. bogneri
B. fimbristipula
B. morelii
B. ovatifolia
B. picta
B. ravenii
B. variabilis

Trailing-scandent

B. elaeagnifolia
B. thelmae

Appendix D

Measurement conversion tables

TO CONVERT LENGTH:	MULTIPLY BY:
Miles to kilometers	1.6
Miles to meters	1609.3
Yards to meters	0.9
Inches to centimeters	2.54
Inches to millimeters	25.4
Feet to centimeters	30.5
Kilometers to miles	0.62
Meters to yards	1.09
Meters to inches	39.4
Centimeters to inches	0.39
Millimeters to inches	0.04

INCHES	CM	INCHES	CM
1/10	0.3	8	20
1/6	0.4	9	23
1/4	0.6	10	25
1/3	0.8	20	51
1/2	1.3	30	76
3/4	1.9	40	100
1	2.5	50	130
2	5.1	60	150
3	7.6	70	180
4	10	80	200
5	13	90	230
6	15	100	250
7	18		

FEET	M	FEET	M
1	0.3	200	60
2	0.6	300	90
3	0.9	400	120
4	1.2	500	150
5	1.5	600	180
6	1.8	700	210
7	2.1	800	240
8	2.4	900	270
9	2.7	1,000	300
10	3	2,000	610
20	6	3,000	910
30	9	4,000	1,200
40	12	5,000	1,500
50	15	6,000	1,800
60	18	7,000	2,100
70	21	8,000	2,400
80	24	9,000	2,700
90	27	10,000	3,000
100	30	15,000	4,600

MILES	KM	MILES	KM
1/4	0.4	70	110
1/2	0.8	80	130
1	1.6	90	140
2	3.2	100	160
3	4.8	200	320
4	6.4	300	480
5	8.0	400	640
6	9.7	500	800
7	11	600	960
8	13	700	1,100
9	14	800	1,300
10	16	900	1,400
20	32	1,000	1,600
30	48	1,500	2,400
40	64	2,000	3,200
50	80	2,500	4,000
60	97		

Appendix E
New combinations and synonymy

To validate the new combinations and synonymy proposed in this work, these taxonomic changes are listed along with the basionyms.

Begonia corallina Carriere, *Rev. Hort.* 47:89 (1875). Synonym. *Begonia macduffiana* L. B. Smith & B. G. Schubert, *Begonian* 52: 135–136 (1985).

Begonia oaxacana A. de Candolle var. *oaxacana, Ann. Sci. Nat. Bot.*, IV 11: 127 (1859). Synonym. *Begonia candollei* R. Ziesenhenne, *Begonian* 36: 35 (1969).

Begonia conchifolia Dietrich f. *rubrimacula* (J. Golding) M. C. Tebbitt, **comb. nov.** Basionym: *Begonia conchifolia* Dietrich var. *rubrimacula* J. Golding, *Begonian* 40: 173–179, 188–190 (1973).

Begonia modestiflora Kurz, *Flora* 54: 296 (1871). Synonym. *Begonia yunnanensis* Léveillé var. *yunnanensis, Repert. Nov. Sp.* 7: 20 (1909).

Begonia modestiflora Léveillé var. *hypoleuca* (L. A. Lauener) M. C. Tebbitt **comb. nov.** Basionym: *Begonia yunnanensis* Léveillé var. *hypoleuca* L. A. Lauener, *Notes Roy. Bot. Gard. Edinburgh* 31: 435 (1972).

Begonia modestiflora Léveillé var. *sootepensis* (Craib) M. C. Tebbitt **comb. nov.** Basionym: *Begonia sootepensis* Craib, *Bull. Misc. Inform.* 57 (1911); Synonym: *Begonia yunnanensis* var. *sootepensis* Craib, *Aberd. Univ. Stud.* 47: 96 (1912).

Begonia modestiflora Léveillé var. *thorelii* (Gagnepain) M. C. Tebbitt **comb. nov.** Basionym: *Begonia sootepensis* Craib var. *thorelii* Gagnepain in Lecomte, *Fl. Indo-Chine* 2: 1104 (1921); Synonym: *Begonia yunnanensis* var. *thorelii* (Gagnepain) J. Golding & C. Karegeannes, *Phytologia* 54: 499 (1984).

Illustrated glossary of terms

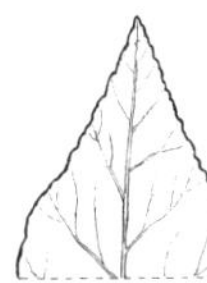

Acuminate Narrowing gradually to a point, with concave sides.

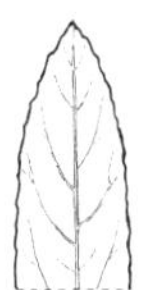

Acute Tapering to a point at an angle less than 90°, with straight sides.

Androecium Collective name for the stamens of a flower.

Angular-ovate Shaped rather like a bricklayer's trowel, broadest below the middle with two equal, straight sides meeting at the apex and two shorter straight sides meeting at the base.

Annual A plant that completes its life cycle, from seed to reproduction, in one year (compare *perennial*).

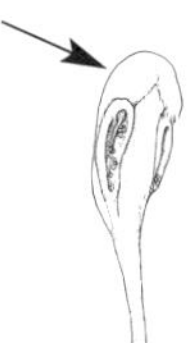

Anther The terminal, pollen-containing part of the stamen.

Apex The tip; the position farthest from the point of attachment.

Apical Located at the apex.

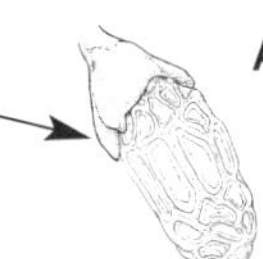

Aril A fleshy seed appendage.

Asymmetric Of a leaf that is not divisible along its length into equal halves.

Attenuate Gradually tapering to a narrow base or apex.

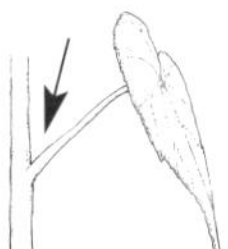

Axil The uppermost angle formed between a leaf and stem.

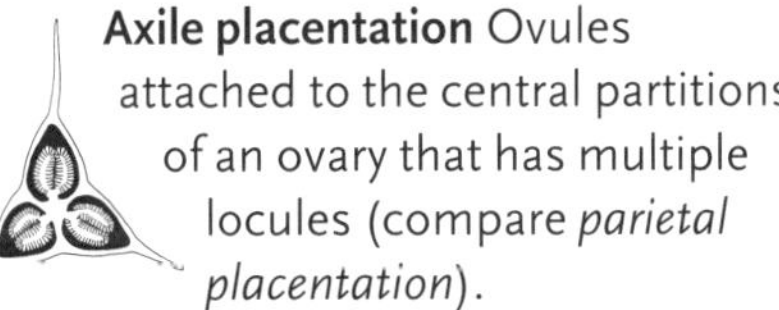

Axile placentation Ovules attached to the central partitions of an ovary that has multiple locules (compare *parietal placentation*).

Axillary Arising from an axis.

Bifid Deeply divided into two.

Bilobed Divided into two lobes.

Bipinnate Twice pinnate.

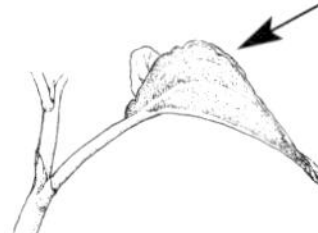

Blade Broad part of a leaf, petal, or sepal.

Bract A reduced leaf or leaf-like structure at the base of a flower or inflorescence. The bracts function to protect the developing flower buds.

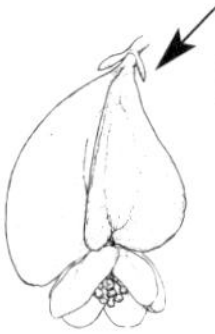

Bracteole A small bract borne either at the base of the ovary or a short distance down the pedicel.

Bulbils A small bulb-like propagule found in the leaf axils of some *Begonia* species, including *B. grandis* and *B. gracilis.*

Bullate Blistered or puckered.

Calyx Collective term for the sepals.

Caudex The axis of a plant consisting of stem and root, sometimes, as in *Begonia dregei*, it is swollen and acts as a storage organ (compare *tuber*).

Chloroplast Tiny structure found inside plant cells. Chloroplasts contain chlorophylls and other photosynthetic pigments that utilize the sun's energy to convert simple inorganic compounds into complex organic compounds.

Ciliate Margin with a fringe of short hairs.

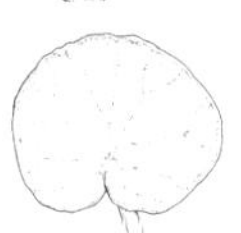

Circular Outline approximately like that of a circle.

Compound With two or more like parts in one organ.

Concave Curved inward; hollowed out.

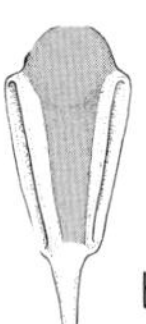

Connective The portion of the stamen connecting the two pollen sacs of an anther, and in *Begonia* sometimes projecting beyond them (shaded in illustration).

Convex Curved outward.

Cordate Heart-shaped, with the sinus at the point of attachment.

Corolla Collective term for the petals.

Creeping Growing along the ground.

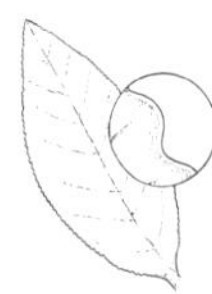

Crenate With rounded teeth along the margin.

Cultivar A cultivated, named, variant of a plant species or hybrid.

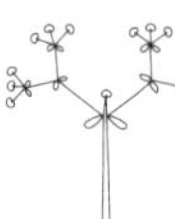

Cymose An inflorescence that is not dominated by a continuously growing central axis (see *racemose*).

Dehiscent Opening when ripe to release the contents, as of fruits and anthers (compare *indehiscent*).

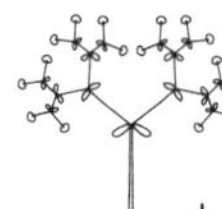

Dichasium (pl. dichasia) A cymose inflorescence in which each branch produces two opposing branches.

Dioecious (dioecy) Having the two sexes on different plants (compare *monoecious*).

Disjunct Occurring in two or more widely separated geographic areas.

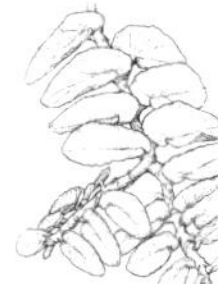

Distichous Vertically ranked on either side of an axis.

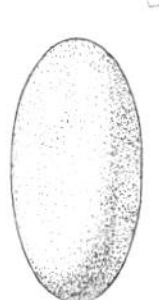

Ellipsoid A solid shape, elliptic in outline.

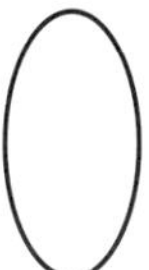

Elliptic A rounded shape that is broadest at the middle and narrower at the two equal ends.

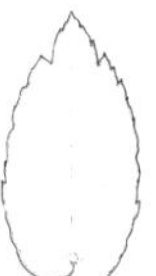

Elliptic-ovate A rounded shape that is broadest at the middle and narrowest at the apex.

Endosperm The nutritive tissue surrounding the embryo of the seed.

Entire A margin of a plant part that is not toothed, notched, lobed, or divided.

Epiphyte A plant that grows on another plant without deriving food or water from it.

Erect Upright.

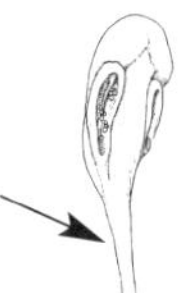

Filament The stalk of an anther.

Form A subdivision of a species usually based on a single conspicuous morphological difference, and which is not geographically separated from other members of the same species (compare *variety*).

Free Not attached to other organs, except at point of origin (compare *fused*).

Fruit A ripe, fertilized ovary containing seeds.

Fused Attached to another organ beyond its point of origin (compare *free*).

Habit The overall form and mode of growth of a plant.

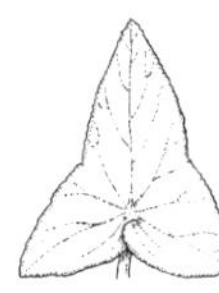

Hastate Arrowhead-shaped with the basal lobes turned slightly outward.

Hooded Of *Begonia* anthers in which tissue from the sides and rear of each pollen sac is expanded to form a cap over the top of the point of dehiscence.

Hybrid Progeny resulting from cross-fertilization between two genetically different individuals, such as two different cultivars or two different species.

Indehiscent Not opening along definite lines or by pores when ripe (compare *dehiscent*).

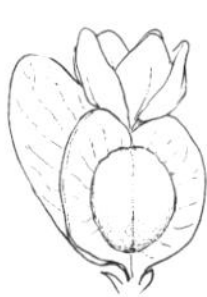

Inferior Of an ovary that is borne beneath the point of attachment of the sepals, petals, and stamens—the situation found in *Begonia* (compare *semi-inferior* and *superior*).

Inflorescence A group of flowers and their branching system, plus associated bracts and bracteoles.

Internode The portion of a stem between the nodes.

Laciniate Cut into narrow, irregular lobes or segments.

Lanceolate Lance-shaped; much longer than wide, with the widest point below the middle.

Lenticel Slightly raised, corky area on a stem or fruit.

Linear Long and narrow with more or less parallel sides.

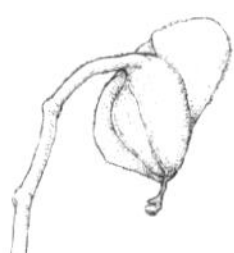

Locule A compartment of the ovary (the illustration has three locules).

Micro- (prefix) Small; not visible to the naked eye.

Monoecious Having the two sexes in separate flowers on the same plant (compare *dioecious*).

Montane A plant that in nature grows in the mountains.

Niche The ecological space that a species occupies. Each species has its own niche, and competition occurs when the niches of different species overlap.

Nodding Bent over to one side and downward.

Node The position on a stem where leaves or branches originate.

Ob- (prefix) Opposite to the typical orientation.

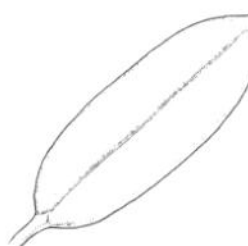

Oblong A shape that is longer than broad, with parallel sides.

Obovate A shape with the outline of an egg, attached at the narrow end.

Obtuse Blunt or rounded at the apex.

Operculum In *Begonia*, a small lid on the seed.

Ovary The lowermost part of the pistil containing the ovules; an immature fruit.

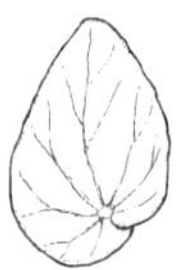

Ovate A shape with the outline of an egg, attached at the broad end.

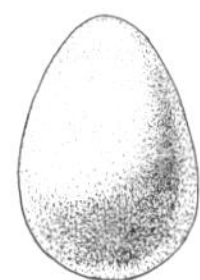

Ovoid A solid shape with the outline of an egg.

Ovule An immature seed.

Palmate Lobed or veined from a common point, like the fingers of a hand.

Palmately compound Of a leaf, divided into distinct leaflets from a common point.

Palmate-pinnate Of leaf venation, the primary veins palmately arranged and the secondary veins pinnately arranged.

Parietal placentation Ovules are borne on the ovary wall or on outgrowths of the wall (compare *axile placentation*).

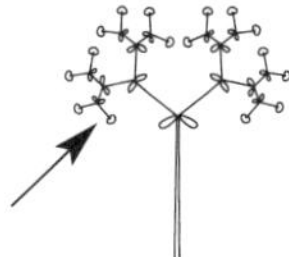

Pedicel Stalk of an individual flower (compare *peduncle*).

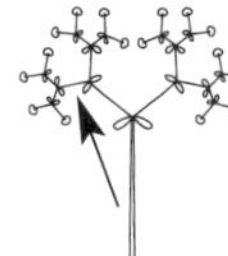

Peduncle Stalk of a group of flowers (compare *pedicel*).

Peltate More or less circular and flat with the stalk sattached to the lower surface rather than the base or margin.

Pendulous Hanging down.

Perennial A plant that lives for three or more years (compare *annual*).

Perianth The collective name for the petals plus sepals; used when petals and sepals can be differentiated; in *Begonia* these organs look similar but may be distinguished anatomically (compare *tepal*).

Persistent Not falling off after it has completed its function.

Petal A segment of the corolla; usually attractively colored or white (compare *tepal*).

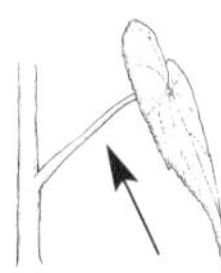

Petiole Leaf stalk.

Pinnate A compound leaf with leaflets arranged in two opposite rows; or, veins of an entire leaf with a similar arrangement.

Pinnatifid Pinnately divided to at least half the distance to the midrib, but divisions not reaching the midrib (see *bipinnatifid* and *pinnatisect*).

Pinnatisect Pinnately divided to midrib (see *pinnatifid*).

Pistil The female reproductive organ of a flower, consisting of a stigma, style, and ovary.

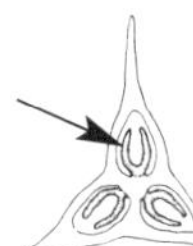

Placenta (pl. placentae) The portion of the ovary that bears the ovules.

Placentation The arrangement of the placentae (see *axile* and *parietal placentation*).

Propagule A seed, or vegetative portion of a plant, such as an offshoot, that gives rise to a new plant.

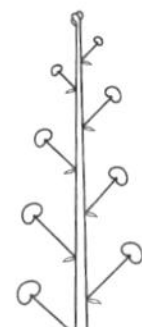

Racemose An inflorescence in which the central axis dominates the lateral flowers or lateral inflorescence branches (see *cymose*).

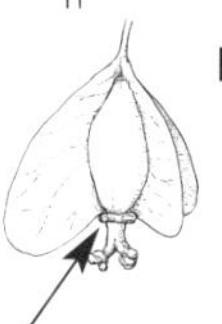

Receptacle Apical part of the pedicel on which all the flower parts are attached.

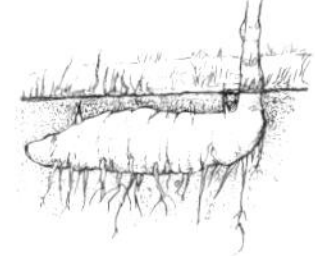

Rhizome A persistent horizontal stem bearing roots and leafy shoots.

Section 1. A taxonomic grouping of one or more closely related species below the level of genus. 2. The process of cutting a piece of plant tissue in order to display its internal structure.

Seed A fertilized ovule.

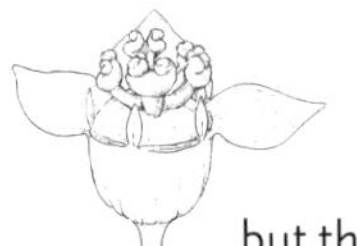

Semi-inferior Of an ovary, of which the lower part is inferior, but the upper part is free and projects above the perianth (compare *inferior* and *superior*). A situation rare in the plant kingdom but found in the *Begonia* relative *Hillebrandia*.

Sepal A segment of the calyx; in most plants green and not as noticeable as the petals, but in *Begonia* usually attractively colored or white and difficult to distinguish from the petals.

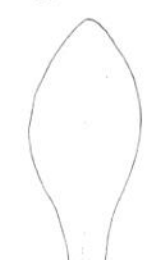

Spatula-shaped Shaped like a spatula.

Stamen The male reproductive organ of a flowering plant.

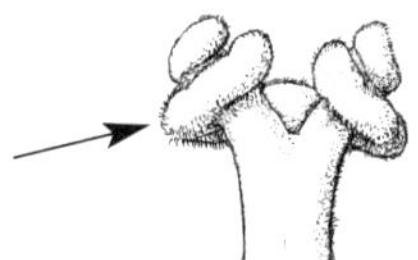

Stigma The apical portion of the pistil that receives the pollen.

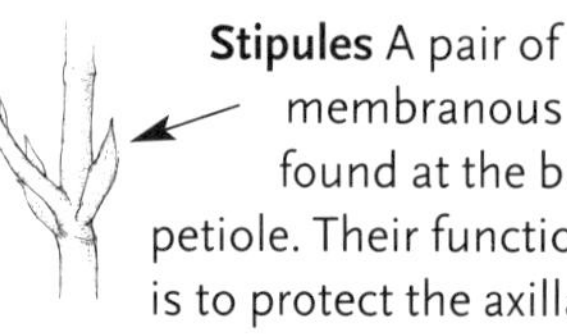

Stipules A pair of leafy or membranous appendages found at the base of the petiole. Their function in *Begonia* is to protect the axillary buds.

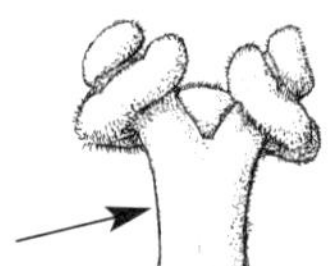

Style Stalk of the ovary that bears the stigma.

Subspecies A subdivision of a species based on a few conspicuous morphological and genetical differences, and a marked difference in distribution from other members of the same species (compare *variety* and *form*).

Superior Of an ovary that is borne above the point of attachment of the sepals, petals, and stamens—not found in the Begoniaceae (compare *inferior*).

Tepal A segment of a perianth; used when the calyx and corolla cannot be differentiated (compare *perianth*).

Terminal Positioned at the apex.

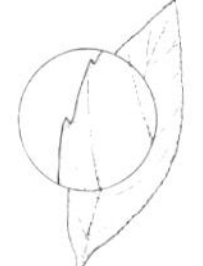

Toothed With shallow tooth-like projections along a margin.

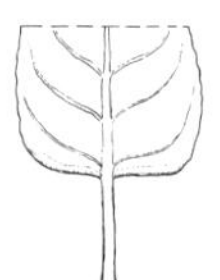

Truncate Flat base (or apex) of a two-dimensional object.

Tuber Thickened portion of stem base, rhizome, or root that acts as a storage organ (compare *caudex*).

Undulate With a somewhat wavy margin.

Variety A subdivision of a species based on one or two conspicuous morphological and genetical differences, and which is often slightly geographically separated from other members of the same species (compare *form* and *subspecies*).

Wedge-shaped Narrowly triangular with narrow end at point of attachment.

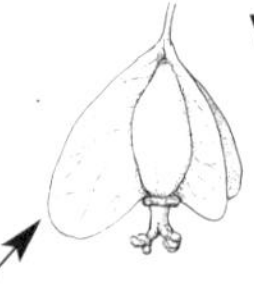

Wing In *Begonia*, a flat marginal protuberance on the ovary or fruit.

Select bibliography

Horticultural works

Arends, J. C. 1970. Somatic chromosome numbers in Elatior Begonias. Publication 341, Laboratorium voor Tuinbouw plantenteel Landbouwhogeschool, Wageningen, The Netherlands.

Brilmayer, B. 1960. *All about begonias*. Doubleday and Company, Garden city, New York.

Butterfield, H. M. 1960. *Growing begonias in California*. Circular 162. University of California, Berkeley, California.

Buxton, B. R. 1946. *Begonias and how to grow them*. Oxford University Press, New York.

Catterall, E. 1984. *Growing begonias*. Timber Press, Portland, Oregon.

Doorenbos, J. 1975. How to produce *Begonia* seed. *Begonian* 42: 7, 159–163, 165.

Elbert, G. A. 1973. *The indoor light gardening book*. Crown Publishers, New York.

Fogg, H. G. W. 1967. *Begonias, Gloxinias, and African Violets*. John Giffor, London.

Fotsch, K. A. 1939. *Die Begonien*. E. Ulmer, Stuttgart. Translated by H. Schlonk, typewritten unpublished copy. 1940. American Begonia Society, California.

Graf, A. B. 1973. *Exotica*. Series 3, 6th ed., Roehrs, Rutherford, New Jersey.

Haegeman, J. 1979. *Tuberous begonias: origins and development*. J. Cramer, Vaduz, Liechtenstein.

Kramer, J. 1967. *Begonias—indoors and out*. E. P. Dutton, New York.

Kranz, F. H., and J. L. Kranz, 1957. *Gardening indoors under lights*. The Viking Press, New York.

Krauss, H. K. 1947. *Begonias for American homes and gardens*. Macmillan, New York.

Krempin, J. L. 1993. *Know your begonias*. Krempin books, Broadbeach Waters, Queensland, Australia.

Langdon, K. B. 1969. *The tuberous Begonia*. Casell, London.

Legro, R. A. H., and J. Doorenbos, 1970. Chromosome numbers in *Begonias*. *Begonian* 37: 203–204; 233–234.

——. 1972. Chromosome numbers. *Begonian* 39: 101–102.
——. 1974. Chromosome numbers in *Begonia* 3. *Begonian* 41: 129–132.
Legro, R. A. H., and J. R. V. Haegeman, 1971. Chromosome numbers of hybrid tuberous begonias. *Euphytica* 20: 1–3.
Misono, I. 1974. *Begonias.* Translated by A. M. DeCola and H. Arakawa. 1978. American Begonia Society, Los Angeles, California.
Stevens, M. 2002. *Begonias.* Firefly Books, Buffalo, New York.
Thompson, M. L., and E. J. Thompson 1981. *Begonias: the complete reference guide.* Times Books, New York.
Wynne, B. 1888. *The tuberous begonia: its history and cultivation.* Gardening World Office, London.
Ziesenhenne, R. 1967. How to register begonias. *Begonian* 34: 226–227.

Taxonomic works

Backer, C. A., and R. C. Bakhuizen van den Brink, 1963. Begoniaceae. In C. A. Backer and R. C. Bakhuizen van den Brink, eds. *Flora of Java.* 1: 307–313. Wolters-Noordhoff N. V., Groningen.
Brade, A. C. 1943. Begonias novas do Brasil. *Arquivos do servico florestal* 2 (1): 21–24.
——. 1944. Begonias novas do Brasil II. *Boletim do museu nacional de Rio de Janeiro: Botânica* 10–23.
——. 1945a. Begonias novas do Brasil III. *Rodriquésia* 9 (18): 12–21.
——. 1945b. Begonias novas do Brasil IV. *Rodriquésia* 9 (18): 23–34.
——. 1948. Begonias novas do Brasil V. *Arquivos do jardim botânico do rio de Janeiro* 8: 227–247.
——. 1950. Begonias novas do Brasil VI. *Arquivos do jardim botânico do rio de Janeiro* 10: 137–140.
——. 1954. Begonias novas do Brasil VII. *Arquivos do jardim botânico do rio de Janeiro* 13: 69–91.
——. 1957. Begonias novas do Brasil VIII. *Arquivos do jardim botânico do rio de Janeiro* 15: 31–40.
——. 1971. Uma espéce nova do genêro *Begonia*, do estado da Bahia, Brasil, e sinopse das espécias Brasiliensas publicadas dos anos de 1944 a 1958. *Bradea* 1 (6): 37–44.
Burt-Utley, K. 1985. A revision of the Central American species of *Begonia* section *Gireoudia* (Begoniaceae). *Tulane Studies in Zoology and Botany* 25 (1): 1–131.
——. 1991. *Begoniaceae.* In D. H. Nicolson, ed. *Flora of Dominica.* 2 (2): 48, Smithsonian Institution Press, Washington, D. C.

——. 2001a. *Begonia.* In R. McVaugh, ed. *Flora Nova-Galiciana: a descriptive account of the vascular plants of western Mexico* 3: 653–695, The University of Michigan Herbarium, Ann Arbor.

——. 2001b. Begoniaceae. In W. D. Stevens, C. Ulloa Ulloa, A. Pool, and O. M. Montiel, eds. *Flora de Nicaragua* 1: 397–402, Missouri Botanical Garden Press, St. Louis.

Calzado, J. S. 2000. Begoniaceae. *Flora de la República de Cuba, serie A, plantas vasculares* Fasc. 3: 3–27.

Candolle, A. de. 1861. Begoniaceae. In K. F. P. von Martius, ed. *Flora Brasiliensis* 4: 338–396.

——. 1864. Begoniaceae. *Prodromus Systematis Naturalis Regni Vegetabilis* 15 (1): 266–408. Victoris Masson et filii, Paris.

Candolle, C. de. 1895. Begoniaceae. In J. D. Smith, Undescribed plants from Guatemala and other Central American Republics XVI. *Botanical Gazette* 20: 538–543.

——. 1908. Begoniaceae Novae. *Bulletin de l'herbier Boissier* 8 (2nd series), 309–328.

——. 1919. Begoniaceae Centrali-Americanae et Ecuadorenses. *Smithsonian Miscellaneous Collections* 69 (12): 1–10.

Chen, C. C. 1993. Begoniaceae. In T. C. Huang, ed. *Flora of Taiwan* 2nd ed., 2: 845–854. Editorial Committee of the Flora of Taiwan, Taipei.

Clarke, C. B. 1880. Begoniaceae. In J. D. Hooker, ed. *Flora of British India* 2: 635–656. L. Reeve, London.

Clement, W. L., M. C. Tebbitt, L. L. Forrest, J. E. Blair, L. Brouillet, T. Eriksson, and S. M. Swensen. 2004. Phylogenetic position and Biogeography of *Hillebrandia sandwicensis* (Begoniaceae): a rare Hawaiian relict. *American Journal of Botany.* 91 (6): 905–917.

Doorenbos, J., M. S. M. Sosef, and J. J. F. E. de Wilde. 1998. *The sections of Begonia including descriptions, keys and species lists* (Studies in Begoniaceae VI). Wageningen Agricultural University Papers. 98-2.

Forrest, L. L., and P. M. Hollingsworth 2003. A recircumscription of *Begonia* based on nuclear ribosomal sequences. *Plant Systematics and evolution.* 241: 193–211.

——. 2004. A molecular evolutionary study of *Begonia. Begonian* 71: 94–99.

Gagnepain, F. 1921. Bégoniaces. In M. H. Lecomte, ed. *Flore général de L'Indochine* 2 (8): 1095–1120. Paris.

Golding, J., and D. C. Wasshausen. 2002. *Begoniaceae, edition 2: part I: annotated species list, part II: illustrated key, abridgement and supplement.* Smithsonian Institution, Contributions from the United States National Herbarium 43: 1–289.

Grierson, A. J. C. 1991. Begoniaceae. In A. J. C. Grierson and D. G. Long, eds. *Flora of Bhutan* 2: 237–246. Royal Botanic Garden Edinburgh.

Hilliard, O. L. 1976. Begoniaceae. In J. H. Ross, ed. *Flora of Southern Africa* 22: 136–144. Department of Agriculture, Pretoria.

Hooker, J. D. 1871. Begoniaceae. In D. Oliver, ed. *Flora of Tropical Africa* 2: 569–580. London.

Houghton, A. D. 1924. A monograph of the Begoniaceae of North America. Unpublished Ph.D. dissertation, University of California, Berkeley.

Huang, S. H., and Y. M. Shui. 1994. New taxa of *Begonia* from Yunnan. *Acta Botanica Yunnanica* 16: 333–342.

Irmscher, E. 1913. Neue Begonien Papuasiens mit Einschluss von Celebes. *Botanische Jahrbücher für Systematik, Pflanzengeschichte und Pflanzengeographie* 50: 335–385.

——. 1921a. Begoniaceae Africanae III. *Botanische Jahrbücher für Systematik, Pflanzengeschichte und Pflanzengeographie* 57: 241–245.

——. 1921b. Plantae novae Sinenses, diagnosibus brevibus descriptae a Dre. Henr. Handel-Mazzetti. *Akademie der Wissenschaften in Wien* 58: 24–25.

——. 1924. Beiträge zur Kenntnisder ostasiatischen Begonien. *Mitteilungen Institut für Allgemeine Botanik, Hamburg* 6: 348.

——. 1925. Begoniaceae. In A. Engler and K. Prantl, eds. *Die Natürlichen Pflanzenfamilien*, 2nd ed.: 548–588. Engelmann, Leipzig.

——. 1927. Beiträge zur Kenntniss der Ostasiatischen Begonien. *Mitteilungen Institut für Allgemeine Botanik Hamburg* 6 (3): 343–360.

——. 1929. Die Begoniaceen der Malaiischen Halbinsel. *Mitteilungen Institut für Allgemeine Botanik Hamburg* 8: 85–160.

——. 1939. Die Begoniaceen Chinas und uhre bedeuting für die Frage der Formbuilding in polymorphen Sippen. *Mitteilungen Institut für Allgemeine Botanik, Hamburg* 10: 431–557.

——. 1949. Beiträge zur Kenntniss der Begoniaceen Südamerikas. *Botanische Jahrbücher für Systematik, Pflanzengeschichte und Pflanzengeographie* 74: 569–632.

——. 1951. Some new Chinese species of *Begonia*. *Notes of the Royal Botanic Garden of Edinburgh* 21 (1): 35–45.

——. 1953a. Neue Begoniaceen, von O. Beccari in Maleisien gesammelt. *Webbia* 9 (2): 469–509.

——. 1953b. Systematische Studien über Begoniaceen des tropischen Südamerikas, besonders Brasiliens. *Botanische Jahrbücher für Systematik, Pflanzengeschichte und Pflanzengeographie* 76: 1–102.

——. 1957. Über raddis Brasilianische Begonien und einige verwandte arten, sowie beschreibung von zwei neuen arten. *Webbia* 12 (2): 445–508.

Jayasuryiya, A. H. M. 1980. Begoniaceae. In M. D. Dassanayaka and F. R. Fosberg, eds. *A Revised Handbook of the Flora of Ceylon* 4: 137–152. Amerind, New Delhi.

Keraudren-Aymonin, M. 1983. Begoniaceae. In H. Humbert, ed. *Flore du Madagascar* 144: 7–108. Muséum National d'Histoire Naturelle, Paris.

Kiew, R. 2001. The limestone Begonias of Sabah, Borneo—Flagship species for conservation. *Gardens' Bulletin Singapore* 53: 241–286.

Koorders, S. H. 1904. Enumeratio specierum phanerogamarum minahassae. *Ntuurk Tijdscher Neder Indie* 63: 90–91.

——. 1922. *Begonia. Flora van N. O. Celebes,* Supplement 2 and 3: t. 93–97.

Merrill, E. D. 1912. The Philippine species of *Begonia. Philippine Journal of Science* 6 (6), section C, Botany: 369–406.

Merrill, E. D., and L. M. Perry. 1943. *Begonia.* In E. D. Merrill and L. M. Perry Plantae Archboldiana XI. *Journal of the Arnold Arboretum* 24: 41–58.

——. 1948. Papuan collection of Clemens. *Journal of the Arnold Arboretum* 29: 160–161.

Plana, V., A. Gascoigne, L. L. Forrest, D. Harris, and R. T. Pennington. 2004. Pleistocene and pre-Pleistocene *Begonia* speciation in Africa. *Molecular Phylogenetics and Evolution* 31: 449–461.

Ridley, H. N. 1906. Begonias of Borneo. *Journal of the Straits Branch Royal Asiatic Society* 46: 247–261.

——. 1922. Begoniaceae. In H. N. Ridley, ed. *The Flora of the Malay Peninsula* 1: 853–864. L. Reeve, London.

Sands, M. J. S. 2001a. Begoniaceae in the Flora Malesiana region. In L. G. Saw, L. S. L. Chua, and K. C. Khoo, eds. *Taxonomy: the cornerstone of biodiversity: proceedings of the fourth International Flora Malesiana Symposium 1998.* 161–168. Forest Research Institute Malaysia, Kuala Lumpur.

——. 2001b. *Begonia.* In J. H. Beaman, C. Anderson, and R. S. Beaman, eds. *The plants of Mount Kinabalu, 4. Dicotyledon families Acanthaceae to Lythraceae.* 147–163, 505–508. Natural History Publications (Borneo), Kota Kinabalu.

Shui, Y. M., C.-I. Peng, and C. Y. Wu. 2002. Synopsis of the Chinese species of *Begonia* (Begoniaceae), with a reappraisal of the sectional delimitation. *Botanical Bulletin of Academica Sinicia* 43: 313–327.

Smith, L. B. 1941. Begoniaceae. In J. F. MacBride, ed. *Flora of Peru.* Field Museum of Natural History, Botany 13, Part 4, No. 1: 181–202.

——. 1973. *Begonia* of Venezuela. *Phytologia* 27 (4): 209–227.

Smith, L. B., and B. G. Schubert. 1941. Revisión de las especies Argentinas del Género *Begonia. Revista universidad de Cuzco* 33: 71–85, tab. 13 and 14.

——. 1945. Revisión de las especies Bolivianas del Género *Begonia. Darwinia* 5: 78–117.

——. 1946. The Begoniaceae of Colombia. *Caldasia* 4 (16): 1–138; 4 (17): 77–107; 4 (18): 179–209.

. 1958. Begoniaceae. Flora of Panama VII. *Annals of the Missouri Botanical Garden* 45 (1): 41–67.

——. 1961. Begoniaceae. In P. C. Standley and L. O. Williams, eds. *Flora of Guatemala. Fieldiana, Botany* 24 (7): 157–185.

Smith, L. B., and R. C. Smith. 1971. Begoniacéas. In P. Raulino Reitz, ed. *Flora Ilustrada Catarinense* I, 128 pp. Itajai, Santa Catarina.

Smith, L. B., and D. C. Wasshausen. 1979. *Begonia* of Ecuador. *Phytologia* 44 (4): 233–256.

——. 1986. Begoniaceae. In G. Harling and L. Andersson, eds. *Flora of Ecuador* 25: 1–66. Swedish Research Councils, Stockholm.

Smith, L. B., D. C. Wasshausen, J. Golding, and C. E. Karegeannes. 1986. *Begoniaceae part I: illustrated key. part II: annotated species list.* Smithsonian Contributions to Botany, 60. Smithsonian Institution Press, Washington, D. C.

Standley, P. C. 1937. Begoniaceae. Flora of Costa Rica. *Fieldiana, Botany* 18 (2): 737–748.

Tebbitt, M. C. 2003. Notes on South Asian *Begonia* (Begoniaceae). *Edinburgh Journal of Botany* 60 (1): 1–9.

——. 2005. Two new species of *Begonia* from Asia and a new subspecies of *Begonia brevirimosa* Irmscher. *Edinburgh Journal of Botany.*

Wilde, J. J. F. E. de. 1985. Taxonomy of the African Begoniaceae, an introduction. *Acta Botanica Neerlandica* 34: 226–227.

——. 2002. *Begonia* section *Tetraphila* A. DC.: a taxonomic revision. *Wageningen Agricultural University Papers* 2001–2002: 5–258.

Wu, C. Y., and T. C. Ku. 1995, 1997. New taxa of *Begonia* L. (Begonieaceae) from China. *Acta Phytotaxonomica Sinica* 33 (3): 251–280; 35 (1): 43–56.

Index of plant names